Knowledge, Action, Pluralism

Sebastian T. Kołodziejczyk / Janusz Salamon (eds.)

Knowledge, Action, Pluralism

Contemporary Perspectives in Philosophy of Religion

PETER LANG
EDITION

Bibliographic Information published by the Deutsche Nationalbibliothek
The Deutsche Nationalbibliothek lists this publication
in the Deutsche Nationalbibliografie; detailed bibliographic
data is available in the internet at http://dnb.d-nb.de.

This publication was financially supported
by Jagiellonian University in Krakow.

Cover image:
© Sebastian T. Kołodziejczyk

Library of Congress Cataloging-in-Publication Data
Knowledge, action, pluralism : contemporary perspectives in philosophy of
religion / Sebastian T. Kołodziejczyk, Janusz Salamon (eds.). — 1 [edition].
pages cm
Includes bibliographical references.
ISBN 978-3-631-62568-2
1. Religion—Philosophy. I. Kołodziejczyk, Sebastian, editor of compilation.
BL51.K6144 2014
210—dc23

2013048300

ISBN 978-3-631-62568-2 (Print)
E-ISBN 978-3-653-01914-8 (E-Book)
DOI 10.3726/ 978-3-653-01914-8

© Peter Lang GmbH
Internationaler Verlag der Wissenschaften
Frankfurt am Main 2013
All rights reserved.
Peter Lang Edition is an Imprint of Peter Lang GmbH.

Peter Lang – Frankfurt am Main · Bern · Bruxelles · New York ·
Oxford · Warszawa · Wien

www.peterlang.com

Table of Contents

6 Table of Contents

Notes on the Contributors

Louis CARUANA is Reader in Philosophy at Heythrop College, University of London. His publications include: *Holism and the Understanding of Science: Integrating the Analytical, Historical and Sociological*; *Science And Virtue: An Essay on the Impact of the Scientific Mentality on Moral Character*; *Darwin and Catholicism: The Past and Present Dynamics of a Cultural Encounter.*

Paul CLAVIER is a Professor of Philosophy at the École normale supérieure de Paris, France. His recent book publications include: *What is the Good?*, *Arguing about Moral Values*, and *What is Natural Theology?*

Marco DAMONTE teaches at at the University of Genoa. His publications include: *Una nuova teologia riformata: La proposta degli epistemology riformati e dei tomisti wittgensteiniani*; *Wittgenstein, Tomasso e la cura dell'intenzionalita.*

Bernd IRLENBORN is a Professor of Philosophy at Theologische Fakultät Paderborn. His publications include: *Der Ingrimm des Aufruhrs: Heidegger und das Problem des Bösen*; *Veritas semper maior: Der philosophische Gottesbegriff Richard Schaefflers im Spannungsfeld von Philosophie und Theologie*; *Religiöse Überzeugungen und öffentliche Vernunft: Zur Rolle des Christentums in der pluralistischen Gesellschaft*; *Gott und Vernunft: neue Perspektiven zur Transzendentalphilosophie Richard Schaefflers*; *Analytische Religionsphilosophie.*

Sebastian Tomasz KOŁODZIEJCZYK is an Associate Professor of Philosophy at the Jagiellonian University in Krakow. He is Editor-in-Chief of the *Polish Journal of Philosophy* and Co-Editor of the book series *Companions to Philosophy* (WAM, Krakow). His publications include: *Conceptual Boundaries of Metaphysics; Idea of Metaphysics* (forthcoming); *Consciousness and Volition* (forthcoming).

Denis MOREAU is a Professor of Philosophy and the Head of the Department of Philosophy at Université de Nantes. Author of 8 books and 11 volumes of translations and critical editions of philosophical works in Latin. His recent publications include: *In the Middle of a Forest: Essays on Descartes and the Meaning of Life*; *The Ways of Salvation: A Philosophical Essay*; *Faith in God and Reason: Two Essays on Philosophy of Religion.*

Roger POUIVET is a Professor of Philosophy at Université de Lorraine and Director of Laboratoire d'Histoire des Sciences et de Philosophie-Archives Poincaré in Nancy, France. He authored and co-edited: *L'ontologie de l'oeuvre d'art; Philosophie de la religion, approches contemporaines; La philosophie de Nelson Goodman; The Right to Believe: Perspectives in Religious Epistemology; Philosophie de la danse; Philosophie du rock: une ontologie des artefacts et des enregistrements.*

Anita RENUSCH teaches at Goethe-University of Frankfurt am Main. She is a leader of Glaube und Gründe research group. She is the author of "Thank God it's the right religion! – Plantinga on religious diversity", in: Dieter Schönecker (ed.), *Essays on Warranted Christian Belief. With Replies by Alvin Plantinga* (forthcoming).

Janusz SALAMON is a Senior Lecturer at Charles University in Prague and Adjunct Professor at New York University. He is Editor-in-Chief of the *European Journal for Philosophy of Religion* and Co-Editor of *Bloomsbury Studies in Global Ethics.* He co-authored and edited the following books: *Solidarity Beyond Borders: Ethics in a Globalising World; Companion to Philosophy of Religion; George Berkeley's A Treatise Concerning the Principles of Human Knowledge* [translation into Polish]; *Future Christianity; Brothers Reunited: Catholic-Jewish Dialogue.*

Vladimir K. SHOKHIN is a Professor of Philosophy at the Moscow State University and the Head of the Department of Philosophy of Religion at the Institute of Philosophy of the Russian Academy of Sciences as well as Editor-in-Chief of the journal *Almanach of the Philosophy of Religion.* Author of 11 books, including: *Stratification of Reality According to Ontology of Advaita-Vedanta; First Philosophers of India;* and *Brahmanic Philosophy.*

Eleonore STUMP is Robert J. Henle Professor of Philosophy at Saint Louis University. Former President of the American Philosophical Association and of the Society of Christian Philosophers. Her recent book publications include: *Wandering in Darkness: Narrative and the Problem of Suffering; The Oxford Handbook of Aquinas* (co-edited with B. Davies); and *Aquinas.*

Richard SWINBURNE is an Emeritus Nolloth Professor of the Philosophy of the Christian Religion at the University of Oxford and Fellow of the British Academy. Among his books are *The Coherence of Theism, The Existence of God, Faith and Reason, The Evolution of the Soul, Responsibility and Atonement,*

Revelation, The Christian God, Providence and the Problem of Evil, Epistemic Justification, The Resurrection of God Incarnate, and *Mind, Brain, and Free Will.*

N. VERBIN is an Assistant Professor at Tel Aviv University and Senior Research Fellow at the Shalom Hartman Institute in Jerusalem. She is the author of *Divinely Abused: A Philosophical Perspective on Job and His Kin.*

Daniel von WACHTER is a Professor of Philosophy and the Director of the International Academy of Philosophy in Liechtenstein. His publications include: *Die kausale Struktur der Welt: Eine philosophische Untersuchung über Verursachung, Naturgesetze, freie Handlungen, Möglichkeit und Gottes kausale Rolle in der Welt; Dinge und Eigenschaften: Versuch zur Ontologie.*

William J. WAINWRIGHT is Distinguished Professor Emeritus at University of Wisconsin-Milwaukee. His publications include: *Religion and Morality; The Oxford Handbook for Philosophy of Religion; Philosophy of Religion; Reason and the Heart; God, Philosophy and Academic Culture.*

Linda ZAGZEBSKI is George Lynn Cross Research Professor and Kingfisher College Chair of the Philosophy of Religion and Ethics at University of Oklahoma. She authored or co-edited: *Epistemic Authority: A Theory of Trust, Authority, and Autonomy in Belief; Philosophy of Religion: An Historical Introduction; Divine Motivation Theory; Intellectual Virtue: Perspectives from Ethics and Epistemology; Virtue Epistemology: Essays on Epistemic Virtue and Responsibility; Virtues of the Mind: An Inquiry into the Nature of Virtue and the Ethical Foundations of Knowledge; Rational Faith: Catholic Responses to Reformed Epistemology; The Dilemma of Freedom and Foreknowledge.*

Preface

The last few decades of the 20th century witnessed a somewhat unexpected renaissance of academic philosophy of religion, especially in the Anglophone countries and in analytic philosophy circles. This period of almost unprecedented flourishing of this branch of philosophy, which in the eyes of many was destined for oblivion, was preceded by a period of diffidence and stagnation, no doubt caused in part by the long shadow of logical positivism which dismissed all claims of the philosophy of religion and metaphysics as meaningless.

The radical change has been brought about by a generation of philosophers led by two towering figures that have dominated the landscape of the late 20th century philosophy of religion: Alvin Plantinga and Richard Swinburne. Plantinga, through his first important book, *God and Other Minds* (1967), initiated the movement towards the rehabilitation of the philosophy of religion, and later developed a version of anti-evidentialist religious epistemology that he dubbed Reformed Epistemology. Swinburne, in a remarkable series of books beginning with *The Coherence of Theism* (1977) worked out an alternative and equally comprehensive treatment of the main problems of the philosophy of religion and philosophical theology, which on one hand can be considered continuous with natural theology in the tradition of Thomas Aquinas, and on the other hand utilises the achievements of a 20th century methodology of science. Of the remaining strands of late 20th century philosophy of religion, two may be thought to have the greatest resonance and significance, if not matching the work of Plantinga and Swinburne in scope and broad appeal. These are John Hick's theory of religious pluralism, comprehensively presented in his *An Interpretation of Religion: Human Responses to the Transcendent* (1989), and perhaps to a lesser extent, the philosophy of religion inspired by the work of the later Wittgenstein.

Echoes of all these four main streams of the late 20th century philosophy of religion – all laying heavy stress on epistemological considerations – can be found in this book. While the present volume, carrying a subtitle 'Contemporary Perspectives in Philosophy of Religion', does not aim at a comprehensive presentation of the newest trends in the philosophy of religion, it is representative of its current state in at least three ways.

Firstly, the content of this book mirrors the fact that the first two decades of the 20th century witness a continuity, rather than a revolution, in philosophy in general, and in the philosophy of religion in particular. The leading scholars in the field in the last decades of the 20th century still lead the field today, while the next generations of philosophers focus on elaboration of particular topics in a conversation with the 'old masters'. The existence of this quasi-scholastic intergenerational cooperation, of which this book is a visible proof, allows one to predict, at least to some extent, what will be the focus of attention of philosophers of religion over the next few decades. Revolutions in philosophy do occur from time to time, but at the moment such revolution does not seem to be emerging on the horizon of the philosophy of religion. What is to be expected is a careful broadening of the debate on particular issues, by taking the established positions as a point of departure, re-examining the argumentation of the predecessors and analysing in a painstaking manner some new claims in an evolutionary rather than a revolutionary manner. The present anthology, which brings together the work of some of the contemporary classics in the field (Swinburne, Stump, Wainwright, Zagzebski) and of scholars one or two generations younger who in many ways follow in their footsteps, is a good example of this trend. The presence of Richard Swinburne in this volume is evidence of one of the characteristic features of his academic activity – and indeed that of the entire generation of British and American philosophers of religion – namely a readiness to lend a support and encouragement to younger scholars in the field, including those from outside the Anglophone parts of the world.

Secondly, the present volume highlights the fact that while philosophers of religion for much of the 20th century gave much of their attention to issues of religious language, partly due to the aforementioned pressure from the logical positivist critics of religious language, contemporary philosophers of religion, having regained their methodological self-confidence, concentrate mainly on the problems of religious epistemology (which includes a broad spectrum of issues, from the justification of religious beliefs to the religion and science debate), philosophical theology (especially God's relation to and action in the world), and religious diversity. In these three broad areas of philosophy of religion, much creative work is being done today and is likely to be done in the years to come. Again, the essays published in this volume demonstrate this dominant tendency in the contemporary philosophy of religion, hence its title: 'Knowledge, Action, Pluralism'.

Thirdly, the list of contributors to this volume demonstrates a relatively recent trend to try to cross the divide between the Continental and analytic philosophical circles which until recently appeared – and still appears to many – unbridgeable. The composition of the team of co-authors of this book is characteristic of the dynamics of this growing collaboration between British and American philosophers on one hand, and Continental European philosophers on the other. Ten out of sixteen contributors to this volume represent countries of Continental Europe, in which philosophy departments – often in contrast to their British or American counterparts – tend to offer a blend of Continental and analytic philosophical traditions as a matter of course. In addition to that, most of the 'European' contributors to this volume have an experience of education at an Anglophone philosophy department (in most cases at Oxford or Cambridge). This methodologically pluralistic background of many of the co-authors of this volume encourages an innovative approach to the issues explored in more familiar ways by the mainstream Anglophone philosophers of religion. On the other hand, all contributors to this volume tend to remain faithful to the 'analytic' ideal of clarity and precision of argumentation, thus making debate across the geographical and methodological divide possible. Again, this aspect of the present volume may be considered indicative of the growing tendency for closer collaboration between Continental European and analytic Anglophone philosophers of religion, especially given the fact that Continental philosophy of religion in the recent decades was hardly a match for the Anglophone philosophy of religion as far as vitality and sheer output is concerned.

As mentioned above, the book gathers a collection of 16 essays centring on the three most hotly discussed topics in contemporary philosophy of religion: (I) religious epistemology, (II) philosophy of God's relation to and action in the world, and (III) the philosophical challenge of religious pluralism.

Given all that has been said above about the 'representative' character of this volume, it is fitting that it opens with an essay by **Richard Swinburne** entitled: *Why Hume and Kant Were Mistaken in Rejecting Natural Theology.* Having identified the general principles of intelligibility and knowledge adopted by Hume and Kant, which seem to rule out the possibility of natural theology, Swinburne boldly states that these principles are all either empty or fallacious. Here are some of the weaknesses of Hume's and Kant's respective critiques of natural theology pointed out by Swinburne.

Hume claimed that all our 'ideas' are compounded of simple ideas, and all simple ideas are derived from 'impressions'; and that any purported idea not so derived is meaningless. But Hume had no rule for which of the many ideas which could be derived from a given collection of impressions are meaningful, or how they can be combined in logically possible ways. Contrary to Hume, the way to show that a proposition s is a logically possible proposition is to show that some more obviously logically possible proposition r entails it; and the way to show that s is a logically impossible proposition is to show that that proposition entails a contradiction.

Hume claimed that to say x causes y is to say that they are kinds A and B such that x is A, y is B, and all A's are followed by B's. BUT (α) that x causes y may be a consequence of a probable hypothesis other than the hypothesis that 'all A's are followed by B's'. A hypothesis H is rendered probable by evidence E insofar as (1) H makes E probable, (2) H fits with background evidence, (3) H is simple, (4) H has small scope. In comparing large-scale hypotheses with each other, only (1) and (3) are relevant. And (β), our experience of causation comes most basically from ourselves causing events. Given (α) and (β) the hypothesis that God caused the universe may be rendered probable by evidence.

Kant held that our categories can only provide knowledge when applied to objects of 'possible' sensible experience, and that knowledge of causation was knowledge of regular succession. BUT it needs the above criteria to show what a 'possible' experience is, as well as to show what non-experiencable possibilities there are. His second claim repeats Hume's mistaken claim. Kant claimed that we could have no knowledge of the unconditioned. BUT his arguments in the Antinomies are fallacious, and he had no conception of how evidence can render a very wide ranging hypothesis probable. Kant claimed that other arguments for the existence of God need to be backed up by an ontological argument to show that any *ens realissimum* exists of logical necessity, and that no such argument can be had. BUT the idea that God's necessity was logical necessity is due to Anselm, and there is no need for any theist to hold it. Thus, concludes Swinburne, Kant's critique of natural theology can be dismissed.

In the essay that follows, entitled *First Person and Third Person Epistemic Reasons: Navigating the Problems of Religious Epistemology*, **Linda Zagzebski** takes up an equally consequential epistemological issue with a more modern twist. In her essay she argues that there are two kinds of epistemic reasons. One kind is irreducibly first personal – what she calls deliberative reasons. The other kind is third personal – what she calls theoretical reasons. She argues that attending to this distinction illuminates a host of problems in epistemology in general and in religious epistemology in particular. These problems include (a) the way religious experience operates as a reason for religious belief, (b) how we ought to understand religious testimony, (c) how religious authority can be justified, (d) the problem of religious disagreement, and (e) the reasonableness of religious conversion.

What Zagzebski means by an epistemic reason is something on the basis of which it is reasonable for a person to settle for herself whether p in so far as her goal is truth, not a practical or moral goal. The two kinds of epistemic reasons can be distinguished by the following features. Theoretical reasons are third personal facts to which we refer in interpersonal discourse. They have no essential connection with believing, and there is no agent control over them. In contrast, deliberative reasons are first personal (or second personal), they are essentially connected to my deliberations about the truth, and they are reasons

I use as an agent. Zagzebski argues that there are deliberative reasons that are more basic than any theoretical reasons I can access. Because of the phenomenon of epistemic circularity, I cannot take anything to be a theoretical reason without self-trust, a deliberative reason. Zagzebski argues that trust in others is a rational commitment of self-trust and it is also a deliberative reason for many beliefs. Other persons can appeal to me to trust them epistemically. If I grant them trust, I have a deliberative reason to believe them. This is the primary feature of the most important subclass of testimony – situations in which one person tells another person that p. The fact that the request for trust and its acceptance gives the person who trusts a deliberative reason to have certain beliefs is crucial to understanding revelation, as well as religious authority. The same model explains what is problematic about reasonable disagreement. Finally, the reasonableness of conversion can be explained by the function of deliberative reasons. Conversion looks unreasonable if the only epistemic reasons are theoretical.

Another distinguished contributor to the volume, **William J. Wainwright**, explores one of the key issues in the epistemology of religious experience in an essay entitled: *The Spiritual Senses in Western Spirituality and the Analytic Philosophy of Religion*. Beginning with the analysis of the doctrine of the spiritual senses in the context of Roman Catholic and Eastern Orthodox spirituality, Wainwright notices that it has been largely unremarked that the doctrine also played a significant role in classical Protestant thought, and that analogous concepts can be found in Indian theism. In spite of the doctrine's significance, however, the only analytic philosopher to consider it has been Nelson Pike, whose treatment Wainwright considers inadequate. Hence Wainwright proceeds to show how the development of the doctrine in Puritan thought and spirituality fills a serious lacuna in Pike's treatment, and concludes with suggestions as to where the discussion should go next.

In his essay *Against Theological Fictionalism*, **Roger Pouivet** refutes theological fictionalism understood as the thesis that religious monotheistic commitment does not necessitate the truth of theism. God could have the same ontological status as a fictional character in a novel or a movie. Such a character does not exist; we know that that character does not exist; but we think about this character and experience emotions (or quasi-emotions) about him and what he does. Like the experience of fiction, religious experience could consist in a game of make-believe. Robin Le Poidevin defends such a theological fictionalism (without using this label) in chapter 8 ('Is God a Fiction?') of *Arguing for Atheism* (1996), partly inspired by Kendall Walton's theory of make-believe (*Mimesis as Make-Believe,* 1990). As Pouivet argues, theological fictionalism is not simply a philosophical or theological theory held by philosophers. It also appears to be a widespread view in Postmodern cultures. The assumption is that we do not have to accept full-blooded theological realism – that God exists, that He revealed himself, that Christ was resurrected, and so on – in order to be religious persons. Such realist claims, it is thought, have been definitively disproven since the Enlightenment and thanks to the human and social sciences. So, theological fictionalism may seem attractive to those who want to preserve what they think of as the spiritual and moral content of religion but who do not accept an ontological commitment to a transcendent being or realist claims about Christ's resurrection, miracles, the Day of Judgment, and so on. Theological fictionalism says, in short, that you can be a *Non-Metaphysical Christian*. God can still be viewed positively as the greatest single creation of the imagination. Fictionalist theology gives sense to the claim that Christ was resurrected, for example, by saying that it is 'true in the Gospels', or 'true in religion'. In this sense, that Christ was resurrected would be a quasi-assertion. To quasi-assert that *p* is to express one's acceptance of *p*, an attitude that is compatible with agnosticism and disbelief. Quasi-assertion is grounded mainly in non-doxastic or non-epistemic reasons, and recourse to this device encourages a non-cognitivist account of religious matters.

Pouivet considers various arguments in favour of theological fictionalism, but concludes that theological fictionalism rests on mistaken assumptions. Above all, theological fictionalism presupposes a non-doxastic account of faith. Faith would not imply full belief, but only quasi-belief or quasi-acceptance. But there is, inescapably, a strong doxastic component in faith. And at the difference of acceptance, belief is essentially realistic. We cannot assert: I believe that *p*, but not-*p* (Moore's paradox). This is the reason why the Bible, understood as a fictional narrative, could not play an authoritative role (distinguished from a cultural role). Paraphrasing John Henry Newman, Pouivet concludes that a fictionalist belief in God – a belief about a God as a character in a narrative, and not about God as a genuine being – would be like 'filial love without the fact of the father'.

The next chapter entitled *From Thinking about God to Experiencing the World: Theory of Transcendentals and the Debate about the Nature of Experience* by **Sebastian T. Kołodziejczyk** is a work of a metaphysician. The author begins by showing how the theory of transcendentals has been invented by mediaeval theologians and philosophers as a tool to be utilized in an effort to grasp and explain the nature of God. However, instead of focusing on its theological efficacy, Kołodziejczyk is interested in exploring its philosophical usefulness and the explanatory power when applied in metaphysics and philosophy of mind, rather than in philosophical theology as such. He shows how the theory of transcendentals sheds light on a much debated problem of so called 'pure experience'. In the first section of his essay, Kołodziejczyk explores the metaphysical and epistemological complexities of pure experience. In the second section the theory of transcendentals is brought into picture. The last part of the essay is devoted to the discussion of the mutual and fruitful relation between the theory of transcendentals and the theory of 'pure experience' favoured by Kołodziejczyk. During the course of the essay, the so-called 'Basic Furniture of Mind Hypothesis' is presented, explored, and defended.

As mentioned above, Reformed Epistemology and philosophy of religion inspired by the work of the later Wittgenstein belong among the main strands of the contemporary philosophy of religion. In his essay entitled *Towards a New Natural Theology: Between Reformed Epistemology and Wittgensteinian Theism*, **Marco Damonte** discusses the merits of both of these approaches to the philosophy of religion. In doing so he formulates a new proposal of natural theology and proceeds to show its capacity to meet the methodological demands characteristic of both analytic and Continental philosophy of religion.

Damonte begins by evaluating the criticisms aimed at the connection between natural theology and the foundationalistic project of modern epistemology. Following the advice of Reformed Epistemologists and Wittgensteinian Thomists, Damonte argues for the necessity of renouncing the evidentialist role of natural theology, and for the possibility to refound this discipline on anthropological foundations. In particular, he proposes to consider natural theology not as a necessary and sufficient condition to assent to religious beliefs, but (1) as an anthropological condition useful for a mature approval and a consistent life of faith, and (2) as an epistemic condition necessary to formulate a theological science. Thanks to this definition it is possible to save the philosophical rigour of natural theology and at the same time to change its role. This proposal supports the equilibrium between *faith in* (existential dimension) and *faith that* (propositional dimension); it allows the passage from argumentation to persuasion; and it encourages the study of specific dogmas (philosophical theology).

Studying this natural theology in depth implies taking into consideration the following points: (A) Analysing Wittgenstein's implicit philosophy of religion. For him religions are forms of life, and theology is a sort of grammar and not a simple addition to our ontological catalogue; (B) Analysing Aquinas's explicit natural theology, since it is not compromised with the project of modern epistemology. His philosophy of being is able to protect the mysteries of faith; (C) Affirming the existence of a natural faculty common to mankind that is able to establish a relationship with God and to affirm something about it. This *sensus divinitatis* can be disclosed both from neurological studies and from human science (phenomenology of the sacred).

Damonte argues that recognizing the legitimacy of religious beliefs, independently from the certitudes of natural theology, makes this discipline free to supply evidence for faith and contributes to making faith intelligible. He is convinced that in the near future philosophy of religion will have to confront itself not with the dispute between theist and atheist, but rather between religious realism and antirealism. He holds that only a natural theology as conceived in this essay is able to avoid fideism and fundamentalism, because it permits the commensurability between religious practices. In particular this natural theology: (a) encourages interreligious dialogue; (b) promotes human spirituality and the importance of a religious education; and (c) induces the acknowledgement of a public role for religions. Damonte concludes by noticing that the themes that the new approach to natural theology he advocates takes into account are recognised as important by both Continental and analytic philosophers of religion, and for this reason it may be conducive towards a fruitful dialogue between representatives of these two traditions.

The first part of the book closes with an essay by **Louis Caruana** entitled *Science, Religion and Common Sense* in which the author challenges Susan Haack's recent attempt to ground the distinction between science and religion on the claim that science is an extended and enhanced version of common sense while religion is not. In her book *Defending Science within Reason*, Haack argues that the grounding of science on common sense is what science has and what religion lacks as regards justification.

Caruana starts by examining Haack's claim that science is in fact an extended and enhanced version of common sense, rather than an independent mode of inquiry that often functions as a corrector of common sense. This first step in Caruana's paper brings to the fore the more fundamental question: What is common sense? His arguments show that Haack's account is misguided not because science is not an extended and enhanced version of common sense, as she says. It is misguided because she assumes a very restricted, and thus inadequate, view of common sense. After reviewing several more realistic models of common sense, Caruana concludes that there are good reasons to think that common sense is rich enough to allow various genuine extended and enhanced versions of it. He shows that just as science can be correctly seen as an extended and enhanced version of common sense, so also, with the same criteria, religion can be seen as an extended and enhanced version of common sense in another direction. Science and religion are not competing extensions of common sense, but extensions of different dimensions of common sense. Science is an extension of the descriptive and explanatory dimension. Religion is an extension of the dimension of common sense that is associated with the concept of person.

The results of this analysis have significant repercussions on broader philosophical issues, as can be seen from the following three points. First, Haack states explicitly that she does not endorse scientism. Yet, she is allegedly formulating a position that, although not as radical as scientistic naturalism, is still sharp enough to discredit religion. An understanding of this nuanced naturalistic approach will probably gain prominence in future philosophy of religion debates, and this paper throws light on the issues involved. Secondly, Caruana's essay suggests that the tension between science and religion can be resolved, in part, by deeper awareness of how these two disciplines are linked to common sense. The main argument does not try to identify, clarify or establish bridges between the two disciplines by linking the peaks of these disciplines, as is often done. On the contrary, it tries to descend to the common platform on which both of them stand, namely common practice and common sense. And thirdly, the entire debate draws attention to the philosophical centrality of common sense. Due to recent positivistic or naturalistic trends, appeals to common-sense are very often assumed guilty until proven innocent. The approach explored in this essay reverses this trend by showing how appeals to common sense can in fact be indispensable to debates concerning meaning, science, religion and pre-philosophical intuition.

The second part of the book opens with an essay by **Daniel von Wachter** entitled *Do the Results of Divine Actions Have Preceding Causes?* In it Wachter deals with the following question: If God brings about an event in the universe, does it have a preceding cause? For example, if the universe began with the Big Bang and if God brought it about, did the Big Bang then have a preceding cause? The standard answer is: yes, it was caused by a divine willing. Wachter proposes an alternative view: God's actions, unlike human actions, are not initiated by willings, undertakings, or volitions, but God brings about the intended event directly. Presenting a solution to the dilemma of free will, Wachter explains what 'bringing about directly' means and shows that the question of what an action begins with is distinct from the question of whether it is a basic action.

In an essay entitled *Atonement and the Cry of Dereliction from the Cross*, **Eleonore Stump** shows that in the history of Christianity, the doctrine of the atonement has been variously interpreted, but the most famous and influential kind of interpretation is that stemming from Anselm's work. On the Anselmian kind of interpretation of the doctrine of the atonement, God's justice does not allow God to forgive human beings for their moral wrongdoing without the punishment those moral wrongs deserve. It is necessary that there be satisfaction for these wrongs before the perpetrators of them can receive God's forgiveness. In this essay, Stump evaluates the Anselmian kind of interpretation of the doctrine of the atonement by reflecting on the divine attribute of love. She argues that, on the account of love given by Aquinas, the central claims of the Anselmian kind of interpretation are antithetical to all love, including the love of God.

In his essay entitled *Salvation as Divine Action: A Philosophical Approach to the Power of Faith in Christ's Resurrection*, **Denis Moreau** proposes a philosophical clarification of the statement 'faith in the resurrection of Christ saves men from sin'. Moreau begins by noticing that the concept of 'salvation' is still present in ordinary language as well as in some modern or contemporary philosophy far removed from Christianity, which uses this concept generally but without specifying its sense. This calls for clarification. It is therefore necessary to distinguish two aspects in the word 'salvation': (a) a negative aspect, by which salvation is understood as liberation and deliverance, rescue, in addition to being torn from a situation of danger where we come under an important threat; (b) a positive aspect, the granting of something good, the entry into a situation considered as beneficial, desirable, the moving from a state of misfortune and hardship to a status of happiness and fulfilment. For other reasons, the notion of salvation also calls for a clarification in the field of Christian theology. Indeed, if the idea that Christ is the Saviour and saves from sin has never been seriously challenged, the question of the *modus operandi* of salvation has become difficult since, especially in Latin Christianity, the theory of 'satisfaction', inherited from Anselm of Canterbury's *Cur Deus Homo*, is being called into question and has been subject to numerous criticisms.

In the second part of the 20th century many authors have suggested that it would be desirable to 'give back the resurrection of Christ, in the treaties [on salvation], the crucial place that it should never have lost (…) to [show that] the resurrection has in itself a salvific dimension" (Henri de Lubac). But this idea has not been fully explored and argued in recent times and Moreau proceeds to develop this thesis in detail, using an analysis which looks at different beliefs about death through a pragmatic lens. Moreau is interested in the efficiency of these beliefs in the lives of those who adopt them. His argument goes through 3 steps: (1) The natural human belief concerning death is that it is the end of life, and that we must, as such, be afraid of it. (2) This frightened belief that death is the end of life has some 'dyspraxic' effects. This is to say that it leads to morally wrong acts which can be called 'bad deeds' or 'sins' (e.g., greed, lust, pride). This state of a man committing sins corresponds to the negative situation described by type (a), from which he needs to be 'saved'. Moreau clarifies this causal connection between fear of death and sins by analysing an argument developed by Lucretius at the beginning of the *De Rerum Natura*, III. (3) A belief indicating that death is not the end of life and that we should thus not be afraid of it is, on the contrary, an 'orthopraxic' belief. This is to say that it liberates from the morally incorrect acts provoked by fear of death, and that it activates, or should activate, in those who embrace this belief, a series of intellectual and emotional processes which improve human existence. The Christian belief that death has been defeated by the Christ is, to the highest degree, an orthopraxic belief of this kind. Leaving the negative state described in (2) and entering into the desirable state described in (3) through the action of an external agent (Christ) and the adhesion to a revelation (of resurrection) can thus be understood as one aspect of salvation as conceived by Christianity.

In an essay entitled *Creation as a Metaphysical Concept*, **Paul Clavier** argues that the concept of creation should be preserved from ideological claims implied in the creationism vs. evolutionism debate. Two different topics have to be disentangled: (1) the probability for living organisms to evolve with or without divine guidance; (2) the ontological dependence of what there is upon a hypothetical (originating and sustaining) cause of its existence. The first topic often (even if not fatally) displays a disastrous mingling of observational evidence with metaphysically premature conclusions (whatever these may be: theistic or atheistic). Giving preliminarily and finally some reasons to cast doubt on the validity of arguing deductively from physical (or biological) states of affairs to God, this paper will be principally concerned with the second topic. The challenge of a rephrased argument to a creator is to find new starting points from which to consider what ontological dependence there might be on a creator.

The doctrine of creation is usually supposed to be: (1) a religious belief proper to western monotheistic traditions; (2) short of any rational justification; or even (3) an irrational superstition, not compatible with scientific evidence. Clavier begins by discussing these preliminary considerations.

Firstly, as Clavier points out, it is true that the doctrine of creation has ruled, like a compelled article of creed, over European philosophy from the 4th century to the Age of Enlightenment (from Augustine to Voltaire). But that people are forced to believe something doesn't forcedly entail the falsity of that belief. The fact that we have been forced, at school, to believe heliocentrism is no sufficient reason to disbelieve it. Only a permanent lack of justification would lead us to suspect that this belief has been inculcated for an advantage, rather than for the truth's sake. Moreover, the belief that the world owes its existence to a cause seems to have been largely unknown out of the spatiotemporal limits of Jewish-Christian-Islamic traditions. But this does not mean that the question cannot arise but in monotheistic cultures. Amartya Sen has recently emphasized the emergence of this very question in the background of the Indian culture and an abbreviated version of the cosmological argument is to be found in Udayana's Nyāyakusumāñjali I,4.

Secondly, it is true that, since Schleiermacher has reduced the meaning of creation to 'the feeling of absolute dependence', many theologians like Karl Barth, Paul Tillich, and Rudolf Bultmann, have renounced the metaphysical significance of the doctrine, which is supposed to be nothing but an 'existential claim'. But philosophers are in no way committed to the choices made by theologians. Although creation was often considered as a basic doctrine without rational justification, some philosophers and apologists, from Tertullian to Samuel Clarke, and until Franz Brentano, have campaigned for humanity's ability to argue for creation out of nothing, without the help of supernatural revelation. It is up to philosophers to define the true metaphysical core of the doctrine.

Thirdly, the picture of creation presented in some contemporary defences of creationism is, according to Clavier, quite misleading and caricatural. In these caricatures, creation is grasped like a physical event. But it should be clear that the very bringing about of everything, if it is likely to occur (in a different meaning of 'occurring'), is to occur at least outside any physical framework. By rights, the methodology of the natural sciences rules out entities like 'God', 'infinite wisdom', 'creation out of nothing', etc. If something like God is to be inferred from physical states of affairs, it can hardly be by means of a deductive argument (there are no physical states of affairs such that it would be logically contradictory that they obtain without there being a God). It is always venturesome to infer a metaphysical conclusion from physical premises. For example, there can be no observational evidence for a supernatural agent intervening in biological processes. Moreover, it is not essential to the concept of creation that the created entity has a beginning of existence. For all these reasons, the concept of creation is worth being studied outside the so often misleading debate of creationism, which entangles science with metaphysics. As J.C. Maxwell suggests: 'Science is incompetent to reason upon creation out of nothing.'

Thus Clavier proceeds to clarify what is involved in the question about Creation: a matter of self-existence rather than a matter of time (1), before assessing the classic cosmological argument to a creator (2), and then Maxwell's argument to the createdness of physical world (3). After a brief rephrasing of the argument (4), he estimates to what extent creation may be held as the best explanation for there being laws of nature (5).

N. Verbin in her *Divine Providence: The View from Within* takes up the problem of suffering and evil by examining the concept of 'divine providence' as it is explicated by two great Jewish thinkers: Moses Maimonides and Simone Weil. She starts with Maimonides and proceeds with Weil.

Understanding God's nature as 'intellect' and our being created in God's image in terms of our 'intellect', Maimonides perceives the nature of God's providence over humanity in terms of the workings of the intellect too, stating: 'providence is consequent upon the intellect and attached to it.' (*Guide of the Perplexed* 3/17). When we come to consider what is involved in the workings of God's providence, the *Guide* is notoriously ambiguous. Certain passages suggest that the divine intellectual overflow protects the individual of perfect apprehension from harm in the sense that no physical harm, e.g., hunger, poverty, injury or sickness befall him/her. Other passages, however, describe the individual of perfect apprehension as free from the *agony* that such ills as poverty, injury or sickness ordinarily bring about, but not necessarily from the ills themselves. On the basis of his comments on Job and on the basis of his comments on the painless deaths of Moses, Aharon, and Miriam, which he characterizes as their being protected from death, Verbin argues that the latter 'contemplative' and non-interventionalist account of divine providence is the one that represents Maimonides's genuine views of divine providence.

Like Maimonides, Weil too divorces 'divine providence' from 'divine intervention' that rewards the righteous and punishes the wicked. Like Maimonides, Weil too conceives of divine providence in terms of our having a certain inner capacity to perceive or assent. This capacity, for Weil, is the only *locus* in which human freedom is exercised. Unlike Maimonides, however, Weil does not believe that the proper use of such a capacity guards us against affliction and despair.

According to Weil, the world was handed over to a blind mechanism that is indifferent to human beings' moral or spiritual perfection. This mechanism throws human beings randomly to the foot of the cross; it makes radical affliction possible. God's benevolent providential care consists in the establishment of this mechanism as well as in our capacity to perceive and respond to the mechanism in a variety of ways: to love or to refrain from loving God amidst radical affliction, to assent or not to assent 'to a right direction'. Weil conceives of these devices as devices of God's providential care since they allow for the realization of what is, in her view, the *summum bonum*: the ultimate love of God. They create the greatest possible distance from God and, thereby, the possibility of bridging that ultimate distance by means of love – love than which no greater can be perceived.

Maimonides and Weil provide challenging and fruitful accounts of divine providence. Despite their different evaluations of suffering, both dissolve the problem of suffering: Maimonides by rendering it insignificant; Weil, by perceiving it as an integral feature in the realization of a higher good. They render perspicuous the internal relation between one's conception of divine providence and one's conception of the *summum bonum*, be it justice, knowledge, or love. Moreover, in presenting non-interventionalist accounts of divine providence, which construe God's providence in terms of a human capacity for knowledge or love, they render much of the current philosophical debate over the compatibility of divine providence with human freedom redundant.

In an essay entitled *Theodicy of Justice as Fairness and Sceptical Pluralism: A View from Behind the Veil of Ignorance*, **Janusz Salamon** takes up two of the most hotly debated issues in contemporary philosophy of religion: the problem of evil and the problem of religious diversity. In both cases he attempts to 'read God's mind' concerning the way God relates to the victims of evils and to adherents of various religious traditions by asking what kind of attitudes or actions of God could in these contexts be considered just or fair. He proposes to consider this question about the meaning of Divine justice and what it might entail within the framework of 'perfect being theology' which would aim at approximating our human view of the human reality to 'God's eye view' on the human reality by way of gradual 'purification' of our human conceptions from their deficiencies and imperfections accounted for by the limitations of our cognitive faculties and perspectival character of our conceptual schemes. Moreover, he suggests that such purification of our conceptions has to be guided by the ethics of belief which takes seriously the challenge of doxastic religious pluralism and is informed by considerations of fairness.

Drawing the attention to the changing character of our moral imagination, he asserts that in order to give meaning to the attribute of Divine justice, we have no choice but to rely on our up-to-date moral intuitions concerning human justice, attributing to God the property of justice by way of the analogy of attribution. In order to identify what kind of up-to-date moral intuitions regarding human justice might be made use of in this context, drawing inspiration from John Rawls's theory of justice as fairness Salamon proposes to resort to thought experiments set up along the lines of the Rawlsian 'original position', in which all individuals involved would be ignorant of their actual position, in this case, their position vis-à-vis the facts relevant to the debates about the problem of evil and religious diversity. Salamon suggests that we should consider afresh various options available to the participants of these debates by looking at them 'from behind the veil of ignorance', allowing ourselves to be guided by our up-to-date moral intuitions concerning what attitudes or actions would be appropriate for God as a perfectly good Being. In so doing he formulates his own responses to the problem of evil and religious diversity which he respectively labels 'theodicy of justice as fairness' and 'sceptical pluralism'.

With regard to the first issue, Salamon suggests that since for all we know God does not intervene in *all* instances or even in *most* instances to prevent evils from happening, and moreover considerations of human free will, the possibility of moral development which arguably presupposes the presence of evil, the desirability of Divine hiddenness, and the undesirability of a massively irregular world, do jointly account for God's refraining in *some* instances from acting to prevent evils from occurring, therefore God's sense of justice as fairness – that is justice as conceived through the lenses of our recent egalitarian and individualistic moral insights into the nature of *human* justice as entailing conditions of impartiality, equal treatment, and freedom from favouritism or bias – effectively prevents God from intervening in *any* instances to change the natural course of the lives of victims of evils. In other words, since intervening in the lives of victims of evils only on rare occasions would not be just or fair, it follows that God *never* intervenes to prevent evils from happening, because for a perfectly good and just Being, such as God, it is not possible to do what is not just or fair.

With regard to the second issue, namely the philosophical challenge of religious diversity, Salamon proposes that God's sense of justice as fairness – or to put it differently, our understanding of Divine justice through the lenses of our new egalitarian and individualistic insights into the moral nature of human persons – falsifies all exclusivist theories of religious diversity that entail soteriological exclusivism (pertaining to chances of salvation / liberation / ultimate fulfilment), moral exclusivism (pertaining to the chances of acquiring moral knowledge and achieving full moral maturity), mystical exclusivism (pertaining to the chances of experiencing God's presence and entering the communion with God), or for that matter any other exclusivism that one can think of that would have a bearing on the chances of the fulfilment of the creaturely potential of human persons.

Salamon labels this approach to the challenge of religious diversity 'sceptical pluralism', because instead of postulating any kind of relativism or revisionism that might undermine one's epistemic confidence in the foundations of one's religious worldview, spiritual practice, and moral commitments, he proposes to adopt a strategy akin to the strategy of 'sceptical theism' and suggests that we should be sceptical of our ability to discern the full truth about the ways God leads various individuals to the ultimate fulfilment of their creaturely potential. In particular, a sceptical pluralist of the kind Salamon envisages will argue that we should be sceptical that our epistemic confidence in our understanding of God's purposes with respect to us individually and our co-religionists somehow limits God in achieving the purpose of leading religious aliens to the fulfilment of their human (God-given) potential in ways that are beyond our intellectual grasp.

As in the case of theodicy of justice as fairness, Salamon suggests that within the context of a thought experiment set up along the lines of the Rawlsian 'original position', in which all individuals involved would be ignorant of their actual position, their moral intuition would lead the vast majority of the participants of such an experiment to choose as morally more plausible such view of a Divine plan for humanity which entails that God positively allows religious diversity to persist and flourish, and consequently God will also make sure that all human persons – whatever their religious beliefs and religious affiliations – will in principle have a chance to achieve the ultimate fulfilment of their human potential, rather than a view on which only relatively few individuals in the course of human history will have a chance to end up in the camp of God's favourites who happened to have the right kind of religious beliefs and the right kind of religious affiliation, as exclusivists of various sorts presume is indeed the case.

In his essay entitled *Religious Inclusivism: A Philosophical Defence,* **Bernd Irlenborn** considers the plausibility of the threefold scheme (exclusivism, inclusivism, pluralism) of the recent debate about the way one can interrelate the multiplicity of divergent religious truth claims. He notes that the first two positions (exclusivism and inclusivism) are related, in so far as they claim the superiority of a single religion. They differ in so far that the exclusivist holds the foreign religion to be completely untrue, whereas the inclusivist holds it to be only partially untrue. Within the theology of religion, the term 'pluralism' includes some or all of the following assumptions: (a) the diversity of opinions and world views is actually insurmountable and to be recognized as normative, (b) the conviction of another is neither inferior nor false in regard to one's own conviction, (c) there is no universally recognized meta position for the evaluation of rival truth claims, (d) religious truth claims are at best only true in a mythological or relative sense.

Irlenborn notes that the validity of this threefold scheme is debated for various reasons. It is said, for example, that this scheme is unusable or that there are more models in addition to these three. Comparative theology or religious relativism are offered as substitutions for or additions to the previous models. An overall criticism of the offered scheme is, in Irlenborn's view, not valid. He assumes that the threefold scheme contains all the meaningful possibilities of affirmative interreligious relationships and that it is heuristically conducive to the analysis of religious truth claims. These relationships can be applied not only at the level of religions, but also at that of individual religious convictions. Here it is possible to differentiate, such that followers of a particular religion in one theological regard think inclusivistically regarding one theological issue (when it comes to the protection of human life, for example), and in another issue they are exclusivistic (e.g. in the thesis that there is only salvation through Jesus Christ). However, this differentiation does not alter the relevance of the threefold scheme.

Irlenborn's discussion of religious inclusivism is complemented by an essay entitled *Exclusive Inclusivism* by **Anita Renusch**. She begins by noticing that religious inclusivism is often presented by its advocates as if it were much more advantageous than religious exclusivism. Though its openness to other religions does not go as far as religious pluralism would require – the theory developed by Hick, Knitter and others – inclusivism is said to outstrip religious exclusivism to a considerable degree. Ever since inclusivism was vindicated for the first time, there have been doubts whether this characterization is right. In her essay, Renusch articulates these doubts more explicitly by clarifying the putative distinction between religious exclusivism and inclusivism. She argues that the claim that there are significant epistemic differences rests on an overly restrictive notion of exclusivism and a misleading use of metaphors like 'an element of truth'. She concludes that the similarities make it advisable for inclusivists to focus their attention on the problems shared with exclusivism instead of dissociating themselves from exclusivism.

The volume closes with yet another essay focusing on the challenges of pluralism, this time not so much the pluralism of truth claims as the pluralism of methods employed in philosophy of religion. In his essay entitled *Methodological Pluralism and the Subject Matter of the Philosophy of Religion*, **Vladimir K. Shokhin** aims at answering the questions of what the proper tasks of philosophy of religion are in the 21st century, given the challenge of methodological pluralism. He begins by noticing that analytical philosophy of religion having great merits in the rational apology of theism does not differ substantially in its subject matters from rational theology or natural theology as founded on one or other epistemological basis (like internalism, externalism etc.). Philosophy of religion in the proper sense has, in contrary, by definition, to have religion and not God as its subject (in the same way as science and education make subjects of philosophies of science and education), which does not, at the same time, exclude apologetics from its purview. One way to mark the area of its tasks in the 21th century could be to turn to the reality of das Religiöse (the term implemented by Fichte during the famous Atheism Controversy in Jena in 1798/9 and having no real English equivalent) as manifesting itself in religiousness (as such), religion (in singular) and religions (in plural).

Shokhin differentiates the main tasks of philosophy of religion as investigating (1) autonomy versus heteronomy of religiousness in the human existence; 2) a possibility to vindicate religion (in singular) besides different traditions; 3) numerous definitions of religion; 4) essential characteristics of religion (as different from its abstract attributes generalized in definitions); 5) religious universals (Divinity, faith, revelation, community, doctrine, salvation, etc.); 6) the phenomenon of atheism (including the paradoxical presence of religiousness in it); 7) classifications of the main types of religious world-outlooks; 8) classifications of religions themselves (like the world religions, national religions, new religions); 9) different criteria for comparison of religions; 10) roles played by philosophy in different religious traditions; 11) criteria of Religionskritik (how does an empirical tradition correspond to its 'eidos'). In addition, philosophy of religion should be interested in 12) arranging the space of adjacent regions of knowledge (both of religious studies and varieties of rational theology) and (in accordance with natural self-reflection of any philosophical area) 13) stages of its own history and exposure of its own clichés (like estimations of Western and Eastern religions as, correspondingly, 'exclusivistic' and 'pluralistic', 'tolerant' and 'intolerant', etc.).

Defining the many tasks of the future philosophy of religion seems a suitable way to end a volume of essays which wants to be an indication of what lies ahead and a testimony to the provisional character of philosophical claims, always open to criticism, deeper analysis and revision.

Sebastian T. Kołodziejczyk
Janusz Salamon

PART I
EPISTEMOLOGY AND RELIGION

Why Hume and Kant Were Mistaken in Rejecting Natural Theology[1]

Richard Swinburne

Natural theology in the sense of arguments from evident features of the natural world to the existence and nature of God has been part of the Christian intellectual tradition for most of its life, and it has roots both in the Old Testament and in Greek philosophy.[2] Not that any of the Christian Fathers, scholastics, and later theologians thought that everyone needed natural theology; but they thought that it was available for any who doubted the existence of God and were capable of understanding the arguments. But this whole tradition became discredited among philosophers and theologians as a result of the similar arguments put forward by Hume and Kant about the bounds to what humans could understand and know. Kant's arguments have had an enormous influence for the past two centuries on the thinking of philosophers on the continent of Europe, and via these philosophers on theologians in English speaking countries as well as on the continent of Europe. Hume's arguments had their greatest influence on the thinking of English speaking philosophers; and the latter influence was at its strongest in the middle years of the twentieth century. I claim that the arguments of both philosophers about the limits to human understanding and knowledge are totally unsound, and so there is good reason for natural theology to resume its proper place in the Christian and – more generally – the philosophical tradition.

I begin with Hume. Hume's very general principle of the bounds of intelligibility is that all our 'ideas' are compounded of simple ideas, and that all simple ideas are derived from 'impressions'.[3] By 'impressions' he means 'all our more lively perceptions [i.e. conscious events] when we hear, or see, or feel,

---

1   This paper has been published previously in (ed.) T. Buchheim and others, *Gottesbeweise als Herausforderung für die Moderne Vernunft* (Tübingen: Mohr Siebeck, 2012); and is republished with the agreement of the editors and publisher of that volume.

2   For my brief account of the development of natural theology within Judaeo-Christian thought, and of some opposition to it, see my *Faith and Reason*, second edition (Oxford: Oxford University Press, 2005), pp. 106-121.

3   David Hume, *An Enquiry Concerning Human Understanding*, (ed.) L.A. Selby-Bigge, second edition (Oxford: Clarendon Press, 1902), section 2.12. (My references to Hume's 'sections' are to the numbered paragraphs of the Selby-Bigge edition.)

or love, or hate, or desire, or will'; while by 'ideas' he means 'the less lively perceptions, of which we are conscious, when we reflect on any of those sensations or perceptions above mentioned'.[4] The ideas produced by impressions can be analysed as composed of 'simple' ideas. We can combine our simple ideas in various ways so as to form complex ideas of things of which we do not have any impression. Thus, to use Hume's example, having had impressions of gold and of a mountain, we can have ideas of gold and of a mountain and then combine them to form the idea of a golden mountain, of which we have not had any impression. But – Hume claims – none of us can have any ideas except ones composed of simple ideas ultimately derived from our own impressions. And since, he assumes, humans have impressions only of certain sensible kinds, we can have ideas only of certain kinds. So 'when we entertain ... any suspicion that a philosophical term is employed without any meaning or idea (as is but too frequent), we need but enquire *from what impression is that supposed idea derived*'; and if no such impression can be produced, that would 'confirm our suspicion' that the term is being employed 'without any meaning or idea'; that is, is meaningless.[5] Hence, Hume claimed, what we can think is 'confined within very narrow limits'.[6]

Hume had a very crude understanding of the nature of thought. It does indeed involve operating with ideas, normally (and especially in the modern world, since Kant) called 'concepts'; but concepts are not faint images of perceptions, understood as the conscious events which occur in us when we perceive. Sometimes using a concept of x may be accompanied by having a faint image of x. But that is never sufficient, and seldom (perhaps never) necessary. Thinking that inflation is increasing doesn't involve having a faint image of inflation; and if one did have a faint image accompanying the thought (e.g. of shopkeepers putting larger numbers on the labels of their goods), that could be an image of many things other than inflation (e.g. the numbers could be the new numbers of the goods in some catalogue). But despite his crude theory of thinking, Hume was probably correct in the general point he was trying to make, that – as a contingent fact[7]- we think only by means of concepts derived (in some sense) from our experience of their application to the (internal

---

4   op. cit. 2.12.

5   op. cit. 2.17.

6   op. cit. 2.13.

7   It cannot be a necessary truth that all our concepts are derived from experience. No doubt I get my concept of 'green' as a result of having seen green things in the past. But suppose a scientist of the future is able to create an exact duplicate of me as I am now. The duplicate would have the same concept of green as I have, and yet he would not have it as a result of having seen green things.

or external) world. As the medievals put it, *nil in intellectu quod non prius in sensu*. But there are two crucial problems with this slogan. One is (to phrase the point in Hume's terms) that our 'impressions' can give rise to many different 'ideas', some of them applicable only to substances and properties very similar in almost all respects to those which caused the original impression, and other ideas which can be applied to substances and properties very different from those in many respects. Suppose Hume has impressions of what are in fact eighteenth-century European humans. These impressions can give rise to an idea applicable to and only to eighteenth-century European humans. But they could also give rise to an idea applicable to, and only to, humans of any time and culture, and also to an idea applicable to and only to persons (i.e. any rational beings, including for example Martians). This problem is – how general are the ideas which we can form from our experience of the world? The other problem is: in what ways is it permissible to combine ideas so as to form other ideas? Can we combine the idea of a person with the idea of a part, and the idea of *not* having something,[8] and the idea of a material object, so as to give rise to the idea of a person who does not have any material object as a part (i.e. is non-embodied)? And could we go further by combining this latter idea with the ideas of power, action, goodness, knowledge, and belief, and the idea of a true sentence (all of which ideas are derivable from impressions), to get the idea of a non-embodied person who has the power to do every good action, no power to do an action which is not good, knows all true sentences, and does not believe any sentences which are not true? If so, we are well on the way to having an idea of God. Hume did not face up to these problems. But whether 'what we can think is confined within very narrow limits' depends on the solutions to them.

Hume's concern with intelligibility is a concern about which words expressing which concepts can be combined in such a way as to form a sentence which expresses a logically possible proposition, one which we may call in an objective sense conceivable. A logically possible proposition is one which does not entail a contradiction. As any given proposition entails an infinite number of propositions, we cannot show that it is logically possible by inspecting them all and not finding a contradiction among them. Rather, to show that some proposition is really logically possible (or, as the case may be, impossible) we

---

8   Hume seems to allow that we do have in some sense a concept of 'not' which he calls 'contrariety' and lists as a 'connection among ideas' *(Enquiry* 19n.); and that general ideas, and so the concept of 'any', are really particular ideas which call to mind other particular ideas *(Enquiry* 125n. summarizing his *Treatise of Human Nature* 1.1.7). But these brief remarks constitute mere 'hints' (see *Enquiry* 125n.) as to how a theory might be developed.

depend on the assumption that a proposition which is apparently logically possible (or impossible), probably is really logically possible (or impossible, as the case may be). If intuitions clash, that is if it is disputed whether or not some proposition p is logically possible, the way forward is to try to show either that p does entail a contradiction *or* that some other proposition q is logically possible and that q entails p. For if q is logically possible, so is any proposition which is entailed by q. One proposition x entails another one y iff (x and not–y) is logically impossible; and so the resolution of these disputes requires further intuitions about logical impossibility; which again depend for their justification on the apparently logically possible (or impossible) being good evidence of the really logically possible (or impossible). If one disputant cannot get the other disputant to agree straight away with his claim that some proposition x entails another one y, he may be able to get him to agree that x entails s, s entails t, and so on until we reach y; since entailment is transitive, that would prove that x entails y. But in all these ways we can only prove a disputed proposition to be logically possible or impossible on the basis of agreement about some other propositions that they are logically possible or impossible. There is no easy maxim (such as Hume, or – later – the logical positivists,[9] thought that they could provide) which will enable us to determine whether some proposition is logically possible or impossible. Only by the methods I have described can we determine by a deductive argument[10] whether it is logically

---

9   Logical positivists claimed that to be 'factually meaningful', which we may understand as 'logically contingent', a proposition had to be 'verifiable'. But if 'verifiable' is understood as 'conclusively verifiable', the claim becomes implausible since very few propositions are conclusively verifiable; and if 'verifiable' is understood as 'such that some possible evidence could make it more probable than it would otherwise be', very few propositions – if any (apart from any which are logically impossible) – would be excluded. Anyway there is no good reason for supposing that any form of verificationism is true; our understanding of a proposition arises not from our understanding of how it could be verified, but from our understanding of its constituent concepts and the grammatical form of the sentence which expresses it. See my *The Coherence of Theism*, revised edition (Oxford: Oxford University Press, 1993), ch. 2.

10   There are probabilistic versions of arguments of these kinds, arguments from the fact that some proposition is logically possible to a conclusion that it is (epistemically) probable that a similar proposition is logically possible, and arguments from the fact that one proposition entails a contradiction to the conclusion that it is (epistemically) probable that a similar proposition does also. For example if one admits that it is logically possible that a human could live forever, that seems to make it (epistemically) probable that it is logically possible that a tiger could live forever. Such an argument is an argument to show that (probably) the relevant proposition does not entail a contradiction; but it does not have the compelling force of a deduction from an evidently

possible that there be more than one space or time, or an effect can precede its cause, or an event can occur without a cause, or whatever; and so only in this way (to put the point in Hume's terms) can we determine the limits to how general are the 'ideas' we can derive from impressions, and to the ways in which we can combine simple ideas to form complex ones.

Hume claimed that we derive our idea of 'cause' from impressions of 'constant conjunction'; that is, regular succession. And he claimed on the basis of the principle discussed above that since our idea of x causing y was formed by impressions of 'objects' (that is, events) like x being regularly followed by objects like y, our concept of cause was therefore itself a concept of regular succession;[11] that is, to say that an event x causes an event y entails that for some A and B, x is A, y is B and that all (or perhaps just most) A's are followed by B's. It is then natural to suppose that the only way we can learn about the cause of a new effect y which is a B is by finding that it is preceded

---

logically possible premiss. One important kind of probabilistic argument to show that some proposition is logically possible is the following. It may be that some observed phenomena would be explained very well by some hypothesis, and so be very probable on normal criteria of what is evidence for what, if the proposition stating that hypothesis was logically possible. Thus the hypothesis that light is both particulate and wavelike may be shown to be (probably) logically possible, on the grounds that if it is logically possible it can explain the various phenomena of light – interference, diffraction, reflection, photoelectric effect, Compton effect, etc., whereas the hypothesis that light is a particle and not a wave or the hypothesis that light is a wave and not a particle can only explain some of these phenomena. Without the supposition that light is both particulate and wavelike the occurrence of some of these phenomena would be very improbable; hence their occurrence is evidence for the truth and so the logical possibility of the supposition. Or someone might deny the logical possibility of a non-embodied person, yet faced with phenomena best explained by the hypothesis that there was a poltergeist (non-embodied person) in the room – e.g. handwriting being formed on a piece of paper without any visible or tactual hand writing it, etc., etc. – might acknowledge the hypothesis as probably true and so probably logically possible. This kind of argument is not an argument from the logical possibility of such phenomena but from their actual occurrence (if they do occur). I discuss this type of argument in *The Coherence of Theism,* pp. 48-50.

11   'We may define a cause to be an object, followed by another, and where all the objects similar to the first are followed by objects similar to the second.' – op. cit. 7(ii).60. Hume does provide, in this passage and elsewhere, also a second definition of 'cause' as 'an object followed by another, and whose appearance always conveys the thought to that other', in other words a cause of an effect is an event which always leads us to think of the effect. But this is not a very plausible definition, and those in the Humean tradition have normally ignored it, and used the former definition to develop the 'regularity theory of causation'.

by some event x which is an A such that – in our experience – all A's are followed by B's and no B's are not preceded by A's; from which we can conclude that x is the cause of y.[12] So, when discussing the suggestion that the universe was caused to exist by God, Hume argues:

> When two species of objects have always been observed to be conjoined together, I can infer by custom the existence of one whenever I see the existence of the other, and this I call an argument from experience. But how this argument can have place where the objects as in the present case [i.e. when God is supposed to cause the universe], are single, individual, without parallel or specific resemblance, may be difficult to explain.[13]

It would seem to follow that we would have to have observed many acts of will of many gods being followed by the existence of universes before we could conclude that our God caused our universe. So even if it were intelligible to suppose that God could cause the universe, it follows that we could have no knowledge that he did.

Now given my earlier point, it does not follow that even if the concept of cause is a concept of regular succession, it cannot be meaningfully applied to regular successions of unobservable events. For we could derive from impressions of regular successions of events not merely the idea of one observable event causing another such event, but the more general idea of one event (whether observable or unobservable) causing another event. So we can certainly speculate about states of atoms causing other states of atoms, even if we cannot learn much about causation at the atomic scale. But if the concept of causation is a concept of regular succession, it is plausible to suppose that it is meaningless even to speculate about single causes, causes which cause effects even though no similar objects cause similar effects.

Hume was however, I suggest, mistaken in supposing that our impressions of regular succession are the only or even the main impressions from which we derive our idea of causation. For we experience ourselves causing effects. A basic action is an action which an agent does intentionally, but does not do by doing anything else intentionally. Me making a simple bodily movement, such as me moving my hand, is normally a basic action – I just do it, do not do it

---

12   I am reading Hume in the traditional way as claiming that the 'necessity' by which a cause is followed by its effect just consists in 'constant conjunction'. Some recent writers claim that Hume has been misunderstood, and that all he was claiming is that we cannot have any more knowledge of the necessity of cause and effect than is provided by constant conjunction. See for example Galen Strawson, *The Secret Connection: Causation, Realism, and David Hume* (Oxford: Oxford University Press, 1989).

13   David Hume, *Dialogues Concerning Natural Religion*, ed. by H.D. Aiken, Hafner, 1948, p. 23.

by doing anything else. (Although of course certain neural events have to happen in order for me to move my hand, I do not intentionally bring these about.) In doing such actions as moving a hand intentionally I seem to be aware of myself as causing an effect (the motion of my hand). And if things are as they seem to be, most basic actions consist in causing (independently identifiable) effects. But there are basic actions which – if things are as they seem to be – do not consist in causing an effect; some actions of trying to bring about some bodily movement are basic actions – for example my trying to move my hand if it is tied down by a rope, or my trying to lift a heavy weight, are basic actions, even if the effect which I seek to cause does not occur. And what is it for me to try to move my hand? It is to do whatever it seems to me will make it causally more likely that my hand will move. There is no separate event which I perform and which I can describe in some other way than as 'doing what it seems to me will make it causally more likely that my hand will move'. In such trying I seem to be aware of myself as exerting causal influence such that if I exerted enough of it, and external circumstances permitted (e.g. if the rope would snap under the amount of force I could exert) I would cause the intended effect. So both in performing easy basic actions and in trying to perform difficult basic actions, I seem to be aware of myself as exerting causal influence. And since it is surely probable that things are as they seem to be (that is, as we find ourselves inclined to believe that they are) in the absence of counter-evidence (a general principle which in effect I have already used in discussing logical possibility) it is probable that I am exerting causal influence when I perform an easy basic action or try to perform a difficult one.

Without this general principle, which I call the Principle of Credulity, that it is probable that things are as they seem to be, we could have no knowledge of the external world, let alone knowledge from memory of which past events were succeeded by which other events, knowledge which Hume supposes that we have in his discussion of causation. We thus derive our idea of cause from the impression of ourselves exerting successful causal influence; that is, causing. We could not discover that we cause the motion of a hand from observing a regular succession, because there is no earlier event which we could discover to have been normally followed by the motion of a hand (except in some cases, the event of trying to move the hand, which – if it succeeds – we must already believe to be an event of causing). We could of course occasionally discover that we were subject to an illusion in believing that we were moving our hand; but discovering the illusion would consist in discovering that something which we already understood as a causal relation really was not one. We must already have beliefs that we cause movements before we could discover that sometimes we don't.[14]

Having acquired the notion of causation from finding that we can cause bodily movements, we may then find that we can cause an event of kind B (e.g. a window being broken) by causing an event of kind A (e.g. a brick being propelled towards the window). We find that once we have caused the A, the subsequent occurrence of the B does not depend on us in any way and so is an effect caused by the A; we cause the A and it causes the B; and since we can cause B's again and again by causing A's, the A causing the B is an instance of a regular causal succession. So we come to see that the concept of causation which we derive from ourselves intentionally causing effects, applies also to regular successions of events over the development of which we have no control. Hence we come to see the B-type events as caused in the same sense as the effects of our basic actions are caused, except that the causation need not be intended.

Our primary awareness of causation is then an awareness of an agent (oneself), not an event, causing an effect.[15] And because our awareness of causation is not an awareness of regular successions of events (which are

14 Hume had an argument against the view that we have a direct awareness of exerting causal influence. He claims that the will 'has no more a discoverable connection with its effects, than any material cause has with its proper effect'. Such a connection 'could not be foreseen without the experience of their constant conjunction'. See his *Treatise of Human Nature*, Appendix. I argue above that a 'will' (or a 'volition' or 'trying') to perform a basic action which consists in bringing about *x* cannot be identified except as that action which the subject believes to be an exertion of causal influence towards the production of *x*; and that when my trying is followed by the occurrence of the required event (*x*), it is probable that my trying is my causing (even in the absence of any evidence of constant conjunctions).

15 This may lead us – correctly in my view – to analyse all causation, not merely causation by intentional agents, as causation by a substance, not by an event. It is the brick, not the motion of the brick, which causes the window to break. The brick causes this because it has the power to transfer its momentum to another substance, and the liability to exercise that power when another substance impedes its motion. So when its motion is impeded by a fragile window, it will transfer its momentum to the window, and the window will break. It follows that 'laws of nature' are generalizations about the powers and liabilities of substances of different kinds; they depend on fundamental laws which concern the interactions of different kinds of particles (electrons, quarks, etc.), differing from each other in their powers and liabilities (e.g. to attract or repel other particles in different ways). For defence of this view see the first four pages of my 'God as the Simplest Explanation of the Universe', *European Journal for Philosophy of Religion*, 2 (2010), 1-24, and in: ed. by A. O'Hear *Philosophical Essays on Religion* (Cambridge: Cambridge University Press, 2011).

the events they are independently of their causal influence), it follows that an agent can cause an effect without that entailing that similar agents would cause similar effects under similar circumstances. So singular causation is possible.

Once we realize that there can be unobservable causes and singular causes, it becomes evident that we need a wider account of the grounds for believing x to be cause of y, than that x is an A, y is a B, *and* that we have observed that (in our experience) A's are followed by B's, and that all B's are preceded by A's, (or rather we need such an account of the grounds for attributing causes to those events which we did not ourselves intentionally cause). These normal grounds, to give a very condensed account of them which would be acceptable to many contemporary philosophers of science, are that it follows from an explanatory hypothesis H which is rendered probable by data, that x is the cause of y. An explanatory hypothesis (or theory) is rendered probably true by data (evidence) insofar as (1) the hypothesis predicts, that is makes probable, much evidence observed to be true and no evidence observed to be false, (2) the hypothesis 'fits in' with any 'background evidence' (that is, it meshes with theories outside its scope which are rendered probable by their evidence in virtue of these criteria), (3) the hypothesis is simple, and (4) the hypothesis has small scope. I understand by 'evidence' the phenomena which the hypothesis, if it is true, would explain; and I contrast this with 'background evidence' which is evidence relevant to theories outside the scope of H. By the hypothesis 'predicting' evidence, we should understand merely that it makes probable much observed evidence and no evidence observed to be false. It is, I suggest, irrelevant, whether the evidence is discovered before or after the formulation of the theory. The scope of a hypothesis is a matter of how much it purports to tell us about the world, in the extent and precision of its claims; the more the hypothesis claims, the less likely it is to be true. Simplicity however carries more weight than scope; scientists consider some theory of enormous scope (e.g. a theory of the evolution of the physical universe from the Big Bang) quite probable if constitutes a simple explanatory hypothesis. There may be no relevant background evidence, and then criterion (2) drops out. One case of this is when a hypothesis has very large scope (as does Quantum theory) and so there is little if any evidence about fields beyond its scope. The relative probability of large scale theories of equal scope, such as theism and rival theories of why there is a universe of our kind, depends on criteria (1) and (3) alone; and so in the case of theories leading us to expect the evidence with the same probability (that is, satisfying criterion (1) equally well), on criterion (3) alone. A theory is simple insofar as it postulates few substances, few kinds of substance, few properties (including powers and liabilities), few kinds of properties, and mathematically simple relations between them. And scientists have often recognized that it is simpler to postulate an infinite degree (one to which there is no limit) of a quantity rather than some very large finite degree – when hypotheses postulating either kind of quantity are equally able to satisfy criterion (1). For example Newton postulated that the force of gravity was transmitted with infinite velocity, while the supposition that it was transmitted with a very large finite velocity would have predicted the evidence equally well.[16]

It follows from this general account that if we have observed many A's followed by B's, no A's not followed by B's, and no B's not preceded by A's, that the theory 'All and only A's cause B's' is the simplest explanation of the data, and so the most probable explanation of the occurrence of another B is that it was caused by an A. But my general account allows hypotheses in terms of unobservables, or of entities which are (in a causally important respect) the only ones of their kind, to be rendered probable by evidence. Hence a hypothesis postulating one simple entity which predicts very many data quite inexplicable otherwise may be rendered probable thereby, and so therefore may be any new explanations which that simple entity provides. Hence, contrary to Hume, natural theology is possible.

I should add that, as well as these very general arguments against the possibility of natural theology arising from his claims about the limits to human understanding and knowledge, Hume had various arguments to the effect that even if we allow that theism could be considered as a possible explanatory hypothesis, it isn't a very probable one. Section 11 of his *Enquiry Concerning Human Understanding* and his *Dialogues Concerning Natural Religion* discuss the form of the argument to design which has as its data the intricate construction of the bodies of humans and animals, and argues thence to God as their designer. In effect he considers it as an argument purporting to satisfy the kind of criteria which I've just advocated, and claims that it does not satisfy them very well. He claims that there are data incompatible with the hypothesis (e.g. human suffering), and other equally probable rival explanations of the data of the intricate construction of bodies

---

16   I discuss what makes explanatory hypotheses probable more fully in my *The Existence of God* (Oxford: Oxford University Press, second edition, 2004), ch. 3; and I give a systematic treatment of this in my *Epistemic Justification* (Oxford: Oxford University Press, 2001), chs 3 & 4. The latter contains a full discussion of the nature and role of the criterion of simplicity. But it is unsatisfactory in the respect that it gives separate accounts of the simplicity of an inanimate explanation (in terms of initial conditions and laws of nature) from that of a personal explanation (in terms of persons, their powers, beliefs, and purposes). I provide a unified account of the simplicity which makes explanations of either kind probable in 'God as the Simplest Explanation of the Universe' (referred to in note 15).

(e.g. in terms of the action of many gods, or of chance). These claims need to be considered in detail – I believe that they all fail.[17] But they are claims which, unlike the claims which I have been discussing so far, do allow any detailed arguments of natural theology to be discussed on their particular merits; they do not rule out the possibility of natural theology in advance.

Hume's general principles about the limits to human understanding and knowledge had a great influence on Kant; and although it is Kant and not Hume who has had such a great influence on continental philosophy, I have spent so much time discussing Hume, because Kant inherited some of Hume's bad mistakes. Kant did of course however have a far more sophisticated philosophy than Hume's crude empiricism. To start with, Kant made the needed distinction between concept and object, in consequence of which his 'concept' was no mere faint image. He tells us that the inputs to our mental life are 'intuitions' and that these are interpreted by concepts. Since, he claims, the only intuitions humans can have are 'sensible intuitions', the categories yield knowledge only insofar as they can be applied to such intuitions – 'The categories, as yielding knowledge of things, have no kind of application, save only in regard to things which may be objects of possible experience'[18] and that – according to Kant – means 'sensible' experience. Although – unlike Hume – he allows, we can have concepts of objects outside possible experience, concepts of an infinitely divisible substance, and of *noumena*, and – more particularly – the concept of a supreme being, we cannot, he held, reason about such objects; and so he adopted a modified form of Hume's view. Kant wrote 'if no intuition could be given corresponding to the concept, ... so far as I could know, there ... could be nothing to which my thought could be applied'.[19] Hence, like Hume, Kant denied that we could have any knowledge of causes apart from ones connecting sensible phenomena in regular ways. Thus: 'the principle of causality has ... no criterion for its application save only in the sensible world'[20] since causation consists 'in the succession of the manifold, in so far as that succession is subject to a rule'.[21] Hence again no scope for natural theology.

---

17   For my analysis and refutation of the eight separate objections which I found in Hume's writings against the argument from design, his principal target in his attack on natural theology, see my 'The Argument from Design', *Philosophy*, 43 (1968), 199-212.

18   I. Kant, *Critique of Pure Reason*, tr. N. Kemp-Smith (London: Macmillan, 1964), B147-8.

19   op. cit. B146.

20   op. cit. B637.

21   op. cit. B183. Of course Kant did not think that all regular successions were causal successions; but he did think, like Hume, that a case of causality consisted of an instance of a causal law which consisted in an event of one particular kind being followed regularly (and indeed invariably) by an event of another particular kind. For the last

His claim however that our 'categories' (i.e. concepts) have no use in providing knowledge except when applied to objects of 'possible' sensible experience, raises the question of how we know which sensible experiences are 'possible'. 'Possible' for Kant is logically possible or objectively conceivable; and Kant purported to have demonstrated some firm results about the limits to conceivable experience, none of which seem to me plausible. For example he claimed that 'we can represent to ourselves only one space; and if we speak of diverse spaces, we mean thereby only parts of one and the same unique space',[22] and that our concept of space yields synthetic a priori knowledge that its geometry is Euclidean.[23] But it seems possible to describe what it would be like to experience life in a closed but unbounded universe (which would not be Euclidean) – it would be such that in whichever direction you go, you would eventually seem to come back to your starting point.[24] And if you found it possible by taking a pill or entering a strange cupboard[25] or just by falling asleep[26] to reach a place which did not belong to the fully explored space of the previous universe, it would be a universe in a different space. The only way to determine whether it is logically possible that we could have such experiences is by the painstaking method described earlier, beginning with the principle that the apparently logically possible is good evidence of what is really logically possible.

But even if a category derived from experience is applied to something which cannot be experienced, it does not follow that we cannot have knowledge of the latter. Whether we can or not depends on whether a hypothesis using that

---

hundred years many thinkers in this tradition have allowed that, as well as deterministic causal laws which consist of an event of one particular kind being followed invariably by an event of another particular kind, there can be probabilistic causal laws which consist in an event of one particular kind being followed with high (physical) probability by an event of another particular kind.

22   op. cit. B 39.

23   op. cit. B 744-5.

24   See the description of the experiences which an inhabitant of a particular kind of closed universe, a 'torus' universe, would have, in Hans Reichenbach, *The Philosophy of Space and Time* (New York: Dover Publications, 1958), section 12. Reichenbach points out (p. 66) that, given the experiences which he describes, someone could insist that the geometry of the universe was Euclidean only by adopting a wildly implausible hypothesis of 'preestablished harmony'.

25   As in the Narnia stories of C.S. Lewis – see his *The Lion, The Witch and the Wardrobe* and *The Magician's Nephew*.

26   As in the story told in Anthony Quinton 'Spaces and Times' republished in: ed. by R. Le Poidevin and M. Macbeath, *The Philosophy of Time* (Oxford: Oxford University Press, 1993).

concept is logically possible (as shown in the way set out earlier) and rendered probable by observed evidence. If a hypothesis about unobservable persons is logically possible and yields many good predictions, that is reason to suppose that it is probably true. And if the probability is high enough, we can (very probably) know that it is true.

Kant's most important use of his principle about the limits to knowledge was his claim that since only the conditioned could be an object of possible experience, we can have no knowledge of the 'unconditioned' (that which is unlimited – such as the whole physical universe throughout space and time), and so we can have no knowledge of God, the supposed cause of all things, unconditioned in his power, knowledge, length of life, etc. Kant claimed to illustrate this by showing how various attempts to acquire knowledge of the unconditioned land us in irresoluble conflicts. The 'Antinomies of Pure Reason' purport to show how if we adduce an argument in favour of some position about the unconditioned we find that there is an equally plausible argument in favour of the opposite position. These arguments all appeal to purported rational principles, and certainly show that either the principle invoked in the thesis or the principle invoked in the antithesis (or both) must be fallacious; but in my view – despite Kant – none of these principles are obvious necessary truths of reason, and evidence can often make one such principle more probable than another. Thus the form of the thesis concerned with time in the first antinomy depends on the principle that 'the infinity of a series consists in the fact that it can never be completed through successive synthesis'.[27] The obvious response is that the principle (seemingly stated as a mathematical truth) is misstated. It should read 'the infinity of a series *with a first member* consists in the fact that it can never be completed through successive synthesis'; and since the first antinomy is concerned with a series with a last member but without a first member, it is not relevant. The antithesis depends on the principle that 'no coming to be of a thing is possible in an empty time'.[28] Kant claims that he has proved in the second analogy[29] that this is necessary, that it is an indispensable law of the empirical representation of the temporal series that the appearances of a past time determine every existence in the following time. His claim is that our ability to distinguish in a succession of perceptions those the order of which depends solely on us (whether we look at this part of a house before that part or vice versa) and those the order of which depends on objective change in the world (seeing the ship

---

27   op. cit. B454.
28   op. cit. B455.
29   op. cit. B233-256.

first higher in the stream, then lower in the stream), requires the assumption of an objective causation in the world (the earlier position of the ship causing its later position).[30] It is true that we can have no knowledge of events unless they have causes or effects from which we can infer them, and we can only make such an inference about the world beyond our immediate experience if in general there are regular causal sequences in the world. But we can learn about some events from observing their effects, and about other events by predicting them from their causes. We do not have to suppose that every event of which we have knowledge has a cause. For example, it may be that tracing back the states of our universe in accord with what are on our evidence very probably the laws of nature leads to a physically impossible state at some earlier time, and so we can conclude that very probably the universe began to exist after that time.[31]

Similar problems beset the version of the first antinomy concerned with Space. The thesis designed to show the impossibility of an infinite space claims that to think of such a space as a whole, we must regard it as consisting of an infinite number of parts, to enumerate which would take an infinite amount of time. Kant claimed to have shown that we cannot justifiably suppose there to be such an infinite time; but we have just seen the fallacy in Kant's argument about this. The antithesis of the argument about space relies on the claim that if 'the world in space is finite and limited' it would exist 'in an empty space which is unlimited'.[32] But that does not follow if space is closed and unbounded, and we could have evidence that space is closed and unbounded – either evidence of experience (see earlier) or evidence that the theory that it is closed and unbounded is probable on various data observed by physicists.

While there are, I believe similar problems of detail with the thesis and antithesis arguments of the other antinomies, the failure of Kant's claims about the first antinomy should suffice to show that there is no general reason to suppose that there must always be equally plausible arguments in favour of rival claims about the unconditioned. And there are two fundamental problems with all Kant's arguments about these issues. The first problem is that he thinks that our knowledge of the world depends on certain knowledge of some necessary principles about the world (e.g. 'every event has a cause'); and this restricts our knowledge of the world to those aspects of it governed by those principles of which we can have certain knowledge. But of course, as

---

30   For exposition of this argument see Paul Guyer, *Kant* (London: Routledge, 2006), pp. 109-112.

31   As argued in my *Space and Time*, second edition (London: Macmillan, 1981), ch.15. We would have no justification for postulating an earlier state of the universe governed by different causal laws.

32   op. cit. B 456.

Butler wrote a few decades earlier, 'to us [i.e. humans, opposed to God], probability [not knowledge] is the very guide of life'.[33] And the second and connected problem for Kant is that he did not have a clear idea of what are the criteria for observed data making probable a theory about the unobservable – which I expounded earlier. There is a simple historical explanation of this ignorance. Kant died in 1804. It was only in 1803 that the first version of an atomic theory of chemistry was proposed by Dalton which gave – by the criteria I expounded – a very probable explanation of the details of observed data (such as the fixed ratios by weight in which substances combined to form new substances). Before Dalton, theories about the unobservable were simply unevidenced speculations. Since Dalton, scientists have produced evidence making probable detailed theories not merely about things too small, but about things too big, too old, and too strange to be observed. Kant had great respect for the physical sciences; if he had known of their subsequent history, he might have acknowledged great scope for human reason to acquire probably true beliefs about matters far beyond the observable.

As well as adducing arguments depending on his principles about the limits of intelligibility and the impossibility of knowledge of the unconditioned, Kant had one further influential argument against the possibility of arguments to the existence of God. He claims that all other arguments of natural theology, which he considers to be merely the cosmological and 'physico-theological' arguments, depend for their soundness on the ontological argument. While he allows that it is 'an admissible hypothesis' to postulate 'an all-sufficient being, as the cause of all possible effects',[34] he nevertheless claims that we would need an ontological argument to show that such a being exists necessarily; that is, of logical necessity; and he assumes that the concept of God is the concept of a being who exists of logical necessity. He thinks that he has shown that no such argument can work, since 'there is not the least contradiction' in the judgment 'there is no God'. 'I cannot', he writes 'form the least concept of a thing which, should it be rejected with all its predicates, leaves behind a contradiction.'[35] He can make no sense of the possibility, let alone have grounds for believing in the actuality, of such a being.

It seems to me, as to Kant and to most modern non-religious philosophers, not merely that there cannot be a sound ontological argument from evident premises for the existence of a logically necessary God, but that there cannot be any logically necessary substance, understood as a logically necessary being

---

33   Joseph Butler, *The Analogy of Religion*, Introduction.
34   op. cit. B640.
35   op. cit. B623.

which can cause or be acted upon causally. It seems to me, for example, evident that it is logically possible that '10 billion years ago there were no rational beings'; it follows from that, since God is essentially an eternal rational being, that it is logically possible that there is no God, and so that it is not logically possible that there be a logically necessary God. Similar arguments will show any supposition of the existence of any suggested logically necessary substance to be logically impossible. Of course a proponent of an ontological argument will deny that '10 billion years ago there were no rational beings' is logically possible, and will offer instead one or more rival premises which seem to him logically possible from whence he will derive his conclusion. The only way to settle this issue is by arguments of the kind discussed earlier. But I do suggest that it is a lot more evident to most people that the premise which I offer is logically possible than that any premise of an ontological argument is logically possible.

I very much doubt however whether any philosopher or theologian before Anselm thought of God as a logically necessary being in anything like our modern sense of that expression which is the sense in which Kant thinks of God as 'necessary'. Aquinas claimed that God was a 'necessary' being, but as he thought of angels who did not exist 'from eternity' and were voluntarily created by God, as necessary beings,[36] he clearly did not mean by 'necessary' logically necessary. He seems to think of a necessary being as one not subject to corruption, that is one which will go on existing forever unless caused not to exist by something else. Aquinas distinguished God from other necessary beings as a 'being necessary through its own nature (*per se*) and not caused to be necessary by something else'.[37] Angels depend for their non-corruptibility on God, whereas God is intrinsically necessary. I suggest that the fact that we cannot make sense of the concept of a logically necessary being has no relevance to the possibility of constructing a cogent argument to a being necessary in some

---

36   See his *Summa theologiae* Ia. 61.3ad3 and Ia.50.5ad3. He holds that human souls are
      also necessarily incorruptible (op.cit Ia.75.6), though he refrains from calling them
      'necessary beings'.

37   op. cit. Ia. 2.3. Admittedly, Aquinas thought that 'God is the same as his own nature
      or essence' (Ia.3.3); but he goes on to claim that anything immaterial, not just God,
      is the same as its own nature. His point is simply that material things are individuated
      by the matter of which they are made, whereas immaterial things are individuated by their
      forms, that is natures. I know of nothing in Aquinas which should lead us to suppose that
      he thought God's existence was a logically necessary truth. He certainly thought that
      the negation of Anselm's 'definition' of God did not entail a contradiction (Ia.2.1.ad.2),
      and I know of no reason to suppose that he thought that the negation of any other
      'definition' (in our sense) of God would entail a contradiction.

other sense, e.g. a being not contingent on the existence of any other being for its own existence, which is a property which all traditional theists have believed God to have.

So, I have argued, despite the great influence which the arguments of Hume and Kant about the limits of intelligibility and knowledge have had on philosophers and theologians, these philosophers have not provided any good reason for denying the possibility of a cogent natural theology. Such a theology will begin from the data of the most general features of the universe, such as that it is governed entirely by simple laws of nature which are such as to lead somewhere to the evolution of human bodies, and that humans are conscious beings having a choice between good and evil. It will argue that the simplest explanation which makes it probable that these data will occur is that the universe is caused (either at a first moment or everlastingly) by an essentially eternal omnipotent, omniscient, and perfectly free being (from which the other divine properties follow), whom we may call God; and so the data make it probable that there is a God – by the criteria described earlier. I believe that such a natural theology can be constructed, and I have argued for it at length elsewhere.[38]

---

38   See my *The Existence of God,* second edition (Oxford: Oxford University Press, 2004); and the short 'popular' version, *Is There a God?,* revised edition (Oxford: Oxford University Press, 2010).

First Person and Third Person Reasons and Religious Epistemology

Linda Zagzebski

I. The Distinction between First Person and Third Person Reasons

1.1.

I assume that believing p is a state in which I have settled for myself whether p. An epistemic reason is something on the basis of which I can settle for myself whether p in so far as my goal is truth, not benefit or some other practical or moral aim. I want to argue that there are two kinds of epistemic reasons, one irreducibly first personal, the other third personal, and that attending to the distinction illuminates a host of philosophical problems, including several that have special importance for philosophy of religion.

What I mean by *theoretical reasons* for believing p are facts that are logically or probabilistically connected to the truth of p. They are facts (or propositions) about states of the world or experiences which, taken together, give a cumulative case for or against the fact that p (or the truth of p).[1] They are not intrinsically connected to believing. We call them reasons because a reasonable person who comes to believe them and grasps their logical relations to p will see them as reasons for p. They can be shared with others – laid out on the table, so they are third personal. They are relevant from anyone's point of view. In fact, they do not require a point of view to be reasons. The connections between theoretical reasons and what they are reasons for are among the facts of the universe. Theoretical reasons aggregate and can be used in Bayesian calculations. What we call evidence is most naturally put in the category of theoretical reasons, although the notion of evidence is multiply ambiguous.[2] But when I mention evidence in this paper, I will mean facts that are in the category of theoretical reasons.

---

1   In this paper I do not distinguish facts from true propositions. If there is a difference, the argument of this paper can be easily amended.

2   For an excellent survey of the different senses of evidence, see Thomas Kelly's entry, 'Evidence', in the *Stanford Encyclopedia of Philosophy* <http://plato.stanford.edu/entries>.

In contrast, what I mean by *deliberative reasons* have an essential connection to *me and only to me* in my deliberations about whether p. Deliberative reasons connect *me* to getting the truth of p, whereas theoretical reasons connect facts about the world with the truth of p. Deliberative reasons do not simply provide me a weightier reason for p than they provide others. They are not reasons for other persons at all. They are irreducibly first personal.

To see the distinction I have in mind, consider experience as a reason for belief. If you have an experience, the *fact* that you have it is a theoretical reason for believing a variety of propositions. You can tell me about your experience, and if I believe what you tell me, I can then refer to the fact that you had the experience as a reason to believe whatever it supports. You and I can both refer to the fact that you had the experience as a reason to believe something, and so can anybody else who is aware of the fact that you had the experience. The fact that the experience occurred is therefore a theoretical reason. It is on the table for all to consider, and all can consider its logical and probabilistic connections to other facts about the world.

However, you are in a different position than I am with respect to your experience because you not only grasp the fact that you had the experience; in addition, you and you alone *had* the experience. That experience affects many of your reasoning processes, emotional responses, and the way you come to have or give up certain beliefs directly, and that is quite proper. In contrast, the fact that you had the experience is something you and I and many other people can come to believe. My way of describing the contrast is that your experience gives you a deliberative reason to form certain beliefs, whereas the fact that the experience occurred gives anybody a theoretical reason to form certain beliefs.[3] Anybody can form the belief that you had the experience, thereby accessing that fact, but nobody but you can have your experience.

Another type of deliberative reason is what are loosely called intuitions in one of its senses. I will not attempt an account of intuition, but what I have in mind is, very roughly, something internal to the mind that responds with an answer to a question, often as a response to a concrete case. For example, if a fat man is stuck in the mouth of a cave, is it morally permissible to blow him out of the cave to save yourself and the other speelunkers from drowning in the rising tide? My intuition might be no, but perhaps yours is yes. I have no position on the strength of an intuition of this kind as a reason to believe what the intuition supports. Maybe it is strong, maybe it is not. But in so far as it is a reason at all, it is a deliberative reason. My intuitions are mine alone, and they

---

3   My use of the terms 'theoretical' and 'deliberative' is not essential to the contrast I am
     making, but the terms call attention to a difference in function that I find helpful.

give me but not you a particular kind of reason for certain beliefs. But again, the fact that I have an intuition can be put out on the table. I can tell you that my intuition is such and such, and that then becomes a theoretical reason supporting some position. So the fact that most people think that Gettier cases are not cases of knowledge is a reason for anyone to reject a theory that has the consequence that the believer knows in a Gettier situation, but your own intuition about such cases is a reason for you alone to draw certain conclusions. Intuitions, then, are like experiences. The intuition and the experience provide the agent with first person reasons to believe something, but the fact that the experience occurred or that the intuition is what it is can be treated as evidence, as a theoretical reason for the truth of some proposition.

I propose that there is another important deliberative reason that is more basic for us than any theoretical reasons we can identify. We can see the need for such a reason by reflecting on the need for a link between third person reasons and something in myself. Theoretical reasons do not operate as reasons for me to believe anything until I take them on board. But *my taking a* certain set of theoretical reasons for p as reasons to believe p is not sufficient in itself to make it likely that p is true. That is because my taking a set of theoretical reasons to be reasons to believe p is irrelevant to the actual connection between those reasons and p unless I have taken them properly – properly identified the facts, figured out the correct logical and probabilistic relations between those facts and p, have appreciated the significance of individual facts, and have not left anything out. But my reasons to believe *that* depend upon the more basic belief that my faculties are trustworthy. And that raises the question of what reasons I have to believe that my faculties are trustworthy. It has been pointed out by others that any such reasons are circular. I have no way of telling that my faculties in general get me to the truth without using those faculties.

A reasonable response to the phenomenon of epistemic circularity is epistemic self-trust.[4] I am not arguing here that no other response is reasonable (although it is my position that no other response is *as* reasonable). But I am claiming that it is reasonable to believe my faculties are generally trustworthy, and it is reasonable to dispel doubt about the trustworthiness of my faculties or hold such doubt at bay, a doubt that naturally arises upon reflection about the phenomenon of epistemic circularity. I think that means that in addition to including the belief that I am generally trustworthy, self-trust includes an affective component, a component of feeling trusting. That is because doubt is partly affective, and it

---

4   See Richard Foley, *Intellectual Trust in Oneself and Others* (Cambridge University Press, 2001) and William Alston, *Beyond Justification: Dimensions of Epistemic Evaluation* (Cornell University Press, 2005).

takes an affective state to dispel it. It is in virtue of self-trust – a state that is partly affective, that I take theoretical reasons I identify to point to the truth of some proposition p, and I am reasonable in doing so.

I said above that a reason to believe p is a state in virtue of which it is reasonable to think some proposition p is true. It so, self-trust is a reason because it is in virtue of self-trust that I believe that what I take to be theoretical reasons for believing p are truth-indicators, and that is a reasonable thing to do. Self-trust *is a* reason, but a reason of a distinctively first personal kind. It is a second order reason because it is a reason to believe that I have properly identified theoretical reasons for a belief. The way self-trust gives me a deliberative reason to think I am properly connected to theoretical reasons shows that there are deliberative reasons that are more basic for me than any theoretical reasons I can identify. Of course, they are not more basic than theoretical reasons, which are facts of the universe. But they are more basic than my use of any theoretical reasons in deliberations about what the truth is.

Deliberative reasons can therefore be first order reasons like experience or intuition, or second order reasons like self-trust. I want to argue next that trust in myself (a deliberative reason) can give me a reason to trust others (another deliberative reason). So a deliberative reason can be a reason to have other deliberative reasons.

How does self-trust give me a reason to trust others? My position is that if, in believing in a way I trust, I come to believe that others have the same faculties I trust in myself, then given the a *priori* principle that I ought to treat like cases alike, I have a reason to trust their faculties. If I reasonably trust their faculties, I have a reason to believe the deliverances of their faculties. Trust in someone else gives me a deliberative reason to believe some proposition p because my reason is based on their similarity to *me* and my trust in myself.[5]

If I am right that trust is partly an affective state, and if I am also right that trust can give me a reason to believe p, then a state that is partly affective can give me a reason to believe p. This is an epistemic reason, not a practical or moral reason. I think that there are probably other affective states that are deliberative reasons for belief. One is the emotion of admiration. I may epistemically admire someone and trust that admiration upon reflection. Admiration for a person can give me a reason to think that she has the truth in some domain that includes p, and it can give me a reason to try to imitate her in a way that includes coming to believe p. In that case my admiration for her is a deliberative reason to believe p.

---

5   I defend the argument of this paragraph in detail in *Epistemic Authority: A Theory of Trust, Authority, and Autonomy in Belief*, based on my 2010 Wilde Lectures and my 2011 Kaminski Lectures (New York: Oxford University Press, 2012), ch. 3.

There are no doubt theoretical reasons to admire her, but those are not the reasons for believing p.[6]

Deliberative reasons to believe p because of trust or admiration for another person are not necessarily reasons to think that the other person has theoretical reasons for p. Of course, it often happens that a person who has the truth whether p also has theoretical reasons to believe p, but my reason to think someone has the truth whether p is not the same as reason to think that she has theoretical reasons to believe p. Even if she has theoretical reasons for p, that is not what I have reason to believe. Deliberative reasons like trust and admiration are higher order reasons to think that I or someone else has the truth whether p, and therefore has reason to believe p, but the reason may be deliberative rather than theoretical.

We have looked at a number of kinds of deliberative reasons: an experience, an intuition, trust in myself, trust in others, admiration. The first two have a third person analogue that is a theoretical reason. The fact that someone had an experience, and the fact that someone has an intuition can be treated by anybody as a theoretical reason to believe p. Trust and admiration are different. The fact that you trust something or admire someone is not a theoretical reason. It is not the kind of reason that can be put out on the table for all to consider in favor of the truth of some proposition. It may, however, be a deliberative reason.

1.2.

There are important differences between theoretical and deliberative reasons that require us to think of them in distinct categories. First, deliberative reasons and theoretical reasons do not aggregate. That follows from the first person character of deliberative reasons and the third person character of theoretical reasons. They cannot aggregate because nobody has figured out how to put the first person and third person points of view together. Deliberative reasons neither increase nor decrease the theoretical case for some proposition p. My deliberative reasons are not facts of the universe that affect the theoretical case for p, and I can grasp that even if I am the one giving the theoretical case. So suppose I am giving the case for the proposition that driving while talking

---

6   The fact that there are theoretical reasons to admire someone in the domain of her believing p is not sufficient to give me a theoretical reason to believe p because reasons are not transitive. If A is a reason for B and B is a reason for C, it does not follow that A is a reason for C. So if A is a set of theoretical reasons to admire Sarah, and admiring Sarah is a reason to imitate her in believing p, it does not follow that theoretical reasons A gives me reason to believe p.

on a mobile phone is dangerous. I would point to the studies by reliable researchers that show that people who talk on the phone while driving have reduced peripheral vision, slower response time, and a higher accident rate than people who do not, but I would not add that I trust the people who did the studies and they believe its conclusion (studies of that sort rarely even mention the personal conclusion drawn by the researchers). The fact that people I trust believe what they believe or have certain epistemic qualities does not make the relationship between the data in the studies and the conclusion stronger. To refer to it when giving the evidence linking mobile phone use and auto safety is beside the point. If driving while on the phone is dangerous, it does not matter what anybody anywhere thinks about it. Of course, I might cite my experience while driving on the phone as a reason for me to believe it is unsafe, and you could cite the fact that I had that experience when giving your theoretical reasons for the same conclusion. But when you cite the fact that I had the experience as a theoretical reason for believing that talking on the phone while driving is unsafe, you are not referring to the same thing to which I refer when I cite my experience.

Although deliberative reasons and theoretical reasons do not aggregate, they are both kinds of reasons to think some proposition is true. Together they can increase or decrease my confidence that p. So if I believe p based on theoretical reasons and then find out that you believe p too, that increases my confidence that p. But while it is true that finding out that you believe p increases my confidence in myself in the way I come to believe p, and therefore increases my confidence in p, it is not additional theoretical evidence for p. If we were listing the facts of the universe that indicate the dangers of driving on the phone, we would not list the people who believe that it is dangerous.

Reasons do not aggregate in the other direction either. I might believe p because of deliberative reasons – say, it is because I epistemically trust you and you believe p. Then I get a piece of evidence that p and that increases my confidence that p. In that case it might appear that the theoretical reason increases the force of my deliberative reason; it increases my trust in you. But that also is a mistake. Getting a piece of evidence for p does not support my trust in you when you believe p. It shows that your conclusion is more likely to be correct, and so I am more confident in p, but even if I got heaps of evidence for p, that should not increase my confidence that you are trustworthy in the way you came to your belief p. I could get evidence that you are trustworthy, but that is not part of the theoretical case for p. It is part of the theoretical case that you are trustworthy.

I am not claiming that the beliefs of others cannot be treated as evidence. I could get evidence that you are reliable in some domain and evidence that you have a belief in that domain. That would give me a theoretical reason to have the belief. It could be put out on the table as inductive evidence for the truth of the belief. That is not the same as the trust I have in you that can give me a deliberative reason to believe what you believe or what you tell me. I have described trust as a state that is partly epistemic and partly affective, and trust in others arises because it is a commitment of my attitude towards myself. A judgment of reliability is a third person judgment that involves nothing about personal relations or agency. In a judgment of reliability a person is treated no differently than a thermometer or a calculator.

Theoretical reasons aggregate with each other since they are third-personal. Deliberative reasons can affect other deliberative reasons, but your deliberative reasons do not aggregate with mine. Nonetheless, your deliberative reasons can affect mine. If I trust you and you tell me that you trust someone else or some authoritative body, I might take that as a reason to trust that person or body. But if I do not trust you and you tell me you trust yourself or someone else, your trust is irrelevant to me. Your deliberative reasons are relevant to me only in so far as they connect with *my* deliberative reasons.

There is another interesting difference between theoretical reasons and deliberative reasons. I have no control at all over the relation between theoretical reasons for p and p, but I exercise executive control over deliberative reasons. It is because of my deliberative reasons that what I believe is up to me.[7] I am not suggesting that deliberative reasons are voluntary, but my agency is involved in deliberative reasons, whereas it is irrelevant to theoretical reasons. By the nature of deliberative reasons, they connect me and the exercise of my reflective faculties with the aim I have in exercising those faculties in the domain of belief. For present purposes I am assuming the aim is truth, although we can also have deliberative reasons to think that our faculties connect us to other epistemic ends such as understanding.

To summarize what I have said so far:
- Theoretical reasons are 3rd personal, deliberative reasons are 1st personal.
- Theoretical reasons have no essential connection to belief; deliberative reasons are essentially connected to my deliberations about what to believe.
- Theoretical and deliberative reasons do not aggregate. Deliberative reasons for me to believe p do not increase the theoretical case for p. Theoretical reasons for p do not increase my deliberative reasons for believing p.

---

7   For a different kind of defence of the position that what I believe is 'up to me', see Richard Moran in *Authority and Estrangement: An Essay on Self-Knowledge* (Princeton University Press, 2001).

- There are deliberative reasons that are always more basic than any theoretical reasons I can identify.
- I have no control over theoretical reasons, whereas deliberative reasons are reasons for me as an agent and I use them as an agent.

Both theoretical and deliberative reasons are reasons, and they are truth-directed. They are epistemic, not practical. Theoretical reasons are facts that support the truth of the proposition p. Deliberative reasons are reasons that support my believing p in so far as my aim is truth. They are reasons that support *my* believing p rather than your believing p. Both deliberative reasons and the theoretical reasons I identify increase my confidence in my belief p.

The distinction I am proposing is not the same as the distinction between first order and second order epistemic reasons. There are both first order and second order theoretical reasons and first order and second order deliberative reasons. As I have said, the fact that an experience occurred is a first order theoretical reason for various beliefs; the experience is a first order deliberative reason. The fact that a certain person is reliable is a second order theoretical reason to believe what she believes; my epistemic trust in that person is a second order deliberative reason.

The distinction between agent-relative and agent-neutral reasons in ethics is closer to the distinction I am drawing here.[8] There are different ways to characterize agent-relative reasons, but sometimes an agent-relative reason is treated as a reason other persons can have, but it has a different force for the agent than for others. For example, everyone has a reason to prevent murders, but the agent has a special reason not to commit a murder herself. In contrast, what I mean by a deliberative reason is a reason only a certain person can have.[9]

---

8   Thomas Nagel is generally credited with introducing a form of this distinction in *The Possibility of Altruism* (Princeton: Princeton University Press, 1970), where he distinguished subjective and objective reasons for action. Derek Parfit introduced the terms 'agent-relative' and 'agent-neutral' reasons in *Reasons and Persons* (Oxford: Clarendon Press, 1984), and Nagel subsequently adopted this usage. For an overview of different approaches to this distinction and their respective merits, see Michael Ridge, 'Reasonsfor Action: Agent-Neutral vs. Agent-Relative', *Stanford Encyclopedia of Philosophy* <http://plato.stanford.edu/entries>.

9   Derek Parfit refers to this difference as the difference between Nagel's distinction and his own very similar distinction. Parfit says: 'Nagel's subjective reasons are reasons only for the agent. I call these agent-relative. When I call some reason agent-relative, I am not claiming that this reason cannot be a reason for other agents. All that I am claiming is that it may not be.' (Parfit, 1984, p. 143). In this respect my distinction is more like Nagel's than Parfit's.

In addition, agent-relative reasons are generally treated as reasons that, while applying in a special way to a particular agent, are reasons for that agent because of some general principle. In this way of looking at reasons, agent-relative reasons are recognizable by persons other than the agent as reasons for that agent independent of the agent's deliberations. So, for example, my agent-relative reason not to commit a murder is not dependent upon my view of the matter. Everyone knows in advance that I have such a reason, and it is not up to me whether that reason applies to me. In contrast, I have proposed that deliberative reasons are connected with the agent's agency, and it is possible that whether something is a deliberative reason for her in some situation is up to her. That is a substantive claim about deliberative reasons that might not affect the way the distinction is made, so perhaps the terminology of agent-relative and agent-neutral epistemic reasons is an appropriate usage for the distinction I have described in this paper. I have no objections to using that terminology, provided that the differences between my way of characterizing the two kinds of reasons and its usage by other authors is recognized.

II. Applying the distinction to problems in religious epistemology

2.1.

The distinction between theoretical and deliberative reasons makes it easier to understand a number of epistemic phenomena. First, it explains *the puzzle of how experience can be a reason for belief*, the enduring problem of the foundation of empirical knowledge. The problem is that the relation between my experience and a proposition I come to believe based on that experience is different in kind from the relation between one of my beliefs and another. There is no way to solve this problem by turning experiences into facts or propositional beliefs in an attempt to make all reasons theoretical. The fact that I have a certain sensory experience of seeing yellow gives me a theoretical reason to believe there is something yellow there, but my grasp of the fact that I have the experience of seeing yellow must itself be justified by the experience of seeing yellow. The foundation of empirical knowledge is not a propositional belief, much less some neutral fact about the universe, but something of an entirely different kind, and the relation between an instance of that kind and a propositional belief differs qualitatively from the relation between one propositional belief and another.

The distinction between two kinds of epistemic reasons can be used to explain this difference. An experience is a deliberative reason for the person who has the experience to form certain beliefs. Those beliefs then give her theoretical reasons to form certain other beliefs when she grasps the relation between those reasons and what they are reasons for. Since we already know that the link between experience and belief has to be different in kind from the link between one belief and another, we seek an explanation for the difference, and the difference between first person and third person reasons gives us such an explanation.

This distinction is important for the rationality of religious belief based on religious experience. A religious experience gives the subject an irreducibly first person reason for belief, one that differs qualitatively from the relation between the fact that the experience occurred and a belief it supports, a relation to which anyone has access, in principle. The distinction between the two kinds of reasons is particularly important for religious experience because religious experience may be uncommon within a population, and that makes it difficult for many people to access the fact that a religious experience has occurred. It is not unreasonable for someone to be sceptical about the evidential support given to a religious belief by the fact that someone else had a religious experience if experiences of that kind are qualitatively different from any experiences that person has had. We usually think that a religious experience is a stronger reason for religious belief for the person who has the experience than for other persons, but I think it is important to recognize a qualitative difference, not merely a difference in degree. In my opinion, discussion of religious experience as grounds for religious belief is advanced by focusing on the way deliberative reasons operate in a rational person. The process is very different when the only relevant reasons are theoretical.

2.2.

The distinction between the two kinds of reasons also makes it easier to understand the *practice of testimony*, which can be interpreted either as giving the recipient a theoretical reason for a belief or as giving her a deliberative reason. Most of the literature on testimony treats it as giving the recipient a theoretical reason. According to the reductionist model, the recipient makes an inductive inference from the evidence that a testifier is reliable in the relevant domain and that she has testified that p, to the conclusion that p. Anything can be treated as evidence, and there is nothing preventing a person from making such an inference. When she does so, she has a third person reason to believe what another person says. Many so-called non-reductionists also see testimony as giving the subject evidence for belief, only they think the evidence is direct rather than inferential.[10] In these evidence models, the testifier is treated the same way we treat a computer or a clock. The testifier gives anybody in similar circumstances a reason to believe the testimony.

But given what I have said, I cannot consistently treat other persons as simply sources of evidence (theoretical reasons) for me. It is because of trust in myself that I must trust them. When I trust someone else and they believe in a way I trust, I have a deliberative reason to believe the same thing. The person I trust may tell me what she believes in a way that expresses an intention that I believe it too. When she does so, she is asking me for trust, and if I grant it, I come to believe what she tells me on her word. There is a relationship between the testifier and myself in which each of us plays a role. The testifier assures me, the recipient, that p is true and that she has taken the responsibility to make the belief justified (or in my preferred terminology, epistemically conscientious). I rely upon her for the conscientious formation of the belief and defer to her if challenged.[11] Since telling involves an interpersonal relationship on this model, there is a sense in which belief on testimony is within the control of the recipient. The evidence view of testimony cannot explain that. The evidential view makes it a mystery how asking for trust and granting it can provide a *reason* for anybody to believe something. It does not seem to be in the right category to be a reason for belief.[12] But we can see why the evidence view of testimony exists. It is the view a person is forced to have if the only epistemic reasons she recognizes are theoretical.

The interpretation of the practice of testimony is important for religious epistemology because divine revelation is testimony from God. On the evidence model of testimony, divine testimony gives the recipient either direct or inferential evidence for the content of the testimony. So belief on revelation can be interpreted as based on an inference that the source of some putative revelation

---

10 This is a point made by Benjamin McMyler, *Testimony, Trust, and Authority,* forthcoming (Oxford University Press, 2011), chs. 2 and 3. McMyler argues that testimony gives the recipient a second-person reason to believe what is testified. I have no objection to calling trust in others a second person epistemic reason for belief. Trust in *you* as a reason to believe something includes an irreducible reference to *me*. The important point for my argument here is that trust in others is clearly distinguishable from theoretical reasons, and it has the properties of first person, deliberative reasons.

11 This model is close to the Assurance model of testimony of Richard Moran, 'Getting Told and Being Believed', in *The Epistemology of Testimony*, edited by J. Lackey and E. Sosa (Oxford University Press, 2005), pp. 272-306.

12 As Richard Moran says, it seems as if my recognizing the speaker's intention ought to be pointless. It does not add to my evidence as interpreter to learn that in addition to his believing p, the speaker also has the intention that I should believe p. See 'Getting Told and Being Believed', p. 15. Moran mentions Paul Grice's much earlier use of that point.

is divine and hence reliable, the position of John Locke.[13] Alternatively, divine testimony can be interpreted as direct evidence for the content of the testimony. Anti-reductionists about testimony typically follow Thomas Reid, who thought of belief on testimony as directly justified in the way he thought perceptual beliefs are directly justified by perceptual experience. On this model, the recipient of divine testimony has direct evidence for the truth of the testimony. Notice that the adherent of this approach agrees with Locke that a revelatory event is evidence for the recipient. The difference is that this view makes the evidence non-inferential, whereas Locke makes it inferential.

But if central cases of testimony give the recipient deliberative rather than theoretical reasons for belief, it seems to me that revelation should be treated differently. The ground of belief in revelation is trust in God, and that gives me a deliberative reason to believe what God tells me. When God tells me that p, God takes responsibility for the truth of p for me and for all other intended recipients of his revelation. God intends that I believe him, and he acknowledges that we who are the recipients place epistemic trust in him by believing him. Our responsibility is to trust appropriately. It is God's responsibility to make the belief true.

There are a number of different ways trust can be an appropriate deliberative reason to believe testimony from God. Some people's trust is grounded in other deliberative reasons such as religious experience or the admiration they have for the Scriptural message.

My view is that trust in another person is justified by my conscientious judgment that trusting that person will survive my own conscientious self-reflection.[14] Believing a person who is currently speaking to me or who has written a book or sent me an email is not very mysterious, but believing God requires a theory of revelation to explain how communication between God and me can succeed. My point here is not to give a theory of revelation, but to point out that a theory of revelation must respect the way in which testimony operates between two persons. If testimony involves a personal request for trust and a granting of trust, that element must be a component of an account of divine revelation.

---

13 See Locke, 'Of Faith and Reason, and Their Distinct Provinces', in *Essay Concerning Human Understanding*, Bk. IV, Ch. 18, Sec. 7. See also Locke's posthumously published essay, 'A Discourse of Miracles.'

14 I defend this idea as the ground for epistemic trust and belief on the authority of individuals and communities in *Epistemic Authority*, cited in note 5.

2.3.

The distinction between theoretical and deliberative reasons also helps us avoid confusion in framing the currently popular topic of *reasonable disagreement*. Suppose I believe p and you believe not p. We get together and compare our evidence, so now we have all the same evidence. Our evidence can include the facts that we have each had certain experiences. We now have the same theoretical reasons. A problem arises when, in addition to the evidence on the table, I know that you believe not p and I trust you in the way you acquired your belief not p. I now seem to have a weaker case for p than I had before.

This situation is not especially problematic if we think of the conflict as arising within one's theoretical reasons. Theoretical reasons may or may not include facts about people's beliefs. Let us suppose first that they do. The issue, then, is that one reliable person who happens to be me believes p, but another reliable person who happens to be you believes not p. This conflict is no different than the conflict that arises when neither of the persons with conflicting beliefs is myself. It is the common problem of a clash in evidence, and it is presumably resolved by awaiting more evidence. In any case, there is no *special* problem when the disagreement between myself and another is interpreted as this sort of conflict within theoretical reasons.

There is another way the person who sees the problem as a conflict within theoretical reasons can look at the situation. They might exclude from the evidence the fact that the believers have the beliefs they have. The idea is that persons are simply conduits for communicating evidence to each other. Once the evidence is on the table, it does not matter what anybody believes. What someone believes is a fact about what they do with the evidence; it is not evidence. It might appear that we are forced to draw this conclusion because we do not treat our own belief as evidence. If I am considering the case for and against p, once I start to believe p, I do not think that then I have additional evidence for p. My believing p does not increase my theoretical case for p. But if *my* believing p has no effect on the case for p, *your* believing p should have no effect either. What people believe is not part of the theoretical reasons for belief. On this approach disagreement is not a problem.

If the only reasons for belief are theoretical, then, disagreement is a problem of evidence pointing in conflicting directions, which is not mysterious or surprising, or it is no problem at all. But reasonable people do experience their disagreement with other reasonable people as a problem, and it is necessary to explain that. Suppose I believe p and I have certain theoretical reasons upon which I base my belief. As I have argued, my confidence in p is not determined solely by those reasons because those reasons by themselves are not sufficient to justify me in believing p in a non-circular way. I must also trust that my faculties have properly handled the evidence, which means not only that I have figured out the correct logical and probabilistic relations between the evidence and p, but that I appreciate the significance of individual pieces of evidence, and that I have not left anything out. I need to trust that I have used my faculties well and have the relevant intellectual virtues. But given that my confidence in my belief p depends upon the above, and given that my trust in myself commits me to trust others who are relevantly like myself, the fact that someone else who is relevantly like me believes not p gives me a reason to trust his belief not p and to distrust my belief p. The problem of reasonable disagreement is therefore a problem that arises among my deliberative reasons.

When we consider deliberative reasons for belief, that gives us a different response to the argument that your belief should not count as evidence for me unless mine does also. If a belief is formed in a way I trust, that *does* give me a deliberative reason to believe it. The perhaps surprising conclusion that if I form a belief p in a way I trust, that gives me a deliberative reason to (continue to) believe p, just as *your* believing not p in a way I trust gives me a deliberative reason to believe not p. The objector who claims that your belief does not give me a reason to believe anything unless mine does also is correct. There is a symmetry between your belief and mine as reasons for belief. Neither belief gives me a theoretical reason to believe. Both beliefs give me a deliberative reason to believe. The problem of disagreement arises when I trust both myself and someone else who has a conflicting belief.

Religious disagreement was recognized as a problem for religious belief well before the topic of reasonable disagreement drew attention from epistemologists. What people did *not* do was to reason as follows: I and my co-religionists are reliable people and we believe p. The believers in these other religions are also reliable people and they believe not p. If that was what they were thinking, the conflict in their evidence would not have been very interesting, as I said. But people also did not take the other approach to disagreement within theoretical reasons mentioned above. That is, they did not say that the conflicting beliefs of other people are irrelevant because beliefs are not evidence. They were presumably worried about something else. Many people found that their experiences of close association with persons in other religious communities led them to place a substantial amount of trust in those persons, and consequently in their beliefs. They interpreted their trust in those others as giving them a *reason* to believe what the others believed, a reason that conflicted with the reasons they already had to believe in their own religion due to trust in themselves. It is very difficult to explain why this kind of experience leads to a clash of reasons for belief unless we are talking about deliberative reasons.

2.4.

The difference between theoretical and deliberative reasons also explains the primary feature of *acting or believing on authority*. According to Joseph Raz, the distinguishing feature of authoritative directives is that they give the subject a pre-emptive reason to obey the authority, where a pre-emptive reason is a reason that replaces the subject's other reasons for and against performing the act. For instance, if I stop at a red light on the authority of the law, then the fact that the law requires me to stop is my reason for stopping, a reason that replaces any other reasons I have for and against stopping at the light.[15] I will not argue here that acting on authority in this way can be justified. My point is only that acting on authority is something people do, and what they are doing is to treat their reasons for acting as the authority dictates in a certain way, one in which the authority's directive becomes *the* reason for the act, replacing other reasons. But it is very hard to see how one reason can replace another when both reasons are theoretical. In order to let one reason replace others, I, the subject, must take the authority's directive as having a certain force for me. I am free to take it as authoritative or not. I therefore exercise the executive function of an agent when I act on authority. My reason to do so must therefore be deliberative.

I argue that the same point applies to believing on authority as to acting on authority. My position is that the belief or testimony of another person whom I conscientiously take to be more trustworthy than myself in some domain can give me a pre-emptive reason to believe what the authority believes or testifies.[16] The distinction between theoretical and deliberative reasons makes it easier to see how this can happen. The fact that the authority has a belief p pre-empts my theoretical reasons for and against p. But pre-emption seems strange if all epistemic reasons are theoretical.

The rationality of taking religious beliefs on authority gets very little attention in religious epistemology and I would like to see that change. I believe that it can be reasonable to take a religious belief pre-emptively out of trust in a religious authority. My reason to take a belief on authority is deliberative. It depends upon a certain connection between the authority and myself, and I exercise the control of an agent when I do so.

The erosion of trust in authority in modern life includes the loss of *reasons* to believe or act as the authority directs. Religious communities have to contribute to our understanding of building and rebuilding the relationships that give persons deliberative reasons to trust authority. In fact, religious

---

15   Joseph Raz, *The Morality of Freedom* (Oxford: Clarendon Press, 1988).
16   I argue for this view in *Epistemic Authority,* ch. 5.

communities may be the most important kind of community in which trust in persons with whom one lacks a direct relationship still exists. I propose that an investigation of the reasons why members of religious communities accept authority in their community will lead nowhere if we expect the reasons to be theoretical, but will be enlightening if we attend to deliberative reasons.

2.5.

Finally, I think that *conversion* cannot be explained except by deliberative reasons. Rarely does anyone convert to a religion because of theoretical reasons he did not previously have. But conversion is sometimes the reasonable thing to do. Trust or admiration for another person or for a tradition or for the sacred texts of a religion is typically the reason for conversion, not just the cause. The fact that conversion can be reasonable is very difficult to explain without reference to deliberative reasons. Of course, someone who maintains that the only kind of epistemic reasons are theoretical will deny that it is ever rational to change one's epistemic stance towards a proposition (belief, disbelief, withholding belief) when one's apprehension and evaluation of the theoretical reasons do not change, but my purpose in this paper is not to convince anyone of the rationality of conversion. I mention conversion as an example of a phenomenon of change of belief that many people do find rational, which deserves more attention in the literature, and which I conjecture cannot be explained except by reference to deliberative reasons.[17]

Conclusion

In this paper I have proposed that distinguishing first person from third person epistemic reasons permits us to get a better understanding of some important problems in epistemology in general and religious epistemology in particular. The problems I have mentioned have something in common. They reveal the way human agency operates in the attempt to get the truth, not just in human action in the overt sense of action. The nature of the self and its executive power

---

17 For a classic historical account of the rise of conversion as a phenomenon in the West, see A.D. Nock, *Conversion* (Baltimore, MD: John Hopkins University Press, 1998). Nock argues that in the ancient world people could be converted to philosophies such as Pythagoreanism, Platonism, Epicureanism, and Stoicism, but not to the ancient Greek or Roman religions. Conversion became important with the rise of Christianity because Christianity included answers to the ultimate questions posed by philosophers, yet it was also in competition with pagan religion since it required people to make a choice.

to manage itself is such a difficult problem, it is unsurprising that epistemologists often prefer to bracket it off from the problems of direct interest to epistemology. But if I am right, we cannot do that without distorting the relationship between epistemic reasons and what they are reasons for. What *I* reasonably take to be reasons to believe some proposition p is not identical to the neutral facts that any reasonable person would take to be reasons supporting p. But as a reasonable person I must figure out how to combine theoretical and deliberative reasons in my epistemic psychology in a way that gives me a determinate answer to the question whether p. It is particularly important that we do not ignore the distinction between the two kinds of reasons in the domain of religious belief since religious belief is a particular person's answer to her own religious questions, yet its content is also the property of all reasonable persons in their common attempt to find the truth.

The Spiritual Senses in Western Spirituality and the Analytic Philosophy of Religion

William J. Wainwright

The concept of the spiritual senses has played a significant role in the history of Roman Catholic and Eastern Orthodox spirituality. It goes back at least as far as Origen, and figures prominently in the work of theologians as diverse as Bonaventure and Urs von Balthasar. What is less well known (indeed almost totally unremarked) is that the doctrine also played an important role in some classical Protestant thought and spirituality. This is important for it suggests that the doctrine is (or at least should be) an important feature of Christian spiritual theology in general, and raises the question of whether similar concepts can be found in other theistic traditions. In spite of its importance, however, the concept has been almost totally neglected by analytic philosophers of religion. My essay will be divided into three parts. I will begin by examining the only treatment of the doctrine by an analytic philosopher that I am aware of (namely, Nelson Pike's). I will then show how the development of the doctrine of the spiritual senses in Puritan thought and spirituality fills a serious lacuna in Pike's treatment, and conclude by saying a few words about where I think the discussion should now go.

I. Pike and the Spiritual Senses

The first two chapters of Nelson Pike's *Mystic Union*[1] describe what are commonly regarded as the three principal forms of mystical prayer. The soul is directly aware of God in each but the degree of intimacy and the place of encounter differ. In the Prayer of Quiet, 'God and the soul are close to each other' (Pike, p. 5). In Full Union and (the culmination of) Rapture, however, they penetrate each other; God and the soul are held in mutual embrace. In the Prayer of Quiet and Full Union, the encounter between self and God takes place *within* the soul of the mystic. In Rapture, it transpires *outside* it. Quiet and Union thus differ with respect to the nature of the encounter but are alike

---

1   Nelson Pike, *Mystic Union: An Essay in the Phenomenology of Mysticism* (Ithaca and London: Cornell University Press, 1992). The descriptive portions of *Mystic Union* rely heavily on the earlier work of Augustin Poulain and Albert Farges.

with respect to its place or domain. In Full Union and Rapture, the *nature* of the encounter is the same but its *place* differs.

Chapter 3 discusses the doctrine of the spiritual senses which asserts that there are 'five spiritual sense faculties' bearing 'some likeness to the exterior senses' (Teresa of Avila) 'by which God's presence in the various states of union is detected' (Pike, p. 42). As Pike understands the doctrine, when the Christian mystic 'claims to have "seen" God, or to have "smelled" or "tasted"' him, she 'means to be affirming that God was detected in the encounter via actual sensations that are at least similar . . . to the bodily perceptions usually identified with these terms' (Pike, p. 44).

Sight, hearing and smell are distance senses. (I not only see things at a distance, I hear what is going on in the next room, and smell what is cooking in the kitchen when I am in the hall. Touch typically requires contact but I can feel the fire while standing at some distance from it.) In the Prayer of Quiet, God and the soul 'are close but not so close as to preclude them coming closer . . . . In Full Union and . . . Rapture, God and the soul are in double embrace' (Pike, p. 49). One would therefore expect that God would be detected by analogues of the distance senses in the Prayer of Quiet, and by analogues of taste and touch in Full Union and Rapture.

According to Pike this is exactly what we find. In the Prayer of Quiet, God is 'heard',[2] 'smelled', and 'touched' 'in the restricted sense appropriate when the object perceived is still at some distance from the perceiver' (Pike, p. 51). (Thus 'Teresa says that the soul feels the heat coming from the "interior depths"' (Pike, p. 50).) In Full Union and Rapture, God is touched and tasted.

There are anomalies, though. First, although sight is the paradigmatic distance sense, spiritual sight is seldom if ever associated with the Prayer of Quiet. It is frequently mentioned in connection with Full Union,[3] however, and is especially associated with Rapture. Second, Pike thinks that the objects of spiritual hearing, touch, taste and smell bear some comparison (if only

---

2   Pike quotes Ambrose who claims to 'hear God's voice' in this state (the Prayer of Quiet) (p. 51). Given Pike's schema, this is of course appropriate since hearing is a distance sense. But how often is 'hearing' referred to at this stage? And when it is, how often does it refer to nothing more than a so-called 'interior locution' (words or thoughts suddenly occurring to one) and not to a direct perception of God himself? (Question: Are the words or thoughts in these locutions *perceived* as coming from God himself. [Cf. My hearing my wife speak], or does one instead *infer* that they do, or simply form the *conviction* that they do. [Cf. I receive a letter from my wife without her signature or address.])

3   But see Poulain's *Graces of Interior Prayer* (St. Louis: Herder, 1950), page 56, where he says that 'as a rule, spiritual visual perceptions are absent in Full Union as they are in the Prayer of Quiet'.

remote) to their ordinary counterparts. The object of spiritual taste, for example, is God's 'sweetness', and the object of spiritual touch is his 'caress' or 'touch'. The exception is spiritual sight whose typical objects are 'power, will, justice, goodness', and the like, that is, properties whose ordinary counterparts *cannot* 'be apprehended in simple acts of [visual] perception'. It thus seems 'that if we are to retain a parallel between spiritual sight and bodily sight, we shall have to introduce an analogue of "*bodily* form" that can be spiritually seen' (Pike, pp. 60-61, my emphasis). The trouble is that references to anything like this seldom (if ever) occur in descriptions of the Prayer of Quiet, Full Union, or Rapture.[4]

The fact that the paradigmatic distance sense (sight) normally comes into play only in Rapture, in which God and the soul indwell one another and are therefore *not* at a distance, and that there are no divine analogues of the objects of ordinary visual experience (colour, shape, etc.) suggests to me that the doctrine of the spiritual senses imposes an overly rigid conceptual scheme on a comparatively unsystematic and fluid use of perceptual metaphors. A number of additional considerations reinforce this suspicion. Let me mention two of the most important.

(1) Pike claims that since God and the soul remain at some distance from one another in the Prayer of Quiet, the spiritual senses most appropriate to this form of union will be distance senses. Touch is involved but 'only in the restricted sense appropriate when the object perceived is still at some distance from the perceiver'. And Pike quotes Teresa who 'says that the soul *feels the heat* coming from the from the "interior depths"', that is '(we can assume) . . . the most interior of the Seven Mansions'. (The analogy is with, e.g., 'feeling the heat of a stove which is at some distance from oneself' (Pike, pp. 50-51).) But while a feeling of interior warmth often is referred to in connection with the Prayer of Quiet, *is* it a feeling of something at a distance as Pike thinks, or instead just a less intense experience of the burning often felt in Full Union or Rapture?[5]

---

4   Though a careful examination of Christocentric mystics like Pierre de Berulle might force one to qualify this claim. See also the Shri Vaishnava theistic mystics' visions of the celestial body of Vishnu.

5   'Since God is an infinite fire of love, when therefore he is pleased to touch the soul with some severity, the heat of the soul rises to such a degree that the soul believes it is burned with a heat greater than any other in the world. For this reason it speaks of this touch as a burn.' The heat in this case is not felt at a distance. Rather, the soul is not only 'conscious of the burn, but it has itself become one burn of vehement fire'. (John of the Cross, *Living Flame of Love*, trans. E. Allison Peers (Garden City, New York: Image Books, 1962), p. 59.)

Augustin Poulain (whom Pike largely follows) implies that the answer is the latter. 'That which constitutes the common basis of *all* the degrees of mystic union', *including the Prayer of Quiet* and Full Union 'is that of the spiritual impression by which God makes known his presence . . . in the manner . . . of *something interior* which penetrates the soul; it is a sensation of . . . saturation, of immersion', and *can be called 'spiritual touch'* (Poulain, pp. 90-91, my emphases). Because 'it is a question . . . here of a spiritual object *which is not remote*' but 'manifests itself by uniting itself with us, dissolving into us as it were', the *appropriate analogy is bodily touch* (Poulain, p. 94, my emphasis).

(2) Is the systematic use of all five perceptual terms typical of Christian mystics generally? Pike's discussion of the spiritual senses reflects his heavy reliance on John of the Cross and especially Teresa. The weight he assigns them isn't unreasonable given the fullness and clarity of their descriptions, their standing in the Roman Catholic community and their importance in the history of Christian mysticism. Their paradigmatic status in Pike's book also has important precedents in the work of Poulain, Albert Farges, Jacques Maritain and others.[6] These mystics and theologians of mysticism aren't fully representative of the Christian mystical tradition as a whole, however.

Gregory of Nyssa, Pseudo-Dionysius and Maximus the Confessor 'do not mention the concept of the "spiritual senses" at all'.[7] Moreover, whereas Karl Rahner and others think we should speak of a doctrine of the spiritual senses 'only when these partly figurative, partly literal expressions such as to touch God, the eyes of the heart, etc. are found' integrated in a 'complete system' of the 'five instruments . . . involved in the spiritual perception of immaterial [religious] realities',[8] this is much too restrictive.

Many ancient authorities who had important things to say about spiritual perception, did not develop anything amounting to a 'complete system' or a body of doctrine of the spiritual senses. In fact most if not all patristic authors, including Origen whom Rahner regards as 'the "founding father" of the spiritual senses tradition, treat the matter casually rather than systematically' (Gavrilyuk, Introduction). Furthermore, there are significant differences between them. 'Some ancient authorities' (as well as the 20th century theologian Balthazar) 'regard the spiritual senses as purified or transformed versions of the physical senses. Others [e.g., Origen] contrast [them] sharply, emphasizing that the physical

---

6   Poulain and Farges, too, stress the doctrine of the spiritual senses.

7   Paul Gavrilyuk, 'Introduction', *The Spiritual Senses: Perceiving God in Western Christianity* (Cambridge: Cambridge University Press, 2012).

8   Karl Rahner, 'The "Spiritual Senses" according to Origen', in Karl Rahner, *Theological Investigations*, vol. 16 (New York: Seabury Press, 1979), p. 82.

senses need to be non-operational in order for the spiritual senses to function properly' (Gavrilyuk, Introduction). Nor is there a uniform list of the *objects* of the spiritual senses. 'God, the eternal Word', the incarnate Word, 'spiritual beings such as angels . . . , transcendentals (the good, the true and the beautiful) and other divine attributes', and God's 'presence in creation, in the sacraments, in the church, and in scripture' have all been suggested at one time or another (Gavrilyuk, Introduction). All this suggests that Christian accounts of the spiritual senses are too rich and too varied to be usefully reduced to any system.

Moreover, in spite of his insistence on the existence of *five* spiritual senses, Farges himself notes that not all of the spiritual senses are equally prominent[9] in each mystic. Which ones play the leading role in any given case varies 'according to the degree of union of each contemplative, and perhaps also with the temperament and character of each' (Farges, p. 284). Take Bonaventure, for instance, who, according to Rahner, has the most fully developed version of the doctrine among the medievals. Sight and hearing relate to the intellect; smell, touch and taste to the will and affections. 'The number five' is a bit 'arbitrary', however, since 'the sense of smell and hearing' are 'more or less superfluous for [Bonaventure's] account of spiritual contemplation and its various levels' (Rahner, p. 127). The important concepts for his analysis are spiritual sight, touch, and taste. Sight is a 'simple vision (*simplex contuitus*)' whose object is 'the immutable first truth' and 'its eternal ideas which form the ultimate principles of all creation' (Rahner, p. 116). Taste is 'the appreciation by the affections' of the operations of grace in the soul, and is less perfect than feeling or touch which is identified with the ecstatic union of love. While 'a direct clear *vision* of God' is essentially reserved for the afterlife, he *can* be directly apprehended by a loving will, and the term 'touch' is appropriately used to indicate both the directness and the darkness[10] of this affective union (Rahner, pp. 117, 127, my emphasis).[11, 12]

---

9   Or indeed always even evident.

10   To the intellect.

11   The accuracy of Rahner's interpretation of Bonaventure has been questioned. For example, Mark McInroy argues that Bonaventure thinks that activities of the spiritual senses help make 'one *ready* for ecstasy' but do '*not* function in ecstasy itself'. (Mark McInroy, from his chapter on Bonaventure in *The Spiritual Senses: Perceiving God in Western Christianity*, op cit.)

12   The fact that Poulain, who insists on the existence of five distinct spiritual senses, assimilates (without explicitly identifying) 'spiritual taste and a spiritual sense of smell' to spiritual touch on the grounds that they too 'are interpretations of certain shades of union' (Poulain, p. 90) suggests that these categories are more open and fluid than he, Farges and Pike think. At the very least his remarks suggest that spiritual touch, taste,

In my view, Rahner was correct in concluding that 'if one assumes five different faculties which correspond analogically to the bodily powers of sensation, then one is going quite a long way beyond the empirical data [of mysticism]' (Rahner, p. 133). The core of the analogy with bodily perception is the direct 'experimental' awareness of a concrete (i.e., non-abstract) and present reality. Our 'exterior senses' don't 'perceive the essences of the objects around us, but only their presence and their physical effect upon our organs, and perceive these directly'. Similarly, the 'holy mystics' perceive the presence of God through his effects upon their souls. 'Here on earth, the intelligence, except as regards itself and its operation, only apprehends directly the abstract and ideal; the senses alone are able to apprehend concrete and present reality, and' do so 'directly.' In an analogous way, the spiritual senses directly apprehend God's 'concrete and present reality . . . . here is the same firmness and certainty of personal grip, the same ardent fullness of contact, of envelopment and penetration'.[13] Note that in this respect, the spiritual senses are not only analogous to the exterior senses, they are analogous to each other.

But to justify the claim that talk of *distinct* spiritual senses of seeing, hearing, smell, touch and taste is not merely 'metaphorical and symbolic' but properly analogical, one would have to show that the sort of direct contact involved in each is properly distinct from that involved in the others and that the kind of contact involved in spiritual seeing, for example, is more like that involved in physical seeing than that involved in physical hearing, smell, touch, or taste. To the best of my knowledge no one has come close to doing this.[14]

In my opinion, then, the notion of the spiritual senses shouldn't be taken too literally. The metaphors may only have been designed to express intimacy (touch, taste), delight (sweetness, fragrance) and varying degrees of perceptual clarity. (Note that we could then explain why the paradigmatic distance sense, sight, isn't used in association with the Prayer of Quiet. Vision has been

---

and smell aren't as sharply differentiated from one another as spiritual sight and spiritual hearing are from each other, and as both are from all three forms of the sensation of spiritual contiguity.

13   Albert Farges, *Mystical Phenomena*, trans. S. P, Jacques from the 2nd French edition (New York, Cincinnati, and Chicago: Benziger Bros., 1925), pp. 279-81.

14   For all of his insistence on the existence of *five* spiritual senses, for example, Farges has not even tried to do this. Poulain does but his discussion is less than fully satisfactory. He says, for example, that spiritual sight is a 'mode of [experimental] knowledge . . . that we are instinctively led to compare . . . with bodily sight', (Poulain, p. 89) but he does *not* say just *how* they are alike. 'Spiritual hearing' is said to refer to the direct communication of God's thoughts to the mystic. But (as we have seen in note 12) spiritual smell, taste, and touch are more or less run together.

traditionally regarded as the most intellectual [and hence clearest] of the senses and one's awareness of God at this stage is relatively obscure.) One should consider the possibility, in other words, that expressions like 'sight', 'smell', 'taste' and so forth refer to only a few phenomenal qualities (the ones I have mentioned perhaps) each of which can be indifferently picked out by more than one perceptual metaphor. What *is* often analogical, however, and *not* merely metaphorical, is the comparison of spiritual perception in general to bodily perception in general.[15]

I conclude that Pike's analysis of the spiritual senses fails because it attempts to fit the language and experiences he discusses into a Procrustean bed which is ill suited to accommodate them.[16] Its biggest lacuna, however, is its failure to address the relevant epistemological issues. Poulain and Farges do, however inadequately. Poulain says, for example, that we have 'an experimental knowledge of the presence of God . . . that is the result of an impression, a spiritual sensation of a certain kind' that bears 'some resemblance' of an analogous kind to the sensations of the 'bodily senses' (Poulain, p. 88). And Farges says something similar. The theory both gesture at is developed most carefully by Jacques Maritain in *Distinguish to Unite, or the Degrees of Knowledge*.[17] Since I have argued elsewhere that the theory in question is inadequate,[18] I would like to turn to a couple of other models of spiritual sensation which at least at first glance might seem initially more promising.

---

15   And note that a number of Christian authors speak of spiritual perception in the singular without implying a specific likeness to any particular one of the bodily senses.

16   In fairness to Pike, I should note that the fault in question primarily lies with the authors (especially Poulain and Farges) he is relying on.

17   Jacques Maritain, *Distinguish to Unite, or the Degrees of Knowledge*, trans. from the 4th French Edition under the supervision of Gerald B. Phelan (New York: Charles Scribner's Sons, 1959). See especially pp. 247-470.

18   William J. Wainwright, 'Two Theories of Mysticism: Gilson and Maritain', *The Modern Schoolman*, 52 (1975): 405-26. Reprinted in William J. Wainwright, *Mysticism: A Study of its Nature, Cognitive Value, and Moral Implications* (Madison: University of Wisconsin Press, 1981), pp. 166-84. I continue to stand by the majority of the criticisms of Maritain that I made at that time. For example, Maritain (apparently) presupposes that all *perceptual* experience involves the presence of a quasi-sensible medium *through* which we apprehend that experience's object. He also appears to presuppose that perception can only occur when the perceived object causally acts upon the perceiver. Neither presupposition is self-evident. The first is clearly false if we grant that our immediate awareness of sense impressions and other mental states is a kind of perception. And if occasionalism is logically possible, then the second presupposition is false as well since, on that view, the presence of a physical object provides the occasion on which God produces appropriate sensory

II. Puritans and the Spiritual Senses

That conversion involved the bestowal of a new spiritual sense was a Puritan commonplace. In what follows I shall argue that Puritans employ 'a sense of the heart' in three different ways. It is often used for a feelingful conviction of gospel truths without any implication of direct or immediate cognitive contact with the divine. But its use more frequently reflects the conviction that a converted heart involves a direct or immediate awareness of God or 'holy things'. There were at least two models for this. The first is a 'Platonic' model which construes the contact as the immediate intuition of a reason thought of as essentially possessing an affective dimension. The second model is sense perception.

While it is often difficult to determine just which of these three senses is intended, I shall argue that the Cambridge Platonist, John Smith (1616-1652), rather clearly intended the second (a Platonic affect-laden intellectual intuition) while the great American theologian, Jonathan Edwards (1703-1758), intended the third (a direct cognition modelled on sense perception).

The Puritan's talk of spiritual senses should be placed in the context of devotional practices that were strikingly similar to those of contemporary sixteenth and seventeenth century Roman Catholics. They 'knew and used classic Catholic devotional works'. Among 'the most popular, judging from the number of editions, were the works of St. Augustine, St. Bernard of Clairvaux', and 'Thomas a Kempis's *The Imitation of Christ*
. . . To a large extent, the Puritan devotional literature that blossomed in the early seventeenth century was modelled on earlier Roman Catholic devotional literature'. 'Continuity' also 'existed in the area of techniques . . . Most important was the use of the imagination and the senses in the exercise

---

effects in the perceiver but isn't their cause. Even so, I am now less inclined to flatly dismiss Maritain's theory than I was in 1975 and 1981. His account of sense perception is at least as plausible as Edwards's Lockean account which I will discuss in section II, and if the Christian mystic *does* become experimentally aware of God's presence through the medium of the effects which God produces in her soul, it is plausible to identify those effects with the consciously experienced effects of infused charity. (For one thing, Christian mysticism is a love mysticism: love is the means of attaining union with God and the union itself is a form of love. For another, the higher stages of contemplation are attained by burying all creatures beneath a 'cloud of forgetting'. All that remains is the mystic's loving awareness of God. If this awareness involves a medium, it seems that we must identify it with love since love is the only thing other than the awareness itself which hasn't been excluded from her consciousness.

known as composition of place', i.e., placing oneself within the scenes of the salvation story on which one is meditating.[19]

For Richard Baxter (1615-1691), meditation involved (1) using the sensory images of scripture to visualize (as well as to imaginatively hear, smell, and touch) divine things while at the same time recognizing the images' inadequacy, together with (2) a single minded concentration on the excellences of heaven or other objects of meditation, with the penultimate aim of eliciting and strengthening holy thoughts, desires and feelings, and (like other Puritans) the ultimate aim of achieving 'union with Christ, a union that was [typically] expressed in mystically erotic imagery from the Song of Songs and Jesus' parable of the ten virgins' (HS, p. 189).[20]

Regular times were set aside for meditation in a place 'free from company and noise', and from other distractions (HS, p. 163). Baxter, for instance, admonishes his reader to 'Get thy heart as clear from the world as thou canst. Wholly lay by the thoughts of thy business, troubles, enjoyments, and everything that may take up any room in the soul. Get it as empty as thou possibly canst, that it may be the more capable of being filled with God . . . say to thy worldly business and thoughts, as Christ to his disciples, "Sit ye here while I go and pray yonder."'[21]

It is difficult to overemphasize the importance which Puritans placed on these spiritual practices. 'Regular secret prayer' was regarded as 'the primary and most necessary means' of grace. John Cotton (1584-1652), for example, argued that 'the end of preaching' was that one 'may learn to pray' (HS, p. 177). Richard Baxter urged that meditation on heaven, i.e., on 'the ravishing glory of saints, and the unspeakable excellencies of the God of glory, and the beams that stream from the face of his son' is the 'duty by which all other duties are improved, and by which the soul digests truth for its nourishment and comfort'. Meditation of this sort involves 'the acting of all the powers of the soul', the will and the affections as well as the understanding. For 'what the better had we been for odoriferous flowers, if we had no smell . . . or what pleasure should we have found in meats and drinks, without the sense of taste? So what good could all the glory of heaven have done us, or what pleasure should we have had

---

19   Charles E. Hambrick-Stowe, *The Practice of Piety: Puritan Devotional Disciplines in Seventeenth Century New England* (Chapel Hill: University of North Carolina Press, 1982), pp. 28-33, 36. Henceforth HS.

20   The five foolish virgins were sometimes interpreted in the wider tradition as the five bodily senses, and the five wise virgins as the five spiritual senses.

21   Richard Baxter, *The Saint's Everlasting Rest* (abridged) (New York: American Tract Society, 1850); reproduced online by the Christian Classics Ethereal Library (1999), chapter xiii, p. 6. Henceforth Baxter.

in the perfection of God himself, if we had been without the affections of love and joy?' (Baxter, xiii, pp. 1-2).

Prayer brings us to communion with God. Thomas Shepard (1605-1649) said, 'I have seen God by reason and never been amazed at God . . . I have seen God himself [in prayer] and have been ravished to behold him' (HS, p. 179). Cotton Mather (1663-1728) spoke of being 'inexpressibly irradiated from on high', of being 'exceedingly ravished', 'raised up into Heaven', of 'delights and raptures', and reported an experience in which he was transported 'into the Suburbs of Heaven' where he was filled with a 'Joy unspeakable and Full of glory. I cannot utter, I may not utter, the Communications of Heaven, whereto I have been this Day admitted: but this I will say, I have tasted that the Lord is gracious' (HS, pp. 285f).

But while talk of spiritual senses is common, even pervasive, it is unclear how literally it was intended. Sometimes our authors' language rather strongly suggests that the most appropriate model of spiritual perception is ordinary sense knowledge. Thus Richard Sibbes (1577-1635) asserts that 'the spiritual life of a Christian is furnished with spiritual senses. He hath a spiritual eye and a spiritual taste to relish spiritual things, and a spiritual ear to judge of holy things, and a spiritual feeling. As everyday life, so this excellent life hath senses and motions suitable to it'.[22] Or consider the Puritan mystic Francis Rous (1579-1659): 'After we have tasted those heavenly things . . . from this taste there ariseth a new, but a true, lively, and experimental knowledge of the things so tasted . . . For even in natural fruits there are certain relishes . . . which nothing but the taste itself can truly represent and shew to us. The West-Indian Piney [pineapple] cannot be so expressed in words, even by him that hath tasted it, that he can deliver over the true shape and character of that taste to another that hath not tasted it.'[23]

John Owen (1616-1683) also employs the language of the senses. But when placed in the context of his thought as a whole, his talk of the spiritual senses is arguably a metaphor for an affect-laden intellectual insight or intuition: 'the true nature of saving illumination consists in this, that it gives the mind such a direct intuitive insight and prospect into spiritual things as that, in their own spiritual nature, they suit, please and satisfy it, so that it is transformed into them, cast in the mould of them, and rests in them' (Walton, p. 202).

---

22 Brad Walton, *Jonathan Edwards, Religious Affections, and the Puritan Analysis of True Piety, Spiritual Sensation, and Heart Religion* (Lewiston, Queenston, Lampeter: The Edward Mellon Press, 2002), p.198. Henceforth Walton.

23 Quoted in Geoffrey Nuttall, *The Holy Spirit in Puritan Faith and Experience* (Chicago and London: University of Chicago Press, 1992) (originally published by Basil Blackwell, 1946, 2nd ed., 1947), p. 139. Henceforth Nuttall.

More detailed models of these two ways of understanding spiritual perception are developed by Jonathan Edwards and John Smith, respectively. Consider, first, Edwards.

Because their hearts have been regenerated by the indwelling of the Holy Spirit, the saints love 'being in general' (i.e., God and the things that depend on him). Their love of being in general is the basis of a new 'spiritual sense' whose 'immediate object' is 'the beauty of holiness' – a 'new simple idea' that can't 'be produced by exalting, varying or compounding' ideas 'which they had before', and that truly 'represents' divine reality.[24]

Edwards sometimes identified true beauty with the pleasure that holy things evoke in people with spiritual 'frames' or 'tempers' or with the tendency they have to evoke it. At other times he variously identified it with what he called the 'consent of being to being', or the 'love of being in general', or 'true benevolence' or holiness. His view on the whole appears to be this. True beauty is identical with benevolence or agreement ('consent') in somewhat the same way in which water is identical with H2O or heat with molecular motion. But benevolence is also the objective basis of a dispositional property, namely, a tendency to produce a new simple idea in the savingly converted. This idea is a delight or pleasure in being's consent to being which somehow 'represents' or is a 'perception' of it. Edwards's account of true beauty thus resembles contemporary Lockean accounts of colour or extension. Spiritual delight is a simple idea or sensation like our ideas of colour or extension. The dispositional property is a power objects have to produce these ideas in our understandings. Benevolence or the consent of being to being is the objective configuration underlying this power and corresponds to the microstructure of bodies that underlies their tendency to excite ideas of colour or extension in minds like ours. Like simple ideas of redness, say, or extension, the new spiritual sensation 'represents' or is a 'perception' of its object. Just as 'red' or 'extension' can refer to the idea, the power, or the physical configuration that is the basis of this power, so 'true beauty' can refer to the spiritual sensation, to the relevant dispositional property, or to true benevolence.

Edwards called the new mode of spiritual understanding a 'sense' because the apprehension of spiritual beauty is (1) non-inferential and (2) involuntary, and Edwards, like Francis Hutcheson, associated sensation with immediacy and passivity. (3) It involves relish or delight, and Edwards followed Locke and Hutcheson in thinking that, like a feeling of tactual pressure or an impression

---

24   Jonathan Edwards, *Treatise on the Religious Affections*, 1746: *The Nature of True Virtue*, 1765, in *The Works of Jonathan Edwards* (New Haven: Yale University Press, 1957-2006), vol. 2, pp. 205, 260; vol. 8, p. 622. Henceforth RA and TV, respectively.

of redness, being pleased or pained is a kind of sensation or perception. Finally, (4) the new mode of understanding is the source of a new simple idea, and Edwards shared Locke's and Hutcheson's conviction that simple ideas come 'from experience'.

John Smith's model of spiritual perception is rather different. He is no more averse to employing the language of the spiritual senses than Owen. He speaks, for example, of 'the senses of the soul', with Plotinus of an 'intellectual touch' of God, and says that 'the soul it self hath its sense as well as the body'.[25] 'There is', he says, 'an inward sweetness and deliciousness in divine truth which no sensual mind can taste or relish . . . Divinity is not so well perceived by subtle wit . . . as by a purified sense, as Plotinus phraseth it.' (SD, p. 15)

Smith's spiritual sensation is best thought of as an *intellectual* intuition, however, an act of 'that *reason* that is within us' (SD, p. 15). 'We must shut the eyes of sense, and open that brighter eye of the *understanding*, that other eye of the soul, as the philosopher calls our *intellectual faculty* . . . the light of the divine world will then begin to fall upon us . . . and in God's own light shall we behold him. The fruit of this knowledge will be sweet to our taste, and pleasant to our palates . . . When *reason* once is raised by the mighty force of the Divine Spirit into a converse with God, it is turned into sense . . . [W]hereas before we conversed with him only. . . with our discursive faculty . . . combating with difficulties, and sharp contests of diverse opinions, and laboring . . . in its deductions of one thing from another; we shall then fasten our minds on him . . . with a serene *understanding* . . . such an *intellectual* calmness and serenity, as will present us with a blissful, steady and invariable sight of him.' What 'before was only faith . . . now becomes vision' (SD, pp. 15-16, my emphases).

Yet if Smith's 'spiritual sensation' *is* best thought of as an intellectual intuition or perception, why employ the language of the bodily senses? Partly because it was traditional. But primarily, I think, because our familiar senses are apt metaphors for the intuition's directness or immediacy and for its affective overtones.

III. Prospects for the Two Puritan Models of Spiritual Perception

How should Edwards's and Smith's models be assessed? Note first that both are models of spiritual perception *as such*, not of spiritual seeing or hearing or touch

---

25   John Smith, *Select Discourses* (London: Printed by F. Flesher for W. Morden, 1660); (New York and London: Garland, 1978 (reprint)), pp. 5, 3.

or tasting or smell, in particular. I shall argue that Edwards's model, while more fully developed than Smith's, is less adequate than his.

In the first place, although it is clear *why* Edwards speaks of the new spiritual cognition as a perception or sensation, it is not clear that he *should* have done so. His first two reasons for construing it on the model of bodily sensation are far from conclusive. Our sensations (and the beliefs directly based on them) appear involuntary and immediate, but so too does our recognition of the fact that 2+2=4. Passivity and immediacy aren't peculiar to ideas derived from (internal or external) sensation.

The other two considerations carry more weight. Locke and Hutcheson identified reason with reasoning. Reason is sharply distinguished from the will and its affections and from the senses. Its sole function is to manipulate ideas received from other sources. Edwards sometimes indicates that he shares these views. Reason does not have an affective dimension and is not the source of new simple ideas. The cognition of true beauty, on the other hand, has an affective dimension since it involves relish or delight, and its object is a new simple idea. If these considerations are sound, then it seems that spiritual cognition should be construed as a kind of sensation or perception.

Edwards's account of spiritual perception is subject to some of the same difficulties as Locke's account of sense perception.[26] But it is also subject to a difficulty of its own. If I am right, the idea of true beauty is both a kind of delight or relish and an apparent cognition. Can something be both? It isn't sufficient to argue that perceptions of objectively real value properties can be inherently affective (and thus pleasurable or painful), for Edwards doesn't think of pleasure and pain in this way. Pleasures and pains in his (and Locke's and Hutcheson's) view aren't qualities or affective dimensions of more complex experiences. They are discrete internal sensations. But if pleasure *is* a kind of internal thrill or delight, how can it *also* be a true 'representation' of something existing 'without' (TV, pp. 622-23)? Ordinary pleasures and pains differ from visual or auditory impressions in lacking what Berkeley called 'outness'; they don't seem to point beyond themselves. Either spiritual pleasure is radically unlike ordinary pleasure in this respect or it isn't an apparent cognition.

Edwards implicitly addresses this issue by attempting to show that 'the frame of mind, or inward sense . . . whereby the mind is disposed to' relish true benevolence for its spiritual beauty agrees 'with the necessary nature of things' (TV, p. 620). The 'frame of mind' in question, however, is benevolence itself. Hence, if we can show that benevolence has a foundation

---

26   It isn't clear that the mind's immediate objects are ideas, how these ideas represent
      or resemble their objects, and so on.

in the nature of things, we can conclude that the spiritual sense, too, is aligned with reality. Edwards has several arguments to show that it does,[27] but his most interesting is perhaps this.

In Edwards's view, 'the Spirit of God . . . communicates and exerts itself in the soul [of the saints] in those acts which are its [God's] proper, natural, and essential acts in itself *ad intra*.' 'The act which is [the Deity's] nature, and wherein its being consists in . . . is divine love', however.[28] This explains how the saints' benevolence is grounded in the nature of things. If the love of the saints just *is* God's love, and God's love is the Holy Spirit, then the benevolence of the saints is an act of the infinite and omnipotent benevolence which lies at the heart of reality.[29]

Another problem isn't so easily overcome, though. That spiritual cognition is best thought of as a kind of sensation or perception on the model of bodily seeing, hearing, tasting and the like, seems inconsistent with other aspects of Edwards's position. A number of Hutcheson's critics took exception to his moral sense theory because they believed that (1) at least some moral propositions are necessarily true, and that (2) necessary truths are discerned by reason.[30] Hutcheson maintained that the moral sense grasps the goodness of benevolent actions and dispositions, that is, perceives that benevolence is (morally) good. His critics objected that 'Benevolence is good' is *necessarily* true, and that necessary truths are apprehended by *reason*, not sense. It is therefore significant that Edwards, too, apparently believed that basic moral truths are necessary.[31] Nor is he likely to have thought that the connection between benevolent actions and dispositions and spiritual beauty is only

27   Four of them are offered in the final chapter of *The Nature of True Virtue*. For a discussion of them, see my *Reason and the Heart* (Ithaca, NY: Cornell University Press, 1995), pp. 34-38.

28   Jonathan Edwards, 'Miscellany 471', in *The Works of Jonathan Edwards*, vol. 13 (New Haven: Yale University Press, 1994), p. 513.

29   While Edwards normally insists on identity or something close to it, a sufficiently close resemblance relation might itself be enough to explain why true benevolence is grounded in the nature of things. If the saints' loving actions and temper mirror God's action and temper, then their benevolence is appropriately related to objective reality because it resembles or is an image of it. Nature's activity on Edwards's occasionalist view is really God's activity. Love is thus 'natural' because it imitates the action of nature itself.

30   See, for example, the correspondence between Hutcheson and Gilbert Burnet.

31   Edwards clearly thought that at least some moral truths are necessary. See his *Freedom of the Will, The Works of Jonathan Edwards*, vol. 1 (New Haven: Yale University Press, 1957), p. 153. His example is, 'It is . . . fit and suitable, that men should do to others, as they would that they should do to them.' It is worth observing that Locke, too, thought that basic moral truths are necessary.

contingent – that holiness or benevolence might not have been truly beautiful. But if 'holiness is beautiful' *is* necessarily true, Edwards seems committed to the implausible view that our knowledge of at least some necessary truths is derived from a sense, i.e., that some necessary truths are perceived by a kind of sensation. It is important to note that the problem here does not arise from Edwards's use of a peculiarly neo-Lockean model of bodily perception. Because the physical senses can't apprehend necessary truths, it would arise from *any* use of models of bodily perception.[32]

One could avoid this problem as well as the one raised earlier by interpreting spiritual cognition as an intellectual intuition with affective overtones in the manner of Smith. A view like Smith's sidesteps the two most pressing problems confronting Edwards – how a feeling of delight can also be an apparent cognition, and how a necessary truth can be grasped by a kind of sensation. It sidesteps them because (1) on Smith's view, the 'sensation' or 'feeling' isn't the cognition itself but, rather, its accompaniment or (better) its affective dimension or resonance, and because (2) there is no mystery[33] in necessary truths and 'platonic' entities such as numbers, universals, archetypes and values, being objects of intellectual intuition.

---

32   Including those of Poulain, Farges and Maritain. One might protest that the objection cuts against Maritain only if 'experimental knowledge' of God, on his view, incorporates a belief in necessary truths, and that it does so is doubtful. For, in the first place, it isn't clear that the experimental knowledge of God incorporates propositional knowing, and even if it does, it is far from obvious that the propositions known are necessary truths. This doubt is reinforced by the fact that the medium through which the mystic apprehends God, on Maritain's view, (namely, the consciously experienced effects of infused charity) are more closely analogous to the sensory effects of physical objects on our bodily senses than to the concepts through which we grasp abstract objects and which we incorporate in propositions. But while the passive reception of the sensory effects of physical objects may be a *necessary* condition of perceptual knowledge, it isn't sufficient. For example, perceptual knowledge of the table I am looking at requires my recognition *that* the object I am experiencing is a table. Similarly here. The knowledge in question is an experimental knowledge of God only if the subject is at least implicitly aware that 'the Divine Reality' is 'present within us' in virtue of its action upon the soul (Maritain, op. cit., p. 272). The mystic's experience thus *does* incorporate propositional knowledge. Moreover, if the propositions known entail that God exists (as they surely must for Maritain, since 'God is present in my soul' entails 'God exists'), and 'God exists' is a necessary truth as the tradition arguably maintains, then Maritain's account of the mystic's experimental knowledge of God is exposed to the same sort of objection as Edwards's.

33   Or at least, less mystery.

But while I find Smith's model more promising, it clearly needs further development. If I am right, Smith employed the language of the spiritual senses because it was familiar and because ordinary sense perception provides an apt metaphor for the intuition's directness or immediacy and affective overtones. Other analogies are at least as apt, however, and should be explored further. The spiritual cognition's directness, for example, is strikingly similar to our immediate recognition of the *prima facie* rightness of an instance of justice or kindness on a view like W. D. Ross's, or our immediate acquaintance with numbers, universals, values and other so-called 'platonic' entities on the views of a number of contemporary epistemologists. Nor are intellectual intuitions always affectless. Kant's respect for the moral law is the affective resonance of the recognition of its obligatoriness in rational beings with inclinations, while classical Platonists thought that reason itself has an affective dimension. Knowing the good involves loving it, delighting in it and putting it into practice – a view which Smith shared. ('Intellectual life, as [the Platonists] phrase it' is a non-discursive 'knowledge . . . [that] is always pregnant with divine virtue, which ariseth out of an happy union of souls with God, and is nothing else but a living imitation of a Godlike perfection drawn out by a strong fervent love of it. This divine knowledge . . . makes us amorous of Divine beauty . . . and this divine love and purity, reciprocally exalts divine knowledge' (SD, p. 20)).

The immediate task for those interested in Smith's model of spiritual perception is thus a close examination of the classical Platonists' account of our knowledge of the forms, the Good and the One, and contemporary literature on the epistemology of intuition in (e.g.) logic and mathematics, ethics and philosophy. If one or more of these accounts is defensible, so too, I suspect, will be Smith's.

It may also be useful to examine similar conceptions in other theistic traditions such as Vaishnavism.[34] Nammalvar sings of the Lord swallowing him, for example: 'The Lord abides in [his] heart, and when it melts, swallows it.'[35] 'He who seized me came, the other day/ and ate my life./ Day after day, he comes, and devours me so fully./ Was that the day that I became his servant?' (9.6.8). Or again, 'He ate my life fully and was filled./ He became all worlds and all life/ . . . and he then became just for me, honey, milk, syrup, [and] nectar' (10.7.2) (CN, pp. 168f., 172f.).

---

34 Vaishnavas are monotheists, and describe God (Vishnu) as omniscient, omnipotent, and all loving.

35 John Carman and Vasudha Narayanan, *The Tamil Veda: Pillan's Interpretation of the Tiruvaymoli* (Chicago and London: University of Chicago Press, 1989), p. 166. Henceforth CN.

But then, as the last line implies, the poet *also* swallows the Lord 'who is beyond all senses and thought' (CN, p. 160). He 'entered my heart filling it./ I have obtained my love ['and contain him']. I ate the nectar, and rejoiced' (10.8.6) (CN 173). 'The Tamil word for "nectar" . . . is *amutu* (from the Sanskrit *amrta*, the substance that gives immortality) and the phrase "nectar of the mouth" is used to mean kissing.' Thus the poet, speaking as one of the god's female lovers (*gopis*) exclaims 'Embrace my beautiful breasts/ with the fragrance of the wild jasmine/ on your radiant chest./ Give me the nectar of your mouth' (10.3.5). '*Amutu* also means "food" and enjoyment' (CN, pp. 170-71). The upshot is that the poet and the Lord include one another. And as in the West, this mutual union or embrace between God and his devotee is expressed by images of taste, touch and smell. Another interesting example is the following.

The Gaudiya Vaishnavas who identify ultimate reality with Krishna[36] believe it is revealed 'in the form of a cosmic drama', known as the Krishna-lila. The heart of this drama is the love play between Krishna and the female cowherds (*gopis*) whose story is told in the *Bhagavata Purana*. The purpose of this revelation 'is to provide humans with a model of, and for, perfection'.[37] This model centrally includes passion which Jiva Gosvamin (fl. 1555-1600) defines as an instance of 'that love which consists of an immense desire of a subject for union with the object of its desire', and which Rupa (fl. 1495-1550) claims provides the 'highest access' to Krishna (Haberman, p. 70).

The devotee internalizes the stories of Krishna by identifying with one of Krishna's companions, thereby attempting to transform his or her identity. The *anubhavas* are the 'spontaneous and natural [external] expressions' of the characters' 'inner emotions'. By imitating, or taking on, the actions of one of the characters in the story, the devotee hopes to 'obtain the salvific emotions of that character and [thus] come to inhabit the world [namely, *Vraja*] in which that character resides' (Haberman, pp. 69f).

To explain more fully: According to Gaudiya Vaishnavism, 'the body . . . is the house of the soul or self (*atman*). Identity is what locates the self in a particular body which resides in a particular world. To participate in the world of *Vraja*', for example, 'one must occupy a body located in that world. And to accomplish this one must develop an identity which connects one to such

---

36   For many Vaishnavas, Krishna is the principle avatara ('descent' or salvific 'bodily' manifestation) of Vishnu.

37   David L. Haberman, *Action as a Way of Salvation: A Study of Raganuga Bhakti Sadhana* (Oxford and New York: Oxford University Press, 1988), p. 45. Henceforth Haberman.

a body . . . Salvation in Gaudiya Vaishnavism' should therefore 'be seen
as the shift of identity from the external . . . body' of ordinary life 'to [one's]
true body which is similar' to that of the exemplary character whose actions one
is imitating (Haberman, p. 73).

Since 'amorous emotion [*madhura-bhava*) . . . contains the essence of all
other emotions', it 'is perfectly represented by . . . the female lovers of Krishna,
. . . the *gopis* of *Vraja*'. Imitation of amorous bhakti (i.e., loving devotion) is
thus modelled on the *gopis*. It is 'divided into two types'. The first involves
'the desire for *direct* . . . enjoyment' and sexual union 'with Krishna' (my
emphasis), and therefore consists in identifying oneself with one of Krishna's
female lovers. The second involves a 'desire to share in the special emotions'
of one of the female *companions or attendants* of his lovers (usually a companion
of Radha, Krishna's favorite *gopi*), and thus to *vicariously* share in the latter's
amorous passion (Haberman, pp. 81-85).

What particularly interests me is that salvation, on this view, involves
the acquisition of a 'perfected body' whose characteristics mirror, while
transcending and transforming, those of one's 'earthly' body. If one's perfected
body *does* mirror one's earthly body, however, it must possess analogues of our
physical senses. What one would like, therefore, is a more detailed account
of just how these analogues of our physical senses function, and the ways
in which they resemble and differ from the latter – models that play a role
similar to those of Maritain or Jonathan Edwards or John Smith, for example.
Doing so would potentially shed further light on the tradition of the spiritual
senses which has been the subject of this article.

Theological Fictionalism: A Postmodern Heresy

Roger Pouivet

Introduction[1]

Theological fictionalism maintains that religious monotheistic commitment does not necessitate the truth of theism. According to this position, God could have the same ontological status as a fictional character in a novel or a movie. Such a character does not exist. We know that the character does not exist, but we think about this character and experience emotions (or quasi-emotions) that concern it and what it does. Like the experience of fiction, religious experience could consist in a game of make-believe. Robin Le Poidevin defends such a theological fictionalism (without using this label) in chapter 8 ('Is God a Fiction?') of his book, *Arguing for Atheism*,[2] partly inspired by Kendall Walton's theory of make-believe.[3] In the first section of this paper, I will review Le Poidevin's version of theological fictionalism.

But theological fictionalism is not simply a theory held by philosophers. It also appears to be widespread in postmodern cultures. The assumption is that we do not have to accept full-blooded theological realism – that God exists, that He revealed himself, that Christ was resurrected, and so on – in order to be religious persons. Such realism, it is thought, has been definitively disproven in the post-Enlightenment period, thanks to the human and social sciences. My second point will consist in inspecting this postmodernist flowering of theological fictionalism.

Fictionalism was already recognized in the *Dogmatic Constitution of the Catholic Faith,* in the text known under the name of its Latin headwords, *Dei Filius*:

> Even the Holy Scriptures, which had previously been declared the sole source and judge of Christian doctrine, began to be held no longer as divine, but to be ranked among the fictions of mythology.

---

1   Parts of this paper appeared under the title 'Against Theological Fictionalism' in *European Journal for Philosophy of Religion,* vol. 3, n. 2 (2011), 427-437. Thank you to Mikael Karlsson and Manuel Rebuschi for very useful remarks on this paper.

2   Robin Le Poidevin, *Arguing for Atheism* (London: Routledge, 1996).

3   Kendall L. Walton, *Mimesis as Make-Believe* (Cambridge, MA, and London: Harvard University Press, 1990).

This indicates that theological fictionalism is the outcome of a modernist view of faith, condemned by the Church if not refuted, but capable of reappearing in new and different guises. The main error of this theory is that it supposes a *non-doxastic account of faith*. Faith would not imply full belief, but only quasi-belief or quasi-acceptance. But I will try to show that there is, inescapably, a strong doxastic component in faith.

I. Compendium of Theological Fictionalism

To explain the position that I call *Theological fictionalism*, Le Poidevin makes use of a debate in the philosophy of science over the status of theoretical entities. Within this debate, he distinguishes realism, instrumentalism, and positivism, and proposes corresponding views about religious matters.

Realism. According to realism, scientific theories are to be taken at face value. If they appear to refer to entities in the world called 'neutrons', then this is what they do. Theological realism is the view that statements about God refer to a transcendent being. Such statements are descriptive and so are true or false.

Instrumentalism. Theories, according to instrumentalism, are merely devices we use to make predictions about how things will behave. So, the entities referred to in theories may just be fictions. Theological instrumentalism says that discourse about God is purely fictional. But the predictive dimension is largely beside the point in theological instrumentalism, unless we have in mind predicting the behaviour of religious persons, which may be anticipated through knowing what they believe.

Positivism. Theories, according to positivism, are either true or false, and so positivism differs from instrumentalism in this respect. But, in contrast with realism, theories need not be taken at face value. Theological positivism says that discourse that is apparently about God is true; but its truths, expressed in symbolic language, are truths about our moral and psychological lives, not about the entities apparently described.

What I call 'theological fictionalism' Le Poidevin calls 'theological instrumentalism'. I think that 'theological fictionalism' is a better name, because the notion of fiction is central to explaining how this kind of view works. Le Poidevin relies heavily upon Walton's theory of fiction as make-believe. According to Walton,

[J]ust as a child make-believes[4] that a group of chairs set in a line is a bus, or that, in chasing after a friend, he is chasing after a desperate criminal, armed to the teeth with a pop-gun and a water pistol, so we, in reading a novel, make-believe that it is reporting the truth. In doing so we, as it were, locate ourselves in the novel. We are there, witnessing the events. We may even assign ourselves a role, and imagine talking to the characters. It is our active participation in the fiction which explains why we become emotionally involved.[5]

Le Poidevin adds:

Walton's solution of the paradox that we can be emotionally involved in something we know to be false is that we play a game of make-believe in which the fiction becomes reality, and part of the game is to feel something akin to real emotions, though they are not the genuine article.[6]

Theological fictionalism is thus the thesis that to engage in religious practice is to engage in a game of make-believe:

We make-believe that there is a God, by reciting, in the context of the game, a statement of belief. We listen to what make-believedly are accounts of the activities of God and his people, and we pretend to worship and address prayers to that God. In Walton's terms, we locate ourselves in that fictional world, and in so doing we allow ourselves to become emotionally involved, to the extent that a religious service is capable of being an intense experience. [...W]e are presented with a series of dramatic images: an all-powerful creator, who is able to judge our moral worth, to forgive us or to condemn, who appears on Earth in human form and who willingly allows himself to be put to death. What remains, when the game of make-believe is over, is an awareness of our responsibilities for ourselves and others, of the need to pursue spiritual goals, and so on.[7]

So, according to theological fictionalism, Christians are not believers, but *make-believers*; they play with a fictional religious world as children play with toy cars, readers with narratives, and filmgoers with moving images. This can be important for their lives, for the sense they have of themselves and of their relations with others, and for their sense of morality and spirituality.

---

4   Walton takes the perfectly good English expression, 'to make believe', and turns it into an artificial, hyphenated verb, 'to make-believe', so that whereas one would normally say, 'a child makes believe that . . .', Walton insists upon saying, 'a child make-believes that . . .'. I do not ask here the question to know if such a simple modification and uglification of English is not a philosophical artefact creating exactly what Walton pretends to describe: our mental activity of make-believe. It would be possible to defend the thesis that we make believe, but it does not mean that there is a mental act consisting in make-believe.

5   Kendall L. Walton, *Mimesis as Make-Believe*, p. 116.

6   Robin Le Poidevin, *Arguing for Atheism*, p. 117.

7   Ibid., p. 119.

Nonetheless, they do not have to claim that what they 'believe' is in fact true about someone or something. Indeed, they do not have to really believe anything. Christian make-belief simply comes down to making sense of stories, characters, interpretations, and so on.

II. Theological Fictionalism as a Postmodern Heresy

Theological fictionalism may seem attractive to those who want to preserve what they think of as the spiritual and moral content of religion but who do not accept an ontological commitment to a transcendent being or realist claims about Christ's resurrection, miracles, the Day of Judgment, and so on. Theological fictionalism says, in short, that you can be a non-metaphysical Christian. God can still be viewed positively as the greatest single creation of the imagination. Anthony Kenny suggests that, 'Set beside the idea of God, the most original inventions of mathematicians and the most unforgettable characters in drama are minor products of the imagination; Hamlet and the square root of minus one pale into insignificance by comparison.'[8]

It is possible that it is not Le Poidevin's intention to give theological fictionalism such a role in religious life. The title of his book, *Arguing for Atheism*, says clearly what he thinks. But it seems to me that Le Poidevin contributes philosophical content to what many Christians today apparently think to be a correct account of Christian religious belief and faith. This is a non-atheistic version of theological fictionalism. It gives sense to the claim that Christ was resurrected, for example, by saying that the event of the resurrection is 'true in the Gospels', 'true for those who accept that sense is to be made of a certain story', or 'true in religion'. 'Christ was resurrected' is understood to be a *quasi-assertion*. To quasi-assert that *p* is to express one's *acceptance* of *p*, an attitude that is compatible with agnosticism and disbelief. Quasi-assertion is grounded mainly in non-doxastic or non-epistemic reasons, and recourse to this device encourages a non-cognitivist account of religious language. Arguably, the grounding of quasi-assertions is typically *pragmatic*: acceptance can provide comfort to oneself and to make one's life easier to live. To *accept* that Christ was resurrected is not to *believe* it – as we believe for example that Cracow is in Poland, or that the moon is not made of cheese – but it could be very helpful to *make-believe* that it was so.

Theological fictionalism gained credit through postmodern theology. By 'postmodern theology', I have in mind, for example, Don Cupitt's account

---

8   Anthony Kenny, *Faith and Reason* (New York: Columbia University Press, 1983), p. 59.

of religion, which is a form of theological fictionalism.[9] He defends
a philosophical perspective in a way that has insinuated itself into theology since
the fifties. But this is not simply a philosophical affair. It seems to me that this
postmodern view has now gained strong influence over religious people,
especially in Western countries. I have no sociological evidence to give
in support of this impression, but my perception is that it is in this way that
many Western Christians – especially those who have received an academic
education – now see theological commitment.

It seems to me that theological fictionalism amounts to a new heresy,
as defined by Alister McGrath: 'not unbelief (rejection of the core beliefs
of a worldview such as Christianity) in the strict sense of the term, but a form
of that faith that is held ultimately to be subversive or destructive, and thus
indirectly leads to such unbelief.'[10] What has developed is a deeply non-
cognitivist and anti-realistic account of faith. It suggests, first, that there are no
religious facts to be discovered, such as the existence of God or the resurrection
of Christ. Secondly, it claims that we create the world through language
and historical realities through narratives. According to the latter-day heretics,
we can say of God what Richard Rorty said about dinosaurs: 'Once you describe
something as dinosaur, its skin colour and sex life are causally independent
of your having so described it. But before you describe it as a dinosaur, or as
anything else, there is no sense to the claim that it is "out there" having
properties. What is out there? The thing-in-itself?'[11] Replace 'dinosaur' by 'God',
'skin colour' and 'sex life' by 'all powerful' and 'absolutely good', and you arrive
at a corresponding non-cognitivist and non-realistic account of Christian
religious 'truths'.

Theological fictionalism explains how one could continue to go to Mass,
to pray, to participate in the Eucharist, without *believing,* but only *make-believing,*
in religious matters. What is important in the end are not true facts, but inward
emotions and perhaps some of the behaviours (kindness, generosity, tolerance,
etc.) supposedly exhibited by Christian make-believers. This corresponds also
to what George Lindbeck[12] called the 'experiential-expressivist' account of faith.
God is not an *object* of discourse, but we can make Him a *condition* of discourse

---

9   See Don Cupitt, *The Sea of Faith* (Norwich: The scm Press, 1984).

10   Alister McGrath, *Heresy, A History of Defending Truth* (New York: Harper Collins,
     2009), p. 33.

11   Richard Rorty, 'Taylor on Truth', in *Philosophy in an Age of Pluralism,* ed. by J. Tully
     (Cambridge: Cambridge University Press, 1994), pp. 20-36 (p. 23).

12   George Lindbeck, *The Nature of Doctrine* (Louisville: Westminster John Knox Press,
     1984).

(and also a condition of a certain behaviour), by entering into a game of make-believe. And religion is just that, according to theological fictionalism.

III. Why Theological Fictionalism does not work

Walton says that what fictions make us feel are not emotions, but quasi-emotions. By 'quasi-emotions', he means emotions that do not suppose that we believe in the situation presented in the fiction. If I am frightened by the colour of the sky, which promises a very big thunderstorm, then I believe that the sky has this colour and that such a sky indicates that there will be a very big thunderstorm. But if I am frightened by a monster on the screen, I do not believe that there is a monster. In fact, I am not really afraid. I enter in a game of make-believe about a monster, and I am *quasi*-afraid, playing at fear, even if I am feeling (phenomenologically) what I would feel in a case of 'true' fear. This means that quasi-emotion is non-doxastic emotion. But perhaps it could also be said that quasi-emotion corresponds to a quasi-belief. I play at believing that there is a monster, and that makes me quasi-afraid.

Aesthetic fictionalism uncouples emotion from belief; theological fictionalism does something parallel and so uncouples faith from belief. We cannot say 'I believe that *p*; but not *p*', as G. E. Moore pointed out. But the theological fictionalist presupposes, without of course clearly realizing, that it is possible to claim: 'I have faith that *p*; but not *p*.' 'To believe' is a factive verb: if I believe that *p*, I am committed to the truth of *p*. But if I have faith in God almighty, it is not necessary for me to believe in the existence of God: making-believe is sufficient. To repeat at the mass that there is a God almighty, or to subscribe to the notion of God almighty Himself, would simply be an emotional prop in a game of make-believe. This would mean that, for faith, quasi-belief and quasi-emotion – the phenomenological content of emotion, without any doxastic component – is all that is needed for our religious life.

But I maintain that this will not do, for it seems for me impossible to 'have faith in *G*' if you do not believe that *G* exists. If *S* has faith in *G*, then *S* believes that *G* exists in a way that renders *S*'s faith in *G* something other than a game of make-believe. That contemporary Westerners are tempted to replace a religious faith that requires realism and metaphysical commitment by fiction-based religion does not imply that the epistemology of doing so is coherent.

I propose four arguments in favour of this critique of theological fictionalism.

The argument from faith as real assent

Faith is doxastic, because it supposes that some propositions – those belonging to the *Creed* in the case of Christian faith – are true. To paraphrase John Henry Newman, a fictionalist belief in God – a belief about a God as a character in a narrative rather than about God as a genuine being – would be like 'filial love without the fact of the father'. Nobody can place their confidence in Superman except the inhabitants of Metropolis, who themselves are fictional. The reader or spectator of Superman adventures cannot place his personal confidence in Superman, because he does not believe in Superman's existence. He may celebrate vicariously the confidence that the inhabitants of Metropolis place in Superman, but this has no *real* significance, because those people themselves belong to the fiction. If we take Jesus Christ to be a fictional character in a game of make-believe, we cannot place our confidence in Him; only characters in the Bible (the apostles for example), conceived of as figures in a story, could do so. And so if we understand Jesus Christ to be a fictional character, we do not have faith in Him, because faith is confidence.

As Newman says in the *Grammar of Assent,* faith is *real* assent, and not merely *notional* assent. Real assent is not directed to characters and stories but to concrete persons and concrete facts. Even if we give real assent to a proposition that is false, to assent in a real manner is to assent to things and not to notions. So the notion of fictional assent is useless for characterizing faith in God. Fictional apprehension and assent are in principle directed to notions, because we take the fictional characters not to be real entities but only to be notions of unreal (or non-existent) entities. Because of the doxastic component of religious faith, to have faith is to believe something, and to believe something means understanding something to be really the case (even if it is not) and not to be merely notional. It is not to claim that the sense of a certain proposition is deep and existentially moving or quasi-moving, but that it is *true*: that Christ is actually the Saviour, for example.

Theological discussion is systematically notional. It does not imply any real assent. That is why a non-believer can be a theologian! He may, for example, suppose hypothetically that the Trinitarian God of Christians exists and will try to see what that implies. This is not very different from asking oneself whether Mme Bovary had mumps when she was a child, or if Superman prefers to use gel or foam when he shaves. A theologian may, of course, be a religious person and a believer, but that is a contingent matter. However, this contingency should not encourage theological fictionalism, because that gives a bad account of the real assent of believers – an account that derives no support from the fact that theology *per se* is notional.

Theological fictionalism originates perhaps in the difficulty of imagining what it would be to understand propositions about God realistically, and especially to understand how a believer can genuinely assent to these propositions. The idea is that perhaps believers assent to such propositions notionally and fictionally. And it also suggests that if they do, they can make-believe without making any metaphysical claims or undertaking to answer to atheist objections. But this is merely meta-theology, not an understanding of what religious beliefs are: I mean *genuine* beliefs implying *real* assent.

The argument from the difference between belief and acceptance

Theological fictionalism as it has been presented does not recognize any difference between belief and acceptance. However, *accepting* that p, unlike *believing* that p, is akin to a decision – the decision to hold a proposition.[13] This contrasts strongly with the essential non-voluntariness of belief. Faith can be said to be voluntary, but only in the sense that it is not against one's will that one believes in God. Having faith in God's grace is not like being brainwashed. You can refuse to believe in God. But that does not mean that adopting religious belief is akin to making a decision to believe. The doxastic component of faith is non-voluntary, in the sense that I cannot decide to believe in God, any more than I can decide to believe that I speak Chinese or that I am a pumpkin, for example. One can *accept* a proposition without believing that it is true, and even while believing that it is false, hence contrary to evidence for its truth. But one cannot *believe* contrary to the evidence of truth, or independently of having considered the question of truth. This is the main reason why simulated beliefs or quasi-beliefs are acceptances, and so are not beliefs at all. Simulated beliefs are no more beliefs than fake money is money. I wonder if the notion of make-believe and quasi-emotion are not, in this sense, very ambiguous, suggesting something like a belief, but not exactly, and something close to an emotion, but not quite the same thing. The use of the notion of 'quasi' (or 'as if') supports the suggestion that something is, and at the same is not, what one speaks about. But this support is strictly rhetorical.

Henry H. Price describes a case that might strike a chord in the contemporary context, at least in the West, where religion is no longer central to one's life, unless one happens to be a priest or a monk:

> Here is a man who half-believes the basic propositions of Theism. ... What makes him that he only half-believes them? ... On some occasions he acts, feels and thinks

---

13   See L. Jonathan Cohen, *An Essay on Belief and Acceptance* (Oxford: Clarendon Press, 1992).

(and draws inferences) in much the same way as a person who does believe these Theistic propositions. But on other occasions he acts, feels and thinks in much the same way as a person who does not believe them, or even as person would has not heard of them at all. ... It would not be fair to describe this man as a hypocrite, someone who pretends or professes to believe what he actually disbelieves or doubts ... His religious attitude is not just a pretended one. But it is, so to speak, a part-time one. It is operative only in some parts of his life but not in others. He is seldom in it except on Sundays.[14]

But the man here described does not adopt a fictionalist stance. He does not simulate. He is sincere, only not continuously, but only intermittently.

It is true there are cases of acceptance where someone has evidence for what he accepts, and yet does not fully believe but only half-believes. Would a fictionalist analysis make good sense of such a case? As Price says, 'We can accept propositions with moderate confidence on evidence known to be less than conclusive, and make use of these propositions, for what they may be worth, for the guidance of our thought and actions.'[15] If I half-believe that *p*, do I simulate that *p*? In this case, I simulate the part that is lacking for a full belief. I *try* to believe fully, like the libertine who is asked, in a famous *pensée* of Pascal, to go Mass and to kneel down, hoping that it would make him a genuine Christian. But this does not mean that faith can be simulated, for faith is not half-belief plus simulation, but it is necessarily full belief. As Aquinas says:

> The act of believing . . . is firmly attached to one alternative, and in this respect the believer is in the same state of mind as one who has science or understanding. Yet the believer's knowledge is not completed by a clear vision, and in this respect he is like one having a doubt, a suspicion, or an opinion.[16]

In faith, there is not full knowledge, that is for sure; but there is full belief precisely *because* there is not full knowledge. This is not acceptance or half-belief, but a *case of certainty without clear vision*. And this does not admit of degrees. Simulated faith is a non-sense.

It is also possible to believe half of a doctrine. One believes some parts of it fully, but one disbelieves some other parts. Possibly, many Christians today believe only a part of Christian doctrine. For example, they fully believe Jesus to be the Son of God, but they might not believe that a non-natural method of contraception is sinful. The question is not here to decide if this attitude is reasonable. But clearly this is quite different from half-belief: half-belief and belief in a half are not the same.

---

14   Henry H. Price, *Belief* (London: Muirhead Library of Philosophy, 1969), p. 306.
15   Ibid., p. 304.
16   St Thomas Aquinas, *Summa Theologica*, IIaIIae, 2, 1.

So, not only is theological fictionalism deeply in error about the nature of faith. but it likewise fails to capture the sorts of attitudes – half-belief or belief in a part – that many Christians have today.

The argument from the dispositional nature of belief and faith

Like acceptance, simulated belief in a fictional scenario supposes that we play with our own mental states. I know that the monster is in fact an artefact on the screen, but I will behave as if I believed that the monster was in front of me. When someone cries when looking at a movie and is asked, 'Why do you cry, it is only fiction?', the answer could be that the very *idea* that something like this could happen is sorrowful. And it is not false that we are able to make ourselves sorrowful simply by focusing our minds on sorrowful ideas. So might it be in the religious case: we make ourselves believers by focusing on religious ideas. This would be good news for theological fictionalism, giving content to the notion of make-believe. A religious make-believer is someone playing with the idea of God, and related ideas. And finally all religious believers are perhaps nothing else than make-believers, and all religious beliefs simulated beliefs.

But such an account of simulated belief presupposes what Henry H. Price called an 'Occurrence Analysis of Belief'.[17] To believe something is to have a certain introspectible mental occurrence or state that one can easily distinguish from other mental states with which it might possibly be confused. So I introspect the difference between a fictional mental state and a realistic mental state, and I can easily make-believe by adopting a certain attitude about my mental occurrence, thereby fictionalizing it. In this case we would be very easily able to simulate having a certain mental state or content without actually having it.

Price distinguishes an *occurrence* analysis of belief from a *dispositional* analysis of belief, which maintains that beliefs are not mental occurrences but are rather dispositions to answer certain questions, or to behave, in certain ways. When it is said of someone that he believes something, we are making a dispositional statement about him. There is no event or act occurring in his mind (or in his brain) over and above the event or act of believing. This is not behaviourism: the occurrences and states in question could be mental. But their 'inner content' is not relevant to the analysis of belief. Beliefs are not something that happen to us, or something we 'do', but something we have or possess

---

17   Henry H. Price, *Belief*.

for a period, even when we are not conscious of having them.[18] Having a belief is in that way like being interested in football or having distaste for seafood. Thus if S believes that p, S does not have a specific mental content but rather has a disposition to answer 'yes', when asked if p, or a disposition to act according to the fact that p. And in that case, how would simulation be possible? In a dispositional analysis of belief, we cannot simulate beliefs. If we simulate, it means that we do not believe at all, simply because believing does not consist to have something in front of the mind, but to have a certain disposition to answer in a certain way or to act in a certain way.

The doctrine of simulated beliefs presupposes an occurrence analysis of belief. Make-believe seems to focus our mental attention on the content of a belief we do not really entertain. We do not have or possess it, but it occurs as if we had it. Imagination seems to be the inner contemplation of mental occurrences in themselves, independently of dispositions. We simulate having a certain mental state or content without having it, because mental occurrences are independent of our dispositions.

I will not here defend a dispositional analysis of belief (even if I think a dispositional account of belief is wholesale correct). But clearly if such an analysis is right, or if a large part of it is right, theological fictionalism conceived in Walton's way must be revised.

The argument from the limitations of make-believe

We saw that we cannot believe at will, but we cannot even imagine at will – contrary to what is often said (on the grounds of a very common romantic account of imagination). I am not at all sure that imagining that God sent us His only son to be crucified, as a Redeemer, to save us from our sins, is something we can easily do. I call this phenomenon 'modal imaginative resistance'. It is directed primarily at the way fictional characters act. Sometimes, when reading a novel or watching a movie, we simply cannot imagine that somebody acts in the way that a certain character does. As Berys Gaut remarks, we can imagine such a scene in the sense of entertaining the propositions which describe it.[19] But at the same time, we can't imagine it in the sense of making a complex imaginative projection involving human action. A story is told, but it makes no

---

18   Price says that 'the difference between the two analyses of belief is not quite so clear-cut as it looks' (*Belief,* p. 244). Surely he is right. But here I want to emphasize the distinction to show that make-believe theory presupposes an occurrence analysis that can be questioned and even rejected.

19   Berys Gaut, 'Art and Cognition', in *Contemporary Debates in Aesthetics and the Philosophy of Art,* ed. by M. Kieran, (Oxford: Blackwell, 2006), pp. 115-126 (p. 119).

sense for us. We do not believe in it and cannot even make-believe in it. I suppose that it is exactly what happens for a lot of unbelievers. They do not think that the religious story is like a novel that makes sense even if it is a fiction. For them, it is like a novel that does not make any sense! And to the extent that this is so, I do not see that theological fictionalism could provide a plausible account of a Christian religious stance attributable to them.

There is a kind of imagination by which we can consider ourselves as being relevantly different than we actually are. And this is of course often what novels and movies invite us to experiment with – to discover, through fictions, human possibilities: what we could be. But this does not always work. And it also seems that fictions tell us important things even when we find ourselves impervious to the possibilities that they offer. Some philosophers – those who consider that we decide to make-believe – exaggerate our abilities at making believe. Sometimes we simply cannot do so, being unable to imagine that things could proceed as presented in a certain sort of novel or film.[20]

Theological fictionalism must explain to us why we make-believe in God if we cannot manage to believe in Him. That people make-believe in Him – in His story, that His son died for us, that one day there will be resurrection of the flesh, and so on – is in no way easier to understand than the fact that people really believe these things. And so, theological fictionalism is in *no way* a better epistemological position from which to explain the religious stance than is theological realism, and is a far worse position from which to raise questions of justification!

The argument against 'as if'

In his chapter on theological fictionalism, 'Is God a Fiction?', in *Arguing for Atheism,* Le Poidevin does not quote Hans Vaihinger's *The Philosophy of 'As If'.*[21] The subtitle of Vaihinger's book is: 'A System of Theoretical, Practical and Religious Fictions of Mankind.' Religious dogmas, Vaihinger says, on the basis of an interpretation of Kant's critical philosophy, are fictions possessing a subjective and practical 'truth'. Belief in gods, or in God, functions as official fictions without which justice would not impose itself, and morality would be impossible. For Vaihinger, Kant's philosophy of religion is based on such an 'as if' attitude. It is a fictionalist one. I will not discuss the question of whether this interpretation is right. I want only to formulate what I think is

---

20   See Roger Pouivet, 'Modal Aesthetics', *Proceedings of the European Society for Aesthetics,* vol. 3 (2011), 15-27.

21   Hans Vaihinger, *The Philosophy of 'As If'* (London: Routledge & Kegan Paul, 1924).

a strong difficulty for such a fictionalist account of religion based on the notion of 'as if'.

Imagine a situation where I will be operated on. I am asked if I am sure that this operation is necessary. I answer: 'I don't believe that the operation that all the doctors recommend will do me any good; only a trained physician or surgeon should have such a belief; but, as a practical matter, I will act *as if* the doctors' advice is good.' (Or, for another formulation, 'I will pretend that the doctors' advice is good'.) As Peter van Inwagen explains, this reasoning presupposes (what he calls) a 'Platonic conception of rationality': 'one's beliefs are not rational unless one is able successfully to defend them against any rational criticism that may be brought against them.'[22] And I am supposed to be unable to have knowledge about the necessity of the operation, or the fact that it would do me any good, for I am not a physician or a surgeon. I can only have an opinion about it. This is the reason why I could only think and act *as if* I believed in the way that those who know, the doctors, believe. So, the only alternative for me would be to fictionalize or simulate my belief; to act 'as if' my belief were true. It would be the same in the case of religion. It is not possible to know whether or not there is a God. (Kant says in the Preface of the Critique of Pure reason that he 'had to deny knowledge in order to make room for faith'.) So I can only simulate moral or pragmatic reasons for there being a God. Unable to defend my belief in God against all rational criticism that may be brought against it, I have no knowledge, I have faith; and this faith is a simulated belief based on non-cognitive, but moral or pragmatic, reasons.

But suppose I were to say: 'I don't believe that the operation all the doctors recommend will do me any good; only a trained physician or surgeon should have such a belief; but as a practical matter I will act as if the doctor's advice was *false*'. As Peter van Inwagen says, 'the person who accepts the doctors' advice "as a practical matter" has not chosen that course of action by tossing a coin'.[23] What does this mean? Surely, it means that even if I do not know, in the way that the physician and the surgeon know, what benefit I would have from the operation, I can still have very good reasons for believing that the operation is necessary. That all the doctors think the operation is necessary is a quite good and solid reason to believe that the operation is necessary and to think that such is the way things *really are*. It also means that it makes no sense to say that to act as if the doctors' advice was bad could be chosen

---

22   Peter van Inwagen, 'Christian Belief and the Platonic Conception of Rationality', in *The Rationality of Theism*, ed. by Godehard Brüntrup & Ronald K. Tacelli (Dordrecht: Springer, 1999), pp. 145-159 (p. 145).

23   Peter van Inwagen, 'Christian Belief and the Platonic Conception of Rationality', p. 150.

indifferently. And if what the doctors advise makes a difference, then to act as if the doctors' advice was good (or bad) is not to depend upon a *fiction*. In fact, when I decide to do as the doctors advise, it is because, based upon their advice, I believe that the operation is not a bad or completely indifferent thing, but likely a good thing. I have good reason to think that what I choose to do is really better and not just fictionally better.

We are not in the epistemic situation where knowledge and faith are opposed, and so where faith could be an attitude based upon fictions with strictly pragmatic justifications. The reason why such a fictionalism is wrong is that we can distinguish the fairly probable from the highly improbable. It may be possible to save the 'as if' analysis of religious belief, but 'as-if beliefs' would not turn out to be *fictional* beliefs. When we act as if something were true, it is because we think that it is more probably true than false. But if something is fictional, we know perfectly well that it is false! Contrary to what is suggested by the fictionalist theologian, we would not think that the way of the world was *as if* God existed if we thought that God did not exist.

Conclusion

Anthony Kenny says:

> Most of us, I imagine, are atheists and not agnostics with respect to the Homeric gods of Olympus. With the possible exception of one or two Oxford professors of Classics, nobody nowadays believes that Zeus, Hera and Aphrodite actually exist in any literal sense. This does not prevent us from enjoying the Iliad and the Odyssey. Nor does it mean that Homer has nothing to teach us about ourselves and about the world we live in.[24]

The Homeric gods of Olympus are fictional. Paul Veyne doubted that Greeks believed in their own myths. Strangely, this supposes that the attitude of Greeks was the same as certain professors of classics, as Paul Veyne is. There is a strong epistemic difference between enjoying myths and fictional characters and believing in gods or having faith in God. Kenny is right to consider that we can learn something important by reading Homer, as we generally can by reading fiction of the better sort, for reasons that philosophers of fiction examine (even if they do not all agree that we do really learn something or that we could not learn it another way). But the non-belief attitude that fiction requires is

---

24   Anthony Kenny, 'Agnosticism and Atheism', in *Philosophers and God: At the Frontiers of Faith and Reason*, ed. by John Cornwell & Michael McGhee, (London: Continuum, 2009), pp. 117-124 (p. 117).

the opposite of the religious attitude, and this gives us a strong reason to doubt that Paul Veyne is right about the Greeks' epistemic life.

Theological fictionalism is supposed to give a faithful account of a possible religious life of Westerners who longer accept the strong metaphysical suppositions of Christian doctrine: the existence of God, the Trinity, Incarnation, Resurrection, and so on. The solution may be seen as that of transforming all these claims into fictional stories that convey a message and provide a meaning to life. But this would be nothing other than atheism with a religious flavour. At best, it would be an account of the cultural dimension of Christian religion.

It would certainly possible to visit Roman churches and Gothic cathedrals with our children, and to say to them: 'Look at these wonderful works of art, my dears! Appreciate all of this beauty!' The children might them ask: 'But, what does all this mean: all these crosses, the statues, and all the rest?' – 'Well, dear children, you must make-believe a certain story to make sense of all this. It is a very long story, contained in a very big book called "The Bible", and I will simply tell you the main episodes. For example, it is said in this story that God had a son, named Jesus Christ, and that he was crucified to save all Humanity from death. Don't laugh, Immanuel, this has a profound meaning! And if you look at these works of art as if there were a God, and a Son of God who died for us, you will be intensely moved by everything you see around you. Do the same as you do when you watch a Superman adventure on TV!' This would be a cultural initiation, exactly as in a course of classics. And for such an initiation, we could perhaps do with simulation. Reading Homer, I can simulate, in a sense, the kind of beliefs traditional Ancient Greeks had about their gods. But it is exactly because I do not have those beliefs that I can *simulate* them. If I do believe, I do not simulate, but *share* the vision of the Ancient Greeks.

If my analysis is right, one understands what makes Theological fictionalism at the same time an attractive account of religious faith and an error – and so a heresy. It is attractive because it eliminates the metaphysical content of Christian faith, which seems to a lot of people very difficult to defend in the face of science and even good sense. But it is an error, because it is impossible to adopt such an attitude and not be finally conducted to unbelief.

From Thinking about God to Experiencing the World: Theory of Transcendentals and the Debate about the Nature of Experience

Sebastian Tomasz Kołodziejczyk

This paper is devoted to one of the most intriguing metaphysical theories – the theory of transcendentals – that was invented by mediaeval theologians and philosophers who searched for tools that might help to explain the nature of God. Here I do not focus on the theological dimension of this idea, but instead I want to show that it is worthy of attention because of its potential philosophical usefulness and its explanatory power. Somewhat surprisingly, the theory of transcendentals seems to shed light on the problem of 'pure experience' that must not have nothing to do with any concepts and theories. Putting forward so-called 'Basic Furniture of Mind Hypothesis' I will argue for fruitful and mutual connection between thinking about God on the one hand, and the world on the other.

My paper is divided into three sections. In the first section, I will consider the idea of pure experience. In the second section, I outline the theory of transcendentals. The last section contains discussion about the relations between the theory of transcendentals and the problem of pure experience.

The theory of transcendentals – both from the historical and the systematic point of view – belongs to one of the most fundamental theories that allow to link thinking about God with formulating the conditions of experience and thinking about the world. This medieval – today underestimated – theoretical construct is based on two assumptions: (1) one can speak about God only in a transcategorial language (as a simple being) and in a transuniversal language (as a being which is beyond any conditions and kinds) and (2) extensions of predicates in sentences about God must be properties, which at least to a minimal degree pertain also to the objects in the world.

The class of transcendentals usually consists of a short list of terms, beginning with being. The other transcendental predicates are: unity, essence, separateness, truth, goodness, and beauty (sometimes also so called disjunctive transcendentals, such as possibility and necessity).

The crucial point here is that with the help of these transcendental predicates one can make meaningful statements both about God and the world: similarly to God, a thing in this world exists, is one and separate, poses its nature; and it is possible to predicate about it in judgments, and to apprehend it as an object of the will and aesthetic judgment.

It is worth noting that the theory of transcendentals was originally used to defend the thesis that God allows evil, without causing evil, because only goodness is real (exists) (Philip the Chancelor, Alexander of Hales; cf. J.A. Aertsen 1996). Only later on the theory of transcendentals has been transformed – especially by Albert the Great and Thomas Aquinas (J.A. Aertsen 1996), and John Duns Scotus (A.B. Walter 1946) – gaining the form that we are interested in here. What these authors began to notice was that the theory of transcendentals connotes the minimal connection between God and the world, and moreover it formulates the conditions of other types of predication (with the help of categorial and general terms).

This last characteristic of the theory of transcendentals is closely related to the problem of conditions of experience and thinking about God analyzed in this essay. Especially in the form given to it by Thomas Aquinas, the theory of transcendentals ceases to play the role of the metaphysical explanation of the existence of evil and its compatibility with God's existence, and becomes a source of answers to the question how an experience of the world and thinking about the world is possible.

I. The Idea of Pure Experience

Donald Davidson in his famous paper 'On the conceptual schemata' says that there are three, not two, dogmas of empiricism. W.V.O. Quine identified two of them in the paper 'Two Dogmas of Empiricism'. Davidson adds the third dogma that is strictly related to the problem we are considering now. It is the dogma of uninterpreted data that is in fact the problem of the existence of pure empirical experience, in which no conceptual factor is involved. Though here I am not interested in arguing for the extremely empirical approach, it is necessary to point out some crucial ideas of this view in order to better understand what kind of solution the theory of transcendentals has to offer.

Let us begin with the main problem that was formulated in a satisfactory way by Bas van Fraassen in his book *Scientific Image*. He writes ([1980], p. 57): "to accept a theory involves no more belief ... than that what it says about observable phenomena is correct. To delineate what is observable, however, we must look to science ... and possibly to the same theory." This problem is called 'the problem of the hermeneutic circle' and there have been many attempts to solve it. The name refers to a kind of trap in the human cognitive process and indicates that any data seem to be interpreted in some way.

The dogma of uninterpreted data sparkles many shades but what is the most fundamental in it is the thesis about direct experience which seems to be simply the thesis about direct sensual perceiving. Robert Hudson ([2000], p. 357) formulates this thesis in the following manner:

(Df) Direct perception is the processes of perceiving an object without the mediation of concepts.

The object given in such direct perception is called 'concept-less' or 'theory-free' object. The question that arises is whether such an experience is possible. Now I will show three main arguments in favour of this position and then some of their defects which cannot be removed without additional assumptions possessing a pre-conceptual and pre-propositional character.

The three main arguments are as follows:

(1) The argument from the independency of routes. As it is a positive argument, I'm not going to explain it in detail. It says that "claims made about an empirical object are more objective, are more valuable epistemically, if the claims are produced by different, although relevantly similar observational or experimental procedures". This position is taken among others by S. Woolgar [1988].

The next two arguments employ the idea of identifying direct experience with experience that occurs without mediation of any descriptive beliefs. Dretske ([1969]; [1993]) and Warnock before him suggested that one should make a distinction between thing-awareness and fact-awareness (Dretske) or, in terms of empirical experience, seeing things and seeing facts (Warnock). Thing-awareness is direct and is possible without any mediation of concepts or theories, while fact-awareness requires theory of some sort. These distinctions offer us two kinds of experience (perception): direct and indirect. Robert Hudson argues, in two steps, for the possibility of the direct experience.

(2) In the first step he takes 'the argument from no explanation' bringing forward the direct perceiving of objects at face value. Opponents of direct experience assert that "The perceptual identification of an object is inexplicable if the perceiver does not possess a descriptive belief that mediates the perception of this object. *Therefore*, for every perception, there is a descriptive belief that mediates the perception" (Hudson, op. cit., p. 365).

Hudson considers the logical structure of this argument and reconstructs it as follows: "Given hypothesis h (e.g. I directly perceive this table), one cannot explain the phenomenon p (my ability to successfully identify this table), *therefore*, hypothesis h is false." Now, he proposes an experiment with a man, Bob, who perceives two identical lamps A and B having only one feature that allows him to distinguish between the two lamps (being to the left of a lamp). If an opponent of direct perception is right (because a descriptive belief is necessary), it means that explanation for seeing lamp A is recognizing it as possessing the aforementioned property (being to the left of a lamp). The question is what happens when we shuffle the lamps without the perceiver knowing it. According to Hudson his opponents should say: the perceiver sees nothing, for it is clear that the perceiver does not see a proper lamp. However, Hudson concludes that "either Bob perceives lamp A or he perceives lamp B; and he does not perceive lamp B (the lamps were changed places each other), thus Bob sees lamp A." In a result Hudson rejects the opponent's argument using their own weapon: "Given hypothesis h (that, for every perception, there is a descriptive belief which grounds the identification of the perceived object), one cannot explain phenomenon p (Bob's ability to perceive lamp A in the post-shuffling situation), *therefore,* h is false" (ibid., p. 366).

(3) The third argument is put forward by different kinds of adversaries of direct perception. They hold that "Without descriptive beliefs, perceptions do not possess the content with which to bear confirmationally or disconfirmationally on other beliefs. *Therefore*, for every (epistemically valuably) perception, there is a descriptive belief that mediates the perception" (ibid., p. 367).

Hudson agrees that, generally speaking, they are right, and for this reason he makes a distinction between conceptually shaped experience and conceptually shapeable experience. This helps to understand his thought experiment with a lamp. We have the sentence 'That is a green lamp'. The advocates of indirect perceiving have to admit that their seeing of the lamp is determined by a descriptive belief 'green lamp', but how about the situation in which that lamp appears as such but it is in fact blue. Hudson asks rhetorically: "what do they perceive, a green or a blue lamp or maybe nothing?" If we agree that perceivers see a green lamp and their experience was shaped by some concepts, it will entail that the sentence "That is a green lamp" is true. This would imply that perceivers are always right, which seems to be a strange idea after all. Concluding, Hudson adds "Now, I am going to take it for granted here that theory-laden, empirical claims are epistemically valuable only if their truth or falsity depends on the way the world is [...]" (ibid., p. 368).

This is not the end of the story. Hudson focuses on the concepts or beliefs which may determine our perception, stressing their content. In fact that what determines perception or experience in general is a content. I agree that this determination is very unpleasant and gives rise to many troubles with solipsism and skepticism in the forefront. But Hudson does not exclude that there is a kind of determination that I call here 'pre-conceptual and pre-propositional determination' and which plays a fundamental role in the process of experiencing the world.

All three arguments for the possibility of direct perception mentioned above have the same flaw. In order to refer to and identify objects we must at least subconsciously to have some sort of tools which enable us to see the world divided into different objects and facts which we may know and talk about (see J. McDowell [1994]). Fodor [1984], for instance, admits that there are so-called core concepts which are located in perceptual modules. Although I don't think that what Fodor is talking about are really concepts, it seems to be a good opportunity to formulate a hypothesis which I label 'the basic furniture hypothesis' – BFH:

(BFH) In order to explain how it is possible to refer to and identify reality in its objective and plural dimensions, there has to exist a basic furniture of our cognitive faculties which pre-conceptually and pre-propositionally determines all experience.

Now this is an appropriate moment to shift our attention to the theory of transcendentals that lends support to the basic furniture hypothesis and helps us to understand why pre-conceptual and pre-propositional determination is something more than only a fairy tale.

II. Theory of Transcendentals

Thomas Aquinas introduces the theory of the transcendentals while discussing the problem of truth. It is worth noting that he does not do it in the context of goodness that is an object of interest of his predecessors, Philip the Chancellor, Alexander of Hales, and his teacher Albert the Great. This is remarkable because truth is strictly connected with knowledge and it means that Aquinas wanted to improve the theory of transcendentals in order to explain some aspects of our knowledge.

I propose to divide Aquinas's text into three parts: (1) methodological assumptions; (2) the concept of being, and (3) the procedure for deriving the rest of the transcendentals.

(1) In establishing the most fundamental concepts of our conceptual schemata, Aquinas uses methodology that he derives from ancient philosophical considerations. In the literature on the subject it is called 'resolutio'. It relies on the analysis leading to first concepts or propositions. Aquinas adopts the procedure of reduction and he mentions two main arguments for it.

He writes (*De veritate*, 1.1 respondeo): "When investigating the nature of anything, one should make the same kind of analysis as he makes when he reduces a proposition to certain self-evident principles (*reductionem in aliqua principia per se intellectui nota*). Otherwise, both types of knowledge will become involved in an infinite regress, and science and our knowledge of things will perish."

When investigating the nature of a thing we have to be able to provide an analysis that shows that there are self-evident principles that constitute the basic 'description' of the thing. For example, let us consider this table. We may produce many different descriptions of this table, and in accordance with the procedure of reduction there is a kind of basic description of this table. Aquinas gives us the subjective, epistemological criterion for it, namely self-evidence. We may easily notice that any descriptive sentences we produce might be not recognized as a basic description because none of them is self-evident for us. It seems to be evident that this kind of description will not use any of the concepts by which we usually characterize things.

The second argument concerns the methodological aspect of achieving knowledge. Aquinas suggests that if there were no first self-evident principles (concepts or propositions), knowledge would be impossible. What is very interesting is that he separates science (lat. *scientia*) from the knowledge of things (*cognitio rerum*). This division uncovers some beliefs that Aquinas is familiar with. The first self-evident principles have to be identified by people both in scientific research and in the natural process of cognition. This means that he establishes his theory as applied to all the fields of human cognitive activity.

There is another interesting methodological view that appears in *The Disputed Questions on Truth*. Aquinas in q. 11 formulates a mysterious doctrine that is hardly understandable to many scholars and specialists of his thought. It seems to be a common opinion that Aquinas does not belong to the nativists, that is, he does not agree with the theory that there is something innate that determines human knowledge about the world. However, in the aforementioned question he states that "preexistunt in nobis 'rationes seminales'."

He mentions two types of 'rationes seminales', simple and complex. The set of simple *rationes* includes such concepts as being, unity, truth and so forth. These concepts are known directly, without any mediation. Members of the second set are principles. They are complex and what we may say in all probability they are reducible to the first simple concepts.

Anyway, we have quite clear methodological assumptions which can be connected with BFH. Now, we have the content of BFH: the mind is equipped with some sort of pre-propositions and pre-concepts which determine our knowing reality.

(2) There is no more basic and more simple concept then the concept of being. Aquinas argues for this point in four ways. We read in *The Disputed Questions*: "Now, as Avicenna says, that which the intellect first conceives as, in a way, the most evident, and to which it reduces all its concepts, is being. Consequently, all the other conceptions of the intellect are had by additions to being. But nothing can be added to being as though it were something not included in being [...]. The Philosopher has shown this by proving that being cannot be a genus. Yet, in this sense, some predicates may be said to add to being insomuch as they express a mode of being not expressed by the term 'being'. It happens in two ways."

Aquinas's four arguments for this point are as follows:

I.   A being is conceived as the first by the intellect. We have to be sure, Aquinas says, that the intellect directly grasps being, simply an existent. Sometimes he tends to say that the intellect grasps being in *actu confuse* which means that there is no conceptual clarity in what the intellect actually conceives.

II. Being is most evident for the intellect. It is easy to understand why it is so. Before we start distinguishing things and predicating full-blooded concepts of them, it must be evident that we conceive an existent. When I look through the window and see the sky over my head, it is not the most evident thing to me that there are birds, clouds, aircrafts, and so forth, but it is evident to me that there are existents which I will recognize in the next steps of cognitive procedure.

III. Until now Aquinas has been speaking of being, now he is beginning to talk about the concept of being. He does it because the concept of being is given immediately when a being is given to our cognitive power. As we can remember from the previous section, the *rationes seminales* are discovered by the agent's intellect through the abstracted data given in experience. But Aquinas adds that all concepts are reducible to being. For them to be reducible in such a way means to be for their referents recognized by the intellect as beings.

IV. In the last argument Aquinas turns over the procedure of reduction we have been talking about so far. He says that all concepts of the intellect are in some sort of combination with being. They supervene upon being. The addition is not an operation on real things. I am not able to add something to being. I may, for instance, add some ingredients to boiling water and then to make soup but this does not mean that the ingredients which are combined and become a mixed substance called 'tomato soup' were not beings before. This means that the only addition is the addition in thought (*secundum rationem*). This addition in fact is the expression of modes of being, which are the ways things are.

We have to be clear about the concept of being. Aquinas takes evasive action here. Although he indicates that both being and the concept of being are first in order of cognition, being is primary in this process. Being is recognized by the intellect immediately, and at the same moment the concept of being is given as well.

(3) Speaking in the most general terms, there are two modes of being. Aquinas names them 'a special manner of being' and 'a mode [...] that is common and consequent upon every being.' The differentiation into ten categories belongs to the expression of a special manner of being, whereas the transcendentals are expressions of that which is common and consequent upon every being. We can observe the latter in detail by dividing it into two parts.

Aquinas writes: "This mode can be taken in two ways: first, in so far as it follows upon every being considered absolutely; second, in so far as it follows upon every being considered in relation to another. In the first, the term is used in two ways, because it expresses something in the being either affirmatively or negatively. [...] To express this, the term 'thing' is used; for, according to Avicenna, thing differs from being because being gets its name from to-be (*esse*), but thing expresses the quiddity or essence of the thing. There is, however, a negation consequent upon every being considered absolutely: its undividedness, and this is expressed by one. For the one is simply undivided being."

The first two transcendentals are established upon reference to being in two manners. If you look at the table now, and imagine that you do not have any knowledge about it, in the absolute and affirmative reference to being (it exists or better it has *esse* – existent) you are able to grasp its *thisness*. We express this primarily by using our index finger, and secondarily through the demonstrative pronoun. Aquinas calls this aspect of our basic experience the absolute and affirmative consideration of being and this is the meaning of the first transcendental *thing* (Lat. *res*). The second consideration relies on an absolute but negative reference to a being. The word 'one' or 'unity (Lat. *Unum*) means reference to a being in such a way that the mind grasps that *this and being* are not divided. Coming back to the table; in the very first experience we conceive *this* as *existing*.

But the mode of being that is common and consequent upon every being may be taken in the second way – according to the relation of one being to another. Aquinas adds that this is done in a twofold manner. "The first is based on the distinction of one being from another, and this distinctiveness is expressed by the word 'something' (lat. aliquid), which implies, as it were, some other things. For, just as a being is said to be one in so far as it is without division in itself, so it is said to be something in so far as it is divided from others. The second division is based on the correspondence of one being to another. This is possible only if there is something which is such that it agrees with every thing. Such a being is soul, which, as is said in *The Soul*, "in some way is all things". The soul, however, has both knowing and appetitive powers. 'Good' expresses the correspondence of being to the appetitive power [...]. 'True' expresses the correspondence of being to the knowing power [...]"

The meanings of the three additional transcendentals have been specified. The first of them, that is named 'something', refers to the plurality of things (a division between things). It is done in a relative and negative consideration. When we look at this, we immediately realize that this is something different from that. Aquinas wants to say that being which is given directly is given in its distinctiveness from other beings; things are given in the richness of plurality and our minds have to be equipped with some tools in order to experience this richness.

The last two transcendentals are controversial. They are based on relative and affirmative considerations. Truth and goodness are recognized as the result of a basic and fundamental relation that occurs in reality. This situation is grasped immediately when a being is given. We are speaking about the mind and its two faculties which relate to being in the correspondence relation. Thomas evidently indicates that when we, for example, experience this table, the possibility of any future knowledge of it we will be able to achieve relies upon the relation between this table on the one hand and the human mind (soul) on the other. This relation is called 'correspondence' and means simply that 'things and souls fit each other'. What is even more interesting, this fitness of our minds is confirmed in the very first moment of experience when they grasp the plurality of things and so the relation between them and itself.

Now we can move to the last section of the essay where I try to make use of the relationship between the theory of the transcendentals and the problem of pure experience discussed in the first section.

III. Hypothesis of the Basic Furniture of Mind

Let us consider the experience of this again. If the theory of direct empirical experience were true, there would be a moment in perceiving the world when we would not have any intellectual involvement in it, which would mean that it is nothing but chaos. The examples with lamps show that we need a basic attitude toward the world. We expect objects and some sort of order between them on the one hand, and between them and ourselves on the other. The basic furniture hypothesis fits well here. Almost all of us have had an experience that is very common to people who walk around the forest in the evening when the sun is setting and it is getting dark. There is a moment when we cannot see anything but suddenly sounds reach our ears. Although we do not know what it is, we are able to say that it is a being, that it is different from other things, that it is what is given to our faculty of knowing and our faculty of desiring. We know all these things but we are still not able to answer the essential question" 'what is it?'. Only a few seconds later we are ready to say: it is a bear or we must have imagined it; there is nothing.

I suggest that the theory of transcendentals lends support to the basic furniture hypothesis (BFH). It offers an understanding of the very fundamental necessary conditions for experiencing and being experienced. The transcendentals seem to be the predeterminations of every particular act of knowing and desiring. Before we formulate the thesis about direct perceiving of objects we have to have a little bit of knowledge about what we actually perceive. What is perceived is being that is recognized by our mind as an existent.

The theory of transcendentals fulfilling the BFH sheds light on both ontological and epistemological dimensions of experience. We may say nothing about the objects we are perceiving with one exception; we are always able to say that they are, they are these or those, they are something, they are objects of our cognitive and voluntary faculties. This pre-conceptual and pre-propositional determination does not mean that we achieve substantial knowledge about these objects. It seems rather that we are equipped with tools which give us immediate and ordered access to reality. When we want to relate what these tools are, we have to do a piece of reflection upon the ways of working and interacting with reality.

At the semantical level all the transcendentals are hidden behind a sentence but it is relatively easy to show they really are there. Let us consider the sentence 'This table is wooden.' It refers to a being (at least a creation of our mind), it refers to a thing, it combines (unifies) an object and its property, it separates one thing from another, it may be evaluated as true, and it refers to something that may be an object of desire. To be very precise we could propose semantical operators that represent the deeper structure. Quine and Woleński showed it for being; I am sure we are able to do the same for the rest of the transcendentals. At the ordinary level of language it is not necessary yet.

In the second section it was said that Aquinas's view on the transcendentals is quite similar to the present philosophers' opinion about the redundancy of truth. This is not surprising for being, thing, something, truth or goodness, as the pre-conceptual and pre-propositional basic furniture of our minds, are absolutely transparent. If we put them in the place of the predicate in a subject-predicate sentence, we do not obtain any substantial information. If someone asks us what is it and pointing at this table he is not expecting an answer 'it is a being' or 'it is a thing' or 'it is something'. His respond will probably be like this: 'I know this thing, please tell me what it is'.

This view leads to some consequences. One of them is the special status of concepts which are derived from the transcendentals. They are not first-order concepts. They really have very little content (as concepts), because they do not represent any feature of things. They are valuable in the very strange cases when for instance we have to find a solution to the problem of whether the things we are talking about are beings. In such situations concepts of the very basic furniture of mind are introduced to first-order sentences and have very strong informative power. To say of unicorns that they are beings means much more for many people than to meet David Beckham in the nearby restaurant. About the latter we know that he is, regarding the former we wish they were.

Concluding Remarks

I have been trying to show that the theory of transcendentals may be treated as the content of the Basic Furniture Hypothesis that seems to be necessary to explain the process of knowing and desiring of human beings. Above all it helps to understand why we are immediately familiar with reality and have no problems with investigating a nature of things in their plurality and mutual relationships. The theory of transcendentals conceived primarily as a way of grasping the nature of God, eventually may be considered as uncovering the fundamental co-relation between being and the mind, recognizing the richness of being in the forms of considerations which are made by the mind. These considerations are the meanings of the transcendental terms, which are *being, thing, unity, something, truth, and goodness*. Without them no knowledge or effective desiring cannot be achieved at all.

References

Aertsen, J.A. 1996. *Mediaeval Philosophy and the Transcendentals. The Case of Thomas Aquinas* (Leiden-New York-Köln)
Armstrong, D.M. 1981. *The Nature of Mind* (Sussex)
BonJour, L. 1985. *The Structure of Empirical Knowledge* (Cambridge, MA)
Chisholm, R. M. 1957. *Perceiving: A Philosophical Study* (New York)
Crane, T. (ed.) 1992. *The Contents of Experience, Essays on Perception* (Cambridge)

Crane, T. 1992b. 'The Nonconceptual Content of Experience', in: Crane (ed.), pp. 136-157

Dancy, J. (ed.) 1988. *Perceptual Knowledge* (Oxford)

Dretske, F. 1969. *Seeing and Knowing* (London)

Dretske, F. 1993. „Conscious Experience", *Mind* 102, 263-83

Fodor, J. 1984. 'Semantics, Wisconsin Style', *Synthese* 58, 231-50

Hudson, R.G. 2000. 'Perceiving Empirical Objects Directly', *Erkenntnis* 52(3), 357-371

Jackson, F.C. 1977. *Perception. A Representative Theory* (Cambridge)

McDowell, J. 1994. *Mind and World* (Cambridge, MA., London, UK)

Peacocke, Ch. 1998. 'Nonconceptual Content Defended', *Philosophical and Phenomenological Research* 63, 381–388

Pitcher, G. 1971. A *Theory of Perception* (Princeton)

Prinz, J.J. 2002, *Furnishing the Mind: Concepts and Their Perceptual Basis* (Cambridge, MA)

Thomas Aquinas. 1952-1954. *The Disputed Questions on Truth*, tr. R. Mulligan, J.V. MacGlynn, R.W. Schmidt (Chicago)

Van Fraassen, B. 1980. *Scientific Image* (Oxford)

Walter, A.B. 1946. *The Transcendentals and Their Function in the Metaphysics of Duns Scotus* (New York)

Woolgar, S. 1988. *Science: The Very Idea* (London)

Towards a New Natural Theology: Between Reformed Epistemology and Wittgensteinian Thomism

Marco Damonte

In the past century, natural theology underwent several attacks. Heidegger accused it of degenerating into onto-theology; post-modernism regards it as harmful meta-narration; neo-positivism affirmed that every proposition about God was senseless and even theologians looked at it with suspicion. In the last decades, the attention of analytic philosophers of religion for natural theology has increased. The aim of my paper is to propose a new natural theology. In order to do this, I will examine first the position of Reformed Epistemologists. They are critical towards the modern project of natural theology, but I consider their works to be a new way to go about natural theology. I will then take Wittgensteinian Thomists into consideration, paying attention to the role, which they recognize, of rationality which leads to religious faith. Finally, I will compare these positions and I will suggest a definition for this discipline, specifying the authors and the themes to be studied in the near future.

I. Suggestions from Reformed Epistemology

Speaking about Reformed Epistemology, I have in mind authors such as Plantinga, Alston, Wolterstorff and Wainwright. Their general project consists in the identification, the criticism, and the replacement of the epistemological paradigm of modernity based on deontologism, internalism and foundationalism. As far as philosophy of religion is concerned, this paradigm is imposed to furnish arguments to have and to keep religious beliefs: rational theology had the task of formulating and defending these arguments. Reformed Epistemologists reject the evidentialistic theories of knowledge and so they reject this way of going about rational theology. So, their criticism of rational theology is radical, but circumstantial, i.e. limited to a use of it.

Reformed Epistemologists propose new epistemological paradigms. For example Plantinga replaces justification with warrant[1] and Alston with a plethora of epistemic desiderata that are directed towards doxastic practices.[2] For

---

1   See Plantinga (1993a) and Plantinga (1993b).
2   See Alston (1993).

the philosophy of religion these theories mean that what is important is not to demonstrate the truth of propositions about religion – or better, about theism – but to recognize their legitimacy. At this level it is possible to consider the attempt to argue for the reliability of religious beliefs as genuine natural theology. In this perspective Plantinga's epistemology of religion,[3] Alston's philosophy of religious language,[4] Wolterstorff's philosophy of communication,[5] and Wainwright's moral philosophy[6] can be seen as unusual forms of natural theology. Moreover, there is another level at which the Reformed Epistemologists contribute to natural theology, and that is the reflection on the role that classical arguments of natural theology, some of which they reformulate, play in their theories. To make a significant example, I can quote Plantinga when he proposes to read Aquinas's Fifth Way as the height of his epistemology:

> Suppose you are convinced (as most of us are) that there really is such a thing as warrant and really are (for natural organisms) such things as proper function, damage, design, dysfunction, and all the rest. You think there really are these things and are unwilling merely to take the functionalist stance: then if you also think there is no naturalistic analysis of these notions, what you have is a powerful argument against naturalism. Given the possible alternatives, what you have, more specifically, is a powerful theistic argument; indeed, what you have is a version of Thomas Aquinas's Fifth Way [...]. 'Whatever lacks knowledge cannot move towards an end, unless it be directed by some being endowed with knowledge and intelligence'; we may construe this as the claim that there is no naturalistic explanation or analysis of proper function. If this claim is correct (and we have seen that it is supported by a consideration of the main attempts to produce such an analysis), then indeed the way to be a naturalist in epistemology is to be a supernaturalist in ontology.[7]

Alston appreciates the role of natural theology in his theory of *perceiving God* as well:

> *Natural theology* is the enterprise of providing support for religious beliefs by starting from premises that neither are nor presuppose any religious beliefs. We begin from the mere existence of the world, or the teleological order of the world, or the concept of God, and we try to show that when we think through the implication of our starting point we are led to recognize the existence of a being that possesses attributes sufficient to identify Him as God [...]. The credentials of this enterprise have often been challenged in the modern era. Hume and Kant are prominent among the challenges. Its death has repeatedly been reported, but like the phoenix it keeps

---

3   See Plantinga (2006).
4   See Alston (1989).
5   See Wolterstorff (1995).
6   Wainwright (2005).
7   Plantinga (1993a), pp. 214-5.

rising from its ashes in ever new guises. [...] As for myself, though I have no tendency to suppose that the existence of God can be demonstratively proved from extrareligious premises, I find certain of the arguments to be not wholly lacking in cogency. [...] This characterization of natural theology sticks closely to the classically recognized 'arguments for the existence of God', but it need not be construed that narrowly. It also includes attempts to show that we can attain the best understanding of this or that area of our experience or sphere of concern – morality, human life, society, human wickedness, science, art, mathematics, or whatever – if we look at it from the standpoint of a theistic, or more specifically Christian, metaphysics.[8]

To sum up the prospect of Reformed Epistemologists for natural theology, I propose the following definition: Natural theology is the study of the legitimacy, of the content and of the consequence of the propositions about God's existence and characteristics. This study uses philosophical methods and starts from the analysis of human (especially cognitive) faculties and from the context of their fulfilment. To appreciate this formulation it is necessary to underline six points. The first regards the knowledge of God which, for Reformed Epistemologists, is originally and usually brought about through the perception of the world, but it is not inferred or deduced from it. This means that this knowledge is, in principle, available and accessible to all mankind, even if this noetic possibility has to be coupled with a willingness of the heart in order to be realized. Moreover, the knowledge of God need not be founded on evidence, because it is already grounded on a specific human ability. Plantinga, for example, following Calvin and Aquinas, speaks of a *sensus divinitatis*[9] and Alston shows that the doxastic practice of sense experiences has the same validity as the doxastic practice of mystical experiences.[10] The reference to a human ability is very important, in fact it suggests that natural theology is not a subject without bonds, but it depends on metaphysical, anthropological, and even theological visions and presuppositions. These disciplines furnish a context that allows for or avoids *de iure* natural theology and very often the denial of the existence of God is due to an issue *de iure and* not *de facto*. For example Marx and Freud refuse to believe in the existence of God not after having analyzed arguments, but because they evaluate it as the consequence of psychological or sociological mechanisms.[11]

The second point concerns the relationship between natural theology and revelation. From an epistemological and an anthropological point of view

---

8   Alston (1991), p. 289.
9   See Plantinga (2000), pp. 167-198.
10   See Alston (1991).
11   See Plantinga (2000), pp. 135-166.

this relationship is not diachronic, but synchronic. The conclusions of natural theology are not preliminarily necessary to have access to revealed propositions, but natural theology is immanent to revelation, and revelation can contribute to natural theology.[12] From an ontological point of view natural theology precedes revelation because it removes obstacles, such as the necessity of the presupposition of atheism, and because it favours its reception. We can say natural theology does not offer an arrogant knowledge, on the contrary it increases the consciousness of human limitations and of the greatness of divine reality. Moreover this discipline respects the latter and protects it from any attempt at rationalization or reductionism.

Another relevant relationship is between natural theology and religious beliefs. This is the third point. Natural theology is *natural* not because it depends on universal and absolute philosophical concepts, but because it reflects and clarifies the capacity of perceiving the divine that every person possesses. Lacking in foundationalistic and evidentialistic presuppositions, natural theology does not aim at forming religious beliefs, but it shows that it is possible to hold them on the grounds of an inborn religious instinct or of a natural awareness of the divine. The reason used by natural theology is a faculty that permits to manage, to show the consistency, and to recognize the legitimacy of beliefs, but it is not the source of religious beliefs.[13] The task of natural theology works if you pay attention to the diachronic dimension of religious notions in their interaction with human history. So this discipline is historical and it is not consolidated once and for all. In brief, natural theology need not have the aim to prove anything, but it can have the aim to indicate and to register.

What exactly is the role of the natural theology proposed by Reformed Epistemologists? The fourth point answers this question. The main role of natural theology is to offer criteria of insight in order to distinguish religious perception and beliefs which are true, reliable and coherent from the false, unreliable and inconsistent ones. Plantinga demands a sort of natural theology based on the method of reflexive equilibrium when he proposes the great pumpkin objection, i.e. when he asks himself: what distinguishes the belief in the existence of God from the belief that we have a great pumpkin every Halloween? Or: what distinguishes the practice of Christian life from the practice of voodoo?[14] To sum up, at an epistemological and at a logical level, natural theology is not either a necessary condition, nor a sufficient one to hold religious beliefs. Instead, this discipline is necessary at an anthropological level in virtue

---

12   See Barr (1993).
13   See Wolterstorff (1984).
14   See Plantinga (2000), pp. 342-351.

of our rational and social nature and in virtue of the historic condition in which we are. For these reasons natural theology has to be encouraged: it is desirable as well as legitimate. In this prospect, a fideistic position is as pernicious as the rationalistic one. Both are antireligious because they deny the possibility of a mutual relationship between God and man.

The last two points concern the connection between natural theology and other aspects of human life. This discipline makes religious beliefs useful in other scientific fields or, more simply, in other fields of human knowledge. The opposite is also correct: thanks to natural theology several disciplines show implications for religious beliefs. In particular Reformed Epistemologists insist on the mutual implication between natural theology and epistemology, anthropology, ontology and metaphysics. Plantinga suggests two dozen theistic arguments and he argues that they are good for at least four reasons:

> first, they can move someone closer to theism – by showing, for example, that theism is a legitimate intellectual option. Second, they reveal interesting and important connections between various elements of a theist's set of beliefs. [...] Third, the arguments can strengthen and confirm theistic belief. [...] Finally these arguments can increase the warrant of theistic belief. [...] They might in some cases therefore serve something like that Thomistic function of transforming belief into knowledge.[15]

Finally, there is a deep and fecund influence of natural theology on religious life. In fact this discipline makes the analysis of the beliefs peculiar to a specific religion possible and promotes it. This analysis improves the understanding and the appropriation of these beliefs which can affect the lives of believers.[16] Moreover natural theology wishes for and favours the contact between different religions (interreligious exchange) and the discussion of philosophical and existential positions alternative to theism, such as atheism, materialism, or naturalism. Natural theology also gives the possibility to confront the beliefs of a religious creed and the principles of the society in which believers live.

II. Suggestions from Wittgensteinian Thomism

Among Wittgensteinian Thomists I'm referring to Geach, Anscombe, Kenny, Haldane, Davies, Brain and, for some aspects, Putnam. Their reflection on natural theology is quite extemporaneous and it is necessary to extract it from their works. Generally we can notice a decisive drift from natural theology to philosophy of theology. This is due to the fact that they tend to start turning

---

15   Plantinga (2007), p. 209.
16   See Wolterstorff (2004).

the relationship between faith and reason into a problem. Wittgensteinian Thomists consider faith and reason as two human cognitive modalities, so they distinguish between them, but they also think of them as inherent to human nature.[17] As a consequence propositions about religious matters and dogmas can (perhaps, must) be formulated and analyzed through both faith and reason. One of the roles of natural theology is to show the convergence and the complementarity of these two human faculties or, in the case of conflict, to indicate a possible solution. In this respect, natural theology has another role, which is to help to not absolutize reason to the detriment of faith or vice versa, but to maintain an equilibrium or, at the worst, a tension, but, in any case, a relationship.

In spite of the peculiarities of each member of Wittgensteinian Thomism, it is possible to identify six constants at least. The first regards the conception of religion which is often considered synonymous with theism. Religion is an original anthropological dimension with which people relate to the world, and that manifests itself through language. So, theism can be considered an interpretative theory of the existence of the universe, of the world and of humankind, even if not an explicatory one. More exactly, theism is not a theory about things, but is a theory on how to see things. In particular it is the most coherent way in which the peculiar capacity of a person to consider the world as a whole is made explicit. To consider the world as a whole is to consider it *sub specie aeternitatis*, to use a Wittgensteinian expression.

Another constant is about features of religious beliefs which are always intrinsically linguistic and for this reason have a cognitive value. These beliefs are expressed through language, but also protected by them, as when using analogy. The second relevant feature of religious beliefs is to be holistic, either internally, i.e. among them, or externally, i.e. in relationship with other beliefs about reality, or better with beliefs produced by other human dispositions. All religious beliefs, both the dogmatic ones and those of a hypothetical natural religion, are conveyed in a propositional way and use concepts, sometimes philosophical notions. This makes the use of natural theology necessary in order to understand these beliefs fairly well and to help the believer's life.

The third point takes into consideration the philosophical presuppositions for natural theology. This discipline assumes a value in a context of epistemological realism which implies a trust in human faculties and in a context of moderate metaphysical realism. In other words, natural theology is possible if we think that people can know what exists as it is, even if not always in a exhaustive manner. Another important presupposition for natural theology which is very

---

17   See Anscombe, *Faith*, in Geach & Gormally (2008), pp. 11-19.

characteristic of Wittgensteinian Thomists, is that reality expresses its richness if it is considered an intentional phenomenon. Causal explanations of reality must be supplemented with an approach that uses the category of intentionality. This implies a reformulation of some traditional arguments for the existence of God and an effort to find out new ways to show the existence of God and to consider his characteristics. For example Haldane suggests the 'Prime Thinker' argument that postulates the existence of an active Prime Thinker to avoid the infinite regress between the reality of a human linguistic community and the necessity to have the predisposition or potentiality to form concepts. Haldane comments on his own argumentation as follows:

> in proposing this argument my aim was not to fashion a detailed and incontestable proof, but, first, to show that design arguments can be carried beyond the usual range of biological functionalism; second, to advance a line of reasoning that should engage the interest of those familiar with contemporary philosophy of mind and language, within which the issue of thought and concepts has been prominent; third, to suggest connection between this reasoning and other aspects of my broadly neo-Thomist case on behalf of theism; and fourth, to encourage others to develop the 'Prime Thinker' line(s) of thought.[18]

Another interesting, anthropologically founded, argument for the existence of God is proposed and maintained by Haldane. He starts from the consideration that the recurrent desire for an answer to the question of being is a religious one and that there is a 'why' for which God is the only possible answer. Less abstractly, cultural anthropology, history, and the arts and literature, as well as specifically religious forms of human organization and practice suggest that more explicitly religious desires are extensively and deeply rooted, so:

(1)   human beings have a natural desire for eternal life in the company of God.
(2)   Wherever there is a natural desire for something that thing must exist (or else the desire would be frustrated).
(3)   Therefore God exists.[19]

What is the relationship between natural theology and the revealed one? This is the fourth point. Given the unity of a human being, natural theology fades into the revealed one. Given the unity of the divine project, revealed theology fades into a natural one. Natural theology has a character of propedeuticity and complementariety with respect to revealed or dogmatic theology. But this does not mean that natural theology is a necessary condition to attain revelation. Natural theology alone is not able to furnish self-sufficient data. It is not able to formulate a complete theory of the divine. Natural theology takes some

---

18   Smart & Haldane (2003), pp. 228-9.
19   Smart & Haldane (2003), pp. 246-7.

elements from the Bible and it helps to protect the Mystery re-vealing it, because
it gives hermeneutic keys to go into it thoroughly, without rationalistic pretention.

At this point (the fifth) it is possible to ask about the role of natural
theology. This discipline assumes the shape of an analysis of the faith data,
excluding from consideration the issue of whether these data are natural
or revealed. In particular, natural theology is the application of logical rigour
to religious beliefs; this rigour is the request of consistency. Geach reminds us that

> even if people claim to be messengers bearing a Divine revelation, that does not
> dispense them from giving reasoned answers to serious enquirers. Christians
> in particular are enjoined to be 'ready always to give an answer to every man that
> asketh you a reason of the hope that is in you, with meekness and reverence' (I Peter
> 3.15).[20]

More specifically, the aim of natural theology is to protect religious beliefs from
idolatry, superstition, common places. Using a Wittgensteinian suggestion, it can
be considered a *linguistic therapy* or a philosophical *examination of conscience*
for theism. Natural theology does not have to try to provide indubitable
or universal certitudes. Because it is devoid of this preoccupation, it can help
to face up to the disputes inside a confession and it promotes communication
between different religions.

Finally, the proposal of Wittgensteinian Thomists is to turn to Aquinas and
Wittgenstein. They consider it relevant to be able to make use of Aquinas'
intuitions. Moreover it is important that natural theology can prove itself
immune from Wittgenstein's criticism and that it succeeds in taking the positive
suggestions he proposes. A good example of this approach is the judgement
of Putnam on Aquinas' and Maimonides' causal argument for the existence
of God. Expounding their argumentation, Putnam observes:

> This is not a 'proof' in the (absurd) sense of *an argument which will convince
> everyone who reads it*, for the very simple reason that the *premises* will not be
> accepted universally; it does nevertheless do a certain service – a service, I think,
> which even the atheist should grant – namely the service of bringing out one *source
> of* our present idea of God, a source which is deep in a very natural conception
> of reason itself. [...] In addition to rejecting the idea that the traditional proofs are
> 'invalid', I reject the idea that they are simply 'question begging'. On the contrary,
> even if in the end you reject the view of reason which is implicit in the proofs – that
> is, the view according to which reason itself tells us that contingent existence
> requires a cause outside itself, and tells us, moreover, that there have to be
> necessities which are not simply 'conceptual' – you ought, I think, to recognize that
> that view of reason speaks to and expresses intuitions which are very deep in us.[21]

---

20   Geach (1976), p. 1.
21   Putnam (1997), p. 489.

III. A New Proposal

Reformed Epistemologists and Wittgensteinian Thomists are able to suggest a new natural theology. Many of the points taken into consideration are common to both these currents. These similarities are such that they cannot be considered extemporary parallelisms. They are much more relevant if we consider that Reformed Epistemology and Wittgensteinian Thomism develop independent research projects. In particular they stress the epistemological question, the linguistic question and, more generally, the question of the relationship between man and world reality. These points require the formulation of a full epistemological theory , but my aim in this section is more modest. I will limit myself to proposing an epistemology of natural theology, namely defining the object, the role and the possibilities of this philosophical discipline.

The criticism aimed at the connection between natural theology and the foundationalistic project of modern epistemology is to the point. Following the suggestion of Reformed Epistemology and Wittgensteinian Thomism, we realize the necessity to renounce (1) the evidentialistic role of natural theology, (2) the modern statement of the relation between epistemology and metaphysics and (3) the dualism, either ontological or anthropological. Only on these conditions is it possible to re-found natural theology on anthropological instances.

First of all I suggest that we distinguish the expression 'natural theology' from that of 'rational theology', even if the philosophical tradition has nearly always identified them.[22] The first expression underlines that the consideration of God consists of a reflection on human nature in its own complexity and in its relationship with reality. On the contrary 'rational theology' gives more attention to the fact that this reflection happens through the faculty of reason alone. The notion of rationality is quite problematic and, in any case, reason is only one of the human faculties: for this reason I prefer to speak of 'natural theology'. Actually, the notion of nature is also complex and it indicates what pertains to humanity and to its own faculties. In this case, the term *natural* is not antithetical to the term *revealed*, on condition that the revelation and its content respect human capacities. The first term is, instead, opposed to the fideistic position because this position lies in an analysis of God through undisputable principles assumed as true independently from any reflection.

The key question is a meta-philosophical question: what is the role of theistic arguments? The answer has two aspects, a negative one and a positive one. First of all it is important to establish what theistic arguments – since they are philosophical arguments – are not able to do. They cannot oblige anyone to believe in something, neither can they be valid for all people in the same way.

---

22   See Clavier (2004), p. 11.

In other words they are not coercive, nor universalistic. Moreover they are not useful to decide *prima facie* the truth or the falsity of a religious belief. This type of belief is original for every person, even if not immediate, and so the only possible question is about its legitimacy. In a positive sense, natural theology assumes the twofold form of:

a. an epistemological inquiry into the validity of religious beliefs;
b. an anthropological inquiry into the human faculties that give rise to religious beliefs.

Natural theology has the aim to sustain the thesis of the legitimacy of religious belief and the thesis of the existence of a human religious capacity and moreover has the function to discuss arguments that are opposed to these two theses. In a synthetic way: natural theology also has the aim to give atheists and agnostics the *onus probandi* for their positions. In this prospect, natural theology assumes the features of a religious epistemology. The conviction is that at the basis of theism there needn't be propositional evidence, because there are proper human capacities and faculties. I regard this point as very important for a dialogue between analytical philosophy of religion and continental philosophy of religion. The first is more interested in propositional aspects, while the second is traditionally engaged in the study of religion as a specific human phenomenon. In the light of what I have said, these two aspects are not juxtaposed, but they are complementary. The reflection on propositional content is possible only if this content is valid and it can be considered valid only thanks to a phenomenological analysis. These themes are traditionally important for the continental philosophy of religion. In the next few years we will be called to confront with these questions, appreciating religion not only as a human phenomenon, but also in its historical and propositional manifestations and also in its claim of truth and in its proposing a way of life based on a way of seeing reality.[23] Note that this approach is not a request of syncretism between continental philosophy of religion, analytic philosophy of religion and classical natural theology used in confessional University, but is a realistic mode to integrate these instances.

The epistemology of religion is the attempt to argue for the legitimacy of religious beliefs, after having critically analysed their manifestation. Having established this legitimacy, the content of religious belief remains to be inquired into, especially through a conceptual analysis of theological notions. This is the task of philosophy of theology. This analysis can also be considered a form of natural theology, in fact (1) it is carried out by philosophical methods and (2) it helps the interaction between the content of religious belief and the content

---

23   See Wainwright (1996) and Ales Bello (1997).

of other beliefs with the same epistemic dignity. In this way, natural theology is not required to be a-religious, but the right of its being religiously featured is admitted. Natural theology distinguishes itself for its capacity to communicate with nonbelievers, even if it is not obliged to come down to its terms. So, religious epistemology becomes a theistic epistemology and actually a theistic metaphysics, as Kretzmann says interpreting Aquinas' *Summa contra Gentiles*.[24] This passage takes place when the consistency of religious beliefs is able to sustain the presuppositions of determined theories or when it is able to determinate coherent consequences from some theories. Plantinga, for example, shows that theism, in particular creation, is the most plausible theory able to explain the validity of our cognitive abilities. Perhaps it may be possible to refer to natural theology as to a philosophy of creation.

The presence of God in the factuality of the world and of people is already compatible with a complex form of deism. The next step is to characterize this presence and to study in detail the relationship between God and man and between God and the world. The present God is a sole, transcendent, personal and creator God as Braine argues.[25] This God decided to reveal himself to man, and so man has the task of receiving, understanding and living this revelation in the concreteness of all his own nature, including intelligence. Natural theology disposes to revelation at least three levels: (1) it discusses the position contrary to the possibility of revelation; (2) it maintains the question on the transcendent sphere and (3) it clarifies the contents to which revelation demands assent. Religious conversion is not the logical consequence of natural theology, and yet without the intellectual conversion that natural theology allows, sometimes religious conversion could not take place. This is Flew's testimony:

> My departure from atheism was not occasioned by any new phenomenon or argument. Over the last two decades, my whole framework of thought has been in a state of migration. This was a consequence of my continuing assessment of the evidence of nature [...]. I must stress that my discovery of the Divine has proceeded on a purely natural level, without any reference to supernatural phenomena. It has been an exercise in what is traditionally called natural theology [...]. In short, my discovery of the Divine has been a pilgrimage of reason and not of faith.[26]

I propose to consider natural theology not as a necessary and sufficient condition to assent to religious beliefs, but (1) as an anthropological condition useful for a mature approval and a consistent life of faith and (2) as an epistemic condition necessary to formulate a theological science. Thanks to this definition

---

24   See Kretzmann (1997).
25   See Wainwright (1986) and Braine (1988).
26   Flew (2007), pp. 89, 93.

it is possible to save the philosophical rigour of natural theology and at the same time to change its role. This proposal supports the equilibrium between *faith in* (existential dimension) and *faith that* (propositional dimension); it allows the passage from argumentation to persuasion;[27] and it encourages the study of specific dogmas (philosophical theology)[28]

Studying this natural theology in depth implies taking these points into consideration:

I.   analysing Wittgenstein's implicit philosophy of religion. For him religions are forms of life and theology is a sort of grammar and not a simple addition to our ontological catalogue;

II. analysing Aquinas' explicit natural theology because it is not compromised with the project of modern epistemology. His philosophy of being is able to protect the mysteries of faith;

III. affirming the existence of a natural faculty common to mankind that is able to establish a relationship with God and to affirm something about it. This *sensus divinitatis* can be disclosed both from neurological studies and from human science (phenomenology of the sacred).

Recognizing the legitimacy of religious beliefs, independently from the certitudes of natural theology, makes this discipline free to supply evidence for faith and contributes to making faith intelligible. In the near future philosophy of religion will have to confront itself not with the dispute between theist and atheist, but between religious realism and antirealism. Only a natural theology so conceived is able to avoid fideism and fundamentalism, because it permits the commensurability between religious practices. In particular this natural theology encourages interreligious dialogue, promotes human spirituality and the importance of a religious education, and induces the acknowledgement of a public role for religions.[29]

Let's see these points in detail.

3.1 Who should we study?

As we have seen, Reformed Epistemologists and Wittgensteinian Thomists agree to give importance to Aquinas and Wittgenstein, but they propose to read their works in an alternative and original way.[30] I think this way is able to construct the scholars' program of philosophy of religion for the next few years.

---

27   See Wood (2004) and Damonte (2009).

28 See Crisp & Rea (2009), Flint & Rea (2009), and Anderson (2007).

29   See Carr & Haldane (2009).

30   See Stout & MacSwain (2004).

Wittgenstein's contribution to natural theology can be appreciated following accurate hermeneutical principles: it is necessary (1) to consider the whole *corpus of* his writings because they have a thematic continuity; (2) to read his works without using the interpretations of his pupils which could be misleading, in particular the so called *Malcolm's fideism* could not be the most plausible interpretation and (3) not to be satisfied with what Wittgenstein explicitly said on the topic, but to contextualize it and to connect it with Wittgenstein's way of philosophizing. Before reading his lectures on religious beliefs, it is relevant to consider his personal religious position.[31] First of all, Wittgenstein's contribution to a new natural theology is an epistemological one. His argument against private language can be used to overcome the evidentialistic role of classical natural theology and his argument about certainty is useful to avoid any extreme form of fideism. A more positive contribution comes from the notions of *linguistic games*, of *criteria*, of *forms of life* and of *family resemblances*.[32] Using this conceptual equipment it is possible to protect the specificity of religion and to preserve it from any form of reductionism, such as the psychological, the sociological, or the scientific. Religion can be considered one of the human forms of life with its dignity and its criteria. Since any form of life is expressed in a language, religion also has its language and so theology is the *grammar* of this language. Moreover the meaning of a sentence is connected to the use of that sentence and so the role of natural theology cannot be separated from the use that believers made of it in their life and also from the pastoral and liturgical aspects. Other relevant questions are about the commensurability between forms of life and about the philosophy of religious language: both of them have to do with family resemblances. To sum up, the principal reason to study Wittgenstein is that he reverses the role of natural theology. This discipline has not the task of inferring God from the world not taking faith into consideration, but it is the attempt to show how, from the believer's point of view, the world is appreciated.

As regards Aquinas, the problem is not to make his natural theology clear, but to study its proposal in quite a deconstructionistic fashion, able to be faithful to his intention and also to be useful in the current debate. The excesses to be avoided are two: Aquinas' natural theology cannot be considered a form of rationalistic onto-theology and it cannot be reduced to a sophisticated apophatic theology. To appreciate his point of view it is suitable to start from his epistemology, which is a form of externalism and of reliabilism. This has two implications for natural theology: first, knowledge of God is mediated from

---

31   Kerr (2008).
32   See Kerr (1986) and Arrington & Addis (2001).

the knowledge of the world and, secondly, our knowledge of Him is always perfectible. According to Aquinas the distinction between natural theology and revealed theology is made on the accepted premises: in the first case the accepted premises are those knowable by human reason, in the latter the accepted premises are the ones positively revealed by God. In this outline, natural theology has nothing to do with the legitimacy of religious beliefs, which has an anthropological basis,[33] but it is the attempt to transform religious beliefs into science. Natural theology is relevant for the relationship between faith and reason in the concreteness of human life:

> Considered in its own right, the object of faith is God himself, but since (in this life) our minds cannot comprehend God directly or immediately, the object of faith, considered from the point of view of human knowers, is not God but propositions about him. On Aquinas's view, assent to the propositions of faith lies between knowledge and opinion. [...] Nothing in this position of Aquinas's denies reason a role in the life of faith. In a tradition going back at least as far as Augustine, Aquinas takes *understanding* the proposition of faith to be the outcome of a process for which faith is a necessary condition. Having once acquired faith in the way spelled out here, the believer is then in a position to reflect philosophically on the propositions of faith, to engage in the enterprise of natural or philosophical theology. But on Aquinas's view it would be a mistake to suppose that faith is *acquired* by such an exercise of reason.[34]

As the structures of *Summae* and their contextualization show, Aquinas' dynamic metaphysics and his speculation on being are the background to speaking about God and not a precondition to do it.[35] Perhaps the so-called Aquinas natural theology is only an arbitrary selection of some themes extracted from a wider philosophical theology. Let's take the five ways as an example. Aquinas does not dedicate too much care to present them and moreover they are not very original: they do not hold an epistemological role, but a pedagogical and a logical one.[36] The aim of these proofs (better: *ways*) is not to legitimate faith, but to present religion as a science. The attempt to create a science about faith is not due to the necessity of justifying religious knowledge, but to the desire of providing the intelligibility of faith, i.e. notions useful for an intersubjective comprehension and investigation into religious beliefs. An in-depth study of the Aristotelic-Thomist conception of science is required because this conception decides the function of natural theology.[37]

---

33   See *Summa Theologiae*, I, q.2, a.1, r.o.1.
34   Stump (1991), pp. 187 and 207.
35   See Kerr (2003).
36   See Kerr (2001).
37   See Jenkins (1997).

Moreover the study of Aquinas is able to contribute to the philosophy of religious language through the notion of analogy and participation and to overcome the suspicion of Protestant thinkers towards natural theology. I would like to conclude with a quotation from Vos:

> For Aquinas faith's assent is a result of the action of the will and its focus is eternal life: faith is in accord not with the light of reason but with its own higher light. Nevertheless, Aquinas does insist that reason has a role in faith. One must in some way grasp that which is believed [...]. Hence, for Aquinas faith is neither a work of reason nor an irrational or foolish act; rather, faith is above reason.[38]

Aquinas teaches us that natural theology has no intellectualistic value, but that it has the aim to support the journey of people toward God, promoting the motion of will.

I am content with these little references, and I consider them sufficient to explain why Wittgenstein and Aquinas cannot be omitted by anyone who wants to deal with natural theology today and in the near future and to indicate the mainline of the work to be done.

3.2 What should we study?

In this section I will identify three disciplinary ambits which must be studied in order to make a new proposal of natural theology. The first is the history of philosophy, the others are taken from epistemology and metaphysics.

Natural theology is a constant in the history of thought, so a diachronic study of it is ineludible. Even if the themes considered are similar, i.e. discussions about the existence of God and about His features, the contexts are very different. What is relevant is not only the specific argumentations, but also their role and their aim. Wittgensteinian Thomists and Reformed Epistemologists agree to focus attention on the modern period, when natural theology changed radically and became a form of evidentialist apologetics.[39] They juxtapose two paradigms: the medieval one vs the Cartesian one. The first thinks of natural theology as a mode of reflecting on faith, as the saying *faith seeking understanding* testifies. The second tries to found religious beliefs on other beliefs considered more certain and, in our days, it is engaged in justifying religious belief following Gettier's requests. This distinction into paradigms is very interesting, but it requires completion. There are other paradigms that deserve to be studied in depth, for example the classical one, the post-modern one, and the one proposed by pragmatism.[40] Moreover the medieval and the modern paradigms

---

38   Vos (1985), pp. 60-1.
39   See Wolterstorff (1986).
40   See Wainwright (1991).

are not so homogeneous as it could appear: Augustine and Aquinas are quite different, and Reid reacted against Locke who is very different from Descartes and Hume, and so on.[41] Different philosophers could be associated in a distinct way considering either one or the other aspect of their thought. For example the line Augustine – Descartes – Locke – Hume – Enlightenment – Kant – Idealism – Phenomenology can be in contrast with the line Aristotle – Aquinas – Reid – Wittgenstein with regard to epistemology, philosophy of mind and anthropology, while the line Plato – Augustine – Aquinas – Newman can be in contrast with the line Tertullian – Kierkegaard – Wittgenstein with regard to the relationship between faith and reason. After the individuation of paradigms it is now necessary to pay attention to each author, including the age of patrology, and modern and contemporary theologians such as Luther, Calvin and Barth.[42] This effort implies a precise historiographical proposal: according to the *principle of recursivity,*[43] it is necessary to protect the peculiarity of the historical event and, at the same time, to grasp its systematic topicality.

The second suggestion is taken from epistemology which, as we have already seen, plays a central role in the new proposal of natural theology. A theory of knowledge is able to lead towards the knowledge of God and moreover it determines the role that natural theology plays for the knowledge of God. What type of epistemology is required for philosophy of religion? Actually, it is not necessary to choose a specific theory, even if not every theory is useful. The relationship between natural theology and epistemology is possible only if the epistemology chosen (1) is able to support theistic beliefs; (2) is able to support the intelligibility of the real and (3) is open to the question about its own foundation, namely it considers itself not self-sufficient. More specifically, the epistemology required can be naturalistic and must possess the following features: have a normative dimension; have a warrant dimension (knowledge as reaction to reality) and a justificatory dimension (knowledge partially determined by self-knowledge); offer conceptual instruments to distinguish beliefs, knowledge and science; offer methodological instruments to determine the criteria of the basicality of our beliefs; understand knowledge as a complex of human abilities more than a set of properties of beliefs; and finally understand knowledge as a intersubjective, fallible and oriented process more than a subjective state of certainty. Contemporary epistemology offers quite a few theories endowed with these features, but I propose to pay

41   See Wolterstorff (2001) and (1996).
42   See Rogers (1995).
43   See Pouivet (2008), pp. 69-96.

attention to the so-called virtue epistemology.[44] This suggestion has a deontological aspect thanks to the notion of responsibility, it appreciates knowledge as an original relationship with reality and moreover it works a posteriori, as a reflection on what we say we know *de facto*. According to virtue epistemology knowing something means establishing an answerable relationship with something other than a cognitive subject, sharing a belief with other people and consenting to the desire of truth inherent in every person. Knowledge becomes a rational appetite and a natural tendency. In particular rationality must be understood as a virtue and as an *habitus* to be cultivated and not simply an instrument to control our knowledge. Another merit of virtue epistemology is its holistic dimension: epistemic virtues are numerous and they include rationality, wisdom, honesty, humility, prudence and courage. In this way, the whole cognitive process interacts with practical aspects and this reminds us that knowledge is a question of education and not only of method. What urges us is to study the mutual relationship between virtue epistemology and natural theology, starting from the connection between virtue and Plantinga's proper function.

One of the more interesting metaphysical implications of the new proposal of natural theology is about realism. For Reformed Epistemologists and Wittgensteinian Thomists philosophical realism is the condition for religious beliefs to have cognitive value, i.e. to give information about reality. For them realism is a presupposition for religious beliefs. Without realism these beliefs lose their independence and become superstructures depending on social, psychological or neural aspects. Metaphysical realism acts on religious beliefs in at least four manners: (1) without realism religious beliefs turn into a mere expression of subjective states and they cannot have any truth claim; (2) without realism the knowledge of the world cannot help to get to the knowledge of God; (3) without realism religious proposition and non-religious proposition about the same object are incommensurable; and (4) without realism reality does not reveal that intelligibility thanks to which the theistic position is possible. Epistemological realism and ontological (moderate) realism as explicitly proposed, among others, by Haldane, allow a religious realism. This position implies that the existence of God is independent from any human thought or belief; that the existence of God does not depend on the fact that people affirm it; that some propositions about God have a literal meaning; that some propositions about God have a transcultural meaning, i.e. they are not culturally or historically determined; that some beliefs about God are more true than others

---

44   See Zagzebski (1996), Pouivet (2008b), Fairweather & Zagzebski (2001) and Damonte (2011).

and that some beliefs about Him could be absolutely true. The cognitive value of theism means the possibility of thinking of theism as a theory able to explain (in the sense of 'give reason for', without any scientistic reductionism) some phenomena, starting from the existence of the world and from displaying its intelligibility. As I have already said, in the near future philosophy of religion will have to confront itself not with the dispute between theist and atheist who at least share the meaning of some religious proposition, but with the more radical dispute between religious realism and antirealism. It is not sufficient to argue the inconsistency of antirealism or to defend the theistic basis of realism. What is necessary is to make the connection between realism and religious propositions clear.

Religious realism seems to lead to a strong religious exclusivism, and actually Wittgensteinian Thomists and Reformed Epistemologists affirm Christian theism to be the most plausible form of monotheism. This could be a serious problem in our intercultural societies, but, on the contrary, it is a very important resource. We have to remember that this sort of realism is strictly connected with the epistemological recognition of the legitimacy of religious beliefs, and based on it. Only because (and not in spite of the fact that) each believer can consider his religious proposition as true is the interreligious and ecumenical dialogue possible.[45] This is one of the most relevant outcomes of the new proposal of natural theology. The second one is the possibility to discuss theological claims, and so to increase the philosophy of theology without fear of rationalizing dogmas. Thanks to religious epistemology and religious realism there is no reason to think that the exclusion of the absurd means excluding the mystery.[46] Actually, philosophy of theology helps to preserve the truth expressed in dogmatic sentences. I suppose and I hope these two last fields of research will engage philosophers of religion in the next few years.

Conclusion

Twenty years ago, Long compared natural theology to a sick woman: she suffered significantly in the eighteenth century, she appeared to be a terminal patient by the mid-twentieth century and only since the end of the 1960s has she been taken off the danger list.[47] During these two decades a lot of work has been done. Miss Natural theology has defined her own object and her own method. More importantly, she has been able to relate herself with relevant philosophical

---

45   See Lindbeck (1984) and Damonte (2009b).
46   See Micheletti (2010), pp. 14 and 37.
47   See Long (1992), p. VII.

fields. I have shown that she is now mature for a social role and that she is competent to be of service to her (philosophical) neighbour.

According to one important strand of medieval thought, we begin with faith, but a faith that is seeking understanding: *fides quarens intellectum*. This ancient saying deserves to be written in the current agenda of philosophers of religion.

References

Ales Bello, A. 1997. *Culture e religioni. Una lettura fenomenologica* (Roma: Città Nuova)

Alston, W. P. 1989. *Divine Nature and Human Language. Essays in Philosophical Theology* (Ithaca: Cornell University Press)

Alston, W. P. 1991. *Perceiving God. The Epistemology of Religious Experience* (Ithaca: Cornell University Press)

_____ 1993. 'Epistemic Desiderata', *Philosophy and Phenomenological Research*, 53: 527-551

Anderson, J. 2007. *Paradox in Christian Theology. An Analysis of Its Presence, Character and Epistemic Status* (Eugene: Wipf & Stock)

Arrington, R.L. & Addis, M. (eds.). 2001. *Wittgenstein and Philosophy of Religion* (London: Routledge)

Barr, J. 1993. *Biblical Faith and Natural Theology* (Oxford: Clarendon)

Braine, D. *The Reality of Time and the Existence of God* (Oxford: Clarendon Press)

Carr, D. & Haldane, J. (eds.). 2009. *Spirituality, Philosophy and Education* (London: Routledge Falmer)

Clavier, P. 2004. *Qu'est-ce la théologie naturelle?* (Paris: Vrin)

Crisp, O.D. & Rea, M.C. (eds.) 2009. *Analytic Theology. New Essays in the Philosophy of Theology* (Oxford: Oxford University Press)

Damonte, M. 2009. 'La teologia naturale come persuasione', in: Cattani, A. & Cantù, P. & Testa, I. & Vidali, P., *La svolta argomentativa. 50 anni dopo Perelman e Toulmin* (Napoli: Loffredo), pp. 155-165

_____ 2009b. 'Confrontation Between Civilization, Religions and Professions of Faith', Études Maritainiennes / Maritain Studies 25: 46-57

_____ 2011. 'From Justification to Warrant, towards Virtue Epistemology', *Epistemologia*, 34: 5-28

Fairweather, A. & Zagzebski, L.T. (eds.) 2001. *Virtue Epistemology. Essays on Epistemic Virtue and Responsibility* (Oxford: Oxford University Press)

Flew, A. 2007. *There is ~~no~~ a God* (New York: Harper Collins)

Flint, T.P. & Rea, M.C. (eds.) 2009. *The Oxford Handbook of Philosophical Theology* (Oxford: Oxford University Press)

Geach, M. & Gormally, L. (eds.) 2008. *Faith in a Hard Ground. Essays on Religion, Philosophy and Ethics by G.E.M. Anscombe* (Exeter: Imprint Academic)

Geach, P.T. 1976. *Reason and Argument* (Oxford: Basil Blackwell)

Jenkins, J.I. 1997. *Knowledge and Faith in Thomas Aquinas* (Cambridge: Cambridge University Press)

Kerr, F. 1986. *Theology after Wittgenstein* (Oxford: Basil Blackwell)

_____ 2001. 'Theology in Philosophy: Revisiting the Five Ways', *International Journal for Philosophy of Religion*, 50: 115-130

_____ (ed.). 2003. *Contemplating Aquinas. On the Varieties of Interpretation* (London: SCM)

_____ 2008. *"Work on Oneself". Wittgenstein's Philosophical Psychology* (Washington: Catholic University of America Press)

Kretzmann, N. 1997. *The Metaphysics of Theism. Aquinas's Natural Theology in* Summa contra gentiles I (Oxford: Clarendon Press)

Lindbeck, G.A. 1984. *The Nature of Doctrine. Religion and Theology in a Postliberal Age* (Louisville: Westminster John Knox Press)

Long, E.T. (ed.) 1992. *Prospects for Natural Theology* (Washington: The Catholic University of America Press)

Micheletti, M. 2010. *La teologia razionale nella filosofia analitica* (Roma: Carocci)

Plantinga, A. 1993a. *Warrant and Proper Function* (Oxford: Oxford University Press)

_____ 1993b. *Warrant: The Current Debate* (Oxford: Oxford University Press)

_____ 2000. *Warranted Christian Belief* (Oxford: Oxford University Press)

_____ 2006. 'How Naturalism Implies Skepticism', in: Corradini, A., Galvan, S., Lowe, E. J. (eds.), *Analytic Philosophy Without Naturalism* (London: Routledge), pp. 29-45

_____ 2007. 'Two Dozen (or so) Theistic Arguments', in: Baker, D.P. (ed.), *Alvin Plantinga* (Cambridge: Cambridge University Press), pp. 203-227

Pouivet, R. 2008. *Philosophie contemporaine* (Paris: PUF)

_____ 2008b. 'Vertus épistémiques, émotions cognitives et éducation', *Education & Didactique*, 2: 1-17

Putnam, H. 1997. 'Thoughts Addressed to an Analytical Thomist', *The Monist*, 80: 487-499

Rogers, E.F. 1995. *Thomas Aquinas and Karl Barth. Sacred Doctrine and the Natural Knowledge of God* (Notre Dame: University of Notre Dame Press)

Smart J.J.C. & Haldane J. 2003. *Atheism and Theism* (Oxford: Blackwell)

Stout, J. & MacSwain, R. (eds.). 2004. *Grammar and Grace. Reformulations of Aquinas and Wittgenstein* (London: SCM)

Stump, E. 1991. 'Aquinas on Faith and Goodness', in: MacDonald, S. (ed.), *Being and Goodness. The Concept of the Good in Metaphysics and Philosophical Theology* (Ithaca: Cornell University Press), pp. 179-207

Vos, A. 1985. *Aquinas, Calvin & Contemporary Protestant Thought* (Massachusetts: Christian University Press)

Wainwright, W.J. 1986. 'Monotheism', in: Audi, R. & Wainwright, W. J. (eds.), *Rationality, Religious Belief & Moral Commitment. New Essays in the Philosophy of Religion* (Ithaca: Cornell University Press), pp. 289-314

_____ 1991. 'James, Rationality and Religious Belief', *Religious Studies*, 27: 223-238

_____ (ed.) 1996. *God, Philosophy and Academic Culture* (Atlanta: Scholars Press)

_____ 2005. *Religion and Morality* (Aldershot: Ashgate)

Wolterstorff, N. 1984. *Reason within the Bounds of Religion* (Grand Rapids: Eerdmans)

_____ 1986. 'The Migration of the Theistic Arguments: From Natural Theology to Evidentialist Apologetics', in: Audi, R. & Wainwright, W. J. (eds.), *Rationality, Religious Belief & Moral Commitment* (Ithaca: Cornell University Press)

_____ 1995. *Divine Discourse. Philosophical Reflections on the Claim that God Speaks* (Cambridge: Cambridge University Press)

_____ 1996. *John Locke and the Ethics of Belief* (Cambridge: Cambridge University Press)

_____ 2001. *Thomas Reid and the Story of Epistemology* (Cambridge: Cambridge University Press)

_____ 2004. *Educating for Shalom. Essays on Christian Higher Education* (Grand Rapids: Eerdmans)

Wood, W.D. 2004. '*Reason's Rapport: Pascalian Reflection on the Persuasiveness of Natural Theology*', Faith and Philosophy, 21: 519-32

Zagzebski, L.T. 1996. *Virtues of the Mind. An Inquiry into the Nature of Virtue and the Ethical Foundations of Knowledge* (Cambridge: Cambridge University Press)

Science, Religion and Common Sense

Louis Caruana

These last decades, the vast literary output on science and religion has concentrated on cutting-edge developments in science, mainly in theoretical physics, cognitive science, and evolutionary biology. Philosophy of religion in this area has therefore struggled with various intricate arguments that are often heavily interlaced with the technical language of these sciences. Against this background, a new kind of argument is now emerging, a form of argument that cuts across these well-established debates because it refers not to scientific discoveries but to the rather mundane idea of common sense. If science is an elaborate, extended, or enhanced version of common sense, while religion is not, can we conclude that science is better than religion? An answer to this question has crucial repercussions in a number of areas of philosophy. For instance, it would throw light on the impact of a new form of naturalism that is gaining popularity, a form of naturalism less associated with positivism and more with pragmatism. It also would redraw attention to the philosophical centrality of common sense as a possible source of justification.

Hence it is timely to deal directly with this question, and a good way to situate the discussion is to start with Susan Haack's book *Defending Science Within Reason*, where she articulates this issue very clearly. I will first give an overview of her main arguments, especially those that deal with religion, and then will proceed with a sustained analysis of the nature of common sense and of its alleged role in justifying science and discrediting religion.

I. Susan Haack's Position

Haack's overall view of scientific inquiry is pragmatic. She explains her agenda early on in the book as one of articulating a healthy middle way between two opposed extreme views. She calls these two views the Old Deferentialism and the New Cynicism. Old Deferentialism is the position according to which science progresses mainly inductively by accumulating true or probably true theories confirmed by evidence. This procedure of science, and variations of it, have been clarified by logical analysis and defended against a number of logical paradoxes that have been wedged against it these last decades. The overall impact of this position is over-optimism, a kind of scientism. The other position, the New Cynicism, is diametrically opposed to this. Blatantly anti-scientific in tone, this New Cynicism rejects the value of inquiry. It endorses relativism, and sometimes even tries to accomplish the logically impossible: it tries to talk intelligently about the rejection of all rationality. Susan Haack stays clear of both these positions and seeks the middle ground because she thinks that both positions not only are extreme positions but also suffer from the same deficiency. They both suffer from a lack of serious engagement with the world. They both are incapable of explaining how through science we can affect the world and be affected by the world. What she means here is explained by the use of an analogy: the analogy of a crossword puzzle. Scientific practice, including evidence and method, is very similar to the entering of words in a crossword puzzle, the entering of the correct words and not just any words, entering words that intersect with others already written, words that are partially supported by previous entries, and words that are themselves partial support for future entries. She calls her middle way *critical common-sensim*, a term she draws from Charles S. Peirce.

Following the lead of many prominent scientists, she holds that science is the long arm of common sense.[1] By this, she means that scientists are not employing some special method of inquiry unavailable to non-scientists. Science is a refinement of everyday thinking. In line with this, she adopts a direct form of realism. She holds that there is one correct description of the world, whether we know it or not, and that the scientific method is our way of discovering more and more details about this correct description. In all this, she remains modest. She acknowledges not only the achievements of science, but also 'the pervasive fallibility, the imperfections and flaws, the sheer untidiness, of this remarkable but thoroughly human enterprise' (Haack 2007: 123). Once she establishes in this way the general features of her overall approach, she proceeds by discussing various peripheral issues related to science, such as the strengths and weaknesses of sociological studies of science, and the tension between scientific and literary cultures. In all this, her position is similar to that of C. S. Peirce.

As regards the specific area of religion, which is our main interest in this paper, she starts by recalling the considerable differences that exist between science and religion. They not only have very different conceptions of the universe; they even have very different views on what constitutes a good explanation. One the one hand, there is science, which has developed ways of extending the power of our senses and ways of enhancing our faculties of reasoning, remembering, and calculating. Science does all this by carefully eschewing appeals to supernatural forces and by resorting only to empirical evidence.

---

1   She refers, for instance, to Albert Einstein who held that 'the whole of science is nothing more than a refinement of everyday thinking' (Einstein 1934-1954: 290).

And on the other hand, there is religion, which, according to Haack, is not primarily a kind of inquiry at all, but a creed built around one core idea, the idea that 'a purposeful spiritual being brought the universe into existence, and gave human beings a very special place. This spiritual being is concerned about how we humans behave and what we believe, and can be influenced by our prayers and rituals' (Haack 2007: 267). Admittedly, theology, as a rational expression of religion, is indeed a form of inquiry, but, like religion, it differs radically from scientific inquiry because it welcomes explanations that involve supernatural features. One needs to note at this point that, when Haack is expressing this difference between science and theology, she does not do so in terms of how these two disciplines function, but in terms of how they relate to everyday empirical inquiry. She writes: 'unlike scientific inquiry, theological inquiry is discontinuous with everyday empirical inquiry, both in the kinds of explanations in which it traffics and in the kinds of evidential support on which it calls' (Haack 2007: 267). The effect of this discontinuity is evident in the way theology, in the course of history, retreated at the same rate as science advanced. In Haack's way of putting it, theology retreated to 'higher ground'. By this, she means that theology kept readjusting its claims and diminishing their content until little or nothing factual is now left.

She turns then to address the debate between creationism and intelligent design theory. Protagonists on both sides of this debate think that there is no compatibility whatsoever between science and theology. She does not spend much time with Biblical literalists. She turns her attention to those scientists who defend religion by allegedly proving that evolutionary explanation is incomplete. Such a defence usually refers to parts of the organism, such as the eye or the DNA molecule, which are considered too internally complex to be producible in stages through natural selection. The argument, in short, is that, since evolutionary changes, by definition, occur only when they confer some survival advantage, and since the internal relations between the parts of such complex units are mutually dependent for the efficiency of the whole, a change in one of these parts can never result in conferring a survival advantage to the organism as a whole. This means that an evolutionary explanation cannot be correct for such cases. The parts must change all together for any survival advantage to be possible. And postulating a synchronized change of a group of variables all together goes against the idea of random mutations, which is a basic feature of any evolutionary explanation. Haack's refutation of this argument is interesting. Instead of entering into the intricate details of such arguments, as many others on both sides of the debate have done, she highlights the virtues of scientists. She concedes that there is no clear answer yet, and then describes how the occasional gaps in scientific explanation do nothing to diminish the determination of scientists, who are perfectly capable of admitting that some given question is not answered yet, and that they are therefore still working on it – the most natural way to proceed in such matters. Theologians are totally different. They can only reiterate: 'It was God who did it.' But this is not an explanation. It is a mere admittance of ignorance. It is just acknowledging that the explanation will remain forever inaccessible. For Haack, this attitude is very cheap; it is no substitute for the scientist's determination to dig further and further. She therefore feels perfectly entitled to reiterate her basic insight: 'supernatural explanations are as alien to detective work and history or to our everyday explanations of spoiled food or delayed buses as they are to physics and biology' (Haack 2007: 279). At this point, a religious believer may want to press the objection that religion is not as alien to human living as this quotation is implying. Religion is as deeply rooted in the history of humanity as any of these simple explanations that Haack is referring to, and has certainly deeper roots in history than science as we know it. To this possible objection, Haack's answer is typically pragmatic. She admits that, because of the ubiquity of religion within human society since earliest times, we need to concede that there must be something in it. She thinks however that, at this day and age when science has progressed so much, people must choose between science and religion – and her choice is clear: 'Religion is no less quintessentially human an enterprise than science; it is much older, and its roots in our psychological makeup perhaps deeper. But its fundamental appeal is to the side of the human creature that craves certainty, likes to be elevated by mysteries, dislikes disagreeable truths, and clings to the flattering idea that we are not just remarkable animals, but the chosen creatures' (Haack 2007: 293).

By now, Haack's overall attitude towards religion should be clear. For her, science is a respectable, extended version of common sense while religion is not. The solid grounding of science on common sense is what science has and what religion lacks as regards justification. Undoubtedly, the crucial factor in her argument is common sense. But what is common sense? Can it really offer Haack the leverage she needs to sideline religion?

II. Common Sense

As a first approximation, we can start with the idea that common sense is the set of rational features common to all human beings. The basic idea behind this preliminary definition is that the word 'sense' within the expression 'common sense' is associated not with the concept of perception but with the concept of reasonability. The principles of common sense understood in this way can be manifested in the way people reason things out in normal circumstances.

To make a list of these principles in detail is not at all straightforward. Consequently, although many people agree that it is perfectly correct to talk about common sense and even that the expression 'common sense' refers to something, not many would be capable of articulating even the major principles it consists in. Some prominent philosophers have had a go at this task, because they were motivated by the conviction that a lot of what we do in our intellectual activity depends on common sense. The result however has never been a complete list of principles. Aristotle and Thomas Reid, for instance, assumed the existence of common understanding, and they even considered it something like a platform on which elaborate philosophical arguments can be built.[2] They went so far as to consider it a foundational source from which conclusions can be drawn about what can be said and what cannot be said, what can be deduced and what cannot be deduced. In the words of Thomas Reid, philosophy 'has no other root but the principles of Common Sense; it grows out of them and draws its nourishment from them. Severed from this root, its honours wither, its sap is dried up, it dies and rots' (Reid 1983: 7). These philosophers did all this however without ever coming close to producing a full list of constitutive principles of common sense. Some may think that this verges on the irresponsible. How can a philosophy be sound if it is based on common sense when the nature of common sense is not clarified first? Although this is an important question, it is not directly related to my aims in this paper. Suffice it to say that I do not think there is any major fault here. The basic assumption is simple. These philosophers, and others like them, assume that common sense includes foundational principles that are universally held and are consequently inviolable and unavoidable. Denying these principles would be self-contradictory, either because these principles can only be denied in artificially construed contexts, far from any real life situation, or because these principles are always being assumed tacitly in the very process of denying them.[3]

---

2   When we are discussing Aristotle, the expression 'common sense' can lead to ambiguity. He often uses the expression 'common sense' to refer to that mental faculty that brings to unity what is perceived in different ways by the different senses. What we nowadays refer to by 'common sense' is not this. For us, 'common sense' refers to those aspects of rationality that are common to all, for instance the principle of non-contradiction. Having said this, however, it is good to recall that this relatively modern use of the expression 'common sense' is also present in Aristotle, even though he does not refer to it by that expression.

3   Useful explorations of the interface between common sense and science include: Gavin 1984, Musgrave 1993, and Rescher 2005. For a more general epistemological account, see Moore 1959, Chisholm 1977, Chisholm 1982, and Lemos 2004.

For the argument I am focusing on in this paper, the main interest is the understanding of common sense by contemporary philosophers like Susan Haack. The way she appeals to common sense is typical of the philosophical tradition she belongs to, namely pragmatism. A typical pragmatist like Charles Sanders Peirce assumes that 'there are indubitable beliefs which vary a little and but a little under varying circumstances and in distant ages; that they partake of the nature of instincts [...] they are very vague indeed (such as, that fire burns)' (Peirce 1931-1958: 498). Peirce adds that these vague beliefs, which are constitutive of common sense, 'have the same sort of basis as scientific results have. That is to say, they rest on experience – on the total everyday experience of many generations of multitudinous populations [...] all science, without being aware of it, virtually supposes the truth of the vague results of uncontrolled thought upon such experiences' (Peirce 1931-1958: 522).[4] The basic idea here is that human beings are all endowed with the elements of common sense and that they express these by vague propositions like 'fire burns'. Through the use of sophisticated scientific methods, such propositions are not falsified but refined. They are stripped of their vagueness, and thereby clarified. For Peirce and his followers, therefore, the continuity between common sense and science is clear and fundamental. And Haack is building her argument precisely on this continuity. For her, science is an enhanced version of common sense as described by Peirce.[5]

But now we have to face the crucial issue. Is common sense correctly exemplified by the belief that fire burns? In other words, is common sense limited to explanation of physical effects in terms of physical causes? Can people appeal to common sense when dealing with issues that go beyond the empirically verifiable? These questions are very important for Haack. She is arguing that there is continuity between science and common sense, and that this continuity justifies science as a legitimate mode of intellectual activity. Science is acceptable, she claims, because it is the long arm of common sense. Anyone who attempts to discredit science will be discrediting common sense, and thereby sliding into irrationality. But could it be that common sense is a broader

---

4   For further insight into Peirce's views, see his two papers 'Pragmaticism and Critical Common-Sensism'; and 'Consequences of Critical Common-Sensism' (both in Peirce 1931-1958, vol, 5). I discuss these issues in Caruana 2000, chapter 8.

5   It is good to indicate here that Haack does not follow Peirce all the way. She seems to think that if one is a pragmatist one is obliged to be a religious unbeliever. Peirce himself, however, defended religious belief in his own way. The climax of his philosophy of religion is probably his 1908 paper 'A Neglected Argument for the Reality of God' (Peirce 1931-1958, vol. 6).

platform than she thinks? If it is, the justification she thinks is reserved only for science may in fact be available also for other modes of intellectual activity.

So my main contention with Haack should now be clear. I want to argue first that common sense is broader than instrumental reasoning, and secondly that, because of this, religion is justified as an enhanced version of common sense just like science.

III. Multidimensional Common Sense

The first step is to ask: how can common sense be broader than instrumental reasoning? To explore some possibilities, let us start with an example. Consider Aristotle's two famous claims: that all people desire to know, and that all people are driven by wonder. Such claims indicate that, for Aristotle, a person who does not desire to know, or who is not driven by wonder, would be lacking in something that is fundamental, lacking in something that is common to all humans. Of course, there are many features that humans share in common, such as having one heart and two lungs. But the features Aristotle is referring to in this context are not biological features; they are mental. A person who does not desire to know or who is not driven by wonder would be lacking in what pertains to the rational or to the conceptual dimension of being human in just the same way as an individual whose reasoning violates the principle of non-contradiction. Consequently, if I am reading Aristotle correctly, we have here an indication that there is more to common sense, understood as common rationality, than just principles that are embedded within explanation in terms of cause and effect.[6]

To explore this further, consider the set of concepts indispensable for inter-personal relations. These concepts are associated directly with the conceiving of other humans as persons: they are associated directly with the conceiving of others as irreducible units that are bearers of a specific group of predicates, predicates associated with love, hate, sympathy, resentment, trust, suspicion, forgiveness, revenge, honesty, hypocrisy, and with other concepts like these. These concepts can function only once the concept of person, as a basic category, is in place. Can we consider this set of concepts dispensable?

---

6   I pick Aristotle as an example because of his particular affinity with today's scientific attitudes, an affinity that can best be seen in his method. He does not begin with being sceptical. He trusts our perceptual and cognitive faculties, and assumes that they put us in direct contact with reality. Starting from experience, he reflects deeply on any puzzles that such experience presents. And yet he does not limit his reflection to any one area of human activity. For him, what humans do by nature is broader than the science of production (see *Metaphysica*, 982b: 11-27).

We cannot. Anyone who tries to live without them would simply drift away from the community that makes meaning possible. Moreover, any attempt to discredit the centrality of these concepts involves an instance of using them – because the very discrediting has to be carried out within a community of persons. Language itself is a communal activity. It is therefore clear that, if common sense is taken to be the set of all that is universally held and that is inviolable and unavoidable, it includes more than just the principles involved in instrumental reasoning in terms of cause and effect. Haack's argument is one-sided because she emphasizes only one dimension of common sense, and thinks that that is all there is to say about common sense.

My second step now is to show that just as science is an enhanced version of the instrumental dimension of common sense (which is just one of the many dimensions of common sense) so also religion is an enhanced version of another dimension of common sense, more specifically an enhanced version of the dimension that involves concepts associated with interpersonal relations. My argument here starts with a couple of observations concerning Haack's reasoning. What is it that convinces pragmatic philosophers like Haack that science can legitimately be called an enhanced version of common sense? First, I would guess, such people are impressed by the fact that the logical form of explanation within science is also found in common sense. It does not require much thought and self-reflection to realise that common sense involves observation, inductive generalizations (most of which are tentative), falsifiability tests, inference to the best explanation, and so on. All these features constitute the engine of sophisticated scientific research. Moreover, philosophers like Haack are also impressed by the fact that science generates the building of instruments that enlarge the range of observation, increase the speed of seeing correlations, and enhance other such operations. Such enhancement is essentially equivalent to enlarging the range of the simple explanations of everyday life.

Now consider religion. The list of basic concepts at work within a religious way of life includes not only the central concept of maximal greatness or infinite perfection, which is usually expressed by the word 'God'. It includes also concepts related to acting rightly and acting wrongly, to attributing praiseworthiness and blameworthiness, to honesty and hypocrisy, to love and hate, to consolation and desolation, to wonder and fear – all these basic concepts are the same in essence as those constituting the dimension of common sense associated with inter-personal relations. We may even add here that in some religious traditions, most notably in Christianity, even the concept of maximal greatness is associated with inter-personal relations. And this fact explains why even children can already have a basic sense of religion, a very simple but genuine sense of religion, from an early age. Moreover, religion is expressed through practices and rituals, both personal and communal, which enlarge or deepen the understanding of the interpersonal relations of everyday life. The sense of personal commitment and fidelity is highlighted, community ideals of goodness and beauty are deepened, global fraternity and personal self-giving are enhanced, ideals concerning loyalty and self-sacrifice are purified.

So the parallelism should now be noticeable. What justifies the idea that science is an enhanced version of common sense justifies also the idea that religion is, in its own way, an enhanced version of common sense as well. Common sense is rich enough to allow various genuine extended and enhanced versions of it. Science enhances common sense in one direction while religion enhances common sense in another direction. Science and religion are not competing extensions of common sense, but extensions of different dimensions of common sense. Science is an extension of the instrumental and explanatory dimension. Religion is an extension of the dimension of common sense that is associated with inter-personal relations.

One might object here that I am naïvely taking religion to be a force for the good. I seem to be arguing that religion enhances inter-personal relations in the sense of making them better. But if we think of the adverse effects religion has had on civilization in the course of history, we will never be tempted to see it as enhancement at all. This objection introduces an important point. Religion emerges within human culture in various ways, and not all these ways are positive. But this fact does nothing to undermine the main line of argument. Concepts associated with interpersonal-relations come in various kinds. If there is love, there is also hate; if there is honesty, there is also hypocrisy. Religion can enhance both the good ways we relate to each other and also the bad ways. And, within the major religions, this ambivalence is well recognized. It is dealt with by self-corrective mechanisms inscribed within their moral traditions. Notice that we can argue in a parallel fashion about science. Although it is agreed that science is an enhanced version of common sense, as defended by Haack, we cannot thereby deduce that science has always been a force for the good. We cannot thereby argue that science has been, and will always be, beneficial for genuine human flourishing. Being based on common sense is no guarantee that things cannot go wrong.

Some may want to object that my line of argument has stretched Haack's understanding of common sense beyond all recognition. She is talking about a set of common rules for inquiry, while I am talking about the set of concepts and presuppositions that are necessary for what might be called successful navigation through life. I concede that this is a legitimate observation, but I add that the distinction between the two accounts is not a weakness in my overall argument. The two accounts are intimately related. Since I am ready to accept that navigation through life, as understood here, is indeed helped by correct strategies of inquiry, my understanding of common sense is broader than Haack's and includes it. What justifies the broader view is the fact that human beings are not characterised only by skills regarding inquiry. They are characterised also by other species-specific dimensions of their activity, including all that is semantic, symbolic, personal, and interpersonal. These dimensions are as foundational a fact of human natural history as the fact that humans reason things out deductively and inductively, and have twenty-three pairs of chromosomes.

In highlighting this fact, I am in fact presenting an argument that is in line with an important trend in current biological thinking, a trend associated with the idea of the extended phenotype. The expression 'extended phenotype' is used by those who claim that considering an organism solely in terms of its constitutive microphysical and chemical processes is seriously limited. The basic proposal is that the phenotype of an organism, in other words its characteristic outward, physical appearance as distinct from its genetic makeup, is not limited to biological processes only; it should include also all the effects that that genetic makeup has on the environment. In other words, we need to accept that the specificity of any organism, when correctly understood, extends way beyond the individual microstructure and even beyond its surface features. For instance, we need to realise that the way beavers build their nest is as much part of the nature of beavers as the colour of their fur, the flatness of their tail, and the structure of their DNA.[7] My broad view of common sense is similar to this. It is an extension of Haack's view just as the idea of the extended phenotype is an extension of the previous limited view of phenotype. In other words, I am urging that, to obtain a correct view of the specific rational nature of human beings, we cannot limit our considerations to how humans deal with simple inquiry of the form 'Why P?'. We need to broaden our range of vision, as it were, and acknowledge also how humans have an important species-specific side to their nature that arises from their complex symbolic way of relating interpersonally, from their appreciation of time, value, and personal commitment, and from the way in which they do not just exist but are infinitely interested in existing (Kierkegaard 1992: 302).

So to conclude, the main question addressed to Haack was this: can common sense be an efficient tool to justify science and discredit religion? I argued that the answer is no. The answer is no not because there is no such thing as common sense, and not because Haack has given a wrong characterisation of common

---

7   The idea of extended phenotype was popularized by Richard Dawkins (e.g. Dawkins 1999). Here I am referring to the basic features of this idea only. I am not endorsing his controversial view that genes are the fundamental units of evolutionary selection.

sense. The answer is no basically because common sense is much broader than what Haack thinks it is. Of course, more work needs to be done. Perhaps there are objections I have not considered. Perhaps some would say that, as regards this issue, Haack's work is not a good place to start. And perhaps there is some argument that shows that religious activity is not in fact related to interpersonal relations after all. Given the strength of the pragmatist tradition, and the impressive philosophical skills of many within that tradition, it seems reasonable to predict that my argument will not convince everyone. Still, it remains to be seen why not. At the very least, I hope to have shown that those who adopt Haack's nuanced naturalistic approach to religion run the risk of ending up with a severely skewed view of what common sense can and cannot support.

References

Aristotle. 1941. *Metaphysica*, trans. W. D. Ross, in *The Basic Works of Aristotle*, ed. R. McKeon (New York: Random House), pp. 681-926

Caruana, Louis. 2000. *Holism and the Understanding of Science* (Aldershot, U.K.: Ashgate)

Chisholm, Roderick M. 1977. *Theory of Knowledge* 2nd ed. (Englewook Cliffs, N.J.: Prentice Hall, Inc.)

Chisholm, Roderick M. 1982. *The Foundations of Knowledge* (Minneapolis: The University of Minneapolis Press)

Dawkins, Richard. 1999. *The Extended Phenotype* (Oxford: Oxford University Press)

Einstein, Albert. 1934-1954. 'Physics and Reality', in *Ideas and Opinions of Albert Einstein*, trans. S. Bargmann (New York, Crown Publishers), pp. 290-323

Gavin, William J. 1984. 'The "Will to Believe" in Science and Religion', *International Journal for Philosophy of Religion*, 15: 139-148

Haack, Susan. 2007. *Defending Science Within Reason: Between Scientism and Cynicism* (New York: Prometheus Books)

Kierkegaard, Søren. 1992. *Concluding Unscientific Postscript to Philosophical Fragments*, vol. 1, Text, ed. and trans. H. V. Hong & E. H. Hong (Princeton, NJ: Princeton University Press)

Lemos, Noah. 2004. *Common Sense: A Contemporary Defense* (Cambridge: Cambridge University Press)

Moore. G. E. 1959. 'A Defence of Common Sense', *Philosophical Papers* (London: George Allen and Unwin)

Musgrave, Alan. 1993. *Common Sense, Science and Scepticism: A Historical Introduction to the Theory of Knowledge* (Cambridge: Cambridge University Press)

Peirce, Charles S. 1931-1958. *Collected Papers,* C. Hartshorne, P. Weiss and A. Burks, (eds.) (Cambridge, Massachusetts: Harvard University Press)

Reid, Thomas. 1983. *Inquiry and Essays*, ed. R. E. Beanblossom & K. Lehrer (Indianapolis: Hacket)

Rescher, Nicholas. 2005. *Common-Sense: A New Look at an Old Philosophical Tradition* (Milwaukee: Marquette University Press)

PART II
DIVINE ACTION AND RELIGIOUS PLURALISM

Do the Results of Divine Actions
Have Preceding Causes?

Daniel von Wachter

I. The divine willing view

Assume that the universe had a beginning and that that beginning was caused by God. Was there then an event that caused the beginning of the universe? More generally, *if God causes an event E in the universe beginning at t, is there then an event C beginning before t which causes E?* The usual answer is yes, I shall argue that the true answer is no. God can bring about events in the universe in a certain sense 'directly' so that they have no preceding cause.

The usual view we find, for example, in Hofmann and Rosenkrantz's book *Divine Attributes* (2002):

> Necessarily, if an agent, A, intentionally [...] brings about an event [...], then A performs such an action either by deciding (or choosing) to do so or by endeavoring (or willing) to do so. Thus, if God exists, then he performs actions [...] via his decisions or endeavorings. (Hoffman and Rosenkrantz 2002: 103)

The authors proceed to argue that to endeavour something is to engage in a 'volitional activity', and 'a volitional activity of God would be an *intrinsic change* in him' (pp. 103 f). Only things in time can change, therefore God is in time.

Richard Swinburne gives a similar argument for God being in time: God's 'acting must be prior to the effects that his action causes' (Swinburne 1993: 216), because causes are earlier than their effects. Also Quentin Smith assumes that there would be divine willings if there were a God, when he investigates 'the relation between [God's] act of willing (an event) and the beginning of the universe (another event)' (Smith 1996: 170).

These authors assume that every action, at least every free action, involves an action event in the agent's mind which causes the intended event. Defenders of agent causation call it an 'undertaking' (Chisholm 1976) or 'trying' (Swinburne 1997: 93), others call it a 'volition', 'endeavouring', or 'willing'. From this assumption it follows that *if God acts, then there are divine undertakings which cause the events which God brings about.* I call this the *divine willing view.* On this view, if the universe began with the Big Bang, then there is a divine undertaking which began before the Big Bang and which caused the Big Bang.

In this article I propose an alternative to this view. To explain and defend it, I shall first present a solution to the dilemma of free will. Then I shall distinguish the question of what an action process begins with from the question of whether an action is 'basic'. I shall investigate, for human as well as for divine actions, what the action process begins with and which actions are basic. I shall defend the view that there are no divine willings and that the beginning of the universe had no preceding cause. More generally, my thesis is that God can bring about events in the universe so that they have no preceding cause. This thesis is independent from the assumption that the universe began with the Big Bang and that the universe had a beginning.

I am presupposing that God is in time and that there was a time before the beginning of the universe. (As for example defended by Swinburne 1993: ch. 12.) On the view that God is outside of time, it would be clear that an event brought about by God does not have a preceding cause. Further, I presuppose that if event x caused event y, then x began earlier than y. Therefore saying that the Big Bang had no preceding cause is equivalent to saying that it had no event cause.

II. The dilemma of free will

The dilemma of free will is that the following two sentences seem to be true:

(A) If an action has a deterministic cause (and thus is the result of a deterministic process), then it is not free, because it is determined and thus the agent has no control over it.

(B) If an action does not have a deterministic cause, then it is not free either, because then it happens by chance and is therefore not under the control of the agent.

By a 'deterministic' cause one usually understands one which necessitates its effect. (A) means that if an action was the result of a deterministic causal process and thus necessitated by preceding events, then it was not free. The agent could not intervene, he 'had no choice', as we say. That is just the sort of scenario we mean when we say that someone is not free. (B) applies the principle that an event is either the result of a deterministic process or the result of an indeterministic, chancy process. By a free action we mean one which has its origin in the agent, the agent chooses which action occurs, motivated through reasons or inclinations. If an action was the result of an indeterministic process, then it occurred by chance and thus it was not up to the agent which action would occur. The agent did not have *control* over the occurrence of the action.

If both, (A) and (B), were correct, then free actions would be impossible, as many have claimed (e.g. Hobbes 1654: 32; Honderich 2002; Strawson 2002).

Compatibilists reject (A). They hold that free will is compatible with the doctrine of determinism that every event is necessitated by preceding events and so is the result of a deterministic causal process. Many compatibilists believe in determinism, that is part of their motivation for embracing compatibilism. Another possible motivation for compatibilism is assumption (B) that if an action is not the result of a deterministic process, then it is the result of an indeterministic process and hence occurs by chance and is not under the control of the agent and is not done for reasons. My view is that (A) is true and that there is a satisfactory reply to (B). So I shall now present an incompatibilist solution of the dilemma which rejects (B) and in this respect makes the refuge to compatibilism unnecessary. My view is *incompatibilist* in the usual sense that it describes free actions as something that is incompatible with determinism as usually understood as the Hobbesian[1] doctrine that every event is necessitated by preceding events. However, I have argued elsewhere (Wachter 2009: ch. 7.6) that the usual notion of determinism describes something that is impossible and that there is another view which can adequately be called 'determinism' and which is compatible with free will. Likewise, there is a more useful meaning for 'deterministic' than the usual one.

The dilemma of free will arises through the assumption, which we can call *mechanicism*, that an event is either the result of a deterministic process so that it is necessitated by preceding events, or the result of an indeterministic, chancy process. We should reject this assumption. We see why if we consider what a free action would be. A free action of a man (or of any agent with a body) which changes some physical state in the universe involves a physical causal process. The intended event is the result of a causal process in the brain, nerves, and muscles. We can call this the action process. If the action process goes back for ever, then the action is not free because it is not under the control of the agent and the agent is forced to do it (regardless of whether he feels forced or free). So the action process must have a beginning, the 'initial event'. The initial event is a complete cause of the intended result of the action. A part of the initial event may be the result of a causal process, but at least a part of it must be not the result of a causal process, neither a deterministic nor a chancy one. We can call this event the 'initiating event'. How does the initiating event occur?

Some philosophers hold that it must be the result of a process which is indeterministic at some stage. Randolph Clarke argues that it has to be caused indeterministically: 'When a decision is freely made [...] there remained until

---

1   As Hobbes (1656: § 2.9.5) said, all events 'have their necessity in things antecedent.'

the making of that decision a genuine chance that the agent would not make that decision.' (Clarke 2000: 21, similarly Balaguer 2009: 4) Others hold that in a free action the decision is caused deterministically but the process of deliberation leading to the decision is indeterministic. (Dennett 1978; Fischer and Ravizza 1992; Mele 1995)

It is true that if an action process were indeterministic, in one of these two ways, then it would be in some sense true that it was possible, until the action occurred, that another action would occur instead of the one that did occur. In this sense it is true that the agent could have acted differently. But this is not what we are getting at when we say that a free agent 'could have done otherwise'. If it is a matter of indeterminacy which action occurs, then it is not up to the agent what he does. An action that occurs by chance is not a free action, because the agent lacks control over which action occurs. If an action is the result of an indeterministic process, then the agent has as little control over it as an agent has over an action that occurs as the result of a deterministic process.

So how does the initiating event occur? If the action is free, then it is neither the result of a deterministic process, nor the result of an indeterministic process. It is not the result of a causal process at all. Is there another way how an event can come about? Yes, the agent might bring about the event directly. That means that the event had no preceding cause, but its occurrence was due to the agent. The agent made it pop up. It would be misleading to say that it was caused by the agent's decision or choice, because that sounds as if the decision was a preceding event which caused it. But we can say that it was the agent's decision or choice. The agent may or may not have intended to bring it about. He must have had some intention governing the action, but perhaps he was not aware of this event at all. We can call an event which in this sense has no preceding cause but is due to an agent a *choice event*. (I have defended this solution already in Wachter 2003b.)

Human actions involve mental events that are suitably called 'willings', 'tryings', or 'undertakings'. If I try to raise my arm but the arm does not move because it is paralysed, then there is still the trying, which is a mental event of a certain type. If I try to raise my arm successfully, then there is an event of the same type. It initiates the causal process leading to the rising of the arm. In human actions the choice events seem to be always tryings. When a man intentionally moves a part of his body, then the action process starts with and through the trying, which lasts until the end of the action, and at all stages the trying has no preceding cause but is a choice event.

Choice events will seem mysterious to many philosophers, because it has become an unquestioned dogma that there is only one way how an event can come about, namely by being caused through preceding events and thus through being the result of a causal process. But there is nothing incoherent or mysterious about choice events. The question is just whether there are choice events, but it is not our task here to examine the evidence for this. Choice events are only mysterious from the point of view that every event occurs through being caused by preceding events. In itself they are no more mysterious than events that are caused by preceding events.

III. Is this 'agent causation'?

One might think that this solution of the dilemma of free will is the same as what some authors have called 'agent causation', but this is not so. Roderick Chisholm and Richard Swinburne, in their defence of 'agent causation', say that an action is free if the 'undertaking' or 'trying' has 'no sufficient causal condition' (Chisholm 1976: 201) or if it is not 'causally necessitated' (Swinburne 1997: 231) or not 'fully caused by earlier events' (Swinburne 1994: 25). That leaves open the possibility that it is a chance event, over which the agent would have no control. In my view, we must dismiss all approaches which assume that chance is a condition for freedom, because chance would diminish control.

Randolph Clarke defends 'agent causation' in the following way: 'There is a relation of producing, bringing about, or making happen in which one event stands to another when the first directly causes the second. For an agent to directly cause an event (such as an action) is for that agent – an enduring substance – to stand in that relation to that event.' (Clarke 2005: 411) But he also says that a free action is 'caused by the agent and [!] nondeterministically caused by events such as the agent's having certain reasons. [...] The action caused by the agent is said to be also caused by the indicated events.' (p. 410)

Does that mean that the action is overdetermined? If not, then there are not two ways how an event can come about, event causation and agent causation. Either the action (or the beginning of the action process) is the result of a causal process, or it is brought about by the agent in the sense of being a choice event. Of course, if the action (or the event with which the action process begins) were the result of a causal process, then it would still be true to *say* that the agent did it or brought it about, but that does not mean that the action came about in a special way, distinct from event causation. Clarke might mean by 'There is agent causation' just that sentences of the form 'Miller brought about *x*' cannot be analysed in terms of sentences of the form 'Event *x* caused event *y*', but this provides no solution for the dilemma of free will at all.[2]

---

2   Chisholm 1978: 622 f and Lowe 2008: 123 explicitly understand 'agent causation' in this sense. Wachter 2003a: 187 criticises this.

If, on the other hand, the action is overdetermined and thus also a choice event, then the agent could have brought about another action instead, one which is not also caused by preceding events. Clarke probably has in mind that human actions are *always* 'caused by the agent and nondeterministically caused by events', but why should that be so? Why and how should the agent and the events be so connected that every action is overdetermined?

I suspect that Clarke accepts the mechanistic doctrine that every event is the result of a (deterministic or indeterministic) causal process. But then there is no good reason for saying that there is agent causation, besides event causation, as another way how an event can come about. In any case Clarke's theory does not claim that the action has a beginning that has no preceding cause, and therefore, in my view, it does not solve the dilemma of free will.

Timothy O'Connor states in his agent causation theory that the agent has it 'directly within his power to cause any of a range of states of intention'. (O'Connor 2000: 72) So there is a causal relation between the agent and some event. However, I cannot find anywhere that he says that this event has no preceding cause.

E. J. Lowe's theory of agent causation is closer to mine. When a human agent, A, caused by acting an event e, such as motion in his hand, then that is an instance of agent causation. For Lowe this leaves open whether some prior events were causes of e, but he finds it 'perfectly conceivable' that 'e occurred as a consequence of A's agency and yet e was not causally determined by prior events (nor, we may suppose, did e have the probability of its occurrence fully determined by prior events).' (p. 29) In another passage he calls agents 'unmoved movers' (p. 12) and 'initiators of new causal chains'. His solution to the dilemma of free will therefore seems to me to be in essence similar to mine, although he says that the agent's causing e has no cause at all (p. 129) because it is no event at all (p. 131), and although he objects to calling agents 'causes' of their volitions[3].

I conclude that, with the exception of Lowe, the contemporary authors who have called their view 'agent causation' do not solve the dilemma of free will because they fail to claim that there is another way how an event can come to occur and that an event brought about in this way by an agent has therefore no preceding cause.

---

3   See Lowe, E. J., 2013, 'Substance Causation, Powers, and Human Agency', *Mental Causation and Ontology*, ed. S. C. Gibb and E. J. Lowe and R. D. Ingthorsson, Oxford UP, 153–172: 152.

IV. God does not need undertakings

So a human action always starts with a choice event that is a trying. Are divine actions like this? Was the Big Bang caused by a trying in God's mind? Imagine someone locked into a room with a switchboard. Pressing buttons on the switchboard makes some machines, which the person can observe through a window, behave in certain ways. All the person can do outside his room, he can do by pressing certain buttons on the switchboard, and he can do it only in this way. Pressing buttons starts certain causal processes which lead to certain behaviours of the machines. He does not know what these processes are, but he knows which buttons he has to press in order to achieve which results.

Similarly, we can act only in certain ways. When you try to raise your arm, then a certain action process is started automatically. We can change the material world only through our body, and we can move our body only through these mental events which we can call tryings or undertakings. The trying, which an identity theorist would take to be identical to a brain event, causes certain events in your nerves and muscles. There is no way you can cut short this process, e.g. by directly making your muscles contract, without there occurring the brain events which usually make your muscles contract when you raise your arm. We may have several possibilities for moving a certain stone, e.g. by pushing it with our hand or by using a stick, but we (or most of us) cannot, for example, just focus on it and move it in the immediate way in which we can move our arms.

God, being almighty and having no body, is not constrained like this. There is no thing which he always has to use in order to bring something about. He does not have to use anything in order to bring about a certain event. He can bring about any event *directly*. God can move a stone by moving some other stone, which then pushes it. But he can also move the stone without using another material object. The movement of the stone then has no preceding physical cause. In the latter case he brings about the intended event more *directly* than in the former.

The divine willing view assumes that the most direct way in which God can bring about an event in the universe, like the beginning of the universe or a miracle, is through an undertaking. But why should God, in order to create a universe, first bring about an event in his mind, an undertaking, which then causes the universe? For us men all choice events are undertakings, which, if the action succeeds, initiate a causal process leading to the intended event. But that is a limitation of power. God can bring about the universe straight away, without delay, as a choice event. God can bring about any event as a choice event. That is what his omnipotence consists in. God is entirely aware of the action, and he brings about the choice event consciously, but there is no event in his mind that is a preceding cause and hence an event cause of the intended event in the universe. We can call this view the 'direct divine action' view. To have a body – more precisely, to be able to act only through a body – is a limitation of one's power. We can make a difference to the world around us only through the chunk of matter which is our body, and we can direct our body only through tryings. But God has unlimited power and thus no body; he can make a difference to the world other than through certain events in his mind and a particular chunk of matter. Whatever God chooses to happen happens without having a preceding cause.

How is this view compatible with the plausible assumption that divine actions can be explained through God's having certain reasons and aims in mind? The defender of the divine willing view can assume that the undertaking or volition contains an intention and an awareness of reasons. He could even hold that the undertaking or volition has divine mental events such as awareness of reasons as preceding *causes*. But in my view this is a false conception of acting for a reason. In acting for a reason we look at a reason in our mind and then respond to it by acting. If some state of our mind or of our brain pushes us to act, then that is not a reason motivating an action, because then the action is not an active response to a reason but a passive effect.[4] If someone does something for a reason, then neither the reason nor the belief in or awareness of the reason is an event cause of the action. The 'acting on' is not reducible to some other relation. It is something mental, something to which the subject has privileged access. If someone saw a reason (or believed to see it) and acted on it, that explains the action. In a very wide sense, such as the meaning of the Greek notion αἰτία, you can still call the reason or the awareness of it a 'cause' of the action, but not in the sense of efficient causation or event causation or law-governed causation. So according to the direct divine action view, God performs his actions with intentions and in the light of reasons, but his having an aim in mind and his being aware of reasons do not cause his action.

V. Basic actions

Is my claim that God can bring about any event as a choice event the same as William Alston's suggestion that any action of God may be basic? And if not (as I shall suggest), are both claims true? We find Alston's suggestion in his article 'Can We Speak Literally of God?' (1981):

---

4   As argued also by Lowe 2008: ch. 8 and Wachter 2009: § 8.4.

[The general concept of a basic action is] the concept of an action that is not performed *by* or in (simultaneously) performing some other action. It is just a fact about human beings (*not* a general constraint on action or basic action) that only movements of certain parts of their bodies are under their direct voluntary control and that anything else they bring off, they must accomplish *by* moving their bodies in certain ways. If I am to knock over a vase or make a soufflé or communicate with someone, I must do so by moving my hands, legs, vocal organs, or whatever. But that is only because of my limitations. We can conceive of agents, corporeal or otherwise, such that things other than their bodies (if any) are under their direct voluntary control. Some agents might be such that they could knock over a vase or bring a soufflé into being without doing something else in order to do so. (Alston 1981: 61)

[A]ll God's actions might be basic actions. If any change whatsoever could conceivably be the core of a basic action, and if God is omnipotent, then clearly, God *could* exercise direct voluntary control over every change in the world which he influences by his activity. (Alston 1981: 61 f)

[An omnipotent deity] could ordain that intentions can directly cause a parting of waters. (Alston 1981: 62)

The last sentence implies that if God lets the waters part in the most direct way, the parting of the waters is caused by his 'intentions'. Presumably 'intentions' are events in God's mind. So Alston does *not* put forward my claim that God can bring about any event, e.g. the parting of waters, as a choice event. Let us have a closer look at what a basic action is and how this relates to choice events. Roughly, to say that Miller's doing x was more basic than his doing y means that it is true to say that Miller did y by doing x. To say that Miller's doing x was a basic action means that Miller did not do x by doing something else, he just did it. (Below, I shall modify this definition with respect to 'doing' and 'trying'.) So being a basic action and x being a more basic action than y applies to actions under a certain *description*. Therefore one can also call one description of an action more basic than another one. It makes no sense to point at someone's moving finger and say 'That was a basic action'. If the person was pointing towards the Sun by moving his finger, then his moving his finger was a basic action, but his pointing towards the Sun was not. To take another example, 'If I sign my name, *that* is done by moving my hand in a certain way, so the action is not basic; but if moving my hand is *not* done *by* doing something else, it will count as a basic action.' (Alston 1981: 55) What is this relationship between the moving the hand and the signing? In some sense these are identical. They are somehow two descriptions referring to the same object or the same action. But they are descriptions of a certain kind. 'Webster caused the movement of neuron B in his brain' (so that his arm rose) is not a more basic action than 'Webster raised his arm', because although both are somehow descriptions of the same event, it is not true in the sense in question that Webster *moved B*.

Richard Swinburne (1997: 87, following Danto 1965 and Baier 1971) distinguishes *teleologically* from *causally* basic actions. That an action under description B is *teleologically* more basic than an action under description A, means that the agent does A following the recipe 'Do B', whilst he does B naturally, not following a recipe. That an action under the description B is *causally* more basic than an action under description A means that the agent does A by doing B with the intention that B has certain effects.

Both these kinds of basicality as well as Alston's notion of a basic action concern the *intention* governing an action. The reason wherefore 'Webster caused the movement of neuron B in his brain' (so that his arm rose) is not a more basic action than 'Webster raised his arm' is that Webster had no intention to move neuron B, he did not think of neuron B in any way. With action descriptions of the form 'Webster did so-and-so' we not only describe who caused what but also an aspect of the intention. The intentions governing our actions cover a certain range, or they have a width, so that several descriptions apply to them. An action description does not describe what this range is but captures only one aspect of the intention. Therefore we sometimes give several descriptions of an action. 'Jones shot a moose yesterday' does not entail 'Jones bent his forefinger', nor does the latter entail the former. Jones could have shot by bending his middle finger, and he could have bent his forefinger in order to switch on the light. Further, the descriptions of the physical events do not entail with which intention the agent acted. Assume that the bullet first killed a sparrow and then a fly sitting on the moose. To say that Jones intentionally killed the sparrow but did not intentionally kill the fly (because he did not even see it) would then provide additional information about the intention.

Swinburne's distinction between two kinds of basicality reflects two aspects or dimensions in intentions. One is that in some actions we follow, as Swinburne says, a 'recipe'. One could include here also recipes of the form 'Do B, then C, then D'. In order to make a soufflé, crack four eggs, whip the egg whites, add a bit of lemon juice, etc. But then my raising my arm 2 cms would be more basic than my raising my arm 10 cms, and there would be no basic action. We better call B, C, and D just 'parts' of the action and restrict teleological basicality to actions where we know that doing B constitutes doing A. For example, in order to enter into a contract, you have to write your name at the right place on a piece of paper with the text of the contract. That an agent follows a recipe of this kind means that he does certain things with certain intentions. In this case certain action descriptions apply so that some are 'teleologically' more basic than others.

'Causal' basicality reflects a different aspect of an intention. Jones killed the moose by bending his finger, believing that this would *cause* the bullet to fly to the moose, enter into his body, and damage the organs so that the moose would die. If an intention contains such a belief about what is likely to cause what, then certain action descriptions apply so that some are 'causally' more basic than others.

Now we see that the question of which action description in an action is most basic (in each of the senses defined) is different from the question of what event an action process begins with and which event is a choice event. The former question is about the structure and the content of the intention governing the action, the latter question is about what event the action process begins with. Alston does not distinguish between these questions. He says some things about the action process, but the question he addresses is whether any action of God could be 'basic'. He says that God could bring about everything 'directly', but he does not claim anything equivalent to my claim that God can bring about any event as choice event, because he writes only that he 'could ordain that intentions can directly cause a parting of waters'. I take it that 'intentions' here refers to a kind of event in God's mind. So it entails that the parting of the waters is caused by an intention in God's mind and thus has a preceding cause. Thus also Alston presupposes the divine willing view and assumes that the Big Bang has an undertaking preceding cause.[5]

Having distinguished the question about basic actions from the question about choice events, we can now answer both questions for man and for God.

VI. Human basic actions

One might want to say that all human basic actions are *tryings*, because it is true to say that 'I raise my arm by trying (undertaking) to raise my arm'. But there is a good reason for not saying this and for taking my raising my arm to be a basic action (as Alston does). 'I raised my arm' and 'I tried (undertook) to raise my arm' are not only rightly called the same action, but unlike 'I killed him' and

---

5   The following passage points towards rejecting the divine willing view: 'Of course, one can think of God as creating light by saying to himself, "Let there be light", or as parting the sea of reeds by saying to himself, "Let the sea of reeds be parted". In that case the basic actions would be mental actions. But [...] we are not conceptually required to postulate this mental machinery. We could think just as well of the coming into being of light or of the parting of the sea of reeds as directly under God's voluntary control.' (p. 61) But Alston then spells this out as intentions causing a parting of waters. This suggests that he does not endorse my claim that a parting of waters can be a choice event and thus have no preceding cause at all.

'I bent my finger' they also refer to the same aspect of my intention. They are like 'He raised his arm' and 'He performed a raising of his arm'. Therefore it is adequate to say that in *human actions involving body movements, the basic actions are not tryings but body movements.*

In human mental actions, i.e. actions that do not involve a body movement, the basic actions are of various kinds. I memorise a phone number by transforming it into a mnemotechnical code; I multiply 31 with 12 by first multiplying 31 with ten and then adding 31 multiplied with 2; I imagine the sound of the dominant seventh chord on A flat by first imagining the A flat, then the major third, then the perfect fifth, then the minor seventh.

Some human mental actions involve a trying, others do not. My calculating the square root of 961 involves a trying. If I fail to calculate it, I have still tried. However, if you make a New Year's resolution to give up drinking Coca Cola, then there is no mental event of trying or undertaking besides the making the resolution. Likewise when you promise to God that for the next seven days you shall get up every morning at 5.30 a.m. to read the Bible and pray, then there is no trying. You either do it, or you do not. You can think about doing it, but to undertake it is to do it.

VII. What do human actions begin with?

The action processes in human actions begin with tryings. The choice event in a human action process is a trying. The trying in a human action has no preceding cause and causes, perhaps together with certain brain events, the intended result of the action. Perhaps the tryings are identical to or somehow linked with simultaneous brain events. Let us consider three possibilities of how the trying may be related to brain events. How these possibilities are to be described also depends on whether one means by an 'event', or a 'state of affairs', just the property of a thing at or during a certain time (or somehow the change of a property) *or* the property plus the (rest of the) thing. To sort this out is not our task here, I shall try to use formulations that are intuitively clear.

Maybe the trying is an event in an immaterial soul and neither identical to a brain event nor linked to a simultaneous brain event, and it is the complete cause of a subsequent change of the properties of some things in the brain (that is, the cause of something that happens with some things in the brain, e.g. a neuron firing), so that the new brain state, B_2, together with other (simultaneous) brain states, B_2^*, causes the intended result of the action. The things that are moved or changed by the trying, or the stuff which the trying affects, exist already before B_2. (A further possibility would be that the trying is the complete cause of some thing a's being F, where a has not existed before but is completely new stuff.)

Maybe the trying is an event in an immaterial soul and neither identical to a brain event nor linked to a simultaneous brain event, and *together with simultaneous brain events*, B_1, it constitutes the initial stage of the action process and thus causes the intended result of the action. (If we want to exclude that possibility (2) is a special case of (1), we have to add that neither the trying nor B_1 is the complete cause of any later event.)

Maybe the trying is identical to, or constituted by, or somehow necessarily linked to, a brain event, which together with other (simultaneous) brain events constitutes the initial stage of the action process and thus causes the intended result of the action.

We do not need to decide here which of these three possibilities is true. In either case, the trying is the choice event and at least a part of the initial stage of the action process. Let us now consider which divine actions are basic.

VIII. Divine basic actions

Alston suggests, as we have seen, that 'all God's actions might be basic actions' (Alston 1981: 61), but I shall argue that there are causally and teleologically non-basic divine actions.[6] God can choose to bring about an event by bringing about another event which then causes it. For example, God can choose to bring about a Big Bang so that, while God sustains it so that it itself becomes a cause (a so-called 'secondary' cause), it leads later to the existence of carbon atoms. Or he can bring about a storm in order to bring about a parting of waters. Like in human actions we can call the causal process leading to the intended result the 'action process'. A difference to human actions is that God is aware of all

---

6   Tanner (1988: 82 ff) claims that each event that is caused by God is brought about directly, as a basic action. Tracy (1994) objects that this excludes the causal activity of creatures and that indirect divine actions are also possible. Two further authors who claim that all God's actions are in some sense basic are Jantzen (1984: 87) and Ellis (1984: 232). Kirkpatrick argues that divine acts need not all be basic. God might utilise 'the causal mechanisms of the world' (Kirkpatrick 1994: 191). That is easily granted, but Kirkpatrick also seems to suggest that there are no divine basic actions or no interventions ('with the possible exception of the original creative act that brings into existence all the causal mechanisms by which all future acts will be carried out' (p. 192)). 'Might it not make more sense biblically and philosophically if we think of God's acts as the utilization of various segments of the causal order in order to achieve divine ends?' That applies to some cases, but it makes no sense, biblically or philosophically, to assume that God never brings about any event in the universe directly.

events in the action process, whereas men are unaware of the events in their brain. Therefore *for each event in the action process it is true to say that God brought it about intentionally.* If A and B are events in the action process and A begins earlier than B, then God's bringing about A is causally more basic than his bringing about B. For example, God's bringing about the Big Bang was causally more basic than his creating the first carbon atom. *The causally most basic action is his bringing about the first event of the action process* (more precisely, his bringing about any event which begins with the action process). This event is a choice event; it has no preceding cause.

Occasionalists, like al-Ghazali, Nicholas of Autrecourt, and Nicholas Malebranche, held that God brings about every event in the universe directly. There is no secondary causation, i.e. causation through created things. On this view there are no causally non-basic actions. But if God sustains things in being so that they can cause something, then God can cause x intending that x shall cause y.

Are there *teleologically* non-basic actions of God? Yes, because some actions one can only do by doing something else. Even God cannot give a promise to Abraham without doing something else, namely speaking to him. Even God cannot punish a man without doing something else, for example ending his life or subjecting him to fire and brimstone. In some of these cases the teleologically most basic action is God's bringing about a certain physical event. However, it is not true to say that God's bringing about a certain physical event is always a teleologically basic action. God's bringing about a universe is not teleologically basic, because he does it by bringing about certain events. Because God is aware of all of the details of an event, his intention refers to them all. As no human description of an event captures all its details, no human description of a divine action ever describes a teleologically basic action. Even if the description were of infinite length, God's intention would contain a richer representation of the event. There are, however, descriptions of divine actions that are teleologically more basic than others.

That God knows all of the details of an event is only one reason why his intentions that govern his actions are much wider than ours. They are maximally wide. God is aware of all reasons for an action as well as of all probabilities of what will cause what. Therefore he does nothing unintentionally; *everything God does, he does intentionally.* Something I say in a talk might encourage someone in the audience to start to study the special theory of relativity in order to examine whether there is really evidence for assuming that the speed of light is always c. But I do not know the man and had not thought of encouraging anyone to do such a thing. It is then true to say that I unintentionally encouraged the man to examine the theory of special relativity. For God no such scenarios arise. Everything he does, he does intentionally. Therefore *by each action God does every action which it is possible that he does by it.* For each divine action the range of the teleologically less basic actions is maximal.

Because God knows all reasons for an action, all probabilities of what will cause what, and all states of affairs obtaining at the time of his action, the width of his intentions is also maximal with respect to causal basicality. In one sense every event in the universe can be said to be brought about by God, because he at least sustained it and its causes. If doing x is causally basic with respect to doing y, then the agent believes that with a certain probability x will cause y (or the event bringing about which constitutes doing y). However, that probability need not be the degree to which y was the motive for doing x. I might throw a lifebelt from the ship into the water hoping that the drowning woman will catch it. Even though the probability of her catching it because of the storm is low, rescuing her is my sole and whole motive.

Because God is perfectly rational, only reasons motivate him. The motive of an action of God is constituted by the sum of the motivating value (or 'force') of all states of affairs that may be brought about by the action. The motivating value of such a states of affairs is proportional to the product of its goodness (or badness) and the probability of it being caused by the action. If God's doing x causes an event y, then it is true to say that God's doing x was causally basic with respect to y to the degree corresponding to its motivating value. Also if God's doing x did not cause y, but there was a probability that it would, the probability of y was a part of God's motivation for doing x (according to the product of their goodness and their probability) – although it is not true to say that God brought about y.

Likewise actions of man are parts of God's motivation for doing the things which make these actions possible (sustaining certain things as well as intervening in certain ways). For good human actions, that is called God's *providence.* If a man does something, then it is normally not true to say that God did it. But it is true that God permitted the action through his sustaining the man, and it can be true that God somehow led him to do it, for example by giving him certain inclinations or insights or commands. Actual as well as possible human actions are parts of God's motivation for some of his actions in accordance to their value and their likelihood (which depends on man's recognition of reasons, his inclinations, his character, and the strength of his will). But, as I said, if it is true to say that x did y, then it is normally not true to say that God did y.

Now let us again consider the question of what God's actions begin with, which is distinct from the question of which divine actions are basic.

IX. What do divine actions begin with?

The divine willing view rests on the thought: 'An action is initiated by an undertaking (or "trying" or "willing"), an undertaking is a mental event, therefore God's actions in the universe are initiated by undertakings, which are events in God's mind.' Of course, also if God acts, in some sense he 'wills' and 'undertakes' the action. But only if 'willing x' and 'undertaking x' are taken to mean 'doing x intentionally', and not if they are taken to mean, as I have defined it in accordance with what the defenders of the divine willing view mean, a mental event of the kind that occurs in human actions. A free action is initiated by a choice event, and that choice event may, but need not be, an undertaking in the mind of the agent. As God is omnipotent and has no body, he can bring about any physical event as a choice event, so that it has no preceding cause. 'God brings about E directly' is to be spelled out as God bringing about that event as a choice event. That event then, alone or together with other events, is the initial stage of the action process.

I conclude that God can bring about any event as a choice event, so that it has no preceding cause and thus no event cause. Therefore, if God brought about the Big Bang (and it was the beginning of the universe), then the Big Bang had no preceding cause. God brought it about directly.

References

Alston, William P. 1981. 'Can We Speak Literally of God?', in: *Divine Nature and Human Language: Essays in Philosophical Theology* (Ithaca: Cornell University Press), pp. 39–63

Baier, Annette. 1971. 'The Search for Basic Actions', in: *American Philosophical Quarterly*, 8: 161–170

Balaguer, Mark. 2009. 'Why there are no good arguments for any interesting version of determinism', in: *Synthese*, 168: 1–21

Chisholm, Roderick. 1976. 'The Agent as Cause', in: *Action Theory*, ed. by M. Brand and D. Walton (Dordrecht: Reidel), pp. 199–211

_____ 1978. 'Replies', in: *Philosophia*, 8: 620–636

Clarke, Randolph. 2000. 'Modest Libertarianism', in: *Philosophical Perspectives, 14: Action and Freedom*, ed. by James E. Tomberlin (Malden: Blackwell Publishers), pp. 21–46

_____ 2005. 'Agent Causation and the Problem of Luck', in: *Pacific Philosophical Quarterly*, 86: 408–421

Danto, A.C. 1965. 'Basic Actions', in: *American Philosophical Quarterly*, 2: 141–148

Dennett, Daniel. 1978. 'On Giving Libertarians What They Say They Want', in: *Brainstorms* (Brighton: Harvester Press)

Ellis, Robert. 1984. 'The Vulnerability of Action', in: *Religious Studies*, 25: 225–233

Fischer, John M. and Mark Ravizza. 1992. 'When The Will is Free', in: *Philosophical Perspectives, 6: Ethics*, ed. by James E. Tomberlin (Atascadero: Ridgeview)

Hobbes, Thomas. 1654. 'Of Liberty and Necessity', in: *The English Works of Thomas Hobbes*, vol. 4. (London), pp. 229–278

_____ 1656. 'Elements of Philosophy, The first section, Concerning Body', in: *The English Works of Thomas Hobbes of Malmesbury*, vol. 1., ed. by W. Molesworth

Hoffman, Joshua and Gary Rosenkrantz. 2002. *The Divine Attributes* (Oxford: Blackwell)

Honderich, Ted. 2002. 'Determinism as true, both compatibilism and incompatibilism as false, and the real problem', in: *The Oxford Handbook of Free Will*, ed. by Robert Kane (Oxford University Press), pp. 461–476

Jantzen, Grace. 1984. *God's World, God's Body*, (Philadelphia: Westminster Press)

Kane, Robert, ed. 2002. *The Oxford Handbook of Free Will* (Oxford University Press)

Kirkpatrick, Frank G. 1994. 'Is the Notion of a Divine Basic Act a Necessary and Sufficient Way of Talking about God's Actions in the World', in: *Religious Studies*, 30: 181–192

Lowe, E. J. 2008. *Personal Agency: The Metaphysics of Mind and Action* (Oxford University Press)

Lowe, E. J. 2013, 'Substance Causation, Powers, and Human Agency', *Mental Causation and Ontology*, ed. S. C. Gibb and E. J. Lowe and R. D. Ingthorsson, Oxford UP, 153–172.

Mele, Alfred R. 1995. *Autonomous Agents: From Self-Control to Autonomy* (New York: Oxford University Press)

O'Connor, Timothy. 2000. *Persons and Causes* (Oxford University Press)

Smith, Quentin. 1996. 'Causation and the Logical Impossibility of a Divine Cause', in: *Philosophical Topics*, 24: 169–191

Strawson, Galen. 2002. 'The Bounds of Freedom', in: *The Oxford Handbook of Free Will*, ed. by Robert Kane (Oxford University Press), pp. 441–460

Swinburne, Richard. 1993. *The Coherence of Theism (Revised edition)* (Oxford: Clarendon Press)

_____ 1994. *The Christian God* (Oxford: Clarendon Press)

_____ 1997. *The Evolution of the Soul (Revised Edition)* (Oxford: Clarendon)

Tanner, Kathryn. 1988. *God and Creation in Christian Theology: Tyranny or Empowerment?* (Oxford: Blackwell)

Tracy, Thomas F. 1994. 'Divine Action, Created Causes, and Human Freedom', in: *The God who Acts: Philosophical and Theological Explorations*, ed. by Thomas F. Tracy (Pennsylvania State University Press)

Wachter, Daniel von. 2003a. 'Agent Causation: Before and After the Ontological Turn', in: *Persons: An Interdisciplinary Approach*, ed. by C. Kanzian, J. Quitterer and E. Runggaldier (Wien: öbvhpt), pp. 276–278

_____ 2003b. 'Free Agents as Cause', in: On *Human Persons*, ed. by K. Petrus (Frankfurt: Ontos Verlag), pp. 183–194

_____ 2009. *Die kausale Struktur der Welt: Eine philosophische Untersuchung über Verursachung, Naturgesetze, freie Handlungen, Möglichkeit und Gottes kausale Rolle in der Welt* (Freiburg: Alber)

Atonement and the Cry of Dereliction from the Cross

Eleonore Stump

Introduction

Any interpretation of the doctrine of the atonement has to take account of those biblical texts traditionally taken to be foundational narratives for the doctrine. Among these texts, one of the narratives that has been the most difficult to interpret is the story describing what is commonly called 'the cry of dereliction from the Cross'. According to the Gospels of both Mathew and Mark, among the things Jesus says on the Cross is 'My God, my God, why have you forsaken me?'

There are so many things puzzling about this line attributed to Jesus that it is hard to know how to spell them all out. Furthermore, there is a rich biblical context for the line in other parts of the narrative in the Gospels, as well as in various places in the Hebrew Bible, including the Psalms and prophets. Here I will leave all of this to one side, helpful and important though it is. I have learned from consulting or considering it; but in this short paper, in the interest of focusing on just one set of problems raised by the story of the cry of dereliction, I will concentrate only on this one line, the cry of dereliction itself. In addition, I will omit consideration of virtually all commentary on this line in the history of interpretation of the Gospels. My purpose here is not historical scholarship on the line but philosophical analysis of it. If the cry of dereliction is to be interpreted within the constraints of orthodox Christian theology, with the traditional assignment of attributes both to God and to Christ, philosophically considered, how is it possible to make sense of it?

Union: Closeness and Psychic Integration

We can begin by thinking in general about closeness between persons. If distance between persons is part of the story of the cry of dereliction, then what is closeness between persons? For that matter, what is union?

Elsewhere I have explored these questions in detail in connection with the account of love given by Thomas Aquinas; here I can only summarize briefly the central points of that discussion.[1]

---

1   See my *Wandering in Darkness* (Oxford: Oxford University Press, 2010), especially chapters 6 and 7.

On Aquinas's account of love, love consists in the interaction of two mutually governing desires, one for the good of the beloved and one for union with the beloved.

Closeness is necessary for the union sought in love. It requires an ability and a willingness on the part of each person in the relationship to share herself, her thoughts and feelings, with the other. But this ability and willingness to share oneself in turn require psychic integration. That is because internal division in the psyche makes a person divided against herself in will or self-deceived in mind or both. Someone who is internally divided against herself in these ways is not united with herself and therefore cannot be united with anyone else either. She will be unable or unwilling to share at least certain parts of herself with anyone else, either because she doesn't really know herself or because she doesn't really want to want something that with another part of her divided self she wants or both.

On an optimistic view of human beings, it is not possible for a person to be internally integrated in moral evil. No one is so evil that there is not some part of his mind and will that retains some hold on the good. Given this view, it follows that all moral wrongdoing fragments a psyche. Since fragmentation in psyche diminishes a person's ability to share himself, it also is an impediment to closeness and union. Closeness and union therefore require integration around the good.

On Christian views, the ultimate good for any human person is union with God. Consequently, for God, the two desires of love collapse into one; they come to a desire for union with the beloved. Given the doctrine that God is perfectly loving and loves every person that he has made, it follows that God also always has a desire for union with every person.

Union: Closeness and Shared Attention

Given these views of love and closeness, it is clear that one obstacle to closeness between a human person and God will come from internal fragmentation in a human being. A person's moral wrongdoing can leave him divided against himself, in a state that wards off closeness with others, including God. Such inner fragmentation is therefore sufficient to undermine or obviate union between persons.

But more than closeness is needed for union. For union itself, significant personal presence is required as well; and significant personal presence includes shared attention. Where shared attention is missing, union is precluded too.

It is difficult to define shared attention, but easy to illustrate it. When a mother looks intently into the eyes of her baby who is also looking intently into hers, there is a kind of shared attention between them. Each of them, mother and baby, is aware of the other and of the other's awareness of her and of the other's awareness of her awareness of the other, and so on. There is something iterative about shared attention.

When there is shared attention between two persons who are already mutually close, then the shared attention between them results in significant personal presence of each to the other and thereby produces union, of one sort or another. By the same token, the absence of such shared attention is an impediment to union. Even between persons who are mutually close, distance can be introduced and union can be warded off by a lack of shared attention.

For union between two persons, then, it has to be the case that each of them is dispositionally close to the other and occurrently sharing attention with the other. Both of these conditions are necessary for union,[2] and the absence of either of them is sufficient for distance between persons. For distance, it is sufficient that one of the persons in the relation lacks closeness or fails to have shared attention with the other.

Distance between Persons and The Cry of Dereliction

Given these reflections on closeness and distance between persons, there are fundamentally three possibilities each of which would be sufficient to account for Christ's experience of distance from God.

First, it could be that
(1) something about God prevents closeness between God and Christ.
   On this possibility, God fails to be close to Christ, at least at the time of the cry; and it is God's doing that he is not close to Christ.

Second, it could be that
(2) something about Christ prevents closeness between God and Christ.
   On this possibility, the distance between God and Christ has its source in Christ, not God. Although God has the desires of love for Christ, Christ fails to be close to God, at least at the time of the cry; and it is Christ's doing that there is this lack of closeness.

Third, it could be that
(3) shared attention between God and Christ is hindered.
   On this possibility, there is distance between God and Christ because one or the other of them lacks the occurrent condition of sharing attention with

---

2   They might also be sufficient for union, but in my extensive discussion of this issue in *Wandering in Darkness*, chapter 6, I did not argue for this stronger conclusion because it is not necessary for my purposes.

the other. In principle, this absence of shared attention is possible even if, at that time, God and Christ each have the dispositions that make for mutual closeness.

This third possibility itself admits of further sub-division, because the responsibility for the lack of shared attention can be assigned to either (or both) of the persons in the relationship. In the case of God and Christ, either

(3a) something about God hinders shared attention between him and Christ

   or

(3b) something about Christ hinders shared attention between him and God.

Someone might object that (3b) is not a real possibility, because on this possibility Christ turns his face away from God, as it were. But no one who turned his face away from someone else, the putative objector supposes, could experience that other as having forsaken him.

But this is a mistaken supposition on the objector's part. A person in great psychological or physical pain can experience as absent even those gathered around him in love to care for him. In *The Lord of the Rings*, Tolkien's description of Frodo's psychic state after he is wounded by the Black Riders makes the point in a sensitive and evocative manner. Something about that wound causes Frodo to be intensely aware of the minds of the Black Riders and to find the rest of the world fading or invisible to his view. In the anguish he experiences then, Frodo feels very lost and alone with the Black Riders. When he finally comes to himself again, he is surprised to find that his friends are around him and have been the whole time.

It was Frodo who in his suffering lost the ability to share attention with his friends; but, in *his* experience, *they* had disappeared from *him*. Anyone who has soothed someone in great pain by saying, 'It's all right! It's all right! I'm *here*!' understands the insightful accuracy of Tolkien's story in these scenes depicting Frodo.

Finally, (3b) itself admits of a yet further division, because it is clear that the obstacle in Christ to the sharing of attention with God could be either (3b1) a function of states of intellect and will in Christ or (3b2) a result of something in Christ other than beliefs and desires of his.

These, then, seem to be the possibilities for explaining distance between God and Christ at the time of the cry of dereliction.

The Possibilities

On possibility (1), at least at the time of the cry of dereliction, for one reason or another, God does not want to be close to Christ and so lacks a desire of love for Christ. In this case, Christ experiences God as distant from him because God really is not close to Christ, however much Christ might be willing to be close to God.

Put this way, however, this possibility is clearly ruled out by the divine attribute of love. God always has the desires of love for every person. God may fail to be united with a person; but if he is, it will be because that other person presents an obstacle to union with God, not because God does not have a *desire* for union with him. And so, as an explanation for Christ's experience of distance between him and God, possibility (1) is excluded by the doctrine that God is perfectly loving.[3]

On possibility (2), at least at the time of the cry of dereliction, closeness between God and Christ is lacking because something in Christ blocks such closeness. However much Christ may want closeness with God, something in Christ turns away from it as well. To the extent that it does, in however double-minded a way, one of the desires of love for God – the desire for union – is diminished or over-ridden in Christ.

Manifestly, however, lacking closeness to God for this sort of reason is a morally bad state in the person who turns away from God. But it is part of orthodox Christian doctrine that Christ is never in a morally bad state. Consequently, it is not possible to attribute to Christ the turning away from closeness with God that possibility (2) would assign him. And so possibility (2) can be excluded as well.

On possibility (3), at least for the time of the cry of dereliction, distance between God and Christ is introduced by a lack of shared attention between them. Even if there is mutual closeness between God and Christ in general, one of them is not present to the other because shared attention between them is hindered at that time.

---

3   This conclusion needs some nuancing, of course. A wife whose husband is unfaithful may move out of their home, in the hope that her absence will cause him to reconsider his behaviour. Similarly, when human persons turn away from God, it is possible for God to withdraw from them as a means to prompt them to be willing to return to him. In such a case, although God is absent, his absence is prompted by the lack of the desires of love for him on the part of human persons. A case of this sort is at issue in this line from Isaiah: 'your evildoings have separated you from your God, and your sins have hidden his face from you.' (59:2) In this sort of case, God withdraws from human persons, but it remains true that God has the desires of love for the persons from whom he withdraws. His withdrawal is a response to their withdrawal from him. Since this nuancing in fact attributes ultimate responsibility for the distance between God and human persons to the human persons, then, it can safely be assimilated to possibility (2).

On possibility (3a), God is responsible for this lack of shared attention. But God can be responsible for it only if God has decided for some reason to block his sharing attention with Christ, since nothing external to God can block God's *willingness* to share attention with anyone.

There are very few attempts to explain why a good and loving God would turn his face away from Christ. The best is probably that given by Calvin. Calvin thinks that God turns away from Christ in order to let Christ feel himself lost, like one of the damned in hell. Since damnation in hell is part of the penalty for human sin, on Calvin's view God lets Christ share in this part of the human penalty too.[4]

On Calvin's sort of explanation, God brings it about that Christ experiences as real what is in fact not real, namely, Christ's rejection and damnation by God. To this extent, however, God deceives Christ. Now it may be compatible with goodness to deceive a morally bad person, as when one lies to the Gestapo to protect the Jewish children in the house. But it is hard to see how it could be compatible with God's goodness to deceive a perfectly good person.

It is true that Calvin supposes God has a good goal for bringing about this experience for Christ, namely, that the suffering the experience entails is somehow necessary for the salvation Christ achieves for human beings. But, as even Calvin must acknowledge, a perfectly good God would not chose means incompatible with his love and goodness to bring about a good goal. If Calvin himself did not accept this very claim, his explanation of the need for Christ's suffering in hell would itself fail. If one did not accept this claim, one could simply reject Anselmian intuitions and attribute to God the salvation of human beings without anyone's bearing the human penalty for sin.

In my view, for these reasons, possibility (3a) can be excluded, too.

We are now apparently left with the two versions of possibility (3b), namely, that (3b1) some state of Christ's intellect and/or will or else (3b2) something in Christ other than his beliefs and desires is responsible for the lack of shared attention between God and Christ. In my view, we can quickly rule out (3b1), for just the reasons canvassed above in connection with possibility (2). If there were nothing external to him constraining him to do so, a perfectly good person would not think it was good or appropriate to turn his face away from a perfectly good God with whom he has mutual closeness, and he would not want to do so either. In no way would such a person want to turn his face from God's.

---

4   See, for example, John Calvin, *The Institutes of the Christian Religion*, tr. Henry Beveridge, vol. 1 (Grand Rapids, MI: Eerdmans, 1970), Book II, Chap. xvi, pp. 443-444.

But (3b2) does not seem promising either. We could try making sense of this possibility by pointing to the great pain caused by crucifixion. But there seems to be an a fortiori argument against this explanation. Since so many others in Christian history seem to have experienced pain at least as great as crucifixion without losing their ability to stay connected to God, it seems implausible to suppose that physical pain alone would have such an effect on Christ.[5]

Mindreading

At this point, it may seem as if we have excluded all the possibilities for making sense of the cry of dereliction. But, in my view, there is in fact one possibility left which is worth exploring in this connection. To see it, we have to understand something about mind-reading, as it often called in contemporary scientific literature.[6] In mind-reading, one person knows intuitively something about what another person is doing and with what motive and emotion he is doing it. Contemporary neurobiologists believe that this kind of knowledge of persons is subserved by a neurologically distinct system, currently thought to be the mirror neuron system. Mirror neurons fire both when a person does a particular kind of action and also when he sees someone else performing such an action.

The kind of knowledge given by the mirror neuron system is not a kind of knowledge *that*. Rather it is a matter of knowing from one's own internal state what someone else is doing and feeling. With regard to knowledge of the emotions of another person, for example, researchers hold that '[because of the mirror neuron system,] observing another person experiencing emotion can ... result in the direct mapping of that sensory information onto the motor structures that would produce the experience of that emotion in the observer. ... [in that case] recognition [of the emotion of the other] is firsthand because the mirror mechanism elicits the same emotional state in the observer.'[7]

---

5   John Calvin says, 'let the pious reader consider how far it is honourable to Christ to make him more effeminate and timid than the generality of men. Robbers and other malefactors contumaciously hasten to death, many men magnanimously despise it, others meet it calmly. If the Son of God was amazed and terror-struck at the prospect of it, where was his firmness or magnanimity?' [*The Institutes of the Christian Religion*, tr. Henry Beveridge, vol. 1 (Grand Rapids, MI: Eerdmans, 1970), Book II, Chap. xvi, p. 445.] Calvin is speaking of Christ's suffering in the garden before his passion, but the point applies as well to Christ's suffering on the cross.

6   For more discussion of mind-reading, see chapter 4 of my *Wandering in Darkness*, (Oxford: Oxford University Press, 2010). In this paper, I am developing and extending some of my remarks there.

7   Rizzolatti et al., 'Mirrors in the Mind', *Scientific American*, 295/5 (Nov. 2006), 60.

The point is easier to appreciate if we think of empathy, which is currently thought to be subserved by the mirror neuron system, too. One person Paula empathizes with an emotion in another person Jerome because the mirror neuron system produces in her an emotional state like the emotion Jerome is experiencing, but taken off-line, as it were. In empathy with Jerome's suffering physical pain, for example, Paula will feel something of Jerome's pain, but she will feel it as Jerome's pain, not as hers. Paula doesn't actually suffer physical pain herself, but in empathy with Jerome the feeling Paula has is a feeling that is in some respects like the suffering of physical pain.

And, in general, in mind-reading Jerome, Paula will know what it feels like to do the action Jerome is doing, what it feels like to have the intention Jerome has in doing this action, and what it feels like to have the emotion Jerome has while doing this action. In all these cases, Paula will know these things through having herself some simulacrum of the mental state in Jerome. Something of Jerome's mental state will be in Paula, but off-line.

In this one respect, mind-reading is like dreaming. If Paula dreams that she is running, her brain will fire those motor programs it would fire if she were in fact running, but it fires them off-line, so that there is no muscle movement in Paula's legs even while her brain is running the motor programs usually used to produce that muscle movement. In the same way, through the mirror neuron system, Paula can have a mental state that mimics Jerome's mental state, but without herself actually being in that very mental state.

In such a case, the mental state in Paula really is Paula's. But, unlike the mental state of Jerome's that Paula is sharing, Paula's mental state is not connected in the usual way to other mental states of Paula's. Among other things, it is not accompanied by the states of will and intellect that mental state has in Jerome. For example, in empathy with Jerome when he has cut his finger badly, Paula may mind-read Jerome's feeling of pain. In that case, Paula will feel some kind of pain too, and the pain will really be Paula's, even if it is only empathic rather than physical pain. But Paula will not believe that it is her finger that is cut, and she will not want medical attention for her finger. So she will not have the states of intellect or will that she would have if she really had those very feelings of pain in her finger that Jerome has.

In the case of dreamed motion, the brain's motor programs for running are off-line in that while they are firing, they are disconnected from the muscles in the legs and so don't produce actual running. In the case of mind-reading, the brain's mirror neuron system runs the programs it would run if Paula were doing what Jerome is doing, but it runs them disconnected from those states of will and intellect Paula would have if in fact she were doing those acts. In this way, Paula shares in Jerome's mental states but without having them as Jerome has them, in virtue of having her own states of intellect and will, not Jerome's, even while she feels what she would feel if she were doing what Jerome is doing.

Mindreading and Moral Evil

It is worth reflecting in this connection that mind-reading between two people Paula and Jerome can also occur when Jerome is engaged in doing actions that are evil or vile or morally repulsive in some other way. That this is so helps explain why watching such actions, in real life or in videos, for example, is so distressing to most people. Graphic videos of violence or abuse are disturbing because such scenes also prompt mind-reading in the viewer. The mirror neuron system gives the viewer some (no doubt limited) sense of what it feels like to do such things. And feeling what it feels like to do such things can be very troubling if the things in question are deeply revulsive to one's sensibilities.

To see better why this is so, it helps to understand that serious moral wrongdoing leaves its effects on parts of the wrongdoer's psyche other than just his intellect and will. There are cognitive faculties besides intellect and will, and wrongdoing can leave them morally worse, too. For example, most people cannot simulate the mind of a person who rapes a child; and we give expression to that incapacity by saying things like 'I can't imagine how a person can do a thing like that!'. But the rapist himself does understand how a person can do a thing like that. He knows what it feels like to do an evil of that sort and, what is worse, what it feels like to *want* to do an act of that sort.

That a person is morally the worse for knowing what such things feel like is clear, although the moral flaw here is not a matter of the agent's having morally wrong desires or morally wrong beliefs about what is good. That is why such a condition is not by itself culpable or worthy of punishment, but there is something morally lamentable about it all the same.[8] Even apart from morally deplorable states of intellect and will, there is a kind of moral flabbiness in the psyche of a person who has engaged in serious evil, and that moral

---

8 Not everything that is morally deplorable is also culpable. That is at least in part because it is possible for a person to be in a morally bad condition without being responsible for being in that condition and therefore worthy of blame for it. A man in an isolated area in some much earlier time in human history might have been completely persuaded that wife-beating in certain circumstances was obligatory for him. When he beat his wife in those circumstances, his psychic state would have been morally deplorable. But most people would hesitate to consider him culpable or worthy of punishment for that act, because we would suppose that he is not responsible for his morally bad psychic condition.

slackness causes others around him to react with revulsion to him even when there is no worry about continued evil on his part.

An extreme case of such moral plasticity can be found in the psychic state of Rudolf Hess at the end of the war. The psychiatrists who examined Hess at Nuremberg testified both to his self-serving cunning and to his 'great instability';[9] and Major Sheppard said of Hess, 'I believe by the nature of his make-up, which reflects cruelty, bestiality, deceit, conceit, arrogance, and a yellow streak, that he has lost his soul and has willingly permitted himself to become plastic in the hands of a more powerful and compelling personality.'[10] The malleability to which Sheppard called attention was itself morally revulsive to those around Hess.

Repentance can reshape previously bad states of intellect and will, but by itself it cannot take away totally the revulsive features in the psyche such as those Sheppard pointed to in Hess. Aquinas called such psychic leftovers of serious evil 'a stain on the soul', and the metaphor is helpful. Something that was lovely in Hess before he participated in the Nazi horrors was lost by his evil actions, and repentance is not by itself sufficient to restore him to the moral fitness he had before his evil acts.[11]

That this is so helps to explain why even if Hess had been completely repentant after the war, people would still have wanted to be at some distance from him. Hardly anyone would have been willing to invite even a totally repentant Hess to dinner if there were children at home. In complete repentance, Hess would have had the states of will and intellect which a morally good person has. But he still would have had the leftover stain on the soul, as Aquinas puts it, and those around him would have shrunk from him in consequence. Even if there is nothing worthy of blame or punishment in a thoroughly repentant wrong-doer, the leftover stain on the soul leaves him in a morally worse condition than he was in before he did the evil in question.

Many things go into this stain, but one central element of it is certainly the knowledge of what it is like to do the evil things Hess did. Mind-reading

---

9   See *Interrogations: The Nazi Elite in Allied Hands, 1945*, ed. by Richard Overy (New York: Viking Penguin, 2001), p. 419.

10   Ibid., p. 401.

11   This is not to say that nothing could take away this stain. In my paper, 'Personal Relations and Moral Residue' [in *History of the Human Sciences: Theorizing from the Holocaust: What is to be Learned?*, Paul Roth & Mark S. Peacock (eds.), Vol. 17 No 2/3 (August 2004), pp. 33-57], I discuss and argue for a certain kind of remedy for the stain, based on Aquinas's particular understanding of the notion of satisfaction. Satisfaction is NOT required for forgiveness. Its effect is to change comparative standing and relational attributes for the person making the satisfaction.

transfers some simulacrum of this knowledge. Seeing a person engaged in a seriously evil act such as the rape of a child, in real life or on videos, is disturbing because the mind-reading capacities of the mirror neuron system are engaged in such cases too. Because mind-reading introduces into the viewer a sense of what it feels like to do the evil acts being seen, and to want to do them, mind-reading the mental states of someone engaged in moral monstrosity will produce feelings that are horrible to ordinarily decent people.

If Paula views and mind-reads Jerome while he is engaged in morally evil acts, then Paula will gain something like a simulacrum of the moral slackness in Jerome even while she lacks those states of intellect and will which enabled Jerome actually to engage in the evil acts. The as-it-were slackness in Paula's psyche is not itself a moral evil on Paula's part, just because Paula lacks the states of will and intellect Jerome has while he does the evil acts in question. Because the mirror neuron system enables Paula to share something of Jerome's mental states off-line, as it were, Paula does not contract the moral evil Jerome has. Paula gains a simulacrum of the stain on Jerome's soul; but since Paula gains this imitation stain without any evil acts of her own intellect or will, she is not blameworthy or otherwise culpable for having it. She has only an off-line re-presentation of Jerome's psychic states, not the real thing.

On the other hand, the feeling that Paula has in such cases is real and is her own. For a morally decent person, the psychic states generated by a mind-reading connection with a person engaged in serious evil will produce psychological pain ranging from distress and revulsion to the catastrophically traumatic. When Tolkien's Frodo is connected in a telepathic way with the minds of Mordor's Black Riders, the horror is so traumatic for him that he never recovers from the experience. The rest of his life is marked by a periodic recurrence of that experience of horror and its suffering.

Human beings are a highly social species, and the mirror neuron system is part of what enables human beings to function as the social animals they are. Mind-reading connects people into smaller or larger social groups which can function as one because the mind-reading unites them psychically to one extent or another. The great good of this system is highlighted by what happens when it is impaired, as it is in autistic children. But the other side of the coin is that the same system also enables a mind-reading union of sorts between the psyche of a morally decent person and the psyche of an evil person, and a psychic connection of that sort will be an affliction of one sort or another for the morally decent person.

Mind-reading, Shared Attention, and Christ's Distance from God

Just as great physical pain can hinder or block a person's ability to share attention with another, even if the two of them love each other and are mutually close, so the psychological pain attendant on a mind-reading connection with a person engaged in serious evil can have the same effect. If Paula is connected with Jerome in the mind-reading way when Jerome is engaged in serious moral evil, that connection can leave Paula unable to share attention with another person Julia, even if Julia is right there for Paula, present to Paula in every respect except for Paula's inability to find Julia in her pain. When Frodo is in the grip of his mind-reading connection with the Black Riders, the whole world around him dims. His loving friends, deeply concerned for him, caring for him, and present with him, fade for him. In the grip of the telepathic connection to the Black Riders, everything else, even the surrounding inanimate environment, begins to disappear for Frodo. The horror of the minds of the Black Riders fills his whole conscious mind and blocks out everything else, until finally he faints from pain.

And so mind-reading and the connection between persons it effects give us another option for understanding the distance between Christ and God at the time of the cry of dereliction on the cross. The love and goodness of God and the love and goodness of Christ seemed to rule out all the possibilities for explaining that distance, except (3b). That possibility assigns responsibility for interrupted shared attention between God and Christ to something having to do with Christ. But it was hard to know how anything having to do with Christ could be responsible for hindering shared attention between Christ and God in a context of mutual love and closeness between them. Morally bad states of intellect and will are ruled out for Christ, and physical pain is insufficient to explain Christ's experience of distance from God too.

But the mind-reading capacities of human beings shows us that, with regard to possibility (3), *tertium datur*. In principle, Christ can be the source of the blocking of shared attention between Christ and God because of

(3b1) something in Christ's intellect and/or will,

    or

(3b2) something external to Christ,

    or – as the description of the mind-reading system makes clear –

(3b3) something relational between Christ and other human beings.

It is Christian doctrine that on the cross Christ bore the sins of all human beings. There are, of course, many explanations of this claim. Virtually all of them suppose that in taking on human sin during his crucifixion, nothing about Christ's intellect and will became truly morally evil. On the other hand, most such explanations also suppose that there is some sense in which the evil of human beings became something Christ took into himself.

The mind-reading system provides one interesting explanation for how Christ could take into himself all human sin at once on the cross without having himself any morally evil beliefs or states of will. If on the cross Christ's human psyche is somehow connected with the psyches of every human being, then at one and the same time Christ will mind-read the mental states found in all the terribly evil human acts human beings have ever committed. Every vile, shocking, disgusting revulsive evil psychic state accompanying all human evil will also be at once in the psyche of Christ, only off-line. He will have in his psyche the simulacrum of all the stains of all the evil ever thought or done, without having any evil acts of his own. One might say that as the ravages of the crucifixion scar his body, this mind-read evil scars his psyche.

The mind-reading system therefore gives one kind of explanation for Christ's bearing all human sin himself while at the same time remaining without moral evil of his own.

But the mind-reading system also provides a way in which to understand Christ's experience of distance between himself and God. There is plausibility as well as sensitivity in Tolkien's portrayal of Frodo's mind as so filled with the minds of the Black Riders that all the world around him fades from his view. Overwhelmed by that telepathic connection, Frodo cannot find his friends, even though they are right there by him, filled with love and care for him. Their mutual love and closeness is not diminished, but Frodo cannot access it, because he loses his ability to share attention with his friends while he is suffering the horror of that telepathic connection.

If Tolkien's story seems plausible as regards Frodo, then it does not seem implausible to suppose that an analogous story, mutatis mutandis, could be told about Christ. The suffering of Christ's psychic connection all at once with all the evil mental states of every human evildoer would greatly eclipse any other human psychological suffering. It would dwarf an experience of suffering such as that brought about by Frodo's telepathic connection to the minds of Mordor, no matter how evil those minds are and no matter how terribly traumatic a telepathic union with such a mind would be. Flooded with such a horror, Christ might well lose entirely his ability to connect to the mind of God. For Christ in such a condition, God would be even more inaccessible than Frodo's friends were to him when the Black Riders occupied his mind.

Furthermore, because in his psychic connection with the evil in every human being Christ would also have a simulacrum of the stains on the soul accompanying all that evil, he would feel the moral ugliness of all that evil in himself. In that condition, why wouldn't he cry that God had forsaken him?

The ugliness of those stains, even in their off-line or simulated form, is a world away from the beauty of God's goodness; and though the movement creating that distance is Christ's, the experience for him will be God's receding from him. For those on a boat moving out to sea, the shore seems to recede, although it is they who are moving, not the shore. An unwilling passenger on such a boat may well feel his home is leaving him as the shore becomes ever more distant, even while something in his mind also knows that it is he who is moving. In the same way, it is possible for Christ to feel that it is God who has gone from him even while it is the overwhelming of his mind by the connection with the evil in human minds that deprives him of his ability to share attention with God.

Conclusion

Philosophical reflection on the biblical narrative attributing to Christ the cry of dereliction from the cross gives an interpretation of one part of the atonement, that process whereby something about Christ's passion and death brought about a solution of some sort to the problem of human sin. On this interpretation, in crucifixion, the psyche of Christ was really united with the psyches of all human beings in all their good and also in all their evil. If this union makes the psyches of human beings accessible to Christ, then presumably, since union is a symmetric relation, the same union also makes the psyche of Christ accessible to every human being. Just as it is not hard to see how a deep psychic connection of a mind-reading sort with all the evil in every human psyche might be a shattering affliction for Christ, so it is not so hard to see that accessibility to the psyche of Christ might be a great redemptive good for human beings.

Wrestling with the story of the cry of dereliction therefore produces some significant insight into the atonement. But, however helpful it is, this insight by itself is hardly a complete interpretation of the doctrine of the atonement. Some of the most important questions about atonement still remain unanswered. What is there about psychic union of this mind-reading sort between Christ and human beings that makes it essential to the atonement? And what is there about crucifixion that is essential to this psychic union? Why couldn't the good brought about by atonement be gotten as well without such psychic union and crucifixion as with it?

By itself, this interpretation of the cry of dereliction cannot provide the answers to these questions, but it does help in discerning what directions could profitably be followed in looking for the answers.[12] It emphasizes the relation, the psychic union, between Christ and human beings as part of the process of the passion itself. And so it also opens the way for a more Trinitarian account of the atonement.

Traditionally, the Holy Spirit has been taken to have an essential role in the process of sanctification, which is one of the ends achieved by the atonement; but it hasn't been clear what the connection is between the passion and death of Christ, on the one hand, and the sanctification brought about by the Holy Spirit, on the other. The interpretation of the cry of dereliction I have argued for is suggestive on this score. On Trinitarian doctrine, the Holy Spirit is united with Christ. And so, if on the cross the mind of Christ is united with all human psyches, then through this union the Holy Spirit is united with them as well. But pursuing a suggestion of this sort requires a book-length project. It is enough for this paper to have shown one way of understanding the cry of dereliction and the suffering that powers its expression.

---

12   I am grateful to William Abraham, Paul Griffiths, and audiences at the American Academy of Religion and the University of Notre Dame for helpful comments on an earlier draft of this paper.

Salvation as Divine Action: A Philosophical Approach to the Power of Faith in Christ's Resurrection

Denis Moreau

I. The Theme of Salvation in Contemporary Discourse

The concept of salvation still occurs regularly in ordinary language. It also appears, typically without being defined clearly, in a number of contemporary philosophical works far removed from Christianity.

It is striking how commonly the notion of salvation and related words (the verb 'to save', the nouns 'saviour', 'salvage') are used in most European languages. In French, people greet one another with the word '*salut*', in Italian they say '*salve*' or '*ti saluto*', in German they say '*salü*' (or '*heil*' '*heil dich*' in the past). Though people using the word in such situations may not know it, this recalls an ancient practice of wishing an interlocutor 'salvation' upon meeting. For instance, Pythagorean philosophers appear to have greeted each other with the word 'health!', *ugiainein* (a greeting also found in the *New Testament*, at the beginning of The Third Letter of John), and Seneca's letters to Lucilius often begin with the formula: '*Seneca Lucilio suo salutem dat.*' The themes of saviour, salvage, salvation, which are etymologically as well as conceptually related to that of salvation, are also increasingly common in political discourse (such and such a person is considered the country's saviour), economic discourse (the salvage of a corporation), as well as computer discourse (we save or salvage data). Finally, on a funnier, but no less meaningful note, French supermarkets sell a shower gel called 'Axe. Difficult Morning, anti-hangover.' The product's packaging states quite clearly that it is intended for people who have a hard time waking up after partying, while the label describes its properties in terms that could come straight from a theology class: '*miracle* shower gel [...] it will *save* your morning and *bring you back to life* after a short and restless night.'

Of course, the very frequency with which the concept of salvation is used means that in a certain way it is spent, close to losing its meaning from being used in too many contexts. But it might also be fair to ask whether this frequency of use doesn't echo, albeit weakly, ancient questions, long-standing concerns. In fact, if someone wanted to develop a Christian apologetic on the basis of the contemporary world's language use and dominant concerns, this theme of salvation would probably be an interesting starting point, a 'good hold' as people use the word 'hold' in rock-climbing.

All the more so because, while this notion of salvation retains, in its technical use at least, strongly religious and more specifically Christian connotations, it crops up in a surprising way in the writings of philosophers who are not particularly known for their support of Christianity, or are even quite critical of it.

Nietzsche is a striking if ambiguous example. As everyone knows, he sees himself as a fierce opponent of Christianity. But in several texts, he advocates a system of thought that, like Christianity, will lead to *salvation* – as long as we interpret salvation in accordance with its etymology, as a healing, the conclusion of a struggle against disease and weakness that yields 'the great health'.[1] The word also occurs in Jean-Paul Sartre, in the famous last page of his autobiography *The Words*: 'My sole concern has been to save myself – nothing in my hands, nothing up my sleeve – by work and faith. As a result, my pure choice did not raise me above anyone. Without equipment, without tools, I set all of me to work in order to save all of me. If I relegate impossible Salvation to the prop-room, what remains?'[2] Similarly, in a rather mysterious footnote at the end of the section in *Being and Nothingness* called 'Second attitude toward others: indifference, desire, hate, sadism', Sartre adds: 'These considerations do not exclude the possibility of an ethics of deliverance and salvation. But this can be achieved only after a radical conversion which we can not discuss here.'[3] Ludwig Wittgenstein, in a text from *Culture and Value* (1937), for his part, wrote: 'If I am to be really saved [erlöst], what I need is certainty, not wisdom, dreams, or speculation [...] For it is my soul with its passions, as it were with its flesh and blood, that has to be saved [erlöst], not my abstract mind.'[4] And finally, Michel Foucault declares, in a way that is both enigmatic and fascinating, 'I know that knowledge has the power to transform us, that truth is not just a way of deciphering the world [...], but that, if I know the truth, then I will be transformed, maybe even saved. Or else I will die. But I believe, in any case, that for me these two are the same.'[5]

These texts have three things in common: the theme of salvation is, for different reasons, unexpected; we understand, as we read them, that it is

---

1   See, for example, *Ecce Homo*, 'Why I am so clever', I; *Thus Spoke Zarathustra*, I and II.

2   Jean-Paul Sartre, *The Words*, translated from the French by Bernard Frechtman (Vintage Books, 1981), p. 255.

3   Jean-Paul Sartre, *Being and Nothingness*, translated and with an introduction by Hazel E. Barnes (Washington Square Press, 1956), p. 534, n. 13.

4   Ludwig Wittgenstein, *Culture and Value*, translated by Peter Winch (Oxford: Basil Blackwell, 1974), pp. 32-33.

5   'Interview', by Stephen Riggins (1982; *Dits et Ecrits*, Paris: Gallimard, 2001), II, 1354.

an important notion, one that reflects a concern essential to the author who uses it; but neither the context of these texts, nor, often, the entire corpus of their authors, give us a clear idea of how we should interpret 'salvation' or 'being saved'. Such conceptual blurriness, if not legitimate, is at least acceptable in the realm of ordinary language. But it is more problematic in a philosophical discourse that aims at conceptual clarity and rigour. To remedy this situation, I propose here a short clarification of the concept of salvation.

II. Clarification of the Concept of Salvation

Historically, among the Greeks and Romans, the word *salvation* first meant the state of being or remaining whole and in good health, 'safe and sound.' To be *saved*, then, was to be healed, and salvation, in the practical sense, meant health – not just physical, but also moral and spiritual health. In a more abstract sense, salvation meant both having reached a desirable way of life, as well as the process of attaining it, by being either removed from a situation or freed from a danger that somehow separated us from it. In a general sense, then, salvation can be understood as the return to a desirable former state that had been lost (as when one is saved from a sickness or a shipwreck), the safeguarding of this state against a threat (as one saves one's freedom from a potential oppressor, or one's life from a danger), or, finally, the improvement attaining this state represents. The meaning of the word salvation can, in short, be analyzed into two parts. Understood in its negative aspect, to be saved means to be delivered and freed, rescued and ripped away from a dangerous situation where looms a serious menace. Understood in its positive aspect, to be saved means being granted some good, reaching a state seen as beneficial or desirable, progressing from trials and wretchedness to a state of happiness and fulfilment. Therefore, I think we should find two elements in any soteriology.

(A) A pessimistic or lucid diagnosis of our present situation as one that is painful and dangerous, a state we are inevitably and structurally thrown into, and out of which we must claw our way. An optimistic theory that held that everything is naturally for the best and will continue that way could not be called a soteriology.

(B) A more optimistic assessment of whether it is possible to leave this grievous state behind. If a theory accepts the pessimistic diagnosis of the human condition described in (A), but judges that we are bound to remain in this state of wretchedness, decay, and misery, then it is not describing human existence from a soteriological point of view.

Within the framework of these two elements, we can highlight a number of criteria to distinguish different kinds of soteriologies. For instance, we can distinguish different types of soteriology based on:

(a) Whether salvation is achieved through oneself (auto-salvation) or through someone else, something external to the self (hetero-salvation). I will return to this distinction, which plays an essential role in differentiating Christian soteriology from most other forms of soteriology developed in philosophical contexts.

(b) The manner of reaching salvation. Individualistic theories hold that it is individuals who reach salvation, and holistic views assume that salvation is achieved collectively, by a group (a community, a nation, a Church, humanity as a whole).

(c) How broadly the class of the saved is extended. Some theories include only a few or a small group among the saved, some include the greater part of humanity, and some universalist or even cosmic doctrines include all of humanity, or even the entire universe, among the saved.

(d) Where salvation will take place: immanent theories hold that salvation is attained in this world, while some reserve salvation for another world.

(e) The nature of the alleged saviour: it can be a god (theo-soteriology), a man or a group of men (anthropo-soteriology), or even something else (extra-terrestrial beings, etc.).

(f) What degree of salvation is attainable: some theories hold that salvation is partial, others that it is total, others integrate the two into a process of salvation in stages or degrees.

(g) The nature of salvation, its content: most often, it is happiness, but even if we leave aside the well-known difficulties in agreeing on a common definition of happiness,[6] there is no logical obstacle to imagining a different content for salvation.

Let us consider, for instance, how the Marxism of the 19th and 20th centuries, interpreted as a theory of salvation (or rather a secularized transposition of a theology of salvation),[7] fits many of these categories. Marxism combines (a) auto-salvation (it is human beings who save themselves) and (e) anthropo-soteriology: it relies on a group of men (the proletariat, or its educated avant-garde) who hold the function of saviour in a period of transition (until the foundation of a classless society) to achieve a salvation which (c) all men or humanity as a whole share. This is (b) the conclusion of a collective process,

---

6   Cf. Aristotle, *Nichomachean Ethics,* I, 2.
7   See Karl Löwith, *Meaning in History: The Theological Implications of the Philosophy of History* (Chicago: University of Chicago Press, 1949), ch. 2.

which consists in (g) a happiness that is (f) complete and (d) obtained in this world.

III. The Specifically Christian Concept of Salvation

The *New Testament* attests that Jesus, whose Hebrew name *Yeshoua* means 'God saves', was quickly recognized by his disciples as the 'saviour' (*salvator, sôter*), the one who saves (*salvare, sôzô*) or brings salvation.[8] These early Christian texts use different themes, different images, to describe the status of the one who is saved, and the nature of salvation. The saved man is an invalid cured by Christ, a slave he frees, a debtor whose debt he forgives, a man possessed whose demonic bonds he looses, a man condemned whom he pardons, a dead man he brings back to life, etc.[9]

One feature distinguishes Christian soteriology very clearly from those that can be found in ancient wisdom, the philosophical classics (e.g., Spinoza),[10] Nietzsche, even, when he advises 'independents' to 'get up on their own',[11] and contemporary thought that emphasizes human or personal *autonomy*. Indeed, for all other soteriologies, salvation is something that man, or in some cases humanity understood collectively, can achieve on his own, by his own actions, by making the best use of his own strengths and natural powers – where the rational powers are often singled out – in a process that is clearly a form of auto-salvation. The end of chapter 9, book IV of *Epictetus's Discourses* neatly synthesizes this conception of salvation: 'Look, you have been dislodged though by no one else but yourself. [...] Turn yourself away to return [...]

---

8   See, for example, Acts of the Apostles, 4:12, and 13:23; I John, 4:14; Gospel of Luke, 2:11.

9   For more fully developed typologies, as well as detailed studies on the theme of salvation in different New Testament texts, see, for example, *Le Salut Chrétien. Unité et diversité des conceptions à travers l'histoire*, ed. by Jean-Louis Leuba (Paris: Desclée, 1995); *Salvation in the New Testament, Perspectives on Soteriology*, ed. by Jan G. van den Watt (Leiden-Boston: Brill, 2005); Alloys Grillmeier, 'Die Wirkung des Heilshandelns Gotte in Christus' in *Mysterium Salutis*, ed. by Johannes Feiner and Dan Magnus Löhrer (Einsiedeln: Benziger, 1969), vol. III-2, pp. 327-390.

10   See, for example, Jean Lacroix, *Spinoza et le problème du salut* (Paris, PUF, 1970). The explicit goal of Spinoza's *Ethics* is to 'lead, as if by the hand, to knowledge of the human mind and its supreme blessedness' (beginning of part II) which is identified as 'salvation' (V, 36, scholium).

11   Posthumous text cited in Didier Franck, *Nietzsche et l'ombre de Dieu* (Paris, PUF, 1998), p. 427. Cf. *Ecce Homo*, 'Why I am so wise', § 2: 'I took myself in hand and I healed myself.' We can also remember the taunt 'Save yourself' shouted at Christ on the cross according to the Gospels (Matthew 27:40).

to freedom [...]. And now, are you not willing to come to your own rescue? [...] If you seek something better, go ahead and continue what you are doing. Not even a god can save you.'[12]

Christian salvation, by contrast, is 'salvation from elsewhere' ('hetero-salvation'). Man cannot reach it on his own, and it requires an external, divine and supernatural intervention: from a saviour, or else from a revelation – if by revelation we understand a body of knowledge that can neither be found in oneself nor gathered by human intellectual capacities alone, but must be received. The Christian approach to the concept of salvation, then, introduces a notion of, if not passivity, at least receptivity or dependence on an other (or an Other), that is, in the broad sense, a notion of heteronomy.

Salvation as understood by Christianity should therefore be defined as 'movement from a negative to a positive state brought about by an external agent [which presupposes] three elements: a terminus, a starting point, and a transforming agent';[13] or else, 'a process whose beneficiaries are moved from a negative situation to a new fulfilled existence by the action of an external agent.'[14] In this case, the external agent is Jesus Christ, who, according to different acceptable translations of a series of Greek verbs used in the New Testament 'frees' (*eleutheroô*), 'saves' (*sôzô*), 'delivers' (rhuomai, *luô*), 'tears away' (*exaireô*) humanity so that it can reach a new way of life.

That Christ is the saviour and that he saves men from sin is an idea that is so obvious to those who accept the Christian faith, that, unlike other concepts also central to Christianity (the trinity, Christ's two natures, etc.), it has never been seriously contested or rejected by any important currents in Christian thought. As a consequence, the great councils that enabled Christians to clarify important but controversial aspects of their faith, and thus to discriminate between orthodox and heretical theses, never made it the object of a dogmatic clarification.[15]

---

12 I am following, with some modifications, W. A. Oldfather's translation in *Epictetus, The discourses as Reported by Arrian, The Manual, and Fragments*, LOEB Classical Library, volume II, pp. 395-397.

13 Paul-Évode Beaucamp, *Supplément au Dictionnaire de la Bible* (Paris: Letouzey et Ané), vol. 11, col. 516.

14 The different components of this definition are taken from Raymond Winling, *La Bonne nouvelle du salut en Jésus-Christ. Sotériologie du Nouveau Testament* (Paris: Cerf, 2007).

15 Among Catholics, the '*schemata* from the preparatory sessions' of the first Vatican council (1869-70) had considered defining redemption, but the texts were neither discussed nor voted on by the council (which was cut short by the Italian army's arrival in Rome). See Jean Rivière, *Le Dogme de la rédemption* (Paris: Gabalda, 1931), pp. 116-120. There is also a mention (without definition) of the theme of 'satisfaction' in a text from the 6th session of the council of Trent.

The creed of the councils of Nicaea and Constantinople tells us only that Christ came « for us men and for our salvation » *(Τὸν δι' ἡμᾶς τοὺς ἀνθρώπους καὶ διὰ τὴν ἡμετέραν σωτηρίαν κατελθόντα ἐκ τῶν οὐρανῶν / Qui propter nos homines, et propter nostram salutem descendit de caelis).*

How the process of salvation works, its *modus operandi*, was thus left so open that it has given rise to a number of speculative accounts, about which it is not always easy to decide whether they are rivals, or whether they bring to light, without fully coordinating or synthesizing their incomplete accounts, different aspects of the concept of salvation. In Latin Christianity, for the last thousand years, the dominant answer to the question of how salvation works was the satisfaction theory proposed by Anselm of Canterbury in the *Cur Deus Homo*, and developed later, most notably by Thomas Aquinas and later Thomists.[16] I find this theory quite powerful, and I think that conceptually it is still relevant. But I don't want to ignore the fact that this explanation has become almost foreign, so to speak, or 'inaudible' for many of our contemporaries. It has in fact become commonplace, for Christians and non-Christians alike, to reject the satisfaction theory of salvation as 'judicial', 'sacrificial', 'vengeful', and 'vindictive'. Our contemporaries criticize its characterization of salvation as a 'compensatory transaction', and the way it seems to worship pain by concentrating all of Christ's saving work in his passion and the sufferings that accompany it.[17] Moreover, in focusing so exclusively on the passion and death of Christ, this theory doesn't really assign to other aspects of his existence – his incarnation and even more importantly, his resurrection considered in themselves – any significant role in the work of salvation.

---

16 See *Summa Theologiae*, III, questions 46-49; see also, for example, Eleonore Stump, 'Atonement According to Aquinas' in *Oxford Readings in Philosophical Theology*, ed. by Michael Rea (Oxford: Oxford University Press, 2009), vol. 1, pp. 267-293.

17 For this type of criticism among writers who attack Christianity, see for example Nietzsche, *The Antichrist*, § 41: '"how could God allow it?' [Jesus' death] To which the deranged reason of the little community [Jesus' disciples] formulated an answer that was terrifying in its absurdity: God gave his son as a sacrifice for the forgiveness of sins. At once there was an end of the gospels! Sacrifice for sin, and in its most obnoxious and barbarous form: sacrifice of the innocent for the sins of the guilty! What appalling paganism!' And in a Christian author, see for example, René Girard, *Des choses cachées depuis la fondation du monde* (Paris: Grasset, 1978), p. 269: 'God [would] not just be demanding a new victim, he [would] be demanding the most precious, most cherished victim: his own son. This claim has probably done more than everything else to discredit Christianity in the eyes of men of good will in the modern world. It might have been tolerable to the medieval mind, but it has become intolerable to ours, and has become the stumbling block *par excellence* for an entire world repelled by the concept of sacrifice.'

Therefore, without rejecting the fundamental importance of satisfaction and atonement in the concept of salvation, it is tempting to look for another explanation, or, more modestly, a complementary explanation of the *modus operandi* of Christian salvation understood as Christ's freeing us from sin.

IV. An Attempt to Explain the Statement
'Faith in the Resurrection of Christ Saves Men from Sin'

It's just this type of explanation I'd like to offer. I have tried to take into account an important trend in contemporary theology, which is really a corollary of the current turn away from satisfaction theories: the rejection of an exclusively sacrificial or expiatory theory of salvation, and the desire to see that the thinking that focuses exclusively on Jesus's passion and marginalizes the resurrection stop dominating the discussion. This agenda, which has been, in a way, the height of fashion in European salvation theology since the 1950's,[18] has been clear in its critical project, clear about what it is rejecting. It has also been clear in its general theoretical aim: 'to restore Christ's victory, and return Christ's resurrection to the central place in treatises on redemption it should never have lost'; '[to show that] the resurrection plays a fundamental role in salvation.'[19] But when it comes to the constructive side of the agenda, to specific explanations in support of the general aim, the results have been more problematic, less successful. I am here attempting one such specific explanation of the statement 'faith in the resurrection of Christ saves us from sin.'

Here, now, is a summary of the argument I have developed to provide a philosophical clarification of this proposition. I will present it in four parts, each one corresponding to a section of my book *Les Voies du Salut*.

(1) The first section offers a defence of a pragmatic approach to belief: beliefs should be considered not only with respect to their truth value, but also with respect to their effects, how they transform the believer and the world in which he acts. I say 'not only...but also' because I don't think we should lose interest in the truth of beliefs, or reject Clifford's principle with its stipulation that the fundamental maxim of the ethics of belief is 'It is wrong always,

---

18   Examples of this tendency born in the inter-war period among Protestant theologians (like Karl Barth) include: François-Xavier Durrwell, Walter Kasper, Joseph Moingt, Jürgen Moltmann (at least in *Theology of Hope*), Wolhart Pannenberg, Karl Rahner, Bernard Sesboüe, Michel Deneken.

19   In this order: Henri de Lubac, *Le Mystère du surnaturel*, ([1965], Paris: Cerf, 2000), p. 20; Bernard Sesboüe, *Jésus-Christ dans la tradition de l'Église* ([1982], Paris: Desclée de Brouwer, 2000), p. 238.

everywhere, and for anyone, to believe anything upon insufficient evidence.' But nothing stands in the way of our connecting our interest in the truth of beliefs to a pragmatic investigation of beliefs. We will then supplement our interest in a belief's orthodoxy (how is its content theoretically righteous, speculatively correct) with a further question about its *eudoxia* (how is it beneficial for the believer who accepts it?). I offer a set of criteria for classifying beliefs from this pragmatic perspective, among which the two most fundamental are the magnitude and the value of a belief's effects. We can thus distinguish between weak beliefs, which have a minimal impact on the believer's life ('beliefs with weak existential implications'), and highly effective ones, which have a significant impact on the life of those who come to believe them ('beliefs with strong existential implications'). We can also distinguish beliefs that produce correct or beneficial behaviour in those who accept them (*eupraxic* beliefs) from beliefs that produce incorrect or harmful behaviour (*dyspraxic* beliefs).

(2) Section II focuses on the notion of death. It takes as its starting point the classical view that any proposition about the nature of death (and more particularly of *my* death) can be an object of belief only, that positive knowledge or science about *my* death is impossible. If we accept this, then we are led to ask, even in this life: which among the available beliefs about death are beneficial and which are harmful? In the remainder of section II, I explain, without much original thought, that we spontaneously and naturally believe that death is the end of life, and that in most cases we are afraid of death so understood. As the expression 'fear of death' is a little bland and not always clear, I try to narrow it down by distinguishing different types or different degrees of fear of death. It ranges from the instinctual reaction we share with other animals, fleeing death as a fundamental threat, an annihilation of what we are insofar as we are alive, to highly intellectualized responses like the great artistic evocations of death (Mozart's *Requiem*, Molière's *Don Juan*) or philosophical investigations like Heidegger's study of *Angst*. The general idea underlying this section is that we are naturally fearful of a death we interpret as the end of life.

(3) Section III shows that this standard belief about death is fundamentally dyspraxic, that is, it leads the believer to behave in ways that are bad and harmful, and which depending on one's lexical preferences, one can call faults, 'bad deeds' or 'sins'. I will call this thesis, that there is a causal connection between the fear of death and sin, 'the Lucretius hypothesis' because the idea is expressed, albeit without any detail about the precise nature of the connection, at the beginning of book III of *De rerum natura*:

... and the old fear of Acheron driven headlong away, which utterly confounds the life of men from the very root, clouding all things with the blackness of death, and suffering no pleasure to be pure and unalloyed (...) Avarice and the blind craving for honours, which constrain wretched men to overleap the boundaries of right, and sometimes as comrades or accomplices in crime to struggle night and day with surpassing toil to rise up to the height of power-these sores in life are fostered in no small degree by the fear of death. For most often scorned disgrace and biting poverty are seen to be far removed from pleasant settled life, and are, as it were, a present dallying before the gates of death; and while men, spurred by a false fear, desire to flee far from them, and to drive them far away, they amass substance by civil bloodshed and greedily multiply their riches, heaping slaughter on slaughter. Hardening their heart they revel in a brother's bitter death, and hate and fear their kinsmen's board. In like manner, often through the same fear, they waste with envy that he is powerful, he is regarded, who walks clothed with bright renown; while they complain that they themselves are wrapped in darkness and the mire. Some of them come to ruin to win statues and a name; and often through fear of death so deeply does the hatred of life and the sight of the light possess men, that with sorrowing heart they compass their own death, forgetting that it is this fear which is the source of their woes, which assails their honour, which bursts the bonds of friendship, and overturns affection from its lofty throne. For often ere now men have betrayed country and beloved parents, seeking to shun the realms of Acheron. For even as children tremble and fear everything in blinding darkness, so we sometimes dread in the light things that are no whit more to be feared than what children shudder at in the dark, and imagine will come to pass.[20]

In a number of analyses that I can't repeat here in any detail, I go on to show that the fear of death understood as the end of life leads to a series of evil actions: avarice or greed, gluttony, lust, homicide, disrespect to father and mother, and pride.

By way of example, here is how we can establish a connection between fear of death and avarice, using a text from Karl Marx as support:

That which is for me through the medium of money – that for which I can pay (i.e., which money can buy) – that am I myself, the possessor of the money. The extent of the power of money is the extent of my power. Money's properties are my – the possessor's – properties and essential powers. Thus, what I am and am capable of is by no means determined by my individuality. I am ugly, but I can buy for myself the most beautiful of women. Therefore I am not ugly, for the effect of ugliness – its deterrent power – is nullified by money [...] I am bad, dishonest, unscrupulous, stupid; but money is honoured, and hence its possessor. Money is the supreme good, therefore its possessor is good. Money, besides, saves me the trouble of being dishonest: I am therefore presumed honest. I am brainless, but money is the real brain of all things and how then should its possessor be brainless? Besides, he can buy clever people for himself, and is he who has power over the clever not

---

20 Lucretius, *De natura rerum*, III, v. 37-90, trans. Cyril Bayley

more clever than the clever? Do not I, who thanks to money am capable of all that the human heart longs for, possess all human capacities?[...]That which I am unable to do as a man, and of which therefore all my individual essential powers are incapable, I am able to do by means of money.[21]

The text reminds us of the specific function traditionally attributed to money: it is the universal mediator, the converter that makes all things commensurate by translating disparate realities and use-values into the same yard stick (the exchange value). To this classical analysis, Marx adds the idea that the act of buying, understood as an act of appropriation, causes the attributes of the property to be transferred to its owner. By merging the two driving ideas of this Marxist analysis, we can answer the question: in this mode of production and exchange, what is the object whose appropriation money fundamentally allows, and whose properties an owner claims for himself, at least at the level of fantasy?

It is time.

Wage-labour, after all, is the employer's use of his capital to 'buy himself' his employees' time as well as the product of their work during that time. A commodity, likewise, is just the fruit of the work-time needed to produce it. It follows that buying and hoarding money (avarice in the strict sense), or objects (in particular, manufactured objects), in other words, being miserly in the broad sense, is really amassing human time, in so far as it is instantiated, and has been, in a certain sense, deposited in those objects. The more money we have, therefore, the more able we are to appropriate other people's time, buying it with wages, or buying it through the mediation of the commodities it has produced, and the more justified we feel in thinking of all this time as potentially our own.

Whether he consumes or saves, and whether his saving is an end in itself or the means to future consumption, the miser doesn't believe that 'time is money'; he is rather moved by the belief that 'money is time', that in the world in which he acts, having money means being able to acquire other people's time, literally, 'saving time' or 'buying time'.

We can thus interpret the amassing of money as a more or less conscious fantasy promise of an indefinite heap of time, the illusory assurance that our existence will continue indefinitely, and so, as a fantasized attempt to escape our fear of death.

This, then, is how a causal and explanatory connection can be established between the fear of death on the one hand, and avarice or greed on the other. Using a number of different theoretical tools, I try to show in section III of my

---

21 Karl Marx, *Economic and Philosophic Manuscripts of 1844. Third Manuscript*, trans. Martin Milligan.

book that the same connection can be established between fear of death understood as the end of life on the one hand, and gluttony, lust, homicide, disrespect to mother and father, and pride on the other.

Section III's general conclusion, then, is that the common belief about death has the characteristic effect of leading human beings to this type of evil act. The fear of death tends to land us in a kind of existential mediocrity, or, in the worst cases, an existential incompetence. In other words, the standard belief about death is fundamentally and globally dyspraxic: it causes us to settle in a negative state that we can also call a state of sin, from which we need to be 'saved', right now, in this life.

(4) In the fourth section, I finally turn to the question of salvation. To be saved from the negative state described in the previous section, one might adopt an orthopraxic belief about death – a belief that frees us from the evil acts we commit out of fear of death, and sets in motion a series of intellectual and emotional reactions that improve human existence. Here my remarks turn avowedly Christian: for I believe that the Christian belief that death has been defeated by Christ is such a belief, orthopraxic in the highest degree.

I do not discuss the question of the truth or epistemic reliability of this belief in my book: I have nothing new to say on this subject.[22] I accept this belief in a hypothetical way, following the method sometimes called philosophical theology. I ask: 'If someone believes that Christ is resurrected, thereby signalling to us that death is not in fact the end of life, then what happens?'

All the elements I have discussed so far are falling into place to form a philosophical explication of how Christian salvation works. The belief in Christ's resurrection abolishes the ordinary representation of death as an absolute end, as well as the fearful relationship that follows.[23] This belief, then, is able to free us from the morally bad consequences (the sins) of the ordinary representation of death and our reaction to it. Thus, going back to the definition already spelled out, salvation is:

A process whose beneficiaries are moved from a negative situation… That is, humanity's situation as depicted by my interpretation of the Lucretius hypothesis: 'led astray' by the ordinary representation of death, and with a propensity to morally undesirable acts.

---

22 On this theme, see, for example, Richard Swinburne, *The Resurrection of God Incarnate* (Oxford: Clarendon Press, 2003).

23 Cf. Athanasius of Alexandria, *The Incarnation of the Word*, 27 (Paris: Cerf, 1973, 'Sources chrétiennes' no. 199), pp. 362-365: 'Death has been destroyed, and the cross represents the victory won over it. It has no strength left, it is really dead. […] Ever since the Saviour resurrected his own body, death is no longer frightening. All those who believe in Christ […] really know that if they die, they do not perish but live.'

... to *a new fulfilled existence*...A man who no longer acts as described by the Lucretius hypothesis has settled into a better realm of existence, one that is qualitatively superior to his former existence, not only because he is now rid of certain negative features, but also because he finds himself in a new set of circumstances conducive to leading a new life, one where dynamisms and capacities that could not be developed in his former existence can flourish. Ancient authors summarized it this way: 'Christ killed the death that was killing man'; 'he cast death's tyranny out of our nature completely by rising from the dead.'[24]

... *by the action of an external agent.* Salvation is brought about by the power of the belief in Christ's resurrection. From an objective or historical standpoint, the external agent, the saviour, can be identified as Jesus Christ. If, on the other hand, we focus on the information contained in the proposition 'Christ is resurrected', then the external agency is a revealed body of faith. For this proposition cannot be deduced from natural principles of human knowledge, nor can it be demonstrated a *priori*, and it is no doubt quite different from an ordinary piece of historical or experiential knowledge. It must therefore be a 'revelation', which means that it presents for belief a body of knowledge that does not and cannot come from 'me', but is given from elsewhere. Of course it belongs to the world, it appears in it, but from a source that is divine, or claimed to be so.

To use a different language: all the analyses I've developed so far now make it possible to explain the proposition 'faith in the resurrection of Christ frees men from sin'. If these earlier hypotheses are granted, then faith in the resurrection of Christ will, or should, set in motion in the individual who accepts it a series of intellectual and emotional transformations that improve his existence. If, as I have argued, the central problem of human life, what leads us astray and ruins our lives, is precisely a certain fearful relationship to death understood as the end of life, then the belief that death has been vanquished – a belief central

---

24 Melito of Sardis, *Peri Pascha* (Paris, Cerf, 1966 'Sources chrétiennes', no. 123), pp. 96-97; Nicholas Cabasilas, *The Life in Christ*, III, 7 (Paris: Cerf, 1989-1990 'Sources chrétiennes' no. 355 and 361), p. 243. The text of this 14th century Byzantine author deserves to be quoted more completely: 'Thus, while men were cut off from God in three ways – through nature, through sin and through death – the saviour allowed them to meet him perfectly [...], by removing one by one all the obstacles that kept them apart: [he removed the obstacle of] nature by sharing in humanity, the obstacle of sin by dying on the cross, and the last obstacle, the tyranny of death, he completely expelled from our nature by rising from the dead.'

and unique to Christianity[25] – must be an excellent way to reach salvation – where salvation is understood as an improvement of existence that begins in this life, not in its eschatological sense (though, of course I don't reject that sense of the word).

Conclusion

In conclusion, let me make four qualifications to the thesis I am defending.

(a) I am not, of course, claiming that we are saved through knowledge, and that salvation is available only to the 'experts' who think seriously about how salvation works. That would be Gnosticism, and I am not a Gnostic. It is faith that saves in my view, and it is 'enough', so to speak, to believe that Christ is resurrected to enter into the process of salvation I describe. Someone who thinks seriously about the problem just adds an explanation of how the dynamics works, or tries to make the process intelligible.

(b) The thesis I am defending does assert that salvation or 'justification' is brought about *by faith*, or, more precisely, by faith in Christ's resurrection with its message that death has been defeated.[26] I am here using the world faith in a strong sense, the sense of the *credere in Deum*, of strong conviction, a deep and sincere adherence that causes noticeable changes in the believer's interactions with the world. It is faith used in this sense that has certain consequences for the believer's salvation in my remarks above. It is, again, faith used in this strong sense that contemporary authors call performative: 'the Christian message was not only "informative" but "performative"'; 'is the Christian faith [...] "performative" for us – is it a message which shapes our life in a new way, or is it just "information" which, in the meantime, we have set aside and which now seems to us to have been superseded by more recent information?'[27] If, by 'performative' (in the broad sense)[28] we understand the property whereby certain beliefs not only represent a state of affairs ('information'), but also produce a change by forming or transforming other beliefs and behaviours, then we can indeed

---

25 See the famous claim by Paul of Tarsus in I Corinthians, 15:14: 'if Christ had not been raised, then our proclamation has been in vain and your faith has been in vain.' (New Revised Standard Version)

26 Cf. Saint Augustine, *Contra Faustum*, 16, 29, Migne PL, vol. 42, col. 336 : 'The very resurrection in which we believe justifies us.'

27 Joseph Ratzinger/Benedict XVI, Encyclical *Spe Salvi*, §2 and §10.

28 In the narrow sense (that of J.L. Austin) used in the philosophy of language, only public utterances (and not mental states) that actualize what they describe, or 'do what they say', are called 'performative'.

speak of the saving character of performative faith in Christ's resurrection: the belief that death has been defeated has the characteristic effect of producing salvation. Being freed from sin – that is, being less tempted, better able to resist temptation, committing fewer or even none of the morally reprehensible acts described above – flows directly from the radical modification in the meaning of death that comes from accepting the belief in Christ's resurrection.

(c) On the other hand, in this defence of salvation through faith, I do not mean to commit myself to a specific position in the age-old (though nowadays mostly becalmed) theological debate about the respective roles of faith and works (i.e., individual actions) in salvation. Even if my thesis can nominally evoke the *sola fide* of the Reformation, since it gives faith the essential role in the production of salvation, it is in fact closer to the position generally thought of as the Catholic one: where the emphasis is on how man is brought into a situation where he can act well, and, using his freedom correctly, (subjectively) appropriate the salvation Christ brings (objectively). In this light, justification becomes the fact of finding oneself in a new practical context, one where obstacles and obstructions to right action no longer bind us when we act, so that it becomes possible for us to be just. On this interpretation, then, justification is more a journey than a consequence of faith in the resurrection that is acquired once and for all; it is not so much a state in which we find ourselves, as the lifelong tension required for becoming just. Collectively, it is less an event we can describe as having happened, than the process in which, according to Christianity, human beings have been involved since the discovery of the empty tomb. The idea that what leads to salvation is revealed implies a certain receptivity, or even passivity, as the intervention of a God or saviour implies heteronomy. But, it turns out, none of these are incompatible with the individual's having, or needing to have some personal agency in the process of his salvation, that is, with the possibility that the individual's actions will have the character of an auto-salvation. Receptivity and passivity are the starting point, necessary conditions for a new mode of action that an individual can't adopt on his own.

(d) Finally, I want to say more about what it means for this discussion of Christ's saving action to shift the focus from the passion to the resurrection – something scholastic theology often saw as nothing more than a happy ending (it's always better when the good guy wins) or else a 'miracle' meant to elicit or strengthen faith.[29] First of all, the shift of focus does not imply that the darkness of Good Friday was useless or superfluous, that Jesus's dying on the cross after a degrading agony was irrelevant, or that nothing essential would be missing if he had died peacefully in his bed before being resurrected a few days later, or even more to the point, if he had proclaimed his victory over death without dying himself. First, as theologians in the first few centuries explained in their arguments against the docetist heresy, the reality of Christ's resurrection and humanity require the reality of his death. Second, the passion insofar as it is sorrowful and negative, and the resurrection, are like two facets of the same event – an event that brings salvation[30] and revelation – which can only be fully understood by focusing alternatively on one or the other of its facets. In its initial phase, this event reveals that salvation is not obtained easily; it is not obtained through the means usually promoted in the world (power, riches, honour, will to dominate), through violence, the desire to punish or to seek vengeance. Christ's passion shows that the road to salvation is hard, and that the fight against evil and everything that leads to it is sometimes painful and can require great sacrifice. The passion reminds us that 'there is here an ordered sequence that Christ himself followed: first the passion, then the glorification. [...] As long as our life here on earth lasts, suffering and death come before joy and resurrection.'[31] As the theologians say, it was 'appropriate', from this point of view, that Christ should die in the agony of the cross. However, the passion (and this includes its role in salvation) can be fully understood only in the light of the later event that gives it meaning. A story in which Jesus was *only* crucified would have a completely different meaning. Or it might not have any meaning at all, like a symbol of the absurdity and cruelty of the world. So, following Karl Barth, I want to warn those who think seriously about Christian justification and salvation against the Nordic

---

29 See, for example, Cajetan's commentary on Saint Paul (On Romans 4:25) *Epistolae Pauli et aliorum apostolorum [...] juxta sensum literalem enarratae* [1531].

30 Ultimately, Thomas Aquinas doesn't disagree: 'as to efficiency, which comes of the Divine power, the Passion as well as the Resurrection of Christ is the cause of justification.' *Summa Theologiae* III, question 56, article 2 ad 4. This same question in the *Summa* parcels out each one's role by distinguishing two aspects in the 'complete' concept of redemption: the passion and death of Christ cause the forgiveness of sins by providing satisfaction, while the resurrection institutes a new life. In every case, finding 'the correct dose' of passion and resurrection respectively seems to be one of the central concerns of Christian soteriology.

31 Hans Urs von Balthasar, *Theodramatik*, 5 vol. (Fribourg-Einsiedeln: Johannes Verlag, 1973-1983), vol. 4.

Melancholy of a (good) Friday theology, abstractly focused on the cross alone and forgetful of Resurrection Sunday.

> The seriousness with which we insist on the starting point of justification is a good and necessary thing, that is, on the fact [...] that we can only go in one direction: from the death [of Jesus] on the cross to his resurrection. And so we must consider first what is past, that is, our death which he suffered, then what is future, that is, the life he received. [...] But we must see to it that this seriousness – there are examples of this both in Roman Catholic and also in Protestant circles – does not, at a certain point which is hard to define, become a pagan instead of a purely Christian seriousness, changing suddenly into a 'Nordic morbidity', losing the direction in which alone it can have any Christian meaning, suddenly beginning to look backwards instead of forwards, transforming itself into the tragedy of an abstract *Theologia crucis* which can have little and finally nothing whatever to do with the Christian knowledge of Jesus Christ. [...] The knowledge of our justification as it has taken place in Him can not possibly be genuinely serious except in this joy, the Easter joy.[32]

Finally, I do not for a moment claim that this explanation of how salvation works is the only valid one or that it excludes all others. It is, for instance, perfectly compatible with the satisfaction or atonement theory. Ultimately, I think that the best description of the Christian conception of salvation is this: 'Christ's incarnation, his life and acts, his passion, death and resurrection, are what make salvation from sin possible.' Of course, one could say that all this constitutes just one event of salvation, the 'Jesus Christ event'. But as soon as we try to explain how this salvation really works, we end up distinguishing different explanatory frameworks; some that focus more on the incarnation's saving power as is the case with so-called deification-theories, others like satisfaction theories, that focus more on the passion. As a philosopher, and following in the footsteps of some of Saint Paul's texts,[33] I have wanted to draw attention to the soteriological value of faith in the resurrection.[34]

---

32 K. Barth, *Die Kirchliche Dogmatik* (Zurich: Evangelischer Verlag Zollikon, 1932-1967) IV, vol. 1, ch. 14, §61, 2.

33 For example, Romans 10:9: 'if you confess with your lips that Jesus is Lord and believe in your heart that God raised him from the dead, you will be saved.' (New Revised Standard Version) On this point, see Stanislas Lyonnet: 'La Valeur sotériologique de la résurrection selon saint Paul' in *Christus victor mortis, Gregorianum* 39-2 (1958), pp. 295-318.

34 Because I want to stick to a philosophical approach, I do not tackle the theme, in all respects difficult, of original sin. The thesis that I defend retains this claim characteristic of Christian theology: between death and sin, there is a causal relationship in the strong sense of productive causality. But it reverses the direction in which the theological tradition, following a possible interpretation of the texts of St. Paul (e.g. Romans, 5, 12)

I don't think that anyone can be certain, with categorical certainty, that the proposition 'Christ is risen from the dead' is true. Accepting it will always imply an irreducible element of faith, something like a bet that answers the existential question 'what may I hope?' as much as the historical one 'what can I know?'. But if this proposition is true, if death really has been conquered by a fully human person, this implies an unprecedented existential transformation, whose full array of consequences, in my view, contemporary philosophers, including those who have paid a lot of attention to the relation between life and death (phenomenology, for instance, in Heidegger) have not analyzed. I have tried here to sketch out a few of those consequences, while at the same time suggesting that there is a real existential benefit to the belief that Christ is risen from the dead, in betting, as Pascal understood the word, that he is *really* risen.

---

has most often considered this relationship: sin (of Adam) would have produced death (the mortality of man, the 'finiteness') that is to say, strictly speaking, the fact of dying and, in an analogical sense, the 'spiritual death' brought about by the breakdown in the relationship with God. If we take 'death' in the strict and biological sense, achievements of modern science seem difficult to reconcile with this view (as, in all cases, the theme of a unique and temporally determined *peccatum originale originans*). My interpretation avoids this problem, considering that sin, as a situation, and from there the sins, as actions, follow from mortality as it is spontaneously understood as a fundamental characteristic, both biological and existential, of humanity. The point is not to identify 'sin' and 'finiteness', but to show how sin stems from a form of spiritual negativity inherent to a certain understanding of finiteness, probably *de facto* inevitable, but not insurmountable.

Creation as a Metaphysical Concept

Paul Clavier

The metaphysical concept of creation should be preserved from ideological claims implied in the creationism vs. evolutionism debate. Two different topics have to be disentangled: 1°) the probability for living organisms to evolve with or without divine guidance; 2°) the ontological dependence of what there is upon a hypothetical (originating and sustaining) cause of its existence. The first topic often (even if not fatally) displays a disastrous mingling of observational evidence with metaphysically premature conclusions (whatever these may be: theistic or atheistic). Giving preliminarily and finally some reasons to cast doubt on the validity of arguing deductively from physical (or biological) states of affairs to God, this paper will be principally concerned with the second topic. The challenge of a rephrased argument to the existence of a creator is to point out new reasons for defeating the claim for a self-existent world, and therefore for arguing the ontological dependence the world might have on a creator.

The doctrine of creation is usually supposed to be: 1°) a religious belief proper to western monotheistic traditions; 2°) short of any rational justification; or even 3°) an irrational superstition, not compatible with scientific evidence.

Let us briefly comment on these preliminary considerations. First, it is true that the doctrine of creation has ruled, like a compelled article of a creed, over European philosophy from the 4th century to the Age of Enlightenment (from Augustine to Voltaire). But that a belief is forced doesn't forcedly entail the falsity of the belief. The fact we have been forced, at school, to believe heliocentrism is no sufficient reason to disbelieve it. Only a permanent lack of justification would lead us to suspect that this belief has been inculcated for an advantage, rather than for the truth's sake. Moreover, the belief that the world owes its existence to a cause seems to have been largely unknown out of the spatiotemporal limits of Jewish-Christian-Islamic traditions. But this does not mean that the question cannot arise but in monotheistic cultures. Amartya Sen has recently emphasized the emergence of that very question in the background of Indian Culture[1] and an abbreviated version of the cosmological argument is to be found in Udayana's *Nyāyakusumāñjali* I,4.[2]

Second, it is true that, since Schleiermacher has reduced the meaning of creation to 'the feeling of absolute dependence',[3] many theologians like Karl Barth, Paul Tillich, and Rudolf Bultmann, have renounced the metaphysical significance of the doctrine, which is supposed to be nothing but an 'existential claim'.[4] But philosophers are in no way committed to the choices made by theologians. Although creation was often considered to be a basic doctrine without rational justification, some philosophers and apologists, from Tertullian to Samuel Clarke, and right up until Franz Brentano, have campaigned for humanity's ability to argue for creation out of nothing, without the help of supernatural revelation. It is up to philosophers to define the true metaphysical core of the doctrine.

Thirdly, the picture of creation presented in some contemporary defences of creationism is quite misleading and caricatural. In these caricatures, creation is seized like a physical event. But it should be clear that the very bringing about of everything, if it is likely to occur (in a different meaning of 'occurring'), is to occur at least outside any physical framework. By rights, the methodology of the natural sciences rules out entities like 'God', 'infinite wisdom', 'creation out of nothing' (see below 3.4). If something like God is to be inferred from physical states of affairs, it can hardly be by means of a deductive argument. (There are no physical states of affairs such as it would be logically contradictory that they obtain without there being a God.) It is always venturesome to infer a metaphysical conclusion from physical premises (see 3.1). For example, there can be no observational evidence for a supernatural agent intervening in biological processes. Moreover, it is not essential

---

1   Amartya Sen, *The Argumentative Indian, Writings on Indian Culture, History and Identity* (London: Penguin Books, 2005), p. 22.

2   See 'Cosmological Argument', SEP. <http://plato.stanford.edu/entries/cosmological-argument/> [accessed 10/01/2013].

3   *The Christian Faith* [1821-22], Ed. by H.R. Mackintosh; J.S. Stewart (Edinburgh: T.&T. Clark 1928), § 39, p. 148.

4   More on this in: George S. Hendry, 'Eclipse of Creation', in *Theology Today*, vol. 28, No. 4 (January 1972), pp. 406-425. Hendry diagnoses a shift from 'createdness' (the fact of being or having been created) towards 'creatureliness' (the distinctive attitude or affect of man feeling the presence of divinity). R. Bultmann describes the former as 'a theoretical worldview that holds that human existence is to be referred back to the existence of God as its cause', and he dismisses it from the scope of faith, pretending that it 'no longer concerns man in the present'. 'Faith in God the Creator', in *Existence and Faith: Shorter Writings of Rudolf Bultmann*, edited and translated by S. M. Ogden (London: Meridian Books, 1961), (pp. 171 sq., p. 176).

to the concept of creation that the created entity has a beginning of its existence (see 1.1, 1.2). For all these reasons, the concept of creation is worthy of being studied outside the so often misleading debate of creationism, which entangles science with metaphysics. As J.C. Maxwell suggests: 'Science is incompetent to reason upon the creation of matter itself out of nothing.'

In the following, we will try to lay down the true state of the question about Creation: a matter of self-existence rather than a matter of time (1), before assessing the classic cosmological argument to a creator (2), and then Maxwell's argument to the createdness of physical world (3). After a brief rephrasing of the argument (4), we will estimate to what extent creation may be held as the best explanation for there being laws of nature (5).

I. Creation: A Matter of Time or a Concern of Self-existence?

1.1 Eternity not opposed to ontological dependency

In order to set out the concept of creation carefully, the problem of whether the universe (or the multiverse) has a temporal beginning must be disentangled from the question of whether its existence is due to something (or someone) else. As Samuel Clarke rightly put it:

> [...] the Question between us and the Atheists is not, Whether the World can possibly have been Eternal? but, Whether it can possibly be the Original, Independent, and Self-Existing Being? Which is a very different Question. For many, who have affirmed the One, have still utterly denied the Other.[5]

All along the history of western philosophy, Plato's 'generation of the kosmos' in his *Timaeus* has alternatively received a historical interpretation, and a timeless one. Aquinas holds that there is no contradiction for anything 'to have existed everlastingly (*semper fuisse*)' and nevertheless 'to be created (*et creari*)' (*De aeternitate mundi contra murmurantes*, 1271). The same point is made in Leibniz's *De originatione radicali rerum* (1697). But of course, the fact that most of the philosophers defending the metaphysical dependence of what there is on a creator, were at the same time more or less compelled to confess a doctrine of a temporal creation, has led to a confusing suspicion of both points.

---

5   *A Discourse Concerning the Being and Attributes of GOD, The Obligations of Natural religion, And The truth and Certainty of the Christian Revelation* [1705] chapter IV, Tenth edition (no place) Corrected, p. 28.

1.2 Beginning of existence, and cause of existence, are to be distinguished

Since most of the monotheistic religions confess a temporal beginning of the universe, the distinction between what is rationally justified and what is dogmatically admitted easily vanishes, so that a temporal beginning is supposed to be a necessary compound of the metaphysical concept of creation. Moreover, it is clear that a beginning of existence *seems to* be begging for a cause of existence more than a beginning-less existence.[6] This has nevertheless been revealed to be a prejudice, or at least a claim wanting of justification.[7] It is not because we are used to asking for a cause when something new suddenly appears in the field of our perception that we are justified in doing so. There must be other grounds for such an inquiry (see below, 3.3). In any case, the issue as to whether the world is created is not a matter of time, it is rather a concern of self-existence.

1.3 The true state of the question

In one of his novels, Benjamin Disraëli describes ironically the pseudoscientific enthusiasm of Lady Constance Rawleigh for a book entitled *The Revolutions of Chaos*:

> everything is explained by geology and astronomy; and in that way. It shows exactly how a star is formed [...] You know, all is development. The principle is perpetually going on. First, there was nothing, then there was something; then I forget the next, I think there were shells, then fishes; then we came, let me see, did we come next? Never mind that; we came at last.[8]

Well, if the premise 'First there was nothing' could obtain with certainty, it seems that an argument from the finite temporal existence a parte ante of the world could succeed. William Craig's work is mostly inspired by this 'argument of the Kalam'.[9] But even if there are serious difficulties with

---

6   Aquinas, *Summa Theologiae*, I, Quaestio 46, art. 1, Resp. Ad 6., 'for anything that did not exist everlastingly, it clearly has a cause; which is not so clear for something which has existed everlastingly (omne enim quod non semper fuit, manifestum est habere causam, sed non ita manifestum est de eo quod simper fuit)'.

7   Although he agrees with the view that there can be no good deductive argument for the universe having a beginning at a time, Richard Swinburne nevertheless presents an inductive one, in chapter 15 of his *Space and Time*, 2nd edn. (London: MacMillan, 1981).

8   *Tancred: or, The New Crusade* (1847), Bradenham edition, vol. X, Peter Davies (London: W.C., 1927), Book II, chap. 9, pp. 112-113.

9   William Lane Craig, *The Kalam Cosmological Argument* (London: MacMillan, 1979); See also 'The Origin and Creation of the Universe, A Reply to Adolf Grünbaum',

the hypotheis of an eternal universe,[10] the premise that 'First there was nothing' is not easily granted. Even if it were, there is an additional problem. As Hume puts it:

> But to say that anything is produc'd, or to express myself more properly, comes into existence, without a cause, is not to affirm, that 'tis itself its own cause; but on the contrary in excluding all external causes, excludes a fortiori the thing itself, which is created. An object, that exists absolutely without any cause, certainly is not its own cause; and when you assert, that the one follows from the other, you suppose the very point in question, and take it for granted, that 'tis utterly impossible anything can ever exist without a cause [...] The true state of the question is, whether every object, which begins to exist, must owe its existence to a cause.[11]

The brute fact that something (without further qualification) begins to exist does not forcedly require an explanation, a reason or a cause, why there is such a thing rather than not. The following picture explores alternative possibilities to the pretended equivalence of 'having a beginning of existence' and 'being created':

The world	Is everlasting a *parte ante* (E)	Is 'new' (not-E)
depends on a creator (C)	Is an everlasting effect (like the foot print of an everlasting foot on the sand of an eternal beach)	Was created at some moment of time, or at the 'beginning' of time
Does not depend on a creator (not-C)	Has always existed on its own (without any external cause)	Has once existed on its own (without any external cause)

The 'C and not-E' combination raises an additional problem. If time is relative to a physical world, it may be said that there is no time so long as there is no world. So there was no time at which the world did not exist. In this sense, there was *always* (at each moment of the time) a world. This would answer the question: 'Why did God not create the world sooner?' or objections against

in *British Journal for the Philosophy of Science*, vol. 43 (1992) No. 2, 233-240; 'The Caused Beginning of the Universe, a Response to Quentin Smith', *British Journal for the Philosophy of Science*, vol. 44 (1993), 623-639.

10   See Richard Swinburne, 'The Beginning of the Universe and of Time', *Canadian Journal of Philosophy*, 26, (1996), 169-189.

11   *A Treatise of Human Nature*, Book I, Part. III, sect. III, ed. Selby-Bigge, revised by P.H. Nidditch (Oxford: Clarendon Press, 1978), pp. 81-82.

a temporal creation, arguing that God would have been idle before the creation of the world, if it had happened at a time, rather than eternally.[12]

1.4 A question of self-existence

The metaphysical issue about creation is not a problem of *timing*, but a question of *self-existence*. But why should we, and how could we, raise such questions? An inquiry into the causes of existence may be revealed to be begging the question. Asking for a cause or reason as to why things exist, or continue to exist, is perhaps already entering the framework of theistic metaphysics. Escaping from this framework requires either to argue for self-existence, or to invoke our inability to discuss such abstruse questions. According to R. Carnap, every question operates within a linguistic framework, and questions about existence (of King Arthur, of Unicorns, of the world itself) are but internal questions, whose answer depends on empirical research: there is no place for metaphysical questions concerning the existence of the framework itself.[13] This is the way Carnap precludes any metaphysical inquiry. Indeed, before discussing such issues as: 'do things exist by themselves or must they owe their existence to a cause?', we have to decide whether the existence of 'things' is an unaccountable fact, or whether we may try to account for their very existence. Making up one's mind on such a topic may once again be a way of begging the question. We shall have to consider if there are any good starting points (arguing from such and such states of affairs) for trying to account for the existence of things.

1.5 Creator or craftsman?

Another important distinction concerns the role of the creator: does he bring about the very existence of everything other than Himself, or does he 'just' (which would already be a job of some difficulty) arrange pre-existing materials in order to compose a universe, like a highly-skilled craftsman? Is he a creator or a world-architect, a demiurge, as described in Plato's *Timaeus*?

---

12   This historical topic has been thoroughly studied by Richard Sorabji, *Time, Creation and the Continuum: Theories in Antiquity and the Early Middle Ages* (London: Duckworth 1983).

13   Rudolf Carnap, *Meaning and Necessity* (Chicago: Phoenix Books, 1958), pp. 206-208.

The world	Depends on a creative principle (*c*)	Does not depend on a creative principle
depends on an organizer (*o*) (demiurge, architect, ...)	Exists (through a *c*) and is organized (by an *o*). Question: *c*=*o*?	Exists uncaused (no *c*) but is arranged by a demiurge (*o*)
Does not depend on any foreign organizer	Exists (in virtue of *c*) but is not organized by any foreign expert (no *o*)	Exists and is ordered on its own (neither *c* nor *o*)

One very interesting point to note is that one may argue that the more familiar view (because of the analogy with our daily experience of working out pre-existing materials) is not the most probable one. It could be easier to conceive of a creation out of nothing (in spite of the lack of analogy with our ways of making) than of an arrangement of previous materials. As we shall see, working out previous materials which exist independently of the worker presents the risk of failure, and makes it highly unlikely that all the materials will be completely submitted to the craftsman's intentions. He will have to compose with them, to take care of the scarcity or excess of the stuff of which he is supposed to make things. So that among the possibilities presented in the preceding figure, the north-east case (no *c* but *o*) may be, although it is the most popularized view (through myths of genesis), the most problematic.

But these constraints concerning the 'making of' the world from previous independent materials may on the other side provide an explanation for the occurrence of monsters, disasters, natural and moral evils, so that the divine craftsman, even if doing his best, would be limited by the capacities of the materials. The explanatory power of the 'no *c* but *o*' crossing has successfully inspired Dualistic or Manichean views of the world.

In order to analyze the concept of creation out of nothing, let us follow Peter Geach, whose investigation of the topic focuses on agent-causation.[14] In fact, it would be misleading to conceive of creation ex nihilo in terms of event causation, the creating event being the initial condition, conducing to the created event, according to laws of nature. Let *x* be an agent, *y* an object, A some predicate and *p* a proposition, we may express causal agency through:

« x caused y to be an A » or « x brought it about that p » for instance:
– Phidias caused the block of marble to be of human form.
– Phidias brought it about that the block of marble had human form.

---

14 P. T. Geach, *God and the Soul*, 'Causality and Creation' (London: Routledge and Kegan Paul, 1969), pp. 75-85.

But of course, in the case of creation out of nothing, there is no block of marble, there is no preceding stuff, neither temporally, nor logically (I mean as a necessary condition), there is nothing presupposed to God's creative action. How then shall we define this very strange kind of causal relationship? Let's follow Geach's suggestion. Geach intends 'to show the difference between *God's creating an A* and *God's making something to be an A* – something presupposed to his action'. In both cases, God brings about that x is an A, but there are two different ways in which we may insert an existential quantifier to bind the « x » in « God brought it about that *x* is an A » The first way is:

I. God brought it about that $(\exists x)$ (x is an A)

    And the second:

II. $(\exists x)$ (God brought it about that x is an A)

Clearly proposition (II) 'implies that God makes into an A some entity presupposed to his action'. Therefore Geach expresses 'the supposition of God's creating an A by conjoining (I) with the negation of (II)' .

So that 'God created an A' = $_{Def.}$ (God brought it about that $(\exists x)$ (x is an A) & ~ $(\exists x)$ (God brought it about that x is an A)).

In Geach's view, it dismisses apparent difficulties arising 'from illicit manipulations of the word "nothing" in "made out of nothing"', but, he adds, 'the idea of creation does not require that such manipulation should be legitimate'. 'Nothing' is not 'the stuff we are made of.'[15] Creation out of nothing is to be conceived in terms of creation not out of anything, which is precisely meant by the clause: ~ $(\exists x)$ (God brought it about that x is an A).

1.6 Creation and continuation

Another topic related to the metaphysical concept of creation is the curious overlapping of creation and conservation. In other terms, this is the issue as to whether we can conceive of a generating cause for some entity's existence which could be different from its sustaining cause. According to James F. Ross:

---

15   See for example: 'Creation "out of nothing" does not mean that there once was a "NOTHING" out of which God created the world, a formlessness, a chaos, a primal darkness. This idea of creation as the shaping of formless matter, is the content of all creation myths. God is conditioned by nothing, not even a "NOTHING". He is self-determining.' Emil Brunner, *The Christian Doctrine of Creation and Redemption.* Dogmatics Vol. II. (London: Lutterworth Press, 1964), pp. 9-10. cf. A.H. Strong: 'Creation is not "production out of nothing", as if "nothing" were a substance out of which "something" could be formed. The phrase is a philosophical one for which there is no Scriptural warrant.' Augustus Hopkins Strong, *Systematic Theology* (Valley Forge: The Judson Press, 1967), p. 372.

'to create *is* to *effect* the *being of* other things.'[16] What about the duration of the effect? Once it has been 'effected', does the 'being' exist on its own?

Things (whatever they may be: material objects, minds, particles, chords, persons,...)	Are wanting for conservation in existence *(S)*	Are not wanting for conservation in existence *(not-S)*
Depend on a creator (an agent or process that makes them exist) *(C)*	Depend (if not everlastingly) on an originating and on a sustaining cause (as long as they exist)	Things, once created (in case of need), continue to exist by themselves (Principle of Ontological Inertia)
Do not depend on anything in order to exist *(not-C)*	Are not wanting for a cause in order to exist, but cannot continue without a sustaining cause of their existence	No need at all: Complete Ontological Independency OR They just exist, and we have no means to investigate further

The crossing *(S)* & *(not-C)* may sound strange: what would it mean for a new entity to be sustained in existence without ever having been originated? Does not a sustaining action, in case of non-everlasting entities, presuppose an originating action? But are there any non-everlasting entities? Why should we not accept the Lavoisier principle: 'Nothing is lost, nothing is created, everything is transformed' in metaphysics, and not only for physical transformations?

The crossing *(C) and (not-S)* does not look strikingly strange, because of our common experience of dealing with perduring entities without making any hypothesis of the cause of their existence. But if one thing did not exist by itself, at the first moment of its existence, how could it be endowed of a power to conserve itself in existence? So the major alternative may be *(C)* & *(S)* versus *neither-(C) nor(S)*.[17]

II. Creation and the Cosmological Argument

Not every argument to a creator is a 'cosmological argument', but every cosmological argument, starting 'from some simple fact about the world, such as that it contains things which are caused to exist by other things'[18] is

---

16 James F. Ross, 'Creation', *The Journal of Philosophy,* vol. 77, n° 10 (1980), 614-629 (p. 626).

17 On this topic, see J. L. Kvanvig, 'Creation and Continuation', SEP.

18 William Rowe, *Philosophy of Religion: An Introduction*, ch. 2, 'The Cosmological Argument' (Belmont, Calif.: Wadsworth, 1978), pp. 16-29 (p. 16). See also S.T. Davis,

an argument to one or more creators. Let us first follow the traditional phrasing of this argument (2.1), before picking out some weak points (2.2); then in the next section, we will follow Maxwell's suggestions (Section 3.1-4) for the rephrasing of the argument, prior to facing some objections (3.5) raised by his theistic conception of the so-called 'foundation stones of the universe', not only ruled, but created by God. Of course, there are many other versions of the argument, but this one deserves much more comments than are usually devoted to it.

2.1 Classical phrasing of an argument to a creator

Let us report Hume's classical phrasing of a 'cosmological' argument to a creator.[19]

(1)   '*Whatever exists must have a cause or reason of its existence; it being absolutely impossible for anything to produce itself, or be the cause of its own existence*'

(2)   '*In mounting up, therefore, from effects to causes, we must [...]*'

(2a)   '*[...] either go on in tracing an infinite succession, without any ultimate cause at all*',

(2b)   '*[...] or must at last have recourse to some ultimate cause, a necessarily existent Being, who carries the REASON of his existence in himself, which determined something to exist rather than nothing , and bestowed being on a particular possibility, exclusive of the rest.*'

(2a)   is soon ruled out: '*In the infinite chain or succession of causes and effects, each single effect is determined to exist by the power and efficacy of that cause which immediately preceded; but the whole eternal chain or succession, taken together, is not determined or caused by anything*'; which is called, without further justification, an absurdity.

So that the argument runs simply as follows: (1) is true; (1) → ((2a) or (2b)); (2a) is false; Then (2b) is true.

2.2 Objections

Hume's rephrasing of Clarke's argument has already been reviewed many times. Nevertheless we may pick out some problems raised by this argument, for they will suggest new starting points for a cosmological argument:

    God, Reason and Theistic Proofs, (Grand Rapids: Wm. B. Eerdmans Publishing Company, 1997), in particular ch. 4 where Davis construes Aquinas third way, by refuting infinite causal regress in hierarchical series.

19   David Hume, *Dialogues Concerning Natural Religion*, [1779, posth.] (Oxford: Oxford University Press, 1993), pp. 90-91.

2.2.1 Firstly, there is a problem with the very possibility of comparing 'nothing' with 'something'. Answering the question 'why is there something rather than nothing?', Leibniz pretends that 'nothing is simpler than anything'. But which criterion of simplicity is being employed here? The intrinsic probability to occur? How could one justify the claim that 'nothing' was more likely to happen than 'something'? How can we then pretend that the existence of something (rather than the so-called 'existence of nothing') is crying out for an explanation? Why should we not consider that a perfectly void universe is less likely to obtain than, say, any possible universe? Moreover, we may compare two different states of affairs (for example one including many things, with another including less entities), but it is not certain that 'nothing occurring to nothing' may be considered 'at all' like a state of affairs. It could be said that the state of affairs where there is nothing at all may obtain by carrying off each component of a standard state of affairs. So that there would be but a slight difference from the state of affair where there is just one atom occupying one place at one unique moment in the spatio-temporal frame. But it still could be argued that the state of affairs *where* 'nothing' occurs still requires, say, a spatio-temporal framework.

How can we compare the probability of there being nothing with the probability of there being anything? This is connected with the problem of ascribing prior probabilities. How must the cake of possibilities be cut up?[20] How is the principle of indifference to be applied in such metaphysical issues? From which packet of cards, from which barrel of marbles can you imagine someone drawing 'nothing'? Isn't it rather 'not to draw anything'? And if there really is a draw of 'nothing', why not many cards or marbles marked 'nothing'? And how many kinds of 'something' are to be a priori supposed?[21]

2.2.2 A second objection would be: why could things not 'carry the reason of their existence' in themselves? Of course, artefacts or chemical compounds must owe their existence to assembling causes. But what about their ultimate components or elements? The presence of a molecule of water certainly has generating causes, but why should its ultimate components not evolve or even exist by themselves? Are we justified in asking for a sustaining cause of their existence? Why shouldn't they be self-sustained?

Commenting on the major studies of William Rowe and William Craig, Jordan Howard Sobel concludes that the claim for a first sustaining cause is

---

20   On this topic, see Richard Swinburne, *Epistemic Justification* (Oxford: Clarendon Press, 2001), pp. 110-123.

21   See Robert Nozick, 'Why is There Something Rather Than Nothing?' in *Philosophical Explanations* (Cambridge, Mass.: Harvard University Press, 1981), pp. 115-164.

strange and doubtful. It may be said that sensible things require generating causes, but not forcedly sustaining ones.[22] John Barrow suggests how one may very simply dismiss a recourse to God as a first uncaused agent: 'Anyone who can live with the concept of a Deity as an uncaused cause can surely live with the a Universe itself as the uncaused cause.' Of course, conceiving the whole world as a unique self-existing substance is a way of escaping the argument (this is Spinoza's way out). But as Barrow himself points out: 'Universe is a collection of things. Not a thing.'[23] As we shall see, this may provide a better starting point for an argument to a creator. The claim for a first sustaining cause may thus be rationally justified.

2.2.3 Then there is the problem of infinite causal regression. Let us recall the distinction between accidentally and essentially ordered causes (generating/ sustaining). The former are successive causes whose causing action does not depend on the precedent. On the contrary, essentially ordered causes are concurrent causes, each of which depends for its causation on the precedent, which must therefore be actually exerting its own causal power.

As Jordan Howard Sobel himself admits 'there cannot be an infinite number of causes that are per se required for a certain effect [...] sustaining causes could not go on infinitely'.[24] Then, of course, in order to dismiss the conclusion, he has to attack the premise that every contingent thing needs a sustaining cause (which leads us back to 2.2.2).

Is it necessary to ward off at all costs the spectre of infinite causal regression? Although he is not at all friendly with theism, J.L. Mackie once remarked: 'If each thing were impermanent, it would be the most improbable good luck if the overlapping sequence kept up through infinite time. Secondly, even if this improbable luck holds, we might regard the series of overlapping time as itself a thing which had already lasted through infinite time, and so could not be impermanent.'[25]

Of course it is not the same to conceive of God as a single cause, or as an infinite process of generating causes. But in the latter case, infinite regression is not a knock-down argument any more. Other objections may concern the physical realization, the very feasibility of an actually infinite causal regression.

---

22   Jordan Howard Sobel, *Logic and Theism: Arguments for and Against Beliefs in God* (Cambridge: Cambridge University Press, 2004), pp. 176-177.

23   J.D. Barrow, *The Universe That Discovered Itself* (Oxford: Oxford University Press, 2000), p. 254.

24   Jordan Howard Sobel, *Logic and Theism: Arguments for and Against Beliefs in God* (Cambridge: Cambridge University Press, 2004), p.190.

25   J. L. Mackie, *Miracle of Theism* (Oxford: Oxford University Press, 1982), p. 89.

Nevertheless, the metaphysical demand for an ultimate cause of the universe, considered as a stopping point of explanation, is not to be confused with the scientific inquiry into the chain of (infinitely?) preceding physical states of affairs.

2.2.4 The fourth problem is: if there are things whose existence is not self-sustained, why should they all owe their existence to one and the same self-sustained being? In what way is a unique creator required?

There is no contradiction in each thing being dependant on its particular first sustaining cause. Of course, this would justify an overpopulated polytheism. Not only water, fire, wind, animals, not only each kind of thing or phenomenon would have its proper first sustaining cause, but every drop of rain that falls, every spark could ultimately depend on its own separate and private first sustaining cause. According to Sobel, 'there should be as many first causes for sensible things as there are sensible things that have efficient causes'. Anyway 'the possibility of a plurality of first members has not been ruled out'.[26]

III. Maxwell's Argument to the Createdness of the Physical World

3.1 Inferring creation from physics?

In his famous 1873 Bradford lecture,[27] Maxwell comments on the great discoveries of molecular science: the perfect combination of gas volumes, the kinetic theory of gas, dynamics of molecules of different masses knocking about together, molecules of air flying about in all directions, at a rate of about seventeen miles per minute. Maxwell emphasizes that, if this molecular bombardment 'were to cease, even for an instant, our veins would swell, our breath would leave us, and we should, literally, expire'. But instead of taking these anthropic considerations further, he prefers to place great stress upon the molecules conforming to a constant type 'with a precision', he says, 'which is not to be found in the sensible properties of the bodies which they constitute'. In Swinburnian terms, he outlines an argument from spatio-temporal order (rather than from design). Maxwell is convinced that the mass and the properties of all molecules of the same kind are absolutely identical and unalterable. 'Each molecule', he claims, 'throughout the universe, bears impressed on it the stamp of a metric system [...]'. Thanks to the spectral analysis of rays emitted from the sun and from the fixed stars by excited molecules of hydrogen, Maxwell is

---

26   John Howard Sobel, *Logic and Theism: Arguments for and Against Beliefs in God* (Cambridge: Cambridge University Press, 2004), pp. 192-193.

27   J.C. Maxwell, *Nature*, 8, 437-41 (1873) [from David M. Knight, ed., *Classical Scientific Papers: Chemistry* (New York: American Elsevier, 1968)].

assured (through induction) 'that molecules of the same nature as those of our hydrogen exist in those distant regions, or at least did exist when the light by which we see them was emitted'. Maxwell believes he has found the so-called 'foundation stones of the material universe, out of which our world is built'. Of course, no metaphysical conclusion is to be deductively inferred from this constitution of the material universe.

3.2 Outdated evidence?

As such, this statement may seem a little too optimistic. This atomism may appear old-fashioned and outdated. Has not Quantum Mechanics changed the deal? This is not certain. As John Barrow often emphasizes, 'this new non-determinist ingredient in our search for the laws of Nature [...] carries with it the key to the stability and the predictability of Nature in the large [...] Quantization of energy levels is also responsible for the uniformity of Nature; [...] If energy were not quantized, every hydrogen atom would be different, and the uniformity of Nature an unrealized idealization'.[28] So we're justified in supposing that there are universal ground states for vast collections of identical elementary particles. Perhaps the foundation stones have been replaced by strings, superstrings, which in their turn will probably be replaced by some more fundamental structures or entities. We nevertheless have reason to admit the existence of natural kinds of underlying constituents, giving rise to universal collections of perfectly similar entities, defined by a small number of structural properties such as their size, mass, electric charge (we could add spin, quantization) and liabilities (be they deterministic or statistical). And, no matter what exactly these entities are (stones, quarks or strings), their very existence remains for us, as for Maxwell, a riddle.

The question is as follows: can we conceive of a material process that would have impressed, throughout the universe, this metric stamp on every available chunk of matter? Maxwell doesn't believe it possible to account for the similarity of molecules by the means of a process of evolution, for evolution necessarily implies, in his view, continuous change, which does not fit with the perfectly discontinuous nature of molecules. According to Maxwell, 'we are unable to ascribe either the existence of the molecules or the identity of their properties to the operation of any of the causes which we call natural.' Indeed, the operation of natural causes *presupposes* the existence of physical entities endowed with

---

28   J.D. Barrow, *The Universe That Discovered Itself* (Oxford: Oxford University Press, 2000), pp. 156-7.

regular properties. Maybe a discontinuous process could do the job, but then the very existence and operation of this process still cries out for an explanation.

3.3 The problem of self-existence raised a posteriori.

So Maxwell agrees with Herschel that 'the exact quality of each molecule to all others of the same kind gives it the essential character of a manufactured article, and precludes the idea of its being eternal and self existent'. Then, Maxwell reaches his metaphysical conclusion: 'because matter cannot be eternal and self-existent it must have been created.' There is another possibility: things could be self-existent, and nevertheless they would receive their properties from a common source. But, as we shall see, this is hard to conceive. Anyway, we may need an additional step for the argument: for identity of properties doesn't necessarily preclude the idea of self-existence. It just makes this self-existence (much) less probable.

This is how Maxwell rescues the cosmological argument. He gives us some reason to contest the possibility for things to exist by themselves. But this is no more an a *priori* reason. It is because of the observed identity of their properties that the cause of their existence is at stake. If you are able to conceive one eternal self-sustained thing, then you have no reason to deny this property to any ultimate constituent of reality; so the universe could be made up of a vast collection of eternal self-sustained things. But in this case, things would exist independently from each other, and any likeness of structural or dispositional properties would become fully unaccountable. The regularity of so many entities falling into a finite number of identical sorts would not be just a mystery, but almost a practical impossibility. How could they fit together spontaneously without a coordinating cause, a common source, usually called a creator, on which they all depend? The inference to a creator provides a metaphysical explanation which simultaneously solves the problem of self-existence and the question of why things must owe their existence to a single cause. But of course, one may be satisfied with the brute fact of the spatio-temporal order of the world, without asking for a further explanation.

3.4 Science is incompetent to reason upon the creation of matter itself out of nothing.

Let us emphasize another interesting remark made by Maxwell:

It is only when we contemplate, not matter in itself, but the form in which it actually exists, that our mind finds something on which it can lay hold. That matter, as such, should have certain fundamental properties--that it should exist in space and be capable of motion, that its motion should be persistent, and so on, are truths which may, for anything we know, be of the kind which metaphysicians call necessary. We may use our knowledge of such truths for purposes of deduction but we have no data for speculating as to their origin.

As Maxwell noticed:

> Thus we have been led, along a strictly scientific path, very near to the point at which Science must stop. Not that Science is debarred from studying the internal mechanism of a molecule which she cannot take to pieces, any more than from investigating an organism which she cannot put together. But in tracing back the history of matter Science is arrested when she assures herself, on the one hand, that the molecule has been made, and on the other that it has not been made by any of the processes we call natural. Science is incompetent to reason upon the creation of matter itself out of nothing. We have reached the utmost limit of our thinking faculties when we have admitted that because matter cannot be eternal and self-existent it must have been created.

Seemingly, Maxwell still mingles eternity and self-existence. But in fact, he is not bound to preclude the eternity of molecules. The 'form in which matter actually exists' (that is 'the exact quality of each molecule to all others of the same kind') provides us with sufficient grounds for supposing it owes its existence – timelessly or not – to a maker. Molecules, or whatever the ultimate constituents of the physical world are, could be everlasting; the repetitiveness of their structural and dispositional properties would nevertheless continue to cry out for an explanation. The simple fact that, as Richard Feynman used to say about electrons, 'once you've seen one, you've seen them all', can hardly be conceived of in terms of a brute fact. But why does Maxwell consider so easily that matter 'has not been made by any of the processes we call natural'? Conceiving of a physical process that manufactures billions of particles endowed with the same fundamental properties (be they deterministic or statistical) is not a theoretical impossibility. Aren't we able to conceive of how elements heavier than Helium happened to be synthesized by stellar or Supernova nucleosynthesis? True, but then we have to explain the structure and properties of the elements stars and Supernovae are made of.

'So,' echoes Richard Swinburne, 'there is our universe. It is characterized by vast, all pervasive temporal order, the conformity of nature to formula, recorded in the scientific laws formulated by humans. [...] These phenomena are clearly things "too big" for science to explain. They are where science stops. They constitute the framework of science itself. I have argued that it is not a rational conclusion to suppose that explanation stops where science does, and so we should look for a personal explanation of the existence, conformity to law, and evolutionary potential of the universe. Theism provides just such an explanation.'[29]

According to Maxwell, the question 'Why is there something rather than nothing?' is neither to be directly investigated, nor a priori answered. The most fundamental characteristics of molecules are not good starting-points for a cosmological argument. Molecules existing in space, capable of motion: this state of affairs is not especially demanding of an explanation. Here the 'why' remains easily balanced by the 'why not'? What else could there be? We have no means of comparison, for we can hardly imagine physical entities with no properties at all (having no relation to space, not even the property of non-locality, no movement). Therefore, a sound cosmological argument, if there is one, won't be a priori. The premise of a reassessed cosmological argument won't be the mere existence of 'anything rather than nothing', but the existence of a small number of vast collections of specific constituents, with the same structural and dispositional properties. As soon as we consider 'the form in which matter actually exists', we have to solve the riddle of universally repeated complex structures. This riddle will be better solved if we admit a common source, a creator, rather than mere chance.

3.5 Objections

3.5.1 An objector could argue that our inability to ascribe the existence of molecules with identical properties to the operation of merely physical causes is just the measure of our provisory ignorance. Doesn't Maxwell postulate a God of the gaps? Is he justified in his recourse to some supernatural entity? How could Maxwell face the objection that the very foundation stones of the universe have naturally evolved, from a self-existing primitive physical entity? In this case, wouldn't the universe be self-explanatory? The problem is that this primitive self-existing entity ought to be endowed with very complex properties and potentialities, which are not 'metaphysically necessary', including liability to self-fragmentation leading to specific kinds of identical entities. Let us say that such an uncaused physical primitive state would already be many things, not just one thing. Well, if the very being on which everything depends is a primitive physical entity, endowed with laws of evolution, and if nothing else is required to explain that it exerts these powers and liabilities, there will be no creator, or a physical one. But why should this first physical high-density state of affairs be precisely likely to give birth to identical entities 'after their kind',

---

29   Richard Swinburne, *Is There a God?* (Oxford: Oxford University Press, 1996), p. 68.

this remains a mystery. Preferring a mystery to a metaphysical explanation is not forcedly a rational way-out.

3.5.2. One could object (as Hume already has): why should a contriver not be sufficient to set the physical world in order? Do you need a Creator to do the job? In the famous Query 31 of his *Opticks*, Newton claims: 'all material Things seem to have been composed of the hard and solid Particles above-mention'd, variously associated in the first Creation by the Counsel of an intelligent Agent. For it became him who created them to set them in order.' Of course, if there is a creator, it befits him to set things in order. But does it necessarily come to him? The answer is no. There is no contradiction in a demiurge trying to subdue materials he has not made. This was the view of Anaxagoras, and to some extent, of Plato. However, as Plato points out, the success of his action would depend on the obedience of the materials he uses. And the chances of success are slight. Independent self-existing things could remain outlaws, rebellious to the watchmaker, blind or clairvoyant. There is no reason why the demiurge would be able to fashion, to shape, all the material. But if he has made it without constraint, there is one reason. Only the one who causes everything to exist will be able, without misfiring, to endow things with specific properties.

3.5.3. Let's now deal with the premise concerning the so-called orderliness of the world. The coincidence of properties, their permanence, could be just an illusory projection of our need for simplification. Identity, sameness, similarity, symmetries, regularities of any kind would occur only, or mainly, in our minds. In that view, scientific theories would have little to do with the uncovering of an objective reality. Like Narcissus, physicists would only mirror themselves, instead of catching any feature of nature. But it would be a miracle if nature so often complied with our autosuggestive representations. Science's power to predict would be utterly unaccountable. There is another objection of the same kind: scientific theories uncover objective reality, but only to a limited extent. Science's power to predict and explain would be nothing but a response to the pressure of natural selection. But, as John Barrow elegantly puts it: if it were the case, science would become less and less successful when applied to environments that were far removed from the circumstances of our struggle for life.

3.5.4. In a short and witty review of Swinburne's *Is There a God?*, Dawkins[30] once attacked the so-called simplicity of theistic explanation. Dawkins contests

---

30   Richard Dawkins, 'Richard Swinburne's *Is There a God?*', *The Sunday Times*, 4th February 1996.

Swinburne's wondering about the orderliness of material objects (that is the repetitiveness and the retaining of structural and dispositional properties of particles of any one type): 'For him it would be simpler, more natural, less demanding of explanation, if all electrons were different from each other; worse, no one electron should naturally retain its properties for more than an instant at a time, but would be expected to change capriciously, haphazardly and fleetingly from moment to moment.' Let us ask: 'Billions and billions of electrons, all with the same properties', so that once you've seen one, you've seen them all, is that a simple or a complex state of affairs? For R.S. it is not simple at all, for R.D. it is simple. So, which Richard is right?

In a sense billions of billions of electrons, all with the same properties is a simple state of affairs: it simplifies the job of physicists. It is not only a simplification of their task, it makes the task possible. The existence of vast collections of entities is a condition for formulating laws of gravitational, electromagnetic or nuclear interaction, predicting their behaviour, at least statistically. Without such a state of affairs, there would be no physics at all (and even no physicists, but this is another point). Nevertheless, this incredibly facilitating state of affairs is not simple in itself at all, in the sense that 'what is simple is less demanding of explanation'. As we have already noticed, that there is something, or many things, rather than nothing, does not as such require an immediate explanation. But the content of 'something' makes a difference to the question. If billions and billions of things have the same properties, this fact requires further explanation than if there were billions and billions of things with billions and billions of different properties. And then, either physics can provide an ultimate explanation, or it will be up to metaphysics.

R.D. reports ironically the theistic explanation in the following terms: 'God comes to the rescue by deliberately and continuously sustaining the properties of all those billions of electrons [...] It is because God is constantly hanging on to each and every particle, curbing its reckless excesses and whipping it into line with its colleagues to keep them all the same.' Dawkins contests that God monitoring and controlling the individual status of every particle in the universe can be a simple hypothesis. But this hypothesis has to be compared with those billions of independent electrons all just happening to be the same. Indeed, we have no idea of how a supernatural agent can play so many strings. But we have no better idea of how so many 'strings' could, independently of each other, play the same symphony.

IV. Rephrasing of the cosmological argument

The preceding considerations may be summarized as follows:

I. Building-blocks of the universe (Empirical premise):

There are vast collections of entities endowed with the same specific properties (or: vast collections of entities falling into a small number of specific kinds)

This statement is:
- Neither a mere idealization (because of science's predictive power)
- Nor merely an adaptation of brains to selective pressure (because of the too wide a range of science's power to predict and explain)

II. Inductive principle to a common source (CS):

The more entities there are, endowed with the same specific properties (or: falling into a small number of specific kinds)

The more likely is their sameness to be explained in terms of a CS
I is better explained by a CS than by mere chance (collections of independent entities haphazardly equal to each other)

At this step of the argument, only the properties, and not the very existence of entities, are supposed to depend on a CS. So we have no concept of creation yet, but only this of a government of nature.

III. Problem of the nature and function of CS:
Generating or sustaining cause?

    I. CS is a common ancestor, a common generating cause of the properties of the entities of the same kind, but unless this CS is self-existent, it will depend in its turn on a deeper source of existence

    II. CS actually sustains the properties of the entities, through secondary causes

Natural or supernatural?

    III. Natural: there is a physical entity or process on which the sameness of the properties of each particle of the same kind throughout the universe ultimately depends (then God would be a physical entity or process)

    IV. Supernatural: there is a metaphysical entity or process on which the sameness of the properties of each particle depends, etc. This claim usually has a cooling effect: better no explanation at all, than a supernatural one. Suppose we could state the impossibility of a merely physical CS, would it be sufficient to call for a supernatural explanation? Of course: 'there is **no physical** process on which the sameness of the properties of each particle ultimately depends ...' does **not** entail: 'there is a **non-**

physical process on which the sameness of the properties of each particle depends...'

IV. Inductive principle to a creator rather than to a contriver:

The power of endowing so many entities with specific properties would depend on the liability of the pre-existing material.

The CS is more likely to exert its endowing power without misfiring if it has brought about the very existence, and not only the properties, of the entities.

The contriver, who will be the most likely to succeed, will be a creator.

(IV) gives us some additional reason to prefer (III-d) and (III-b) because it seems difficult to ascribe to a physical entity (III-c) the property of bringing about out of nothing the very existence of something, and a fortiori vast collections of entities falling into a small number of specific kinds.

V. Creation as Ultimate Explanation for There Being Laws of Nature

Another attempt to justify the thesis that the world is created may be an inquiry into the best explanation for there being laws of nature. In his *Tractatus Logico-Philosophicus* (1922), Wittgenstein is very suggestive about the pretended ultimate explanations provided by modern science:

> 6. 371 At the basis of the whole modern view of the world lies the illusion that the so-called laws of nature are the explanations of natural phenomena.

> 6. 372 So people stop short at natural laws as at something unassailable, as did the ancients at God and Fate. And they are both right and wrong. But the ancients were clearer, in so far as they recognized one clear terminus, whereas the modern system makes it appear as though *everything* were explained.

Well, if clarity is evidence for the strength of explanatory power, the theistic ultimate explanation may challenge the naturalistic one.

5.1 Self-explained laws?

It may be said that the laws of nature explain everything but themselves, according to Einstein's famous claim: 'the most incomprehensible thing about the world, is that it is comprehensible.' But is this incomprehensible thing better explained by God and Fate? In which sense are God and Fate a clearer terminus than the brute fact that there are laws of nature? Why on earth would God and Fate stop the demand for further explanation? If 'God' is just another description for the same state of affairs as the mere existence of laws of nature, the consideration would lead us to what Einstein called a 'feeling of cosmic religiosity', a deep admiration for the God of Spinoza; that is, nature considered as brute necessary orderliness, but not a Creator, endowed with Will.

Here we are: is it clearer to ultimately explain nature through a supernatural power, or to renounce an ultimate explanation? Is it clear that, given the laws of nature, there must necessarily be a lawmaker for them to exist? For centuries, the existence of a Creator was held to be a self-evident truth, or an inescapable conclusion. The ways of God were inscrutable, but the ways to God were obligatory rail tracks without sidings. Swinburne's rephrasing traditional arguments as inductive ones[31] represents a new deal.

Let us remark that, if it were a necessary conclusion from universally admitted premises that God exists, then all atheistic scientists would be themselves blind watchmakers or ungrateful discoverers. Is that probable?

5.2 No Creator, No Laws?

Laws of nature do not dictate, but just state how physical entities behave, given certain initial conditions. In any case, the very nature of these laws is controversial. Laws of nature may codify physical necessity, or express accidental generalizations. Do they just report conjunctions of past events? Do they allow us to expect conjunctions of future events? Do they express correlations between universals, or regularities in the causal powers and liabilities preserved by substances? It is not certain that any of these conceptions is more friendly to theism than another. Unless you conceive of the laws of nature as decrees of God's will, which is a way of begging the question, there is no direct argument from the laws of nature to a divine lawmaker. But surely the laws of nature would not be at stake if there were no similar events happening to similar entities, or frequently enough instantiated universals, or typical entities exerting specific causal powers.[32]

5.3 Nature's metaphysical dependency and the operating of mere physical causes: creation without creationism

Let us consider Newton's admiration for the arrangement of the planets. He couldn't but confess the invisible hand of God as responsible for the arrangement. (Darwin himself sometimes confessed that he could not conceive of evolution

---

31   Richard Swinburne, *The Existence of God*, 2nd ed. (Oxford: Oxford University Press, 2004).

32   Nancy Cartwright, 'No God, No Laws', Proceedings of the International Conference 11-13 October 2004, *God and the Laws of Nature* (Milano, 2005), pp. 183-190.

without a God providing guidance.) The divine Watchmaker was supposed to wind up the astronomical (or biological) clock. But how? Is his intervention describable in terms of physics or biology? Of course not. God's agency is not to be included in the course of a scientific explanation. Kant and Laplace were much better physicists, when trying to understand the arrangement of the planets from a physical point of view. And then, the alternative is:

(1) either you succeed in further explaining the orderliness by discovering a new kind of entity, or a still unperceived or undetected interaction, whose properties explain (but not ultimately), the observational data.

(2) or you are condemned to admit your (provisory?) ignorance. But postulating God as physical cause or process is as little help as postulating a God of the gaps.

In this sense, Kant was right when preventing us from searching for any unconditioned cause in the field of conditioned phenomena. So there is no place within the limits of a scientific account for supernatural causes and events. A scientist is right in taking no account of God's alleged interpositions when he has to explain a physical transformation. He may sometimes confess: such natural effects have not yet been explained in natural terms. Or even: it is highly improbable that they could ever be explained in natural terms. But the low probability of finding a naturalistic explanation does not entail ipso facto the high probability of a supernaturalistic one. So one may be satisfied with Darwin's claim (1842): 'What would the Astronomer say to the doctrine that the planets move not according to the laws of gravitation, but from the Creator having willed each separate planet to move in its particular orbit?' On the other hand, there is no contradiction between nature's metaphysical dependency on God and the operating of mere physical causes. From a theistic point of view, the Creator has willed each separate planet to move in its particular orbit according to the laws of gravitation, and given fully determined initial conditions. 'According to the laws of gravitation' does not mean that things behave in order to conform. On the contrary, getting rid of God would presuppose that the universe is completely self-existent (and not only self-contained, because the origin of this self-containedness characteristic would still require an explanation).

So we may say that naturalism is the only correct method for scientific research, searching for laws but not for a Divine lawmaker. But, of course, naturalism may not be the correct ontology; that is, the correct answer to the question 'what is there?'. Let us recall the conclusion of Darwin's *Origin of Species*:

> To my mind it accords better with what we know of the laws impressed on matter by the Creator, that the production and extinction of the past and present inhabitants of the world should have been due to secondary causes, like those determining the birth and the death of the individual. [...] There is grandeur in this view of life, with its several powers, having been originally breathed into a few forms or into one; [...][33]

That God must have brought about the world and provided guidance may be the metaphysical explanation of why this state of affairs has occurred rather than anything else; but how He intervenes is completely out of the range of scientific research, since scientific research is concerned with physical entities, and physical principles. Describing and explaining how matter-space-time-energy-fields behave can in no way involve God's intervention as a physical cause. Nevertheless, if God is metaphysically responsible for the existence of matter-space-time-energy-fields, all these structures or entities will depend on His Power and Wisdom. One could maintain that 'He created everything perfect in number and measure and weight', although there will be no possibility of introducing creation as a scientific datum. However, the claim for creation, that is for the metaphysical dependency of everything on God's Will and Power may even satisfy some scientific criteria (for instance, the criteria of the confirmation theory).

Of course, explaining the existence of nature and nature's law through the existence of God the creator supposes that the low prior probability of the hypothesis (we have no available analogy to 'making something exist out of nothing': even a birth is to be explained in terms of pre-existent cells, whose existence, as far as we can physically investigate, are never created out of nothing) is largely compensated by its explanatory power.

---

33   C. Darwin, *The Origin of Species by Means of Natural Selection* (1859) (London: Penguin Classics, 1985), p. 458.

Providence Interiorized:
Maimonides, Kierkegaard and Weil on Divine Providence

N. Verbin

The concept of 'divine providence' has occupied a central place in philosophical and theological debates for over 2000 years. Philosophers and theologians inquired, among other issues, about the nature of divine providence, about its compatibility or incompatibility with divine foreknowledge, with human freedom, and with the reality of suffering and affliction, as well as about the very existence of divine providence and what it means to assert it. Despite the rich heritage of debate and discussion, the contemporary debate in the Anglo-American world is limited in scope. It is largely concerned with the validity of Molinism, presupposing a highly circumscribed conception of 'divine providence'.

In a characteristic passage, Thomas Flint makes the following comments concerning the nature of an 'orthodox' conception of divine providence, taking it for granted that divine providence has to do, first and foremost, with *divine agency*:

> The notion of divine providence that orthodox Christians have typically come to endorse – a notion I shall refer to as the *traditional notion* (or *traditional picture*) of providence – is essentially a picture of how a God who is perfect in knowledge, love and power exhibits those perfections through the detailed control he exercises over his creation... according to this traditional picture, then, to see God as provident is to see him as knowingly and lovingly *directing* each and every event involving each and every creature towards the ends he has ordained for them (Flint 1998: 11-12).

Flint does not merely insist on a general sense of 'direction' or design. The type of providence that he characterizes as 'orthodox' places everything and everyone under God's sovereign and direct control:

> God exercises sovereignty over his world in a very strong and specific sense. God does not simply give his creatures the initial powers and arrangement and then, like the deity of the deists, sit back and let things develop on their own. Nor does his control extend only to certain general features of the world, the specifics being out of his hands. (…) Rather, traditionalists insist that God is sovereign in the sense that every event, no matter how large or small, is under God's control and is incorporated into his overall plan for the world (Flint 1998: 13).

Divine providence, for Flint, has to do, first and foremost, with divine agency, divine action, sovereignty, or control. Plantinga, Hasker, Craig, Persyk, Rhoda and others make similar assumptions about the nature of divine providence, giving rise to similar conceptions of its nature (Craig 1987; Craig 1988; Hasker 2004; Perszyk 2011; Plantinga 1974a; Plantinga 1974b; Rhoda 2010).

My purpose, in this paper, is to disturb and transform this one-sided picture of divine providence by examining conceptions of divine providence that shift the *locus* of 'divine providence' to the human agent as the bearer of a certain capacity. In so doing, I intend to portray a more complete picture of the logical/ grammatical features of 'divine providence'.

I assume that in order to understand a concept in general and the concept of 'divine providence' in particular one need not formulate a set of necessary and sufficient conditions by means of which it can be defined. A description of the different threads that make it up and of the complex ways in which it shows itself and relates to other concepts may be more helpful. I, thus, embark on the project that the later Wittgenstein had himself employed and considered appropriate for philosophers of religion to employ – the project of 'assembling reminders' (Wittgenstein 1968: §127).

I selected my reminders for their specific purpose, namely, to challenge the contemporary presumptions concerning the meaning of 'divine providence' – and to counterbalance them. The reminders that I selected – Maimonides, Kierkegaard and Weil – belong to different religious traditions and they are committed to different philosophical outlooks. They were selected for their similarities as well as for their differences. All three reminders 'interiorize' God's providence. In so doing, they provide a corrective to the current analytic overemphasis on divine-agency. Their different manners of 'interiorizing' God's providence, however, enable us to trace some of the different contours of the concept and to appreciate its richness and complexity. The 'reminders', therefore, provide a cure to what the later Wittgenstein had characterized as a 'one sided diet' of examples (Wittgenstein 1968: §593), facilitating a more perspicuous view of the grammar of 'divine providence'.[1]

I shall argue, by means of these reminders, that 'divine providence' is best understood as a 'family resemblance' concept with blurry boundaries and a great variety of manifestations: it is sometimes internally related to 'passion' and at other times to 'intellect'; it is sometimes internally related to 'happiness' and on other occasions to 'affliction'. Divine control and sovereignty, as well

---

1   For more on the Wittgensteinian notion of 'perspicuous representation' see Wittgenstein 1993b.

as divine foreknowledge, sometimes play a peripheral role and the human capacity to exercise freedom enters into the discussion in different manners.

The paper has three parts. The first is concerned with Maimonides's conception of divine providence and the manners in which it relates to Maimonides's negative theology. The second part focuses on some of Kierkegaard's remarks on divine providence and the ways in which they relate to his conception of neighbourly love; the third is concerned with Simone Weil and with the role of love and affliction in her conception of providence. I end with a few brief remarks about the relationship between the three 'reminders' and the manners in which they bring to light some of the logical features of the concept of 'divine providence'.

I. Maimonides

Maimonides discusses 'divine providence' in different chapters in different parts of his *Guide of the Perplexed*.[2] The relation between the different discussions is a complicated one and it gives rise to, at least, two different sets of questions: 1) Questions that have to do with the specific sense in which the individual of perfect apprehension is guarded from harm, or, in other words, questions that have to do with the specific sense in which providence and happiness are inter-related; and 2) Questions that have to do with the relation between Maimonides's conception of divine providence and his negative theology, especially his denial of a spatio-temporal relation between God and the world. I will address these two questions after I lay out the less controversial components of the Maimonidean conception of divine providence.

For Maimonides, the primary *locus* in which God's providence is exercised is the human subject, or, to be more precise, the workings of his intellect.[3] Understanding God's nature as 'intellect' and our being created in God's image in terms of our 'intellect', Maimonides states:

> [P]rovidence can only come from an intelligent being... Accordingly everyone with whom something of this [intellectual] overflow is united will be reached by providence to the extent to which it is reached by intellect (III/17, p. 474).

---

2   This discussion partly relies on Verbin 2010, Ch. 3, and Verbin 2011.

3   This statement is by no means self-evident, since it is clear that God's providence, first and foremost, has to do with the outpouring of the *divine* overflow. However, given that the outpouring of the divine intellectual overflow (through the active intellect) is constant, and given that the human vessels that receive it vary in their capacity to do so, we may correctly state that the primary *locus* in which God's providence is exercised is the working of the human intellect. In other words, we may state that for Maimonides, providence has to do with the capacity to receive the divine intellectual overflow.

Divine providence, according to Maimonides, 'is consequent upon the intellect and attached to it' (III/17, p. 474).

This famous Maimonidean principle is explicated in several manners in the *Guide*: 1) Maimonides insists that divine providence watches only over the individuals belonging to the human species, since only they are endowed with intellect; 2) He insists on a correspondence between the degree of one's intellectual perfection and the degree to which one enjoys God's providence; 3) He maintains that divine providence is absent when the individual's intellect does not focus on God although 'its withdrawal then is not like its withdrawal from those who have never had intellectual cognition' (III/51, p. 625) and, 4) Maimonides insists that the nature of the distraction has a bearing upon the nature of the harm that befalls on the one who is distracted. He concludes:

> If a man's thought is free from distraction, if he apprehends Him, may He be exalted, in the right way and rejoices in what he apprehends, that individual can never be afflicted with evil of any kind. For he is with God and God is with him. When, however, he abandons Him, may He be exalted, and is thus separated from God and God separated from him, he becomes in consequence of this a target for every evil that may happen to befall him. For the thing that necessarily brings about providence and deliverance from the sea of chance consists in that intellectual overflow (III/51, p. 625).

What does 'deliverance from the sea of chance' involve? What types of evil cannot afflict the individual of perfect apprehension? The *Guide* is notoriously ambiguous in its manner of addressing these questions. Some passages explicate 'deliverance from the sea of chance' in physical terms, emphasizing that the individual of perfect apprehension is not permitted, e.g., 'to be devoured like the beasts' (III/51, p. 626) or to be harmed by 'the plotting of men' (III/51, p. 626). Other passages explicate 'deliverance from the sea of chance' in a contemplative non-physical manner, so that the individual of perfect apprehension is mentally unaffected by whatever befalls him, including the physical injury, loss and harm that he may endure.[4]

---

4   The tension between the two explications of the principle that 'providence is consequent upon the intellect' has troubled the *Guide's* readers since the 12th Century. Shmuel Ibn Tibbon, Maimonides' contemporary and first Hebrew translator, had written to Maimonides, asking for clarification concerning Maimonides' theory of providence. He suggested several possible interpretations of Maimonides' views on providence and asked for his judgment concerning the most appropriate. No answer, however, has survived. See Diesendruck 1936. For more recent attempts to deal with the issue see, e.g., Raffel 1987; Reines 1972; Strauss 2004.

The former, physical explication is strongly highlighted in Chapter 51:

> Thus it has become clear to you that the reason for a human individual's being abandoned to chance so that he is permitted to be devoured like the beasts is his being separated from God. If, however, *his* God is *within him*, no evil at all will befall him. For He, may He be exalted, says: *Fear thou not, for I am with thee; be not dismayed, for I am thy God, and so on.* He says: *When thou passest through the waters, I will be with thee, and through the rivers, they shall not overflow thee, and so on.* The determination that when *thou passest through the waters and I will be with thee, the rivers shall not overflow thee,* is accounted for by the fact that everyone who has rendered himself so worthy that the intellect in question overflows toward him, has providence attached to him, while all evils are prevented from befalling him. It says: *The Lord is for me, I will not fear; what can man do unto me?* And it says, *Acquaint now thyself with Him, and be at peace,* meaning to say: turn toward Him and you will be safe from all ill (III/51, p. 626).

The succeeding reference to the song on mishaps strengthens the impression that Maimonides maintains that God's providence involves protection from physical harm:

> Consider the *song on mishaps*: You will find that it describes this great providence and the safeguard and the protection from all bodily ills, both the general ones and those that concern one individual rather than another, so that neither those that are consequent upon the nature of being nor those that are due to the plotting of man would occur. It says: *That He will deliver thee from the snare of the fowler, and from the noisome pestilence. He shall cover thee with His pinions, and under His wings shalt thou take refuge; His truth is a shield and a buckler. Thou shalt not be afraid of the terror by night, nor of the arrow that flieth by day; of the pestilence that walketh in darkness, nor of the destruction that wasteth at noonday.* He then goes on to describe the protection against the plotting of men, saying: If you should happen to pass on your way a widely extended field of battle and even if one thousand were killed to your left and ten thousand to your right, no evil at all would befall you... (III/51, pp. 626-627).[5]

---

5   I maintain that the evil, which does *not* fall on the wise person in, e.g., the battle-field is not the evil of injury or of death. Rather, it is the evil of estrangement from God. The wise person is not safe from the material arrows of the battle-field, which are of no importance. He is safe from the poisonous 'mental' arrows that occasions and locations such as the battle-field may aim at him. Being wise, he is able to perceive divine justice, divine reward and punishment even in circumstances which seem to exhibit their absence, since he does not identify God's providence with God's interference in the ordinary state of things to cause physical and mental distress to the wicked and joy and happiness to the righteous. He does not conceive of divine justice as involving divine acts of protection or retribution. Rather, he conceives of divine justice, of reward and punishment, as inherent features of one's own state, of one's

Maimonides's commentary on the book of Job, however, presents an incompatible conception of protection from harm, laying out the second, contemplative sense of 'deliverance from the sea of chance'. It is this explication of providence and of the type of deliverance that it involves, which, I believe, expresses Maimonides's genuine view of the nature of divine providence.[6]

In chapters 22-23 of the *Guide*, Maimonides discusses the bearing of the book of Job on his conception of divine providence. He argues that Job's afflictions do not amount to a counter-argument against his view of providence. According to Maimonides, Job's suffering did not have to do with his physical illness, with the loss of property and children, but with his non-apprehension of the sublime, with his ignorance:

> The most marvelous and extraordinary thing about this story is the fact that knowledge is not attributed in it to Job. He is not said to be a wise or a comprehending or an intelligent man. Only moral virtue and righteousness in action are ascribed to him. For if he had been wise, his situation would not have been obscure for him... (III/22, p. 487).

Job's afflictions do not render divine providence impossible or improbable. Job denied God's providence when he had been unwise, when he lacked apprehension. After the divine revelations, after he came to acquire wisdom, he ceased to suffer; he ceased to complain; he was delivered from the sea of chance and its harms:

> When he knew God with a certain knowledge, he admitted that true happiness, which is the knowledge of the deity, is guaranteed to all who know Him and that a human being cannot be troubled in it by any of all the misfortunes in question. While he had known God only through the traditional stories and not by the way of speculation, Job had imagined that the things thought to be happiness, such as health, wealth, and children are the ultimate goal. For this reason he fell into such perplexity and said such things as he did (III/23, pp. 492-493).

---

intellectual perfection, which have to do with what one is able to achieve by one's use of one's intellect. Being wise, no evil befalls such a person.

6   We may assume that the contradictions have to do with the fifth or the seventh causes for contradictions that are mentioned in the Introduction to the *Guide*. I find Maimonides's discussion of the deaths of Moses, Aaron and Miriam, (III/51), which he characterizes as 'salvation from death', his discussion of Job, (III/22-23), and his discussion of the possible fate of the prophet who may be put to death on account of his commitment to the teaching of the truth (II/38) as conclusive evidence in support of the contemplative understanding of providence. Since my purpose is to emphasize a dominant strand of philosophical/theological thinking, in which God's providence is interiorized, it is sufficient for me to demonstrate that the contemplative strand is a dominant component within the *Guide of the Perplexed*.

The individual of perfect apprehension is not protected from sickness, poverty or social degradation. Rather, he is protected from the agony and despair that such *realia* may bring about. Since the individual of perfect apprehension 'is with God and God is with him', he is happy. Realizing that property, good health and social status are insignificant, he is not pained by their loss.

In his 'Lecture on Ethics', Wittgenstein describes three experiences that seem to those who have them to bear intrinsic absolute value. Among these he mentions the experience of feeling absolutely safe, feeling safe in the hands of God (Wittgenstein 1993a). The early Wittgenstein, however, believes that the only necessity is logical necessity and that 'Even if everything we wished were to happen, this would only be, so to speak, a favour of fate, for there is no *logical* connexion between will and world. . .' (Wittgenstein 1988: 6.374). Wittgenstein recognizes the manners in which human beings are vulnerable to the contingencies of the world; he recognizes that we are never absolutely safe from physical harm. Nevertheless, from a certain perspective-less perspective, one may feel 'safe in the hands of God'. When viewing the world *sub specie aeternitatis*, when recognizing that everything in the world incarnates the ineffable logical structure of the world, one may, indeed, feel absolutely safe. From such a perspective-less perspective, one may see the problem of the meaning of life vanish and feel content and happy.[7]

Maimonides, eight hundred years before and from within a wholly different philosophical and religious outlook, seems to have proposed a similar immunity to contingency and chance and a similar view of happiness. Divine providence, according to Maimonides's contemplative explication of the principle that 'providence is consequent upon the intellect' is God's gift of reason, by means of which human beings may receive the divine intellectual overflow and attach themselves to God (through the active intellect). When doing so, they transcend the world and its contingencies, transcend their body and the processes of deterioration to which it is susceptible, transcend time and space, transcend even death and become absolutely 'safe in the hands of God', absolutely happy.

Maimonides's comments on the deaths of Moses, Aaron and Miriam, in which he characterizes their manner of dying as 'salvation from death', emphasize the radical nature of such 'deliverance from the sea of chance':

> [The Sages], may their memory be blessed, mention the occurrence of this kind of death, which in reality is salvation from death ... with regard to Moses, Aaron, and Miriam (III/51, p. 628).

The arrows of the battlefield, of sickness and death do not touch the individual of perfect apprehension. They may touch the body; they may inflict pain

---

7   For more on the relation between Maimonides and Wittgenstein, see Verbin 2011.

on the body; they may even destroy the body; but they cannot reach the intellect that is attached to the body; they cannot reach one's true selfhood; they cannot disrupt the intellectual overflow. Thus:

> [W]hen a perfect man is stricken with years and approaches death, this apprehension increases very powerfully, joy over this apprehension and a great love for the object of apprehension become stronger, until the soul is separated from the body at that moment in this state of pleasure (III/51, p. 627).

Death and dying, whether they are caused by the arrows of the battlefield, the snare of the fowler or by natural causes, are not agonizing experiences for the individual of perfect apprehension. For him, the moment of death is a moment of intense pleasure and love, during which his intellect is freed from its attachment to the body, freed to comprehend the divine more fully than it could ever have comprehended when it was attached to a body. The individual of perfect apprehension, therefore, dies 'by the kiss of God':

> Because of this the Sages have indicated with reference to the deaths of *Moses, Aaron, and Miriam* that the three of them died by a kiss. They said that the dictum [of Scripture], And *Moses the servant of the Lord died there in the land of Moab by the mouth of the Lord, indicates that he died by a kiss.* Similarly it is said of *Aaron...* And they said of *Miriam* in the same way... The three of them died in the pleasure of this apprehension [of God] due to the intensity of passionate love (III/ 51, pp. 627-628).[8]

The sage who receives God's providence to its fullest is wholly protected from the sea of chance, from every type of harm, including death. Nothing and no one can undo him. Nothing and no one can cause him terror and distress, and separate him from God. He is happy in the pleasure of his passionate intellectual apprehension of God.

What is the nature of this intellectual apprehension of God in which God's providence shows itself, which protects the individual of perfect apprehension from the ills of this world and even from death? Given Maimonides's negative theology, given his denial of divine attribution in the first part of the *Guide*, 'intellectual apprehension' cannot be conceived of in terms of the acquisition of propositional knowledge that shows itself in true utterances about God and God's nature.[9] Propositional knowledge is the ladder that the individual of perfect apprehension climbs over in his ascent toward the 'supreme pleasure of apprehension due to the intensity of passionate love'. Such a state of 'supreme pleasure of apprehension' clearly goes beyond propositional reasoning, beyond propositional knowledge. It is a climax of apprehension

---

8   I am grateful to Ron Margolin for this point. See Margolin 2011: 404.
9   See part I, chapters 51-60 of the *Guide*.

as well as a climax of love; it is a moment during which the distinction between reason and passion collapses, a moment of passionate *contemplation*, an experience of something that shows itself, a type of passionate seeing.

Maimonides uses different metaphors to characterize this climactic moment of apprehension:

> Thus, all the philosophers say: We are dazzled by His beauty, and He is hidden from us because of the intensity with which He becomes manifest, just as the sun is hidden to eyes that are too weak to apprehend it (I/59, p. 139).

It is a moment of dazzling beauty, of revelation and hiddenness, a quickly fleeting moment:

> Sometimes truth flashes out to us so that we think it is day, and then matter and habit in their various forms conceal it so that we find ourselves again in an obscure night, almost as were at first. (I/Introduction, p. 7).

Not only is the climactic moment of intellectual passionate apprehension a moment during which the distinction between 'reason' and 'passion' collapses but it is also a moment during which the dichotomies between 'transcendence' and 'immanence', 'infinity' and 'time' collapse.

In Part I, Chapter 52, Maimonides emphasizes that since God is not a body, nor is God attached to a body, there is no spatio-temporal relation between God and the world:

> There is no relation between God, may He be exalted, and time and place; and this is quite clear. For time is an accident attached to motion, when the notion of priority and posteriority is considered in the latter and when motion becomes numbered, as is made clear in the passages especially dealing with this subject. Motion, on the other hand, is one of the things attached to bodies, whereas God, may He be exalted, is not a body. Accordingly there is no relation between Him and time, and in the same way there is no relation between Him and place (I/52, p. 117).

Thus:

> There is, in truth, no relation in any respect between Him and any of His creatures... How then could there subsist a relation between Him, may He be exalted, and any of the things created by Him, given the immense difference between them with regard to the true reality of their existence, than which there is no greater difference? (I/52, p. 118).

On the other hand, God is apprehended (in a non-propositional manner) by the human intellect. The divine intellectual overflow flows into the human being. In other words, there does seem to be a relation between God and the world. Maimonides, indeed, emphasizes the flowing of the divine intellectual overflow: 'its action is constant as long as something has been prepared so that it is receptive of the permanently existing action, which has been interpreted as an overflow' (II/12, p. 279). The prophets, who are *embodied* intellects, who occupy a location in space and time, are prepared to receive it: 'In the same way it is said that He caused His knowledge to overflow to the prophets' (II/12, p. 279). The climactic moment of supreme apprehension in prophecy seems to be a moment of 'relation' or 'connection'.

Maimonides, however, emphasizes that 'apprehending God', absorbing the intellectual overflow, is not a 'moment' that occurs in space and time. He emphasizes that the divine intellectual overflow does not have a spatio-temporal relation to the world, since it is not a bodily entity nor is it attached to a bodily entity, which alone can occupy a location in time or space. He insists that the term 'relation' is unsuitable.

Thus, the supreme moment of apprehension, in a sense, transposes the individual of perfect apprehension away from his body, 'outside' space and time. It is, in a sense, both in time (by virtue of its attachment to the body) and in eternity (by virtue of the fact that it is a reception of a non-bodily divine intellectual overflow, that bears no relation to time and space); it is both a moment of immanence and of transcendence. Indeed, it is a moment during which ordinary language with its ordinary categories, distinctions and dichotomies, collapses:

> Glory, then to Him who is such that when the intellects contemplate His essence, their apprehension turns into incapacity; and when they contemplate the proceeding of His actions from His will, their knowledge turns into ignorance; and when the tongues aspire to magnify Him by means of attributive qualifications, all eloquence turns into weariness and incapacity (I/58, p. 137).

The climactic moment of passionate apprehension that is both immanent and transcendent, both in time and in eternity, is a moment in which dichotomies are blurred and speech collapses into pregnant silence.

To summarize, divine providence, for Maimonides, does not involve a deity who intervenes or interferes in the contingent world; it is not a matter of divine action, sovereignty, or control. Rather, divine providence involves a deity who instils reason and the capacity to use it and climb up by means of it, into some of His creatures. It involves a deity who instils, in some of His creatures, the capacity to go beyond the world, beyond suffering, dying and death, toward happiness; beyond language, beyond propositional knowledge, toward that which shows itself but which cannot be uttered in propositions; and 'beyond' space and time to eternity, to 'enduring permanence', remaining permanently 'in that state of intense pleasure' (III/51, p. 628).

II. Kierkegaard

Similarly to Maimonides, Kierkegaard too does not characterize God's providence in terms of God's agency, or sovereignty, in terms of God's interference in the ordinary state of things, to guard the righteous and punish the wicked, to ensure reward and retribution. As with other matters, Kierkegaard turns away from metaphysical dogmas toward 'subjectivity', interiorizing the life of faith and its effects. Divine agency gives way to human subjectivity; and omnipotence and omniscience give way to love, faith and hope in some of his remarks on God's providence.[10]

In a journal entry from 1854, Kierkegaard states:

> Providence is omnipresent, and so in one sense the nearest of all. But in another sense he is infinitely far away. That is to say, he does not wish to intervene with power, but he omnipotently constrains his own omnipotence, for it pleases him to see what can become of the whole existence. In a certain sense he is like a scientist with his experiment: perhaps the scientist has it in his power to get his result in another way, but he wants to see if it can be produced by this particular experiment, he constrains himself to watch the experiment, he waits in patience... (Kierkegaard 1965: 273-274).[11]

This may lead one to deny the existence of divine providence:

> In a certain sense one can therefore say that there is no providence, just as it is as though there were no experimenter, or the experimenter were nobody, since he does not intervene but just leaves it to the same steady powers to unfold. (Kierkegaard 1965: 274).

Kierkegaard, nevertheless, affirms the existence of divine providence, insisting that the non-interventionist nature of divine providence does not entail divine indifference: 'just as the experimenter and the maieutic teacher are anything but indifferent, so too God is infinitely concerned' (Kierkegaard 1965: 274). Kierkegaard insists that both concern and non-intervention are features of God's providence:

> And yet the experimenter is utterly attentive and in a flash he is there – which is only a weak image of God's presence, while in another sense he constrains himself from intervening with omnipotence (Kierkegaard 1965: 274).

Kierkegaard does not presume to address the metaphysical question 'Why does God not show His infinite concern by intervening in the ordinary state of things?';

---

10   Kierkegaard uses 'divine providence' in various ways throughout his writings. In this paper, I focus solely on those contexts in which he distances himself from divine action conceptions of providence and 'interiorizes' God's providence.

11   Søren Kierkegaard, *Journalen*, NB 34: 29; see <www.sks.dk/nb34> [accessed 27.12.2012].

or, 'Does the lack of divine intervention entail a lack of divine power, goodness, knowledge, or the very absence of divine providence?' Instead, Kierkegaard interiorizes God's providence. Divine providence is not a matter of divine power, action or agency; rather it is a matter of 'divine presence'; it is not so much transcendent but immanent; and it shows itself in 'infinite concern' and 'attention'.

If we wish to understand this Kierkegaardian 'reminder' we must explore the nature of the 'infinite concern' and 'attention' that characterize God's providential presence. I propose to do so by examining Kierkegaard's most detailed analysis of concern and attention as these show themselves in love, in God's love and in our love for our neighbours, as discussed in Kierkegaard's seminal work on love, his *Works of Love*. I shall argue that God's providential presence has to do with *our* capacity to love our neighbours.

The relation between 'divine providence' and neighbourly love is explicitly expressed, in various manners, in *Works of Love*:

> everyone (…) is first and foremost to place himself in the position where Providence can use him if it so pleases Providence. The position is just this, to love the neighbour or to exist essentially equally for every human being (Kierkegaard 1998: 84-85).[12]

God's providence is not a matter of divine sovereignty, action or intervention here; rather, it has to do with the *human* capacity to love, 'to exist essentially equally for every human being', to be attentive and concerned with every human being's needs. According to Kierkegaard, we become instruments in the service of God's providence when we realize this capacity, when we fulfil the love commandment. Thus, when we love our neighbour we fully realize our humanity, and become the primary *locus* in which God's providence shows itself. Kierkegaard proceeds:

> I wonder… whether a single one of those whom Providence has used as instruments in the service of truth (…) has arranged his life in any other way than to exist equally for every human being… Truly, only by loving the neighbor can a person achieve the highest, because the highest is to be able to be an instrument in the hand of Providence [Styrelse] (Kierkegaard 1998: 86).[13]

Providence works by means of human love; it is consequent upon love and attached to it, to paraphrase Maimonides. It is conceptually related to love and it shows itself in its presence. Our capacity to love is our *imago dei*, for Kierkegaard.

---

12   Hong and Hong have translated *Styrelse* here as 'Governance'. Since Kierkegaard does
      not seem to distinguish between '*Forsyn*' and '*Styrelse*', I used, here, the term 'providence',
      as was done in a previous translation of *Works of Love*. For more on the meaning
      and use of these terms, see also McKinnon 1973.

13   Here, too, I translate *Styrelse* as 'providence'. See footnote 12.

'Love is...devotion and sacrifice...', according to Kierkegaard (Kierkegaard 1998: 107). It is a basic attitude, a fundamental attitude or decision, which goes deep into our manner of living and acting. It is internally related to trust and hope.[14] Similarly to trust and hope, it is to encompass everyone, everywhere, at all times. Thus, just as hope is not limited by what is probable and trust is not limited to the so-called trustworthy, love too, is not limited to the so-called lovable. It is not limited to those that we preferentially tend toward in our intimate relationships, e.g., family members, friends or lovers; it extends beyond our preferential relationships to include all, be they strangers, enemies or lovers. Kierkegaard, therefore, distinguishes between erotic love and Christian love.

Kierkegaard's insistence on the equality in loving does not, however, entail the abolishment of preferential relationships. Rather, it seeks to safeguard these relationships from turning into self-serving relationships in which the other (lover, friend, parent or child) is not seen as a separate centre of gravity, with desires, needs and wishes of his or her own, but is used as a means to fulfil our own needs, desires or aspirations. It seeks to safeguard our attention and concern for the other in his or her otherness. Since our preferential relationships are in as great a danger as our non-preferential relationships of deteriorating into instrumental relationships, they have to be safeguarded. Thus, the goal is 'in erotic love and friendship, preserve love for the neighbor' (Kierkegaard 1998: 62).[15]

Love is both an attitude of concern and attention to the other's needs and a way of seeing the other. It takes love to see love; it takes the pure eyes of loving trust to discover loving trust in the world. Love and its works are not medium-sized objects, self-evident for all to see, like tables or chairs. Thus: 'we must believe in love – otherwise we simply will not notice that it exists' (Kierkegaard 1998: 26). Perceiving loving trust in others is a feature of our relating to others with loving trust; and perceiving love is an aspect of loving: 'Like is known only by like; only someone who abides in love can know love and in the same way his love is to be known' (Kierkegaard 1998: 26). Although love and its works are not 'objective' public *realia*, although there are no guarantees that can infallibly attest to the presence of love, love can be recognized by its fruits. The trusting lover is called upon 'to work so that it

---

14   For a discussion of the manner in which it is like and unlike a decision and of its relation to the will, see Ferreira 1991.

15   For a helpful discussion of Kierkegaard's attitude toward our preferential relationships, which emphasizes these relationships as an important *locus* for the fulfilment of the commandment to love, see Ferreira 2001. For a critique of Kierkegaard's views on preferential relationships, see Krishek 2009.

could be known by its fruits, whether or not these come to be known by others' (Kierkegaard 1998: 13).

Kierkegaard uses seemingly contradictory formulations to bring out the logic of loving, to emphasize that 'love's element is infinitude' (Kierkegaard 1998: 180). He states, on the one hand, that the true lover, when loving, runs into infinite debt: 'the one who loves by giving, infinitely, runs into infinite debt' (Kierkegaard 1998: 177); on the other hand, 'The one who truly loves has become richer...' (Kierkegaard 1998: 241). Both formulations emphasize that the grammar of love is the grammar of infinitude. Thus, when love is perceived as a debt, it has to be perceived as an infinite debt; when it is perceived as a pure giving, like the giving of a gift, it has to be understood as the kind of giving that does not impoverish the giver, does not reduce or diminish him but renders him richer. It is not susceptible to the rules of the financial market, in which one person's gain is always another person's loss. Thus: 'Love's element is infinitude, inexhaustibility, immeasurability' (Kierkegaard 1998: 180).

Moreover, human love is grounded in God's love. When we love our neighbour truly, God functions as the 'middle term' between us and the one we love:

> Worldly wisdom is of the opinion that love is a relationship between persons; Christianity teaches that love is a relationship between a person – God – a person, that is, that God is the middle term... To love God is to love oneself truly; to help another person to love God is to love another person; to be helped by another person to love God is to be loved (Kierkegaard 1998: 106-107).

Kierkegaard insists that 'The love-relationship requires threeness: the lover, the beloved, the love – but the love is God' (Kierkegaard 1998: 121). In Maimonidean terms, our love for our neighbour is the overflow of divine love to us, and through us to those around us, uniting us with each other and with God. Thus, for the Kierkegaardian lover, 'to love is indeed the highest good and the greatest blessing' (Kierkegaard 1998: 241).

Since our love for our neighbour is grounded in God, who is love, since 'love's element is infinitude', since it is 'the highest good and the greatest blessing', it is in loving and in the type of apprehending that loving involves, that we transcend ourselves. In other words, loving the neighbour, a particular neighbour, is both temporal and a-temporal; it is an act or attitude that shows itself in a particular time and place, toward a particular neighbour with particular needs, and also an a-temporal, infinite, transcendent mode of being that is grounded in the infinite, in God. Thus, in Kierkegaardian love too, the dichotomies between 'time' and 'eternity', 'transcendence' and 'immanence' collapse.

Despite the collapse of these dichotomies, the blessedness of love does not guarantee happiness. Kierkegaard does not share the Maimonidean optimism concerning the relation between blessedness and happiness. On the contrary, the blessedness of love is likely to lead the Kierkegaardian lover to suffer greatly. Sacrifice and loss are likely outcomes of loving:

> [I]f someone in this Christian world merely wants to strive in some measure to fulfill the duty of remaining in love's debt to one another, he, too, will be led out into the final difficulty and will have the world's opposition to contend with (Kierkegaard 1998: 201-202).

The loving trust that characterizes the Kierkegaardian knight of faith of *Works of Love* does not guard him against the world. As Simone Weil puts it: 'supernatural love ... does not protect the soul against the coldness of force, the coldness of steel' (Weil 1987: 56). The Kierkegaardian lover is vulnerable and passionate. He can be mocked, injured and tortured. In fact, he is likely to be mocked, injured and tortured. After all, he is not guided by the same principles that guide his fellow human beings; he opts for trust, being fully aware of the possibility that his trust may be ridiculed and abused. Moreover, unlike the Maimonidean sage, the Kierkegaardian lover *is* troubled 'by any of all the misfortunes in question' (Maimonides 1963: III/23, p. 492). Although 'love's element is infinitude', he does not transcend his sensations, emotions and passions, neither does he eradicate, suppress or disconnect himself from them. He does not exercise *apatheia*. He experiences his sensations, emotions and passions to their fullest. Thus, the life of the Kierkegaardian lover may turn into a glaring offence to those around him:

> In the divine sense Christianity is the highest good and therefore also, in the human sense, an extremely dangerous good, because understood in a merely human way, it is ... an offense, a foolishness... Wherever the essentially Christian is, there is the possibility of offense... (Kierkegaard 1998: 198).

Despite the painful consequences that may follow, despite the painful cost, in the deepest sense, true love can never be deceived: 'In love to believe good is ... no error' (Kierkegaard 1998: 221). This is true even when what is believed appears to be false; even when hope remains unfulfilled; even when trust leads to injury, even when love is not reciprocated. People are afraid of being fooled by others, taking them to be better than they are. The opposite attitude, however, is of greater harm, according to Kierkegaard, since the opposite attitude turns them into suspicious misanthropes incapable of love. Because the lover fears this error, he believes all things and is immune against the most dangerous error, which leads to utter destruction, namely ceasing to love, ceasing to hope and to trust – breaking one's ties with eternity. Thus, 'the one who loves, just by believing everything, can be secured against every deception' (Kierkegaard 1998: 225); he 'defends himself against illusion precisely by believing all things' (Kierkegaard 1998: 236). It is impossible to deceive him since loving trust is precisely that which he is out to give, recognizing it as the ultimate good and the ultimate blessing.

In this sense, the Kierkegaardian lover, living in love, living in trust and hope, remains unharmed for, as Maimonides puts it, He is with God and God is with him (Maimonides 1963: III/51). As long as his fundamental attitude of loving trust remains intact, he remains unharmed, since it is that fundamental attitude which is the *summum bonum*. Kierkegaard emphasizes that 'the best is love itself, and one can always keep that if one will be the truly loving person' (Kierkegaard 1998: 238). Thus:

> If to love is the highest good and the greatest blessedness, if the one who loves, just
> by believing all things, remains in the blessedness of love – how then would he be
> deceived in time or in eternity? (Kierkegaard 1998: 244)

The Kierkegaardian lover lives by an entirely different set of principles; he evaluates his life, his success and failure, his losses and gains by a different criterion from those around him. Living up to it is blessedness and the very realization of divine providence, which is likely to involve horrendous suffering.

To summarize, Kierkegaard, in some of his writings, does not construe divine providence in terms of divine agency, in terms of God's interfering or intervening in the ordinary state of things. For him, at least sometimes, it has to do with God's *presence*, which shows itself in the capacity to love, which human beings share with God. It has to do with the capacity to attend to everyone, to be concerned with everyone, without making distinctions. It is a matter of an attentive-concerned loving attitude. Love – human love – is the primary mechanism through which God's providence operates and the primary *locus* in which divine providence shows itself.

Kierkegaardian love, similarly to the Maimonidean intellect, is a *'locus'* in which the dichotomies between 'emotion' and 'apprehension', 'transcendence' and 'immanence', 'time' and 'eternity' collapse. Loving takes place in time; it shows itself in concrete acts of love, in the specific ways in which one is attentive to the needs of another; at the same time, it is grounded in eternity, in God's love. It is both imminent and transcendent, both in time and in eternity.

While for Maimonides, God's providence shows itself in the happy individual of perfect apprehension who dies in the pleasure of apprehending God, for Kierkegaard, it is the *unhappy, afflicted lover* who manifests God's providence. Insisting that true love, at least in this world as it is, entails suffering, Kierkegaard maintains that: 'Christian love is hated, detested, and persecuted by the world' (Kierkegaard 1998: 120). The images of Moses, Aaronand Miriam, who die by the 'kiss of God', in the pleasure of apprehending Him are replaced by the image of the afflicted Christ on the Cross.

III. Weil

Similarly to Maimonides and Kierkegaard, Simone Weil, too, divorces 'divine providence' from its presumed ties with divine action, reaction or intervention. Similarly to Maimonides and Kierkegaard, Weil construes divine providence in terms of a God-given capacity to perceive, apprehend, or love, a divine gift, which enables human beings to transcend the natural world and find their way back to God. Weil perceives God's providence in terms of that gift. Unlike Maimonides, however, Weil does not believe that it provides a guarantee against affliction: physical or mental; thus similarly to Kierkegaard, she relates God's providence to both affliction and love, maintaining that the two are internally related to one another.[16]

Weil explicitly denies divine intervention in the ordinary state of things, to secure reward and retribution. She emphasizes that 'God changes nothing whatsoever' (Weil 1987: 101). She states:

> God sends affliction without distinction to the wicked and to the good, just as he sends the rain and the sunlight. He did not reserve the cross for Christ.... No event is a favor on the part of God... (Weil 1987: 101).

And:

> If I thought that God sent me suffering by an act of his will and for my good, I should think that I was something, and I should miss the chief use of suffering which is to teach me that I am nothing. It is therefore essential to avoid all such thoughts, but it is necessary to love God through the suffering (Weil 1987: 101).

According to Weil, God does not intervene in the world and God's providence is *not* to be understood in terms of divine agency, sovereignty or control. The world, according to Weil, was handed over to a blind mechanism that is indifferent to human beings' moral and spiritual perfections. This mechanism throws human beings *randomly* at the foot of the cross: 'A blind mechanism, heedless of degrees of spiritual perfection, continually tosses men about and throws some of them at the very foot of the Cross...' (Weil 1951b: 69). God's providence proceeds by means of this blind mechanism. An internal relation between 'divine providence' and 'divine intervention' is thereby denied by Weil.

---

16   The following analysis relies on my discussion of Weil in Verbin 2010, Ch. 3.

Proceeding by means of the operations of the blind mechanism that it installed, God's providence creates the very possibility of affliction. The reality of affliction is part of the 'divine plan'. Divine providence is, therefore, compatible with radical affliction, with horrendous suffering: 'It does not mean that God's Providence is lacking. It is in his Providence that God has willed that necessity should be like a blind mechanism' (Weil 1951: 69).

Affliction, according to Weil, is different from suffering. It has a physical, emotional and social component. It is 'physical pain, distress of soul and social degradation, all at the same time' (Weil 1951: 77). It is the breaking down of body and soul, which makes God appear completely absent (Weil 1951: 66). It 'leaves a being struggling on the ground like a half crushed worm' (Weil 1951: 65); it 'deprives its victims of their personality and makes them into things' (Weil 1951: 69).

God's providence, therefore, does not involve particular divine acts, which are directed at guaranteeing a certain fit between one's conduct and one's well-being. God does not interfere to alter the course of events, to reward or to punish, nor does God interfere to afflict the righteous with suffering and despair: 'He did not reserve the cross for Christ' (Weil 1987: 101). Rather, God's providence has to do (1) with the installation of a blind mechanism that disregards perfection, intellectual, moral or spiritual, and (2) with the installation of a human capacity to perceive and respond to that mechanism in a variety of ways, to love God amidst radical affliction, to keep one's eyes 'turned toward God through all the jolting' (Weil 1951: 69), to assent 'to a right direction' (Weil 1951: 77) or to refrain from doing so.

By installing the blind mechanism that creates the very possibility of affliction, God's providence creates the possibility that the greatest possible distance between God and human beings is established, since the afflicted believer feels wholly distant from God, and completely abandoned by Him. Affliction allows both for the greatest possible distance between human beings and God and for the overcoming of that distance in love; it allows for the possibility that the world is transcended and the lover comes into the presence of God. In other words, when the afflicted, feeling wholly estranged from God, turns his gaze toward God and loves him, he realizes the greatest possible love of God, love than which no greater can be perceived. Weil states:

> Of the links between God and man, love is the greatest. It is as great as the distance to be crossed. So that the love may be as great as possible, the distance is as great as possible. That is why evil can extend to the extreme limit beyond which the very possibility of good disappears. Evil is permitted to touch this limit. It sometimes seems as though it overpassed it. This, in a sense, is exactly the opposite of what Leibniz thought. It is certainly more compatible with God's greatness, for if he had

made the best of all possible worlds, it would mean that he could not do very much (Weil 1987: 81-82).

Affliction and horrendous suffering are not a problem that has to be resolved but an ingenious solution, according to Weil, 'a marvel of a divine technique' (Weil 1951: 77) that allows for the greatest possible love to be realized. Weil maintains that it is our only hope:

> God can never be perfectly present to us here below on account of our flesh. But he can be almost perfectly absent from us in extreme affliction. This is the only possibility of perfection for us on earth. That is why the Cross is our only hope (Weil 1951: 71).

The hope lies in a certain freedom that we have, despite our being handed over to necessity, to the blind mechanism that governs the world. The freedom is the freedom to realize our capacity to love God, to 'continue to want to love' Him (Weil 1951: 77). We are ruled by necessity, except for this freedom, according to Weil: 'we are nailed down to the spot, only free to choose which way we look' (Weil 1951: 69). The freedom to choose which way to look is the freedom to love, for Weil. Weil emphasizes that 'love is a direction and not a state of the soul' (Weil 1951: 77); it is directing oneself toward God while being emptied of one's self during affliction, thereby allowing free passage in us to God's love.[17]

Such freedom may seem highly limited; it is not. The one who 'keeps his eyes turned toward God', like Maimonides's individual of perfect apprehension, and like the Kierkegaardian lover, is susceptible to the contingencies of the world. He may gain or lose everything that he has in an instant. He may be struck by poverty, illness and disgrace. Unlike the fool, however, unlike the one who does not keep his eyes turned toward God through all the jolting, and does not love Him, he can transcend the contingent world while remaining susceptible to the laws that govern it. He is able 'to walk on the water without violating any of the laws of nature'. She states:

> God has provided that when his grace penetrates to the very center of a man and from there illuminates all his being, he is able to walk on the water without violating any of the laws of nature. When, however, a man turns away from God, he simply gives himself up to the law of gravity. Then he thinks that he can decide and choose, but he is only a thing, a stone that falls (Weil 1951: 71).

---

17   Weil states: 'God can only love himself. His love for us is love for himself through us. Thus, he who gives us our being loves in us the acceptance of not being' (Weil 1987: 28). The capacity to offer such acceptance, i.e., to offer the 'I', can be realized during radical affliction.

It is by turning one's gaze in the right direction while afflicted that one may literally transcend oneself, transcend the self that was destroyed during affliction, and return to God.

The Weilian self-transcendence, similarly to the Maimonidean and the Kierkegaardian self-transcendence, collapses the dichotomies between 'transcendence' and 'immanence', 'eternity' and 'time'. The Weilian lover continues to exist within his body, in a particular time and location. He continues to 'have' a body. He, nevertheless, exists also in eternity:

> He ... finds himself nailed on to the very center of the universe. It is the true center, it is not in the middle, it is beyond space and time, it is God. In a dimension which does not belong to space, which is not time, which is indeed quite a different dimension, this nail has pierced a hole through all creation, through the thickness of the screen which separates the soul from God. In this marvelous dimension, the soul, without leaving the place and the instant where the body to which it is united is situated, can cross the totality of space and time and come into the very presence of God (Weil 1951: 78).

The climactic moment of radical affliction during which one turns one's gaze toward God is a moment that is both in time and in eternity; it is both immanent and transcendent; above all, it is a moment during which the greatest possible love is realized. Weil believes that this climactic moment is the moment of Jesus' death on the Cross – the ultimate manifestation of God's providence, for Weil.

The Cross marks the ultimate moment of radical affliction, the experience of the greatest possible distance from God, and the overcoming of that distance in love, for Weil. She states: 'The abandonment at the supreme moment of the crucifixion, what an abyss of love on both sides!' (Weil 1987: 79); and: '"My God, my God, why has thou forsaken me?" There we have the real proof that Christianity is something divine' (Weil 1987: 79).

Weil distinguishes between the Cross and martyrdom:

> Those who are persecuted for their faith and are aware of the fact are not afflicted, although they have to suffer... The martyrs who entered the arena, singing as they went to face the wild beasts, were not afflicted. Christ was afflicted (Weil 1951: 69).[18]

The martyrs felt an intimate connection with God during their ordeal; the crucified Jesus felt abandoned by God on the Cross; feeling estranged and abandoned by God, he could overcome the greatest possible distance from God and realize a love no greater than which can be perceived:

> One might choose no matter what degree of asceticism or heroism, but not the cross, that is to say penal suffering. Those who can only conceive of the crucifixion under

---

18   For more on Weil's distinction between martyrdom and the Cross, see Verbin 2012.

the aspect of an offering do away with the salutary mystery and the salutary bitterness of it. To wish for martyrdom is far too little. The cross is infinitely more than martyrdom. It is the most purely bitter suffering – penal suffering. This is the guarantee of its authenticity (Weil 1987: 80).

The capacity to transcend the world that has thrown one at the foot of the Cross, the capacity to cross the totality of space and time and come to the very presence of God, without leaving the place and the instant during which the body is pierced like 'a butterfly which is pinned alive into an album' (Weil 1951: 77), manifests the ultimate grace of God's benevolent providence, for Weil.

To summarize, divine providence, for Weil, is not, first and foremost, a matter of divine action, reaction or interaction; it is not, first and foremost a matter of divine sovereignty. Weil's God does not interfere in the world and its mechanical operations, altering the course of events, rewarding the righteous or punishing the wicked. God's providence has to do with the installation of a blind mechanism that disregards perfection, intellectual, moral or spiritual, and with the installation of a human capacity to respond to that mechanism in certain ways, to keep one's eyes turned toward God through all the jolting and love him. When the afflicted lover uses his freedom to perceive, to turn his gaze in the right direction and love God, he is able to transcend the world: 'he is with God and God is with him', although he remains susceptible to the contingencies of the world. He is able to walk on water without violating any of the laws of nature. He has reached 'the highest good and the greatest blessedness' (Kierkegaard 1998: 244).

God's providence lies in that interior realm, which is intellect and the capacity to go beyond its propositional manifestations, toward 'the intensity of passionate love', for the happy Maimonidean sage; it lies in love, which shows itself in one's trusting all, hoping for the best for all, caring for all, for the Kierkegaardian *afflicted* lover; and it lies in love, which shows itself in Weil's afflicted lover, who turns his gaze in the right direction, toward God, loving Him in utter despair.

The three 'reminders', Maimonides, Kierkegaard and Weil, provide a strong counter-balance to the so-called 'orthodox' picture of divine providence, which focuses on the 'control he exercises over his creation' (Flint 1998: 12). They reveal the richness and complexity of the concept; they show the various manners in which reason, passion and love, happiness and affliction, freedom and necessity feature in it, and the limited role of 'omnipotence', 'omniscience' and 'foreknowledge' in various discussions of its nature. They show that 'providence' is best understood as a 'family resemblance' concept with blurry boundaries and a great variety of manifestations. They also show that our ordinary distinctions, e.g., between 'reason' and 'emotion', between 'transcendence' and 'immanence', 'eternity' and 'time' sometimes collapse when God's providential, non-interventionist care for His creation is discussed.

Whether we endorse the optimistic Maimonidean picture of what such care involves or the more pessimistic pictures that Kierkegaard and Weil propose is an altogether different matter.

References

Craig, William Lane. 1987. *The Only Wise God: The Compatibility of Divine Foreknowledge and Human Freedom* (Grand Rapids, Michigan: Baker Book House)
_____ 1988. *The Problem of Divine Foreknowledge and Future Contingents from Aristotle to Suarez* (Leiden: E. J. Brill)
Diesendruck, Zvi. 1936. 'Samuel and Moses Ibn Tibbon on Maimonides' Theory of Providence', *Hebrew Union College Annual*, 11: 341-356
Ferreira, M. Jamie. 1991. *Transforming Vision: Imagination and Will in Kierkegaardian Faith* (Oxford: Clarendon Press)
_____ 2001. *Love's Grateful Striving: A Commentary on Kierkegaard's Works of Love* (Oxford: Oxford University Press)
Flint, Thomas P. 1998. *Divine Providence: The Molinist Account* (New York: Cornell University Press)
Hasker, William. 2004. *Providence, Evil and the Openness of God* (London and New York: Routledge)
Hong H. V., and E. H. Hong (trans. and eds.). 1967-1978. *Søren Kierkegaard's Journals and Papers*, Vols. 1-6 (Bloomington: Indiana University Press)
Kierkegaard, Søren. 1965. *The Last Years: Journals 1853-1955*, ed. and trans. by Ronald Gregor Smith (London: Collins)
_____ 1998. *Works of Love*, trans. and ed. by Howard V. Hong and Edna H. Hong (Princeton: Princeton University Press)
Krishek, Sharon. 2009. *Kierkegaard on Faith and Love* (Cambridge: Cambridge University Press)
Maimonides, Moses. 1963. *The Guide of the Perplexed*, trans. by Shlomo Pines (Chicago: University of Chicago Press)
Margolin, Ron. 2011. *Interior Religion: The Phenomenology of Inner Religious Life and its Manifestation in Jewish Sources (from the Bible to Hasidic Texts)* (Ramat Gan and Jerusalem: Bar Ilan University Press and Shalom Hartman Institute) [In Hebrew]
McKinnon, Alastair. 1973. 'The Concept of Fate in Kierkegaard', *Cirpho Review*, 1: 47-58
Perszyk, Ken. (ed.) 2011. *Molinism: The Contemporary Debate* (Oxford and New York: Oxford University Press)
Plantinga, Alvin. 1974a. *God, Freedom and Evil* (New York: Harper and Row)
_____ 1974b. *The Nature of Necessity* (Oxford: Clarendon Press)
Raffel, Charles M. 1987. 'Providence as Consequent upon the Intellect: Maimonides' Theory of Providence', *AJS Review: The Journal of the Association for Jewish Studies*, Vol. XII/1: 25-71

Reines, Alvin J. 1972. 'Maimonides' Concept of Providence and Theodicy', *Hebrew Union College Annual*, Vol. XLIII: 169-206

Rhoda, Alan. 2010. 'Gratuitous Evil and Divine Providence', *Religious Studies*, 46/3: 281-302

Strauss, Leo. 2004. 'The Place of the Doctrine of Providence According to Maimonides', *Review of Metaphysics*, 57/3: 537-549

Verbin, N. 2010. *Divinely Abused: A Philosophical Perspective on Job and his Kin* (London and New York: Continuum)

_____ 2011. 'Wittgenstein and Maimonides on God and the Limits of Language', *European Journal for Philosophy of Religion*, 3/2: 323-345

_____ 2012. 'Martyrdom: A Philosophical Perspective', *Philosophical Investigations*, 35/1: 68-87

Weil, Simone. 1987. *Gravity and Grace* (London and New York: Ark Paperbacks)

_____ 1951. 'The Love of God and Affliction', in *Waiting on God* (London: Routledge and Kegan Paul), pp. 63-78

Wittgenstein, Ludwig. 1968. *Philosophical Investigations*, trans. G. E. M. Anscombe (New York: Macmillan Publishing Co.)

_____ 1988. *Tractatus Logico Philosophicus*, trans. C. K. Ogden (London and New York: Routledge)

_____ 1993a. 'A Lecture on Ethics', in *Philosophical Occasions 1912-1951*, ed. by James Klagge and Alfred Nordmann (Indianapolis and Cambridge: Hackett Publishing Company), pp. 37-44

_____ 1993b. 'Remarks on Frazer's Golden Bough', in *Philosophical Occasions: 1912-1951*, ed. by James Klagge and Alfred Nordmann (Indianapolis and Cambridge: Hackett Publishing Company), pp. 119-154

Theodicy of Justice as Fairness and Sceptical Pluralism: A View from Behind the Veil of Ignorance

Janusz Salamon

Introduction

In this essay I sketch out the contours of my response to two of the most hotly debated issues in contemporary philosophy of religion: the problem of evil and the problem of religious diversity. Although with regard to both of these debates I take a clear stance and make substantive claims, I discuss them here primarily by way of examples that allow me to make some more general suggestions concerning the course that the philosophy of religion might take in the years to come. In this sense the present essay – which as the original sense of this word implies is a first attempt to map a research project that calls for detailed elaboration – is both in its content and its form defined by the context of the volume for which it has been written and which has among its main aims to provide some clues as to where and what kind of fresh ideas one might expect to see emerging on the horizon of the 21st century philosophy of religion. I believe this consideration sufficiently justifies what otherwise might be seen as a controversial decision to focus – despite the length constraints – on a broad picture, and I hope that the resulting less than rigid approach to the subject matter will be compensated by the breath of the claims being made.

But before I turn to identifying the direction in which my more general comments about the future philosophy of religion will be pointing, it will be helpful to summarize the positions I take concerning the problem of evil and religious diversity which are indicated in the title of the essay.

With regard to the first issue, I suggest that since for all we know God does not intervene in *all* instances or even in *most* instances to prevent evils from happening, and moreover considerations of human free will, the possibility of moral development which arguably presupposes the presence of evil, the desirability of Divine hiddenness, and the undesirability of a massively irregular world,[1] do jointly account for God's refraining in *some* instances from

---

1   I refer here to the most significant recent contributions to the debate about the problem of evil, such as Alvin Plantinga's free will defence (cf. e.g. A. Plantinga. *God, Freedom, and Evil*. Eerdmans, 1977), John Hick's 'soul making' theodicy (cf. e.g. J. Hick. *Evil and the God of Love*. Palgrave Macmillan, 1977), Peter van Inwagen's idea about the natural evil resulting from the necessary regularities of the physical world governed

acting in the world in order to prevent evils from occurring, therefore God's sense of justice as fairness which entails conditions of impartiality, equal treatment, and freedom from favouritism or bias, effectively prevents God from intervening in *any* instances to prevent evil. To put it somewhat differently: our recent insights into the nature of human justice give us strong reasons for thinking that God *never* intervenes to change the natural course of life of human and other sentient beings to prevent evils from happening, because doing so in only relatively few cases, when God is apparently prevented from doing so in all cases – even cases of horrendous of evil – would not be just or fair, and for a perfectly good and just being it is metaphysically not possible to do what is not just or fair.

I label this approach to the problem of evil 'theodicy of justice as fairness', because in proposing that in our efforts to grasp the idea of Divine justice after the Holocaust we have to take into consideration our newly acquired egalitarian insights into the indispensable worth of each individual and the related insights into the nature of justice as fairness, I draw inspiration from John Rawls's theory of justice as fairness.[2] In doing so, I suggest that within the context of a thought experiment set up along the lines of the Rawlsian 'original position', in which all individuals involved would be ignorant of their *actual* position (vis-à-vis their experiences of being victims of evils and their beliefs about evil being on some occasions prevented by God from affecting their lives), their moral intuition would lead the vast majority of the participants of such an experiment to choose as morally more plausible such a view of Divine providence which entails that God *never* intervenes to change the natural course of events to prevent evils from happening, rather than a view on which God intervenes on rare occasions to change the natural course of life of relatively few individuals and in a way that from a human point of view cannot be perceived differently than either an expression of arbitrary and baseless favouritism or of some kind of 'Divine utilitarianism' which allows God to 'sacrifice' countless individual victims of evils in order to achieve some overall positive outcome. In doing so the participants of our thought experiment would favour theodicy of justice as fairness over theodicies which entail that God *sometimes* does intervene to prevent evils from happening and which claim that we have no

---

by laws of nature (cf. e.g. P. van Inwagen, *The Problem of Evil*. Oxford University Press, 2006), and arguments for desirability of Divine hiddenness put forward by various authors (cf. e.g. D. Howard-Snyder, P. Moser, *Divine Hiddenness: New Essays*. Cambridge University Press, 2002, also: R. McKim, *Religious Ambiguity and Religious Diversity*, Oxford University Press, 2001).

2   Cf. John Rawls, *A Theory of Justice*, Revised Edition, Harvard University Press, 1999.

reason to expect that God should make sure that we grasp the reasons God has to act in the world in such an outrageously selective way.

With regard to the second issue, namely the philosophical challenge of religious diversity, I propose that God's sense of justice – or rather our understanding of Divine justice through the lenses of our modern insights concerning the moral nature of human persons – falsifies all exclusivist theories of religious diversity that entail soteriological exclusivism (pertaining to chances of salvation / liberation / ultimate fulfilment), moral exclusivism (pertaining to the chances of acquiring moral knowledge and achieving full moral maturity), mystical exclusivism (pertaining to the chances of experiencing God's presence and entering the communion with God), or for that matter any other exclusivism that one can think of that would have a bearing on the chances of the fulfilment of the creaturely potential of human persons.

I label this response to the challenge of religious diversity 'sceptical pluralism'. I do so because instead of postulating any kind of relativism or revisionism that might undermine one's epistemic confidence in the foundations of one's religious worldview, spiritual practice, and moral commitments, I propose to adopt a strategy akin to the strategy of sceptical theism[3] and suggest that we should be sceptical of our ability to discern the full truth about the ways God leads various individuals to the ultimate fulfilment of their creaturely potential. In particular, a sceptical pluralist of the kind I envisage will argue that we should be sceptical that our epistemic confidence in our understanding of God's purposes with respect to us individually and our co-religionists somehow limits God in achieving the purpose of leading other people – especially religious aliens – to the fulfilment of their human (God-given) potential in ways that are beyond our intellectual grasp. Moreover, a sceptical pluralist will propose that we should grant that our inability to think of a good reason for allowing religious diversity to persist and indeed to flourish is indicative of whether or not God might have a good reason for allowing it. If there is a God, he knows much more than we do about the relevant facts regarding the diversity of religious beliefs and practices and regarding their soteriological, spiritual or moral efficacy in allowing various individuals to fulfil their human potential, and thus

---

3   Cf. e.g. M. Bergmann. 'Skeptical Theism and the Problem of Evil.' *Oxford Handbook of Philosophical Theology*. Eds. T. Flint and M. Rea. Oxford University Press, 2009, pp. 374–402; W. Alston. 'The Inductive Argument from Evil and the Human Cognitive Condition,' *Philosophical Perspectives* 5, pp. 29-67; K. Durston. 'The consequential complexity of history and gratuitous evil,' *Religious Studies* 36, pp. 65-80; S. Wykstra. 'The Humean Obstacle to Evidential Arguments from Suffering: On Avoiding the Evils of 'Appearance,' *International Journal of Philosophy of Religion* 16, pp. 73-93.

it would not be surprising at all if God has reasons for allowing religious diversity to persist and flourish that we cannot fathom.

As in the case of theodicy of justice as fairness, I suggest that within the context of a thought experiment set up along the lines of the Rawlsian 'original position', in which all individuals involved would be ignorant of their actual position (this time vis-à-vis their worldview, religious beliefs, religious affiliation, and other factors relevant to the case), their moral intuition would lead the vast majority of the participants of such an experiment to choose as morally more plausible such view of a Divine plan for humanity which entails that God positively allows religious diversity to persist and flourish, and consequently God will also make sure that all individuals – whatever their religious beliefs and religious affiliations – will in principle have a chance to achieve the ultimate fulfilment of their human potential, rather than a view on which only relatively few individuals in the course of human history will have a chance to end up in the camp of God's favourites who happened to have the right kind of religious beliefs and religious affiliation, as exclusivists of various sorts presume is indeed the case.

In the first chapter I set the stage for a detailed elaboration of my responses to the problems of evil and religious diversity by showing that since attempting to 'read God's mind' regarding the way God sees and relates to the victims of evil and adherents of various religious traditions we are always explicitly or implicitly doing perfect being theology, therefore in doing so we ought to utilise our *new* insights into the realm of values (such as the egalitarian and individualistic insights into the nature of human persons). This is so, because in ascribing meaning to Divine attributes such as Divine goodness and Divine justice which we predicate about God by way of analogy of attribution, we have no choice but to rely on our *current* moral intuitions as to what *human* goodness and justice entails in the first place. Thus in trying to approximate our human view of things to 'God's eye view' of the matter, we can take advantage of the peculiar relation between the realm of facts and the realm of values that obtains only in the case of God as a perfect being. This peculiar relation between 'Divine axiology' and 'Divine ontology' makes perfect being theology a theoretically effective method, as I hope will be evident from my application of it to the debates about the problem of evil and religious diversity.[4]

---

4   Speaking about perfect being theology, I will have in mind a method of arriving at true or verisimilitudinous – in the Popperian sense – beliefs about God by assuming that God is the most perfect or maximally great being and then asking what consequences for God's nature follow from this assumption. The great-making properties that the maximally great being cannot fail to possess will be properties that it is intrisically

I. Evolving Moral Imagination and the Meaning of God's Goodness

Going back to the future of the philosophy of religion, I will make few methodological recommendations and then I will return to theodicy of justice as fairness and to sceptical pluralism in order to show how these two theories I put forward are shaped by the concerns expressed in my methodological recommendations.

First of all, I believe that the academic discipline of the philosophy of religion does not need to be restricted to a debate about the existence and attributes of the eternal and immutable God conducted in such a way that would allow philosophers of religion to ignore the wealth of *new* insights into human experience coming from a variety of sources, including human and natural sciences, arts and literary studies, and indeed from the philosophical inquiry, especially from these branches of philosophy which interact with the sciences. Instead, philosophy of religion, having a Socratic mission to help *contemporary* people to reflect *critically* on their religious beliefs and practices, is in need of constant confrontation with the new scientific discoveries and intellectual trends that shape the context in which a belief-holder in question is immersed, or else may be accused of betraying its critical calling and becoming merely a tool of apologetics.

Here I want to focus on just one category of such new insights that should inform philosophy of religion which, by being responsive to the concerns of the contemporary public, remains intellectually relevant, namely the new insights into the nature of the human individual that emerged somewhere at the intersection of political theory, moral philosophy, and moral psychology and has changed dramatically the social landscape of our planet. The way a human person and her place in a society and in the Universe is perceived today is so different from the way it had been perceived 5, 10 or 15 centuries ago, that it would be deeply disappointing if the philosophy of religion done in the 21st century would not differ much from a similar intellectual enterprise done in the context of, say, the High Middle Ages.

Thus I propose that in approaching the central problems of contemporary philosophy of religion which concern in one way or the other the way God *relates* to human persons, we should incorporate the recently gained insights into the nature of human persons (such as individual moral autonomy, the indispensable value of an individual vis-à-vis community, or the equal worth

---

better to have than to not have. For this reason, at least with regard to God's moral properties, such as the properties of 'goodness' and 'justice', we have to apply our human intuitions about perfection in order to arrive at any beliefs about God.

of all individuals), which underlie the apparent evolution of our ideas about morality and justice and which guide the profound global changes in social and political life. I suggest that in this respect much of the contemporary philosophy of religion appears to be somewhat lagging behind other academic disciplines, clinging to the moral intuitions formed in much earlier eras of human history, characterized by strictly hierarchical social structures and for this reason marked by the absence of the egalitarian and individualistic views which today we are increasingly inclined to take for granted.

The above proposal has primarily a methodological character, because it concerns the way in which our (changing) moral intuitions inform our understanding of the claims about the attributes of God (especially the Divine attributes of omnibenevolence and omnipotence) which are involved in assertions about the way God relates to and acts in the human world. What this claim amounts to is a rejection of the possibility of any 'theology from above' strictly understood, if this term would be taken to refer to a set of propositions about the way God relates to his creatures which would have an ahistorically fixed meaning and so would be unable to be affected by the evolution of our human moral intuitions about the nature of human persons. Instead I suggest that such propositions are always interpreted within a context of an explicit or implicit perfect being theology, which entails that understanding how a perfectly good being is expected to relate to other beings will depend on our particular moral intuitions concerning what being good in relation to human and other sentient beings might amount to.

The dependence of our intuitions concerning the evaluation of God's actions directed towards human persons on our intuitions concerning moral evaluation of human agents can be uncontroversially established against the background of the analogical theory of religious language, according to which the perfections we attribute to God, such as goodness or justice, are attributed to God on the basis of our prior attribution of such terms to human beings. Having said that, it seems that the claim that our moral intuitions concerning goodness and justice with regard to human agents cannot fail to affect our understanding of the Divine attributes of goodness and justice will remain valid whatever theory of religious language one will adopt.

That our moral imagination – that gives shape to our particular moral intuitions which we have to rely upon when attempting to identify God's attributes and purposes – is not unchangeable is evident from the undeniable fact that today a far broader range of acts directed towards other human persons draws from the public a response of moral outrage, than would be the case in more or less distant past. By way of example, let us remind ourselves that for all we know the belief that God approves of human sacrifices was at some point of religious history nearly universally held. That sacrificing innocent human beings may please God (or gods) appeared thinkable not just to the Aztecs, Mayas, Vikings and the likes, but also to the Greeks (as is evident from the story of Agamemnon) and the Hebrews (as is evident from the story of Jephte, only somewhat less evident from the story of Abraham, and perhaps to some extent even from the story of Jesus). Now let us compare it with the moral intuition of Dostoyevsky's Ivan Karamazov, for whom the suffering of innocent children makes such a moral mockery out of this world (supposedly) planned and willed by God, that even if this suffering would somehow ultimately contribute to some positive total outcome (or even to the 'best of all possible worlds'), he 'respectfully returns God his ticket'. I can think of contemporary people whose moral imagination might make them to be inclined to 'return God their ticket' in response to the extreme suffering of animals, or might make them to refuse to 'join God in heaven' in which there would be no place for their beloved pet animals, because their moral intuition would make them think that the morally perfect God could and should be more generous than that.

Incidentally, it is inessential that *differences* in moral beliefs of the kind just mentioned may be identified across cultures, not just across times, because a global pattern of changes in one direction is discernible in a way that clearly supports the claim that human moral intuitions concerning what God would be expected to do or not to do are likely to evolve together with our intuitions with regard to what kinds of treatment of other human beings are good or not.

Lastly, let us turn to a less anecdotal example of evolution of moral imagination that is more directly relevant to our present purpose which includes considering the evolution of human understanding of Divine justice. I have in mind the near universal acceptance of human *inequality* within the context of religious worldviews, traditions and institutions. There is no need to provide extensive arguments of a historical nature to establish the claim that religions have an (un)impressive record of opposition to social changes leading to greater social equality and recognition of equal worth of every human person. Once certain new achievements of humanity – such as the establishment of democratic forms of government or securing basic human rights and freedoms, including freedom of belief – become so much a part of the shared moral imagination that they begin to be taken for granted, religions often accommodate their position and begin to hold that these new moral insights were in fact always implicit in their teachings. I believe that in such cases they are indeed always right, because new moral insights of humanity to the degree they are true, are always indirectly new insights into the perfect goodness of God, whose goodness at an earlier point was less adequately conceived (and always remains such to a greater or lesser degree). However, what should not be overlooked in this example is that by *de facto* accepting the idea of the moral progress of humanity (in terms of moral beliefs, if not in terms of the application of these beliefs in moral practice), religious people implicitly admit that their *present* moral intuitions – through the lenses of which they see not just their own moral obligations to others, but also 'see' the moral character of their God – are in principle always open to revision, change, and hopefully improvement (which will amount to approximating in an asymptotic way to a 'God's eye view' on the moral realm).

This revisability of our moral insights, that underlie and shape some of the most important beliefs about God's moral character and the moral status of human persons vis-à-vis God, is the crucial point I want to make in this part of the essay, since later I want to suggest that these beliefs in turn inform the way one is inclined to think about such issues as the problem of evil and religious diversity.

However, let me first elaborate further on the unavoidability of the reliance on our human moral intuitions in our 'reading God's mind', whether by doing perfect being theology or interpreting the Scriptures.

Among the properties that theists attribute to God, goodness and justice appear to be the two most 'anthropomorphic' ones. There are important thinkers (e.g. Aristotle, Sankara, Spinoza) who do have a clear conception of the Absolute and who do not attribute properties of goodness or justice to the Absolute in a way that would call for and make possible analogical predication, which constitutes the basis of attribution of such predicates to the God of theism. Also, the religions of the pre-Axial Age did not stress the centrality of these 'moral' attributes in their conception of the Divinity, and their Divinity was considered worthy of worship in virtue of its power, rather than its goodness. In fact, it is this very shift from the focus on the power of the Divinity to the focus on the moral perfection of the Divinity (and the accompanying shift from the ideal of a religious human person as possessing magical powers which allow him to influence the Divinity to the ideal of a saint as an outstandingly ethical person whose moral character facilitates a mystical contact with the Divine), which accounts for this most profound and dramatic change in the history of religion. No comparable change took place since then and we still can be said to live in the same era in the history of religion that had its beginnings some 25 centuries ago and which is characterized by intense focus on moral perfection as the central component of the conception of holiness, both when applied to God and to human worshippers of God. Incidentally, this theistic focus on the centrality of the moral perfection of God is the very reason why only in the context of theism the problem of evil and the need for theodicy (literally: a demonstration of God's justice) arises in the first place.

Thus we attribute to God these 'anthropomorphic' qualities of goodness and justice, and our possibilities to 'purify' these particular predicates from their anthropomorphic imperfections in the process of attributing them proportionally to God are limited, because if we move too much in the direction of 'negative theology' by stressing the radical dissimilarities between Divine goodness and justice and human goodness and justice, we risk that so much meaning will get lost that we will be unable to say anything meaningful about God. Still, no other option is available, because while we may feel that we know what we are talking about when we define Divine omniscience and omnipotence as, say, unlimited knowledge and unlimited power, and we can do it without relying on our understanding of human knowledge and human power in such a way that this understanding will be open to constant revision over time, definitions of Divine goodness as unlimited goodness and Divine justice as unlimited justice will remain vacuous without attending to our *current* conceptions of human goodness, and this need will be even greater with regard to justice, since the meaning of this term will be even more difficult to fix and will be open to greater variations across times and cultures.[5] Incidentally, that our understanding of goodness and justice predicated in the human context evolves over time is evident not just from the profound changes in the conceptions of social justice, but also from the profound changes in the religious conceptions of human holiness.

These changes in our understanding of human and Divine goodness and justice will take place within a hermeneutic circle, where new insights into the nature of human goodness and justice will affect the way we conceive of Divine goodness and justice, and vice versa. It seems that the dialectical moral progress (which may refer to acquiring new moral insights absent at an earlier stage of human history or to the universalisation of moral insights which at an earlier stage were applied in a more restricted way) takes place when new moral insights are gained either at the religious level (as when new insights into the Divine goodness and justice leads someone – e.g. a Hebrew prophet – to advocate a change in the way moral obligations towards other human beings are conceived) or at the moral level (as when new insights into

---

5   As it happens, I'm putting final touches on this text having just visited the site of the Buchenwald concentration camp. The notorious slogan that is displayed at its gate: 'Jedem das Seine' ('to each his own') is something of a definition of justice to be found in Plato, Aristotle, and Cicero, and clearly has been intended as such by the Nazis. Here we have an example how different meanings can be attributed to the term 'justice'. One may presume that at least some of the people responsible for bringing about the horror of the Nazi concentration camps believed in God and that their understanding of Divine justice was appropriately shaped by their understanding of human justice.

the moral nature of human persons lead someone to advocate a change in the way the moral character of God and the way God relates to human beings is conceived).

One might suggest that this spiral dynamics of the moral progress is entailed in the Judeo-Christian idea of *Imago Dei*, grounded in the biblical assertion (in three passages of the Book of Genesis 1:26-27; 5:1-3; 9:6) that human beings are created in the 'image' and 'likeness' of God. Even though God's transcendence – which calls for the application of the analogy of proportionality in making any assertions about God on the basis of the qualities shared by human beings with God – seriously limits our ability to 'see God's face' in the mirror of our humanity, that is to identify Divine attributes by attending to fundamental human attributes (especially if one believes in some sort of 'Fall' or corruption of the human nature after its creation), still it may be argued that at least as much of the trace of the Divine in humanity is left, namely human openness to the realisation of the original potential for imitating God in his goodness, truth, and beauty (and whatever other transcendental concepts might be applied to both God and human beings).

It seems that to detect this human openness to infinite fulfilment, it suffices to attend to our awareness of our own finiteness, incompleteness, and mortality with its accompanying threat of annihilation of all meaning. Be that as it may, our main concern here, at least for the moment, is with our ability and the necessity of dialectical progression from insights into the human nature to insights into God's moral character and vice versa. This much should be uncontroversial: one's view of human nature determines to a significant degree one's view of God's nature, of God's moral character, and of the way God relates to the human world, and also one's 'image of God' may inform in a profound way one's view of the human nature, human dignity, and more generally humanity's place in the cosmos.

From our discussion so far we should be able to draw a number of conclusions relevant to the debate about the future of the philosophy of religion in general, and to the ongoing debate about the problem of evil and religious diversity in particular.

It is clear that philosophy of religion – and, for that matter, theologies of various religions – cannot in a long run retain its relevance to a critically-minded contemporary public without endorsing the idea that we think and speak about God and God's purposes and actions employing human concepts and human language, which makes our God-talk provisional and historically conditioned. This is true also when it comes to making assertions about God's moral character, God's moral demands upon humanity, and God's relation to and action in the world, since such assertions rely on our evolving moral intuitions which are affected by the overall changes in human self-awareness and self-consciousness.

Our human conceptions of goodness and justice typically precede our interpretation of the truths of the Revelation (however this is conceived) regarding Divine goodness and justice, and without the employment of these such conceptions would remain incomprehensible. Therefore unless one is prepared to pay the price of endorsing some extreme 'literal' interpretation of the Scriptures that does not allow the question of interpretation even to arise, one should be prepared to open the religious discourse to contributions from all kinds of sources of new insights into the nature of the human person, including human, social and natural sciences, which will weigh in on the interpretation of the Scriptures, making it provisional, that is in principle always open to revision in the light of new insights.

One benefit of such an opening up of religious discourse should be the resulting avoidance of radical divergences between religious and 'secular' discourses regarding the same aspect of the human reality (and this may be especially relevant to the debates about the problem of evil and religious diversity we attend to in this essay). There seems to be no obvious reason to expect the existence of a gulf between these two kinds of discourses – religious and secular – about the human condition. Especially in the light of the aforementioned tendency that religions often at the end of the day endorse new insights and new claims that they initially resisted, there are no reasons to assume that future new insights into the reality of human existence will not prove to be valuable and able to be accommodated by religious believers and incorporated into a religious discourse.

Moreover, given the changing nature of our moral imagination and its relevance for our efforts to identify God's attributes and purposes by using the method of perfect being theology, there is no reason to expect the philosophy of religion to be, by nature, a 'conservative' discipline – as it is often perceived – committed to defending the rationality of the beliefs that religious believers happen to hold already, rather than being a profoundly progressive force focused on challenging people to examine critically their current beliefs. A philosophy of religion that will take into consideration the contributions of 'secular' sources, such as human, social and natural sciences, will be likely to challenge – in the spirit of the Socratic ideal of critical inquiry – the established views and claims, approaching them with plausible suspicion that they incorporate insights formed in conditions and contexts that make them at least in part obsolete. For example, an outdated, parochial view of God as a tribal Divinity from whom action in the spirit of favouritism is to be expected, or a view of God as a feudal sovereign, will weigh in heavily on one's approach to the questions concerning religious diversity, as well as the questions concerning the ways God attends to and deals with the victims of horrendous evils. In such cases exposing the problematic and implausible elements of one's belief system, rather than defending *en bloc* its epistemic rationality (which, as Reformed epistemologists have shown, is not always a tall order) seems to be the appropriate task of the philosophy of religion.

II. Theodicy of Justice as Fairness: Facing Reality and Taking Responsibility

Having indicated why and how new moral intuitions can generate new ideas in the philosophy of religion, we should be able to see clearly the rationale behind bringing the Rawlsian insights into the nature of justice to the debates about the problem of evil and religious diversity. Rawls's theory of justice as fairness has one fundamental characteristic that makes it a source of valuable insights into the meaning of justice that cannot be ignored in the discussion of Divine justice, namely it takes into consideration our modern intuitions concerning equal worth and indispensable dignity of every human person to a degree that was absent from other theories of justice, including the utilitarian one, not mentioning the earlier conceptions of justice – such as the ones to be found in Plato or Aristotle – which took human inequality for granted and/or were prepared to give precedence to the claims of a community over the claims of individuals.

As I suggested in the previous chapter, in our efforts to grasp something of the meaning of Divine justice, in order to be able to answer the question what kind of treatment of human beings by God is God likely to consider just, we have to begin with the most plausible and up-to-date conception of human justice (that is, what kind of treatment of human beings by other human beings we consider just). Following my own advice, I pick up John Rawls's conception of human justice as (currently) the best available approximation to the truth of the subject matter. To the degree to which our modern conception of human justice is an approximate truth, we are justified in assuming that it is the best approximation to how God sees the matter. In this particular case, since I find the conception of justice as fairness to be the most plausible of the available contemporary conceptualisations of relations between human persons that we perceive as just, it follows that I'm justified in suggesting that our understanding of what kind of treatment of human persons by God is God likely to perceive as just has to be analogically related to the view of the matter implied in Rawls's theory of justice as fairness. In short, Rawls's egalitarian and individualist insights into the nature of human justice must inform our understanding of Divine justice.

As mentioned above, the debate about the so-called problem of evil is at its core a debate about just treatment of the victims of evil by God. Since it is assumed that God is indeed perfectly just (without such assumption the problem of evil does not arise in the first place), what is questionable is *our* adequate understanding of Divine justice, and more broadly, of the way God relates to humanity and each individual human person. I suggest that our understanding of Divine justice is inadequate to the extent it does not incorporate the conditions of fairness, such as impartiality, equal treatment, and freedom from favouritism or bias.

As I have already indicated in the introduction, I believe that since for all we know God does not intervene *all the time* or even *most of the time* in the natural course of life of the victims of evils to prevent evil from happening – and I believe that God can be said to have good reasons for refraining from intervention on *some* occasions – therefore due to considerations of justice as fairness it would not be right for God to intervene on only some rare occasions in order to prevent evil from happening in the lives of *few* individuals, while the vast majority are apparently left in the face of evil without God's active assistance. If God has legitimate reasons – and God has to have them – not to intervene to prevent the sorts of evils exemplified by the horrors of the Holocaust which would leave even the biblical authors defending God's justice speechless, then the only way to make some sense of the talk about Divine justice after the Holocaust is to conceive the relationship between God and the human world in a way that retains fairness as the parity of treatment of all individuals by God. Given the pattern of the occurrence of horrendous evils in the history, the only fair option one can think of is a world in which God *never* intervenes in the natural course of human lives to prevent evils from happening. Needless to say, if God fails to intervene to prevent horrendous evils, it would be morally outrageous to suggest that God intervenes to prevent minor evils from happening.

What I will do in the remaining part of this chapter, will be, on one hand, considering possible counterarguments against my position, and, on the other, drawing the implications of the theodicy of justice as fairness for the Divine-human relationship in general, and implications for understanding Divine providence in particular.

One possible criticism of the theodicy of justice as fairness – which is a theodicy, rather than a 'defence', as it suggests actual rather than possible reasons for God's never intervening to prevent evil from happening – is the likely response to it by a sceptical theist. A sceptical theist will reject my suggestion that we have no choice but to rely on our intuitions concerning human justice when trying to establish what Divine justice might entail. Instead, a sceptical theist will argue that our ability to intuit what human justice may entail has no bearing on our ability to discern God's reasons for acting or refraining from acting in any particular instance, including in the instances of the occurrence of horrendous evils. A sceptical theist holds that if there is a God, then God is a being that knows much more than we humans do about the relevant facts, and hence it would not be surprising at all if God has reasons for doing or allowing something that we cannot grasp, and moreover God has no obligation to share with us his reasons.

The objection of a sceptical theist can be dismissed on at least two grounds. Firstly, most of the biblical authors do not seem to see a problem in using human moral intuitions to understand God's view of good and evil, justice and injustice. The biblical *locus classicus* which highlights the unavoidability of such an approach is Abraham's reaction to God's announcement that he is about to destroy Sodom to punish its sinful inhabitants. The exchange between Abraham and God may be considered one of the philosophically most memorable fragments of the Hebrew Bible, since in it Abraham apparently points towards the same conclusion as does Socrates in *Euthyphro*, namely that our human understanding of good and evil must *precede* any apprehension of God's moral character.[6]

The text in the *Book of Genesis* 18:23-25 reads as follows: 'Then Abraham came near and said, "Will you indeed sweep away the righteous with the wicked? Suppose there are fifty righteous within the city; will you then sweep away the place and not forgive it for the fifty righteous who are in it? Far be it from you to do such a thing, to slay the righteous with the wicked, so that the righteous fare as the wicked! Far be that from you! Shall not the Judge of all the earth do what is *just*?".'[7] Thus we see that Abraham takes it for granted that his moral intuition regarding such an obvious matter as killing innocent inhabitants of Sodom cannot differ from God's view of the matter. Killing innocent inhabitants of Sodom just cannot be 'right' and 'the Judge of the earth' – by which Abraham clearly means: 'a God that is perfectly just' – is unable to do what is not right. So sceptical theism is clearly foreign to Abraham, otherwise in this situation he would have to refrain from making any comments about any course of action God could take, because he would have to assume

---

6   Of course, on a theistic interpretation of reality, there is no option of God being immoral or amoral, and moreover human moral intuitions may ultimately be seen as metaphysically grounded in God, despite being epistemically independent of any revealed Divine commands, so strictly speaking Abraham does not face here any Euthyphro-type dilemma.

7   Quoted from *The Bible*. New Revised Standard Version, Harper Collins, 1989.

that even if his moral intuition would tell him that certain courses of action are clearly morally wrong, he should always be sceptical about his ability to discern God's reasons for acting or refraining from acting in *any* particular instance. Even though one should not overlook the fact that on a number of other occasions Abraham's moral intuitions were such that today we wouldn't be inclined to share them with him (intuitions concerning slavery, polygamy, inhuman treatment of his slave-wife Hagar and their son Ishmael, to mention just a few), surely Abraham's trust in his own moral intuition and the resulting intercession on behalf of the righteous inhabitants of Sodom is an attitude one would expect from the Father of Faith, whose relationship with God has been described as one of *covenant*.

This brings me to the second ground of my refutation of the potential sceptical theist's criticism of the theodicy of justice as fairness, which is that a sceptical theist presupposes a model of the Divine-human *relationship* which from the point of view of our modern moral imagination appears to be morally unacceptable. Sceptical theism implies not only that we should not expect to be able to identify God's reasons for refraining from intervention to prevent evil from happening, but also that ultimately we cannot know for sure what is God's moral assessment of any given situation. Let us consider what is perhaps the most extreme example of horrendous and (apparently) gratuitous evil known to history, namely the case of the German Nazis killing more than one million Jewish children. It seems that a sceptical theist would have admit that from his point of view the following analysis of the case would make sense. God is justified in permitting such evil to happen, if (a) it was a part of God's exceedingly complex – and hence *beyond our grasp* – overall providential design of things that best forward the chance of salvation for all involved, or (b) the evil in question had in a long run good enough consequences which justify it – again consequences totally *beyond our grasp*, although not beyond the grasp of God, or (c) God did in fact intervene to save few hundred thousand other Jewish children, and God did not act arbitrarily saving some but not other children, but *we are not in a position to know* all the relevant facts that God knows to appreciate the fact, that God saved the maximal number of children that was possible to save, given other considerations, such as free will of the perpetrators, the need for God to remain hidden to preserve human freedom, etc.

It is one of the central claims of this project that we should allow ourselves to be guided by our modern moral intuitions in being suspicious of any theological claims (such as the ones just mentioned) that entail models of the Divine-human relationship that are clearly opposed to our contemporary conceptions of the indispensable dignity and equal worth of every human person. God as a perfect being may be infinitely greater in every respect than human beings, but when it comes to giving meaning to the Divine attributes of goodness and justice, God cannot fail to be *at least* as good and as just as our human moral intuitions concerning moral ideals expect him to be. Again, we can use a Rawlsian 'veil of ignorance' type of procedure to determine what kind of model of the Divine-human relationship would be chosen as optimal. I suggest that the model of the Divine-human relationship that is likely to be selected 'behind the veil of ignorance' will – despite the metaphysical gulf between God and his creatures – be the one that will be to the greatest degree informed by our modern democratic, egalitarian and individualistic moral insights. This model will draw on our most positive human experiences of close intimate interpersonal relationships built on partnership, openness, trust, communication of intentions, solidarity, freedom, autonomy, and respect for individuality.

Perhaps the most central element of such an optimal model of the Divine-human relationship will be God's respect for metaphysical uniqueness, indispensability, irreplaceability (for a want of better words) of every individual human person. There is no need to argue at length that such a model of the Divine-human relationship does not allow God to be an ethical consequentialist who would be free to calculate in a utilitarian fashion what kind of individual sacrifices God's overall providential design of things calls for and justifies. Having ascribed to every individual human person an absolute value, God is no longer free to dispose of them as pawns in some kind of Divine chess game which will have a happy end, except that before it will reach an end it reminds one of a slaughterhouse – to use Pierre Bayle's imagery – rather than a chess game. God cannot *use* any of his creatures – creatures that he not only respects, but loves with infinite love – as means to some end, even if this end would be bringing into existence the best of all possible worlds (which, needless to say, must necessarily be a world in which each creature is always a goal in itself and never merely a means). God cannot consent to the annihilation of one man to save a nation, nor can he consent to one deer dying a slow and painful death in a forest fire, so that other animals could learn a lesson that fires may be dangerous. A perfectly good God cannot be concerned only with achieving certain goals (even if these goals are all about bringing about what is good for creatures). *How* these goals are achieved is equally important, because surely treating the creatures in the right kind of way must itself be one of the main goals of creation, given the moral character of God as a morally perfect being.

Another thing from the list of postulates of a sceptical theist that God – which would act in accordance with our optimal model of the Divine-human relationship selected 'behind the veil of ignorance' – could not do is withholding permanently the possibility of human beings – who willy-nilly participate in a cosmic drama of history in which the stage is set up by God – acquiring knowledge about God's reasons for doing or not doing things as he does. What I mean by this is that God cannot do (or refrain from doing) things that affect human beings for reasons that of their nature could not be communicated to those affected. A perfectly good God cannot have any other reason for intervening or not intervening in particular way in the human world than the good of those affected. One can find in some religious traditions metaphorical images of the Divine purposes – like Divine dance or Divine play – which do not presuppose such anthropocentric understanding of Divine action, but it is hard to think of a plausible theistic understanding of Divine action, that is not creature-centred. Thus the goods that God has to have in mind are, so to speak, 'goods for us'. God cannot 'use' his creatures to achieve goods that are good only for God, or goods that are good for some angels or extraterrestrials, because that would amount to treating us as means to an end. But if the reasons for God acting or refraining from acting are goods for us and God takes us seriously and respects our autonomy, then he can do things that affect us only for reasons which he can, at least in principle, communicate to *us*. The only acceptable (on our model of the Divine-human relationship) qualifications to that rule (that God shares his reasons with those affected by his actions or his refraining from action) would be the ones having to do with protecting freedom of human will, since in the case of finite beings, as we are, knowledge of certain facts might sometimes restrict our freedom, and for this reason our limited knowledge or lack of knowledge may sometimes be a condition *sine qua non* of our freedom and autonomy, as is argued – convincingly, as I think – in the debate about Divine hiddenness. In short, our optimal model of the Divine-human relationship which would be chosen 'behind the veil of ignorance' presupposes that God 'shares his mind' with his creatures, and the only question that remains is 'when' and 'how', not 'whether'.[8]

At this stage one might ask: given that human history is apparently full of horrendous evils, and keeping in mind that the central claim of the theodicy of justice as fairness is that God's sense of justice prevents God from intervening in *any* instances to change the natural course of events to prevent

---

8   Jesus seems to have something similar in mind when he tells his disciples: "I do not call you servants any longer, because the servant does not know what the master is doing; but I have called you friends, because I have made known to you everything that I have heard from my Father." (Quoted from *The Bible*. New Revised Standard Version, Harper Collins, 1989.) Leaving behind the master-servant model of the Divine-human relationship and rethinking philosophical theology through the lenses of the 'covenantal' relationship of 'friends' or partners is what this essay aims to suggest.

evils from happening, what then is so positive about this view of the human reality in which God does *not* intervene that made God choose to create this kind of world, rather than to realise some other available option, including not creating human and other sentient beings at all? I see this world in which God out of respect for equality and absolute value of each human person does not intervene to prevent evils as indeed a preferable option to a world presupposed by some other theodicies, such as sceptical theism. We have already mentioned some positive characteristics of the relationship between God and creatures in our optimal world selected by perfect being theologians 'behind the veil of ignorance'. Let me spell out some other features of this optimal world (which is, of course, the *actual* world).

First of all, the relationship between God and human beings inhabiting the world in which God, due to considerations of justice as fairness, does not intervene to prevent evil from happening may be helpfully defined as a relationship of covenant, to use a biblical term. By this I mean a relationship in which despite the metaphysical gulf between God and the creatures, God treats creatures as *partners* to a maximal possible degree. In fact, the metaphysical difference between God as the infinite being and creatures as finite beings is the *only* source of qualifications of this relation that prevents one from speaking about God and creatures as *equal partners*. I suggest that the world presupposed in the theodicy of justice as fairness is more of a world in which God and creatures are partners – as opposed to other types of relationships formed in less egalitarian and democratic contexts, such as king and subjects, master and slaves, lord and servants, or father and children – and for this reason it is a world morally more agreeable than the world presupposed in some other theodicies.

I presuppose that this covenantal relationship is established by God the Creator as a free gift of love, and as such can be thought of as a bridge above the metaphysical gulf defined by the metaphysical difference between God as the necessary being and creatures as contingent beings. Two things follow from this.

One is that by deciding to establish such a covenantal relationship of partners, God freely chooses to limit himself in what he can or cannot do in this relationship without contradicting the character of this relationship, and by doing so God elevates the creatures to such metaphysical heights and so significantly 'shortens' the metaphysical distance between himself and creatures, that it no longer can be said that creatures have no claims to God's treatment adequate to their metaphysical status as possessing absolute value (which in our contemporary 'secular' parlance – rooted in not so secular philosophy of Immanuel Kant – is expressed in terms of indispensable value and equal worth of each human person). That by creating partners for himself God constitutes them as possessing absolute metaphysical value should not be seen as overtly controversial, because God cannot love something that has no absolute value, and indeed even in our creaturely love by loving the Other we constitute the Other as possessing absolute value, making him or her unique, indispensable, irreplaceable. Even we can do it, that is to say, even we have a power to *create* by constituting another as a bearer of absolute value, and this act of constituting is done by the loving one, not the loved one, hence the metaphysical 'limitations' of the loved one do not deprive the loving one of this creative power. Which brings me to a suggestion that even greater metaphysical gulf that exists between God and other non-human sentient beings does not deprive God of the power to constitute each non-human sentient creature as absolutely valuable and capable of being loved by God, who cannot love anything that has no absolute value.

The potential of this covenantal relationship of partners may also be conceived in a very exalted terms, worthy of a perfect being theologian. Actually, some of the mainstream Eastern Orthodox thinkers, such as Vladimir Lossky, Georges Florovsky, or John Zizoulas, elaborating on Ancient Christian patristic ideas, came up with a portrayal of the Divine-human relationship that couldn't be more exalted. They see the Divine-human relationship as possessing a potential for infinite fulfilment – which they appropriately call deification (*theosis*) – and a most intimate participation in the Divine life (*koinonia*).

In short, the world in which God does not intervene to prevent evils from happening may possess some profoundly attractive features, which may actually be seen as more attractive than a world in which God himself would directly take care of the hungry, the sick, and the afflicted, but did not open to them a profound perspective of full participation in the Divine life.

But one may ask: couldn't God do both? It is plausible to think that the answer to this question is 'no'. The theodicy of justice as fairness presupposes many of the features of the world as portrayed by John Hick in his soul-making theodicy. In order to grow spiritually and to achieve the personal maturity that is a condition of the future union with God, we need to encounter evil both as an expression of our creaturely finiteness and contingency, and as an appropriate context for developing selflessness, integrity, and capacity for genuine love and solidarity with other human beings and the entire creation.

But my main reason for suggesting that we should accept that God does not intervene in human affairs to prevent evils from happening is twofold.

Firstly, I think that after the Holocaust it is *irresponsible* to stick to the traditional interpretations of Divine providence grounded sometimes in not just pre-modern, but pre-theistic picture of the world in which gods were taking direct care of trees growing, streams flowing, and stars falling. Surely it must be an act of extreme irresponsibility to teach children – in the age of genocides, which is hardly over – that God has a comprehensive providential plan and nothing happens without God's permission, when it is sufficiently clear that God is unlikely to stop us when we will be about to blow up the planet or annihilate the human race. Instead, what is called for at the present stage of human history – and what most probably God expects from the stewards of his Creation – is facing the facts and taking *full* responsibility for the future of humanity and the future of all sentient beings, whose suffering only we ourselves can reduce.

Secondly, approaching the issue of responsibility from a different angle, I think that 'behind the veil of ignorance' we will be inclined to think that the world which contains evil and in which God does not intervene to prevent it, is preferable to a world which contains evil and God intervenes in it only on occasions, because in the former God puts much greater *responsibility* for the world in the hands of humanity and this is an expression of God's seriousness about the status of the Divine-human relationship as a covenant of partners. We are familiar with an experience of becoming more mature when taking upon ourselves serious responsibility for other people. When exercising such responsibility we begin to see ourselves and the world very differently, than when we cultivate a view of the world as seen by a powerless and immature child which is taken care of and unable to take responsibility for itself and others. The exalted status of human beings as God's partners and the future perspective of the communion with God calls for creating conditions that facilitate our significant growth in maturity. Hence, we have reason to think that God responds to this need of ours by giving us *full* responsibility for the earthly fate of humanity and for the shape of the world we inhabit. Therefore we have reasons to be sceptical about theodicies which portray God as, on one hand, pulling all the strings and taking care of even trivial matters, but, on the other hand, refraining from acting when millions of innocent people are being slaughtered, or, on one hand, supposedly having detailed plan regarding everything that happens, but, on the other hand, concerned with leaving space for actions of such free human beings as Hitler or Stalin. Such portrayals of God's relation to the human world lack the simplicity and plausibility which is needed to convince us 'behind the veil of ignorance' where we are choosing among our moral intuitions concerning the way in which a perfectly good God should relate to the human world.

What is necessary to make the view of the world free of God's intervention in human affairs a *religious* view is preserving the possibility of religious experience and retaining some kind of notion of Divine providence. Neither of these constitutes a problem for the theodicy of justice as fairness. Firstly, given the nature of the relationship between God and his creatures as portrayed in this essay, one may expect that God will be interested in making his loving Presence to be experienced by his creatures (in ways that are appropriate, given the metaphysical and epistemic constraints involved in finite beings experiencing the Presence of the Absolute). As to the meaning of Divine providence on this picture of the Divine-human relationship, it would have to be primarily some kind of 'providence from within', which would amount to God guiding, inspiring, and strengthening us, as we take full responsibility for our life. So understood, Divine providence would itself be continuous with religious experience, and none of them presuppose God's direct intervention in the natural course of lives of his creatures. This was, of course, about so-called 'particular' providence, that is pertaining to individuals. When it comes to the so-called 'general providence', according to which God is continuously upholding the existence and natural order of the Universe and sustaining all human and other sentient beings in existence, the theodicy of justice as fairness does not call for any significant revision of the traditional view of this aspect of Divine providence.

As to the possible worry that this 'hands-off' kind of God will be kept insufficiently busy, if he will not be expected to intervene in human affairs to prevent evils from happening, exactly because the theodicy of justice as fairness faces reality as it is without trying to present it in brighter colours (as do some other theodicies by pointing to possible good consequences of even the most horrendous evils), theodicy of justice as fairness presupposes that God will in due time have to redeem all gratuitous evils in order to make the ultimate fulfilment of the human potential of the victims of evils possible. Following in the footsteps of Kant, I suggest that we should postulate the existence of such possibility beyond death, and this time God will have to take full responsibility for establishing such possibility.

But everything on this side of Lethe God left in our care, and repairing the world (*tikkun olam*) is ours, not God's, task.

III. Sceptical Pluralism: Making Room for Freedom and Solidarity

In the Introduction to this essay I have already stated the main propositions entailed by the theory of sceptical pluralism. In the first two chapters I have elaborated at length on the main considerations that have to be taken into account when approaching the debates about the problem of evil and religious diversity in the spirit of an ethics of belief formed 'behind the veil of ignorance'. In what follows, I will limit myself to spelling out only briefly the most important consequences of the position I advance and I will contrast it with some alternative responses to the philosophical challenge of religious diversity.

As was the case with theodicy of justice as fairness, I suggest that in order to settle the truth of the matter regarding religious diversity we should proceed by doing theology through the prism of axiology, that is trying to 'read God's mind' concerning the way God relates to the adherents of various religious traditions by asking what kind of attitudes or actions of God could in this context be considered just or fair. Thus here again I propose to consider this question (what Divine justice might entail) within the framework of perfect being theology which aims at approximating our human view of reality to 'God's eye view' of reality by way of gradual 'purification' of our human conceptions from their deficiencies and imperfections (accounted for primarily by the limitations of our cognitive faculties and perspectival character of our conceptual schemes). I suggest that such purification of our conceptions regarding religious diversity should be guided by the ethics of belief which takes seriously the challenge of doxastic religious pluralism (i.e. coexistence of conflicting religious truth-claims with a rough *parity* of epistemic justification) and should be informed by considerations of fairness.

It is my contention that adapting for the purpose of the analysis of religious disagreement the Rawlsian idea of deliberation 'behind the veil of ignorance', we unavoidably end up in an anti-exclusivist camp in the debate about religious diversity. For the purpose of this essay it suffices to define religious exclusivism very broadly, as a belief that only one particular religious tradition (or sometimes, though rarely, a family of closely related religious traditions) is in some sense true and soteriologically efficacious in an *unqualified* way and hence has a privileged position vis-à-vis other religious traditions. Such provisional definition of exclusivism is sufficient for our purposes, because *any* version of religious exclusivism one can think of will be rejected 'behind the veil of ignorance' (that is when all involved in the thought experiment set up along the lines of the Rawlsian 'original position' will be ignorant of their *actual* religious beliefs and religious affiliations).

First of all, religious exclusivism will be rejected 'behind the veil of ignorance', because incorporating into the conception of Divine justice the conditions of fairness, such as impartiality, equal treatment, and freedom from favouritism or bias, and taking into consideration the contingency of religious beliefs of the vast majority, if not all, of religious believers (by which I mean the accidental nature of the circumstances which have a decisive impact on the formation of one's religious beliefs and on one's religious affiliation), one will have every reason to think that God's attitude towards adherents of various religious traditions would be profoundly unfair, if exclusivism were true.

Secondly, the covenantal model of the Divine-human relationship as partnership – which, as I argued in the previous chapter, is likely to be chosen 'behind the veil of ignorance' as the most plausible model to adopt in the light of our new moral insights into the nature of interpersonal relationships – entails that we should expect God to respect the absolute value and dignity of *each* human person, which surely would not be respected by God, if being in epistemic error (concerning the truth about religious matters) by no fault of one's own would have such dramatic consequences for the chances of the ultimate fulfilment of one's human potential, as religious exclusivists typically imply.

As already mentioned, this model of the Divine-human relationship does not allow for utilitarian treatment of individuals (and whichever religious tradition happens to be privileged in an exclusivist manner, religious aliens are likely to constitute the vast majority of humanity), therefore 'sacrificing' individual 'religious aliens' within the framework of some particular overall Divine plan of salvation will be out of question.

Moreover, the covenantal model of relationship presupposes the possibility of openness, trust and communication of intentions (perhaps in the Divine-human relationship it will be more appropriate to speak about 'discoverability' of Divine intensions), while the situation in which the vast majority of humanity finds itself on the exclusivist picture of religious diversity looks more like a situation of permanent deception, since adherents of each religious tradition typically find themselves believing that they hold correct religious beliefs and follow the right path to the religious goal (and however this goal may be defined in various religious traditions, it always implies the possibility of the ultimate fulfillment of the human potential). As the advocates of the Reformed epistemology and others have argued convincingly, religious beliefs (and other propositional beliefs, for that matter) are typically *not* directly under one's voluntary control, and moreover they are typically formed under conditions and circumstances which are not under control of the belief's holder. If one adds that even those adherents of various religious traditions who have a chance (and most of them do not) to attend in a serious manner to the conflicting truth-claims challenge typically end up confident in a rough parity of epistemic justification, if not in superiority of their epistemic situation, then it seems that we are left with only two options that are compatible with the character of the Divine-human relationship of partnership: (a) either we assert that an appropriate degree of openness, trust and communication of intentions does indeed exist in this relationship, and the adherents of various religious traditions are *not* being deceived by God when they firmly hold to their religious beliefs they found themselves believing involuntary, from which it will follow that beliefs of adherents of *various* religious traditions are in some sense correct; or (b) the beliefs in question are in some sense or to some degree not correct, but they are incorrect only to the degree to which holding incorrect (or less than fully correct) religious beliefs is *irrelevant* for the chances of the ultimate fulfilment of the human potential, in which case, although one will be able to conclude that in the Divine-human relationship the possibilities of openness and communication of the truth about the subject matter under consideration are limited (and there may be variety of reasons for that, such as the imperfection of human cognitive faculties, desirability of Divine hiddenness to preserve human freedom, etc), still the *essential* elements of the Divine plan for humanity *are* discoverable, and the epistemic confidence of the adherents of various religious traditions who believe they grasped the Divine intentions that concern the fulfilment of their human potential can be justifiably relied on. Neither of these two options, (a) and (b), is available to an exclusivist.

To sum up, the considerations that emerge from the analysis of the challenge of religious diversity 'behind the veil of ignorance' speak against the plausibility of religious exclusivism and lend support to an anti-exclusivist stance.

Let me now explain why I choose the term '*sceptical* pluralism' to describe the position I take on this issue. The deliberation 'behind the veil of ignorance' is in itself insufficient to formulate rationale for sceptical pluralism. As I have just shown, such deliberation provides only arguments for rejection of exclusivism. Since my overall approach to the challenge of the religious conflicting-truth claims relies on the 'original position' type thought experiment (and on the assumption that we need to rely on our up-to-date moral intuitions when giving meanings to God's attributes such as Divine goodness and Divine justice), consequently I propose *twofold* typology (exclusivism, pluralism) of responses to religious diversity as sufficient for mapping adequately the debate under consideration, and indeed superior to the now-standard treefold typology (exclusivism, inclusivism, pluralism) introduced three decades ago by Alan Race and Gavin D'Costa.

First of all, I propose that the provisional definition of pluralism (a version of which I advocate in this essay) should be formulated in purely negative terms, as a denial of exclusivism. It is the exclusivist who first formulates his position and makes substantive positive claims (ascribing epistemic and soteriological superiority to one religious tradition, stating that adherents of some religious traditions hold false religious beliefs and are in high risk of eternal damnation, etc.). Therefore given the rough parity of epistemic justification which the parties involved in the conflict of religious truth-claims enjoy – a parity which even Alvin Plantinga, the most influential philosophical defender of religious exclusivism, will be ready to acknowledge[9] – the burden of proof will rest with the exclusivist, who – against the background of our modern egalitarian and individualistic insights – will have to provide plausible explanations and scenarios which would give us some clue as to why a perfectly good God might like to limit the chances of the ultimate fulfilment[10] of the human potential of the vast majority of the members of human race which by no fault of their own happen to hold religious beliefs which are not correct. Now, while an exclusivist has no choice, but to make substantive positive claims in order to spell out his position, a pluralist can refrain from making positive claims other than denying the truth of exclusivism. He can limit himself to defending an anti-exclusivist stance.[11] Refraining from making substantive positive claims and from trying to answer the question *how* God will bring it about that all human persons – whatever their religious beliefs and religious affiliations – will in principle have a chance to achieve the ultimate fulfilment of their human potential, helps to avoid running into troubles that pluralism of the kind advocated by John Hick has

---

9   Cf. Alvin Plantinga, 'Pluralism: A Defense of Religious Exclusivism', in Philip L. Quinn and Kevin Meeker (eds), *The Philosophical Challenge of Religious Diversity*, New York: Oxford University Press, 2000, pp. 172-92.

10   When speaking about 'the ultimate fulfillment of the human potential', I don't refer merely to the post-mortem salvation/liberation in the eschaton, but I presume that the potential for ante-mortem human flourishing is not of no significance for the ultimate fulfillment of the human potential, and that forming the right kind of alignment with God here and now is crucially important for human flourishing, therefore disparities in the chances of forming such an alignment here and now will have an important bearing on the chances of the *ultimate* fulfillment of the human potential. This is an important consideration, because it calls into question the plausibility of the solution to the problem of religious diversity offered by some Christian inclusivists, who wish to retain all the elements of the full-blown exclusivism, with the exception of one concession, namely allowing that the God of Jesus Christ prepared a nice surprise for the religious aliens who proved themselves to be people of good will, but failed to hold the correct religious beliefs: such people will in the eschaton discover that they were wrong, but nevertheless they will be granted salvation by the God of Jesus Christ.

11   In doing so the pluralist can adopt a strategy akin to the strategy employed by the defenders of anti-evidentialism in epistemology of religion (here again, Alvin Plantinga may serve as a good example). For this reason the position I advance might as well be labelled 'sceptical anti-exclusivism', rather than 'sceptical pluralism'.

difficulty to avoid, especially the troubles resulting from the excessively revisionist character of his theory.[12]

When pointing out to the revisionist consequences of Hick's pluralistic hypothesis, I have in mind the kind of revisionism which may be avoided without giving up the core tenets of pluralism. As is evident from what has been said in the previous chapters, I adopt a view of religion according to which *some* religious beliefs are *permanently* revisable, but (a) they are being revised, as it were, *from within* a religious tradition in the light of perfect being theology, which no religious tradition can afford to ignore without denigrating human reason in a way that will be totally out of tune with the contemporary intellectual climate, and (b) they are being revised primarily in the light of new *moral* insights. Consequently, unlike Hick, who by adopting the Kantian epistemological framework makes substantive *metaphysical* claims, I propose to refrain – as far possible – from making such theoretical commitments and substantive positive claims which are difficult to defend, and moreover are unnecessary for establishing pluralistic position understood in negative terms as a rejection of religious exclusivism.[13]

It is this objective to evade the difficulties to which Hick's version of religious pluralism is exposed that motivates my move towards *sceptical* pluralism, which involves framing the response to the challenge of religious diversity by adopting a strategy akin to the strategy of sceptical theism. However, it has to be stressed that sceptical pluralism does not entail anything like radical agnosticism about God's nature and God's purposes concerning his creatures. On the contrary, as we have seen, the first step towards establishing our anti-exclusivist position was made by drawing moral insights from perfect being theology, and for this reason *all* elements of the theory of sceptical pluralism have to be in harmony with the deliverances of perfect being theology. Thus a sceptical pluralist is not at all sceptical about the truth of the matter when it comes to the question of *what* is God's intention concerning adherents of various religious traditions (it is, needless to say, the ultimate fulfillment of their God given human potential), because this much we will be able to discover guided by perfect being

---

12   I discuss this aspect of Hick's pluralistic hypothesis in 'John Hick's Philosophy of Religious Pluralism: A Critical Examination', *Forum Philosophicum International Journal* 8(2003), pp. 67-80.

13   While my overall position on religious diversity differs in a number of respects from that of Philip L. Quinn, I believe that my theory of sceptical pluralism does take into account some of Quinn's key concerns and suggestions. (Cf. 'Towards Thinner Theologies: Hick and Alston on Religious Diversity', *International Journal for Philosophy of Religion* 38 (1/3) (1995), pp. 145-164).

theology 'behind the veil of ignorance'.[14] What a sceptical pluralist is sceptical about is our ability to discern the truth regarding *how* God will bring about the realisation of his intention to lead various individuals to the ultimate fulfilment of their creaturely potential. In particular, a sceptical pluralist of the kind I envisage will argue that we should be sceptical that our epistemic confidence in our understanding of God's purposes with respect to us individually and our co-religionists (and this includes *our* understanding of God's purposes supposedly communicated by God in the Scriptural Revelation of *our* religious tradition) somehow limits God in achieving the purpose of leading other people – especially religious aliens – to the fulfilment of their human potential in ways that are beyond our grasp.

Since sceptical pluralism – as a theory of religious pluralism motivated, in the first place, by concerns with God's fairness vis-à-vis the chances of the ultimate fulfilment of the human potential of adherents of various religious traditions – presupposes our (at least partial) ignorance as to *how* God will bring about the fulfilment of the Divine plan concerning humanity, therefore the threefold typology of the responses to religious diversity loses its rationale. Now all responses to religious diversity will fall into two categories: (a) responses which affirm the possibility of the *ultimate* fulfilment of the human potential of adherents of various religious traditions, and (b) responses which deny it. Now the basis of the distinction between various theories of religious diversity will be *whether* they allow for such positive solution to the problem of religious doxastic pluralism, and not so much *how* they envisage the realisation of the Divine plan. A more detailed question which will have to be attended to is whether the fulfilment of the human potential of adherents of various religious traditions for which a given theory of religious diversity allows is indeed

---

14   It is my reliance on perfect being theology 'behind the veil of ignorance' that explains why there is nothing paradoxical about my rejection of sceptical theism as a response to the problem of evil on one hand, and drawing inspiration from its sceptical strategy in my treatment of the problem of religious diversity on the other. As I see it, in both cases the deliverances of perfect being theology 'behind the veil of ignorance' suggest that we have no reason to be sceptical about God's basic intentions, and in both cases we have reasons to be sceptical about the truth of the 'traditional' theistic views of God's attitudes and actions directed towards the victims of evil and adherents of various religious traditions. So the fundamental difference between the approach of a sceptical theist and my own lies in what we think we should be sceptical about. A sceptical theist is, as it were, more sceptical than I am when it comes to identifying God's basic intentions, while I recommend scepticism with regard to our knowledge and understanding of the ways God may bring about the realisation of his intentions. I believe that this kind of scepticism may be easily accommodated by any religious tradition that is not entirely alien or hostile to apophatic theology.

an *ultimate,* that is an unqualified fulfilment, since introducing any sort of gradation of the fulfilment of human potential (e.g. allowing for a partial fulfilment of the human potential in the case of religious aliens, while reserving the ultimate fulfilment of such potential to the adherents of one privileged tradition) will fall short of the demands of Divine justice as fairness intuited by us 'behind the veil of ignorance'. By now it should be clear that all so-called 'inclusivist' theories of religious diversity, depending on what answers to the above questions they imply, will fall either into the exclusivist or the pluralist category.[15]

Having narrowed the field of the debate about religious diversity to just two options (exclusvism and anti-exlusivism or pluralism), and having already indicated the main difference between sceptical pluralism and Hick's pluralism, let me now point out the main difference, as I see it, between my approach to religious diversity and that of the exclusivists of the Plantinga kind.

Plantinga assumes that in order to get an exclusivist off the hook it suffices to show that an exclusivist is not *necessarily* committed to any moral or epistemological failures, and it will follow that he is not necessarily at fault in continuing to believe what he believes (and this typically involves a belief about the eternal damnation of religious aliens, or at least the lack of the chances of the *ultimate* fulfillment of their human potential), despite his being aware that the billions of people who do not share some of his core religious beliefs are at least equally intelligent, knowledgeable and moral as himself and his co-religionists. Plantinga compares an exclusivist to a sighted person in a society of blind people: he is justified in believing that the sky is blue because he sees it. That the blind (i.e. religious aliens) make truth-claims that conflict with beliefs of the sighted person, and that he is unable to convince them, does not make the sighted guilty of moral or epistemological failure.

---

15 By way of example, in 'Light Out of Plenitude: Towards an Epistemology of Mystical Inclusivism' (*European Journal for Philosophy of Religion* 2 (2010), pp. 141-175), I put forward an epistemological theory of religious experience, labelled 'mystical inclusivism', in which I argued that "inclusivism with respect to the issue whether adherents of different religious traditions can have veridical experience of God now, is more plausible than the Alstonian exclusivism". This, of course, makes the theory anti-exclusivist, but since I argued for this thesis 'from the point of view of a theist', I called it inclusivist, rather than pluralist. Today I would be inclined to reformulate this last point and I would say that in defending the thesis that adherents of different religious traditions can have veridical experience of God now, I am guided by insights of perfect being theology (rather than the assumptions of theism), which would allow me to call this theory 'mystical pluralism', rather than 'mystical inclusivism'.

Due to the space constraints of this essay, instead of attending to all controversial consequences of the portrayal of a believer that Plantinga's exclusivism entails, let me just point out the key similarity and the key difference between the approaches of the Plantingian exclusivist and a sceptical pluralist. Both make much of the human finiteness and contingency in general, and of the limitations of human cognitive faculties in particular. Moreover, both are likely to favour externalist accounts of the epistemology of religious belief (relying on unprovable 'insights' and 'intuitions', perhaps incorporating J.H. Newman's idea of 'implicit reasoning', Plantinga's own epistemology of 'proper function', or something along the lines of 'pure heart' epistemology implicit in the writings of some Eastern Orthodox thinkers). However, the Plantingian exclusivist's sense of human finiteness (and the externalist character of his epistemology) leads him to focus on the 'miracle' of his 'chosenness' which accounts for the uniqueness of his privileged access to the truth about God and consequently to salvation (i.e. the ultimate fulfillment of the human potential). He is not disturbed by the apparent unfairness which underlies this portrayal of Divine providence and human destiny. In contrast to the exclusivist, a sceptical pluralist's sense of human finiteness makes him doubt the anthropomorphic and self-serving intuitions concerning Divine providence and leads him to focus instead on the shared destiny of all finite and contingent creatures, on compassion in perceiving the human predicament, on hope founded in belief in God's infinite generosity for all his creatures, and on human solidarity. A sceptical pluralist is thus pulled in a different direction by his moral intuitions formed 'behind the veil of ignorance'. He *is* disturbed, indeed appalled, by the apparent unfairness which underlies the exclusivist's portrayal of Divine providence and human destiny, and he refuses to believe that such a morally outrageous plan could even cross the mind of a perfectly good God. If God have created imperfect, finite and contingent beings (and it is one of the contentions of perfect being theology that God could not create other perfect beings, hence if God decided to create, he could create only imperfect, finite and contingent beings), Divine fairness does not allow God to 'punish' creatures for their failures that derive from their metaphysical deficiencies.

One last consideration – again emerging from 'behind the veil of ignorance' – which has a bearing on the sceptical pluralist's solution to the problem of religious diversity has a more positive overtone and has to do with the nature of human freedom. As we have seen from the debate about the problem of evil, philosophers of religion tend to see human freedom as just about the most important gift of God for his human creatures. It is my suggestion that as was the case with Divine and human justice, so also our efforts to give meaning to human and Divine freedom calls for 'evolving interpretation' that will necessarily follow dialectical progression from insights into our human nature to insights into God's moral character and vice versa. There can be no doubt that the fact that the vast majority of human beings, in all times and places, formed their views of human nature in the condition of unfreedom, had a significant impact on their views of the Divine-human relationship and the role of freedom in it. Our modern moral insights into the human nature justify the suspicion that the modest and restricted role which religions often ascribe to freedom in the relation between humanity and God (and to relations within hierarchically structured religious communities which are perceived as appropriately mirroring the hierarchical nature of the Divine-human relationship), and the stress they put on human obedience to the overpowering 'will of God' which, as it were, tends to suck all freedom out of these relations, is a heritage of the era of unfreedom which hopefully is passing away. Perfect being theology 'behind the veil of ignorance' will – in the spirit of the doctrine of *Imago Dei* – suggest maximal expansion of the meaning of human freedom, setting as the only external restriction on human freedom (as opposed to logical or physical restrictions) considerations of goodness and justice. In the light of the above, there is no reason to think why freedom which in God's case involves the ability to create or not to create, choosing from among great variety of possible worlds, should not involve in the case of human individuals the ability to realise one of many possible *good* lives, choosing from among variety of *correct* ways of relating to the Absolute[16], and leading a moral life shaped by a different ordering

---

16   Needless to say, perfect being theology 'behind the veil of ignorance' will suggest that God's fairness and infinite generosity extents to non-believers. Since due to space constraints I did not address this particular issue in this essay, let me only indicate how this issue might be approached in the light of perfect being theology 'behind the veil of ignorance'. As to *moral* conditions of the chances of the ultimate fulfillment of the human potential in the case of unbelievers, little has to be said. On a perfect being theology view of moral life, a moral life *is* an imitation of the perfect goodness of God, whether one believes in God or not, hence religious belief is not necessary for moral life. When it comes to fundamental 'knowledge' of the Absolute, I would suggest that it is available to non-believers through their grasp of the Absolute Truth, Goodness, and Beauty (subject to the same limitations as the 'knowledge' of God available to a believer). I would point to the analogical nature of various kinds of religious and transcendental experiences (i.e. experiences that involve concepts of Goodness, Truth, Beauty, and perhaps other transcendental concepts) and I would develop a theory of such experiences along the lines of the insights to be found in some Eastern Orthodox thinkers who speak about 'iconic experiences', which are experiences of human reality which disclose something of the Absolute Reality, even though they are not translatable to the second-order concepts and thus akin to mystical experiences. In 'Chopin's

of values (in the spirit of Isaiah Berlin's value pluralism) than equally moral but different life led by other individuals.

Such pluralistic vision of religious reality which makes room for freedom and diversity, combined with a realistic, 'hands-off' interpretation of the relation of God to the human world (as implied by the theodicy of justice as fairness), highlights the need for human solidarity and global responsibility. Such religion of freedom and solidarity seems to conform to God's call to humanity which resonates throughout the Sacred Scriptures of all religious traditions: 'Be perfect, as I am perfect'.

Absolute: An Essay in Metaphysics of Music' (in: R. Darowski (ed.), *Philosophiae et* Musicae, Cracow, 2006, pp. 629-646), I have suggested how such non-religious insights into the Absolute Reality might be possible in the context of the transcendental experiences of Beauty.

Religious Inclusivism: A Philosophical Defence[1]

Bernd Irlenborn

Introduction

The theology of religion traditionally recognizes three affirmative ways of interrelating the multiplicity of divergent religious truth claims: exclusivism, inclusivism, and pluralism. The first two positions are related, in so far as they claim the superiority of a single religion. They differ in so far that the exclusivist holds the foreign religion to be completely untrue, whereas the inclusivist holds it to be only partially untrue. Within the theology of religion, the term 'pluralism' includes some or all of the following assumptions: (a) the diversity of opinions and world views is actually insurmountable and to be recognized as normative, (b) the conviction of another is neither inferior nor false in regard to one's own conviction, (c) there is no universally recognized meta position for the evaluation of rival truth claims, (d) religious truth claims are at best only in a mythological or relative sense true.[2]

The validity of this threefold scheme is debated for various reasons.[3] It is said, for example, that this scheme is unusable or that there are more models in addition to these three. Comparative theology[4] or religious relativism[5] are offered as substitutions for or additions to the previous models. An overall criticism of the offered scheme is, in my view, not valid. It is not the place here to give detailed reasons for this view. I will assume that the threefold scheme contains all the meaningful possibilities of affirmative interreligious relationships and that it is heuristically conducive to the analysis of religious truth claims.[6] These relationships can be applied not only at the level of religions, but also at that of individual religious convictions. Here it is possible to differentiate, such that

---

1 This article is a modified and expanded version of B. Irlenborn, 'Religious Diversity: A Philosophical Defence of Religious Inclusivism', in: *European Journal for Philosophy of Religion*, 2 (2010), 127-140.

2 J. Hick, *An Interpretation of Religion: Human Responses to the Transcendent* (New Haven/London: Palgrave, 2004), pp. 362-376.

3 Cf. G. D'Costa, *Christianity and World Religions. Disputed Questions in the Theology of Religion* (Oxford: Wiley-Blackwell, 2009), pp. 34-37.

4 Cf. for comparative theology F. X. Clooney, *Comparative Theology. Deep Learning Across Religious Borders* (Oxford: Wiley-Blackwell, 2010).

5 Cf. J. Runzo, *Reason, Relativism, and God* (London: Macmillan, 1986).

6 Cf. R. McKim, *On Religious Diversity* (Oxford: Oxford University Press, 2012), pp. 10-13.

followers of a particular religion in one theological regard think inclusivistically regarding one theological issue (when it comes to the protection of human life, for example), and in another issue they are exclusivistic (e.g. in the thesis that there is only salvation through Jesus Christ). However, this differentiation does not alter the relevance of the threefold scheme.

Currently within the Catholic tradition, since the Second Vatican Council and in the wake of the considerations of Karl Rahner, inclusivism has been the preferred position of the magisterium.[7] On the other hand, one notices a surprising lack of consideration or distance in relation to the inclusivistic concept in the field of analytical philosophy of religion. Regarding the philosophical analysis of religious pluralism, most theistic philosophers within the analytical tradition take the side of either pluralism or exclusivism. To highlight this, one need only look to the preface of their collection of essays on this subject, where Philip L. Quinn and Kevin Meeker name pluralism and exclusivism as the 'most fully developed positions'.[8] For David Basinger there are only 'two basic responses to the reality of religious diversity: religious exclusivism and religious pluralism'.[9] The inclusivist position experiences no similar reception within the analytical philosophy of religion. For example, Quinn and Meeker stress that in comparison to the two competing models: 'inclusivism faces a less certain future.'[10] For John Hick, the inclusivist position represents an 'astonishing doctrine', because it aims to bring together a claim to superiority with the recognition of the truth claim of other religions.[11] For the exclusivist Harold A. Netland inclusivism contains a number of 'somewhat ambiguous principles', which become interpreted in various ways by inclusivists.[12] In the large-scale *The Oxford Handbook of Religious Diversity* are

---

7   Cf. K. Rahner, 'Christianity and the Non-Religions', in: *Theological Investigations*, vol. 5 (London: Darton, Longman and Todd Publishers, 1966), pp. 115-134.

8   K. Meeker/P. L. Quinn, 'Introduction', in: K. Meeker/P. L. Quinn (eds.), *The Philosophical Challenge of Religious Diversity* (New York: Oxford University Press, 2000), pp. 1-37 (p. 27).

9   D. Basinger, *Religious Diversity: A Philosophical Assessment* (Aldershot: Ashgate, 2002), p. 4.

10 Meeker/Quinn, 'Introduction', p. 27.

11 J. Hick, 'Religious Pluralism and Salvation', in: *Faith and Philosophy*, 5 (1988), 365-377 (p. 376).

12 H. A. Netland, 'Inclusivism and Exclusivism', in: C. Meister/P. Copan (eds.), *The Routledge Companion to Philosophy of Religion* (New York: Routledge, 2010), pp. 226-236 (p. 228).

entries for religious pluralism, exclusivism, and relativism, but not for inclusivism.[13]

The reservations towards inclusivism in the analytic philosophy of religion have at least three motives. Firstly, the inclusivist position is not philosophically considered and analysed as such. Rather, at least among many analytical philosophers of religion, it is simply mentioned under the title 'soft exclusivism'.[14] Secondly, exclusivism, as a direct competitor of inclusivism with its claim to the superiority of its own religion, is well represented within the ranks of analytical philosophers.[15] In turn, this tendency towards exclusivism has various motives, to be found on the one hand in the logical orientation of analytical philosophy, and on the other hand in the very affirmative and bold confessional ties of a number of analytical thinkers.[16] A third reason for the reservedness of analytical philosophers of religion with respect to inclusivism lies in the fact that within the threefold scheme, as Jonathan L. Kvanvig points out, this model is the most philosophically difficult to clarify.[17] Logically, the easiest to assert and defend against opposition seems to be exclusivism. As Peter van Inwagen states: 'The only way to avoid being a religious exclusivist (other than denying the principle of non-contradiction) is therefore to have no religious beliefs.'[18]

Within this article, I wish to argue against the above presented reservations and in favour of the inclusivist model. Perhaps, because Christians have defended it solely on the basis of theological grounds, inclusivism has not received adequate attention in the debates in philosophy of religion. Thus, I shall

---

13 C. Meister (ed.), *The Oxford Handbook of Religious Diversity* (Oxford: Oxford University Press, 2011).

14 Basinger, *Religious Diversity*, p. 5.

15 Cf. for example A. Plantinga, 'Pluralism: A Defense of Religious Exclusivism', in: T. D. Senor (ed.), *The Rationality of Belief and the Plurality of Faith* (Ithaca/London: Cornell University Press, 1995), pp. 191-205; P. van Inwagen, 'Non Est Hic', in: Senor (ed.), *Rationality*, pp. 216-241; W. L. Craig, '"No Other Name": A Middle Knowledge Perspective on the Exclusivity of Salvation through Christ', in: Quinn/Meeker (ed.), *The Philosophical Challenge*, pp. 38-53; J. I. Gellman, 'In Defense of Contented Religious Exclusivism', in: *Religious Studies*, 36 (2000), 401-417; H. A. Netland, *Dissonant Voices: Religious Pluralism and the Question of Truth* (Vancouver: Regent College Publishing, 1997); P. K. Moser, 'Religious Exclusivism', in: Meister (ed.), *The Oxford Handbook of Religious Diversity*, pp. 77-88.

16 A good example of this is Alvin Plantinga and his profession of Calvinism. Cf. Plantinga, 'Pluralism'; Plantinga, 'Reply to Professor Hick', in: J. Hick (ed.), *Dialogues in the Philosophy of Religion* (Basingstoke: Palgrave, 2001), pp. 52-56.

17 J. L. Kvanvig, 'Religious Pluralism and the Buridan's Ass Paradox', in: *European Journal for Philosophy of Religion*, 1 (2009), 1-26 (p. 3).

18 P. van Inwagen, 'Reply to Professor Hick', in: Hick (ed.), *Dialogues*, p. 60.

proceed not from a theological, but from a philosophical perspective. As Quinn and Meeker have emphasised, although many religious persons hold the inclusivist view, 'no one has yet undertaken to provide the same detailed defense of inclusivism that is evident in Hick's defense of pluralism or Alston's defense of exclusivism'.[19]

In this essay, I shall develop a response to this deficiency and formulate a number of philosophical arguments towards a defence of inclusivism. In comparison to the prominent concepts of Hick and Alston, my response to the aforementioned deficit can only be an outline. Here is not the place to refer to the extensive debates about pluralism and exclusivism or to give detailed reasons why pluralism and exclusivism are not, in my view, 'the most fully developed positions' for coping with conflicting religious truth claims. I only present a few arguments which respond to this lack of an elaborated philosophical defence of inclusivism and which help to show that this position is independent and well-founded, according to the standards of analytical thinking. Particularly in relation to the challenge of religious plurality, inclusivism seems to me, in comparison to the other competing models, to be more philosophically demanding, theologically convincing and politically justifiable: It is the only position, in relation to the other two, which makes it possible to mediate divergent religious truth claims in such a way that neither are they as a whole relegated to mere mythological assertions, thereby contradicting the self-understanding of religious people (as in John Hick's pluralism), nor are the claims of one religion deemed to be true and all other claims deemed to be false without any further possibilities of conceptual differentiation (like in the 'closed' or 'restrictive-access' exclusivism[20] of William L. Craig or Harold Netland).

I am going to call the position that holds that there is a compatibility among competing religious truth claims '*epistemic* inclusivism', because it pertains primarily to epistemological considerations about religious truth claims and not to theological considerations about the way of salvation. In the first section, I analyse the idea of inclusivism. In the second section I sketch a philosophical view of inclusivism and give reasons for thinking that it constitutes the most viable position in response to the challenge of divergent religious truth claims. The third section presents a brief conclusion.

---

19 Meeker/Quinn, 'Introduction', p. 27.

20 Two types of exclusivism are to be distinguished: *closed* or *restrictive-access* exclusivism, which holds that truth and salvation can only be found in the home religion, and *open* or *universal-access* exclusivism, which considers truth and salvation possible even for adherents of other religions. Cf. D'Costa, *Christianity and World Religions*, p. 7.

II. The Idea of Inclusivism

If neither pluralism nor exclusivism are appropriate responses to the problem of religious diversity, what reasons would there then be to support a position of epistemic inclusivism? I would like to defend the following position: The inclusivist position opens up the only conceptual possibility of a believer upholding the exclusivity of her own truth claims (against pluralism), without declaring the divergent belief, or the central truth claims of that belief, to be false (against exclusivism). Inclusivism and exclusivism share the view that the doctrines of the home religion are true and truth claims of other religions incompatible with them are false. But inclusivism differs from (at least a traditional and restrictive-access) exclusivism on the question, 'whether it is possible for an alien religion to include any true claim among its doctrines and teachings'.[21] According to inclusivism, the exclusivity of a truth claim of the home religion excludes incompatible alien truth claims, though not a possible inclusion of the truth of the home religion in the alien belief system. The inclusivist can accept the fact of religious diversity and manage that fact conceptually without having to deny the superiority of her own standpoint. This kind of inclusivism should not be understood, as David Basinger claims, as a derivative 'soft exclusivism', but as a model in its own right that remains distinct from exclusivism and pluralism. Correct terminology is important here. Any position that acknowledges, theologically, the salvific force, or, philosophically, the inclusivity of at least one of its own basic truth claims within the tenets of a different religion, should be considered as an inclusivism and not as a form of universal-access exclusivism or 'soft exclusivism'.

Yet how can one think that the other religious belief is possibly only *partially* true? Is such a view, and therefore the inclusivist position as a whole, at all tenable, bearing in mind the principle of bivalence contained in classical logic, according to which any proposition is either true or false, but not true and false at the same time, and therefore not 'partially' true? The inclusivist standpoint maintained by the Catholic Church for instance is based firstly on Biblical witness, and then on theological reflection concerning the radius and centre of the divine salvific will. Regarding the truth claims of other religions, the Second Vatican Council states:

> The Catholic Church rejects nothing that is true and holy in these religions. She regards with sincere reverence those ways of conduct and of life, those precepts and teachings which, though differing in many aspects from the ones she holds and sets forth, nonetheless often reflect a ray of that Truth which enlightens all men.

---

21   P. J. Griffiths, *Problems of Religious Diversity* (Oxford: Blackwell Publishers, 2001), p. 57.

Indeed, she proclaims, and ever must proclaim Christ 'the way, the truth, and
the life' (John 14:6), in whom men may find the fullness of religious life, in whom
God has reconciled all things to Himself.[22]

This notion revolves primarily around St. Justin's Christian interpretation
of the stoic idea of the *logos spermatikos*. Theologically, this idea states that
there are or may be 'grains' of truth in other religions; a 'ray of that Truth'
(*radius illius veritatis*) that Christians recognise in Christ shines through them.[23]
This passage implies a distinction between *alethic* inclusivism and *relativistic*
inclusivism. Both versions hold that (a) there exists an absolute truth or set
of true assertions about God. Only the latter holds that (b) no religion is able
to ascertain fully the absolute truth or the complete set of true assertions about
God and (c) every religion can at best ascertain partially the absolute truth or the
true assertions about God.

'Inclusivism' in the Catholic sense refers to an alethic, that is truth-inductive
inclusivism, which defends the position that one particular religion is able
to ascertain, as the passage says, 'the fullness' of God's truth in Jesus Christ.
The following statements apply to this version of inclusivism: (i) There is
the absolute truth about God with a set of corresponding true statements, (ii)
a particular religion (here Christianity in its Catholic tradition) possesses
a superiority, because in comparison to other religions or denominations it
contains a maximum amount of true and life regulating faith convictions, which
can be connected with such an understanding of God.

But this might turn out to be more complicated than it seems at first glance.
In light of the fact that within the Catholic tradition the concept of truth, without
relativising the truth claim of the Church's own teaching, is construed
historically, insofar as 'every truth attained is but a step towards that fullness
of truth which will appear with the final Revelation of God'.[24] This distinction

---

22   'Ecclesia catholica nihil eorum, quae in his religionibus vera et sancta sunt, reicit.
     Sincera cum observantia considerat illos modos agendi et vivendi, illa praecepta
     et doctrinas, quae, quamvis ab iis quae ipsa tenet et proponit in multis discrepent, haud
     raro referunt tamen *radium illius Veritatis*, quae illuminat omnes homines. Annuntiat
     vero et annuntiare tenetur indesinenter Christum, qui est "via et veritas et vita" (*Io*
     14,6), in quo homines plenitudinem vitae religiosae inveniunt, in quo Deus omnia Sibi
     reconciliavit' (emphasis added), in: 'Declaration on the Relation of the Church
     to Non-Christian Religions *Nostra Aetate*', no. 2. See also the 'Decree on the Mission
     Activity of the Church *Ad gentes*', no. 11.
23   Cf. *Nostra Aetate*, no. 2.
24   'conscia sit omnem veritatem captam unam dumtaxat stationem esse plenam ad illam
     veritatem quae ultima in Dei revelatione ostendetur', in: John Paul II, 'Encyclical
     Letter *Fides et Ratio*', nos. 2-3.

between a 'truth attained' (*veritas capta*) and the 'fullness' of truth (*veritas ultima*) would entail, unintentionally, not alethic but a version of relativistic inclusivism. This distinction can be expressed within the metaphor of the cited document of the Second Vatican Council *Nostra Aetate*. So, read in light of this distinction, we see that Christians, too, do not yet see all rays of the Truth that is the event of Christ, but, in contrast to non-Christians, they do now see at least those rays that reveal it to be the event of *Christ*. This metaphorical view might explain why the Catholic tradition adheres to an alethic inclusivism. However, in the sentence of the Encyclical Letter *Fides et Ratio* about the distinction between the *veritas capta* and the *veritas ultima* it remains problematic, how under these conditions key tenets of Christian faith can be conceived of as being fundamentally final and irrevocable. This problem indicates that the talk of the *logos spermatikos* remains more of a metaphor, which does not take us very far in analyzing the basic problem of an inclusivist position.

The first question to be addressed is the meaning of inclusivity or inclusion in the term 'inclusivism'. Based on to the quoted passage of *Nostra Aetate*, inclusivity denotes the notion that a particular set of truth claims or at least one truth claim of a religion P (here Christianity in the Catholic tradition) is contained, or included, in a different religion S. 'Inclusion' is tantamount to 'containment'. So literally, 'inclusion' means that a truth claim or a set of truth claims of P is contained in S. The relation of inclusion is stated by a particular religion that assesses the occurrence of its own truth claims within the set of truth claims of different religions. It requires an outright interreligious commitment on the part of the inclusivist to analyse carefully the truth claims of different religions before stating any form of inclusivity.

How can the notion of inclusion be stated more precisely? Since set theory construes 'inclusion' as a particular relationship of containment between two sets of elements, it might be helpful to clarify the idea of inclusivism in light of this insight from set theory. A set A includes a set B ($A \supseteq B$), if B is a subset of A and is contained in A. If there exists at least one element of A which is not contained in B, then A is also a proper superset of B, or, equivalently, B is a proper subset of A. This relation is antisymmetric, because if A $\supseteq B$ with A $\neq$ B, then $B \supseteq$ A is false. Assume, as an example, a relationship of inclusion between a religion S with its truth claims $S_1, S_2, S_3 \ldots S_n$ and a religion P with its truth claims $P_1, P_2, P_3 \ldots P_n$. If P is a proper subset of S, all the truth claims of P must be contained in S (so that $S_1 = P_1$, $S_2 = P_2$, and so forth) and there exists in S at least one truth claim S_{n+1}, which is not contained in P.

However, it is clear that the model of inclusion of set theory thus articulated is not applicable to the issue of religious inclusivism. Even if the latter entails an antisymmetric relation between two religions (with a set of truth claims or only one truth claim of P as a subset of the truth claims of S), P could not be considered as a proper subset of S insofar as not *all* truth claims of P are contained in S. In this regard, the idea of inclusivism refers more to the intersection of two different sets, which contains all elements – i.e. truth claims – of P that also belong to S. But on the other hand, the concept of intersection does not express an antisymmetric relation as it is implied in the notion of inclusivism.

Consider an example. Religion P entails the three central and basic propositions $\{a, b, c\}$. Religion S entails $\{b, c, d\}$, religion T $\{c, d, e\}$ and religion U $\{d, e, f\}$. Here, P's truth claims b and c are included in S, and its claim c in T. No truth claim of P is included in U – but it would be possible for an adherent of P to suppose that, for the time being, no truth claim of P has yet been identified as contained in U. Even with this simple example, we can draw three conclusions for the position of inclusivism: there might be (1) one religion all of whose (or whose core) truth claims are true, (2) different degrees of inclusivity with regard to the number of truth claims of P that are contained within different religions, (3) a hierarchy of religions from the perspective of P according to the number of the truth claims of P that they contain. It should be mentioned that this interpretation is simplified in that it focuses solely on the number of occurring truth claims. It is also possible – though I am not going to do so – to emphasise the meaning of truth claims within different religions and infer from that particular hierarchies.

My explication of the core ideas of epistemic inclusivism shows us that there are epistemic advantages of inclusivism in comparison to exclusivism and pluralism.[25] With regard to exclusivism, the position of inclusivism is better differentiated in terms of the relation between one's own religion and other religions. The restrictive-access exclusivist analyses solely, under the principle of self-contradiction, the compatibility of the central truth claims of a different religion with his own core truth claims. In the case of incompatibility between these two sets of claims, the restrictive-access exclusivist tends to deny the truth and salvific force of the whole other religion – otherwise (as a universal-access exclusivist) he would hold a form of inclusivism (as I have defined it). Inclusivism allows to assert the absolute truth of one's own religion while affirming that salvation is also possible for non-Christians. For the restrictive-access exclusivist the only logical action, when confronted with a foreign

---

25 Recall that I am referring to a traditional and more restrictive or closed form of exclusivism. A 'traditional exclusivist' holds that only her own religion is true if there are no core claims of an alien religion which are compatible with the core claims of Christianity (for example, the claim that salvation is only available through faith in Christ).

religious truth claim, is to declare it false without any further differentiation. Obviously, in the case of a contradicting relationship of the foreign truth claim to one's own, this course of action is logically appropriate. Now, the explicit denial of one's own truth claim by the foreign truth claim is neither the beginning of nor the rule in inter-religious dialogue. It is often in this discourse either unclear or not immediately recognized, (i) whether this foreign religious truth claim is actually contrary to one's own truth claim (in which case only one of the two could logically be true) or (ii) whether it is subcontrary[26] (in which case both could logically be true), or lastly (iii) whether it is contrary and thereby logically incompatible, but on an underlying level able to be isolated into two or more partial statements, of which at least one is true. How this can happen shall become clear in the next section. That means, in the case of incompatibility between two sets of truth claims, the restrictive-access exclusivist tends to deny the truth and saving power of the other religion as a whole. Inclusivism allows the claim of the superiority of one's own religion together with the affirmation of the possibility of salvation also for those of other beliefs through a particular hierarchy, which is dependent upon the inclusion of one's own religious truth claims in the system of foreign religious truth claims. Thus, any form of universal-access exclusivism should be called 'inclusivism' if it identifies the inclusivity of, at least, one of its own truth claims within the tenets of a different religion.

With regard to pluralism, the sketched idea of inclusivity allows a religious person first to refer to her self-understanding and maintain the (non-mythological) truth of her single religion, and second to define a hierarchy of religions different from her true religion, which are not completely false, but, on a sliding scale, partially true.

II. An Epistemic Framework for Inclusivism

The described advantages of inclusivism are convincing only if this model receives a solid philosophical foundation, which, at this point, can only preliminarily occur. Despite these advantages, this model of inclusivism still needs a more solid philosophical underpinning. How is it possible for the inclusivist to hold, on the one side, the exclusivity of truth claims of her own religion which excludes incompatible alien religious claims, and, on the other side, an inclusion

---

26 A subcontrary contradiction is the relationship between two particular judgements, of which one is affirmative and the other is negative (e.g. 'some people are educated' – 'some people are not educated'). Characteristic of subcontrary judgements is that both cannot be false, although both can be true.

of a truth claim or a set of truth claims of her religion in the alien belief? As it was shown, the inclusivist maintains that only her religion R is true and that there is a hierarchy of religions which are, on a sliding scale, either partially true (depending on the number and the meaning of the true claims contained in R) or even false (because no truth claims of R are contained). I would now like to introduce three defining aspects of epistemic inclusivism.

(1) *epistemic inclusivity*

It is possible that different religions refer to the same God in different ways. This can be illustrated with a simple example: At t_1 observer A sees from a distance that a tower looks round, whereas to observer B, who is even further away, the tower appears rectangular.[27] At t_2, the persons get closer and both see that the tower is, in fact, round. Hence, at t_1 two contrary beliefs are held, but, as is revealed at t_2, the two observers have been successfully referring to the same object. This clearly emerges as we consider the conditions of perception of the truth claim. At t_1 observer B was able to give sound reasons for his belief, while from A's perspective it is clear that B is not mistaken in referring to the same object, but is mistaken in his description thereof. From his perspective, A has sound reasons to assume both that he is correct at t_1 and that B is referring to the same object (for instance because B is pointing at it). At this point it is helpful to distinguish three types of reference based on John Searle's theory of reference in *Speech Acts*:

(a) fully consummated reference, which identifies the object unequivocally,
(b) successful reference, which though not complete is successful,
(c) unconsummated and failed reference, which fails to lead to an identification of the object.[28]

Compared to both Quine's general scepticism with regard to the success of the act of reference (even within the system of one's own language), and the causal theories of reference developed by Kripke and the early Putnam, Searle's descriptive theory of reference has the advantage of conceptualizing the identification of the object of reference as a performative act, which with the aid of descriptors or markers can lead to unequivocal identification. Thus,

---

27 The example originates from Sextus Empiricus, *Outlines of Pyrrhonism*, chap. XIII (Cambridge, Mass.: Harvard University Press, 2000), p. 69 (I am grateful to Erik Baldwin for this hint).

28 J. Searle, *Speech Acts. An Essay in the Philosophy of Language* (Cambridge: Cambridge University Press, 1969), p. 82. Searle does not explicate separately the third form of reference.

according to Searle, successful reference is *potentially* fully consummated reference.[29]

It is precisely this transition that is at the stake in the example given above. The situation at t_1 is a case of successful reference: The tower is successfully identified as the object of reference by both A and *B*, though only *B* refers to it in an incomplete mode. Epistemic inclusivism might rephrase the performative act of reference as follows: From the internal perspective of a religion *E*, reference to God within the religion *F* can be conceived of as a case of successful, though not complete, reference.[30] It points in the right direction, allowing identification and thus distinction between God and idol, yet, from the internal perspective of *E*, still remains provisional compared to *E*'s own more precise reference.[31] Consider, as an example in the field of religion, the following belief: (B) 'The one God is not triune.' Both the Christian inclusivist and exclusivist share the view that (B) is incompatible with the Christian doctrine of the Trinity and, thus, agree that it is false. But, in contrast to the restrictive-access exclusivist, the inclusivist, by a more careful analysis, can still distinguish between (B$_1$) 'There is a God' and (B$_2$) 'God is not triune'. With regard to (B$_1$) he can acknowledge that there is an 'element' of the Christian faith included in (B). So, in terms of reference, the inclusivist may argue that – because of (B$_1$) – (B) is a case of a successful reference to the object of the Christian belief, in which case (B) is in fact able to identify the Christian God, but remains incomplete because of (B$_2$). The restrictive-access exclusivist cannot grant there is an element of truth in (B). See, for instance, the following definition:

> *Exclusivism* maintains that the central claims of Christianity are true, and that where the claims of Christianity conflict with those of other religions the latter are to be rejected as false. Christian exclusivists also characteristically hold that God has revealed himself definitively in the Bible and that Jesus Christ is the unique incarnation of God, the only Lord and Savior. Salvation is not to be found in the structures of other religious traditions.[32]

---

29   Ibid., p. 82.
30   Of course this is not to say, as John Hick's pluralist theology of religions might, that all religions refer successfully, though necessarily imperfectly, to a transcendent reality.
31   Can religion *E* still revise its strong and central beliefs? From *E*'s internal perspective, its own truth claim is, at root, the certainty that no such revision will take place, either at t_3 or at t_n. However, the foundational certainty that this involves relates only to the successful identification of the object of reference 'God', not to the scope of the set of propositions that can be predicated by it.
32   Netland, *Dissonant Voices*, p. 9. See also ibid., p. 112: 'Christian exclusivism ... contends that where the central claims of Christian faith are incompatible with those of other religious traditions the latter are to be rejected as false. Thus, for example, it

Exclusivists and inclusivists share the view that claims which are incompatible with their own religious claims are false. But the inclusivist is not automatically forced to therefore reject the other religion. With regard to the incompatible claim of other religions, the inclusivist is able to examine carefully whether it is based (a) on a fully consummated reference, which identifies God in accord with one's own religion, or (b) on a successful, albeit incomplete reference (and is therefore at least partially true), or (c) on an unconsummated and failed reference (and is therefore false). Thus, accepting incomplete reference to the same object permits the inclusivist to accept that 'false statements' about that object may be partially true. This view is available only to the inclusivist but not to the exclusivist, otherwise the latter would hold some sort of 'covert inclusivism'. This idea of an incomplete though successful reference does not only apply to particular truth claims but also to religions as theories.

(2) *doctrinal contingency*

Understood as theories, religions are under-determined and, with respect to the scope of the set of propositions that they uphold, not necessarily complete. For instance, if we understand the belief system of a religion as theory T_1 with the truth claims $S_1, S_2, S_3 \ldots S_n$, then from an internal perspective it is not ruled out that T_1 might, in light of 'progress towards the fullness of truth' develop into T_2 with the truth claims $S_1, S_2, S_3 \ldots S_n, S_{n+1}$ (broadening of the set of propositions) or $S_{1*}, S_{2*}, S_{3*} \ldots S_{n*}$ (unfolding or revision of certain propositions or attitudes). Within the Catholic Church, numerous examples of this can be found in the history of dogma. Examples of broadening include for instance the mariological dogmas of the 19th and 20th centuries. Examples of revision include attitudes towards the freedom of religion. And examples of unfolding include the understanding of revelation. This insight entails recognition of a certain form of doctrinal contingency: From the internal perspective of a given religious community, its own teaching is true at t_1, while it is not excluded that this truth may be capable of being expressed more comprehensively and precisely at t_2. In the terminology of *Fides et Ratio*, one could say that the *veritates captae* are for that reason true and irrevocable, because they refer to the *veritas ultima*. It cannot be ruled out that attained truths could be more precisely defined or that they could quantitatively increase in the future. The extent of this tentativeness, with regards to the central truth claims of a religion, must be determined by the religious community itself with

---

has traditionally been said that the Muslim and the orthodox Christian cannot both be correct in their respective beliefs about the identity of Jesus of Nazareth.'

its respective authorities. If a religious tradition disputes such underdeterminedness and thus the possibility of extending or deepening of its core beliefs, then it can only be described as radically exclusivist.

(3) *openness to learning*

The first two aspects can be strengthened by a coherentism regarding the epistemic justification of religious convictions. The logical exclusivity of a conviction does not imply an epistemic exclusivity of the set, or rather system, in which this conviction appears. Such a system cannot be *de iure* exclusive, i.e. shutting out any possible expansion or deepening, due to the finite conditions of knowledge, even when it *de facto* rejects any justification and closes itself off to the correction of former insights or to the inclusion of new ones. That such an openness to learning does not necessarily imply a revision of one's central convictions became clear through the first aspect. According to the basic intuition of coherentism, the justification of a conviction is viable within a set or system of convictions. This set is not only consistent, but also coherent:[33] the individual convictions are interconnected through various, above all inferential relationship paradigms. Nevertheless there needn't be any epistemic parity: central, exemplary or strong convictions are bound together with peripheral, singular, and weak convictions by various links. The set is highly inclusive and not closed off. Rather, it is open for the integration of further convictions, as laid out in aspect (b). In this sense, it might be helpful to offer coherence as a criterium (not as a definiens) of truth claims.[34] It opens up the possibility of interpreting the concept of 'approximately true',[35] which, according to the principle of bivalence, would be meaningless. In this respect, an inclusivistic theory must not claim an epistemic exclusivity and can nonetheless hold on to the logical exclusivity of their point of view.

---

33 Cf. W. J. Wainwright, 'Doctrinal Schemes, Metaphysics and Propositional Truth', in: T. Dean (ed.), *Religious Pluralism and Truth* (New York: State University of New York Press, 1995), pp. 73-85 (p. 80).

34 Cf. N. Rescher, *The Coherence Theory of Truth* (Washington: University Press of America, 1982), pp. 23f.

35 Cf. L. BonJour, 'Reply to Solomon', in: *Philosophy and Phenomenological Research*, 50 (1990), 779-782 (pp. 779f.). See also: L. B. Puntel, 'The Rationality of Theistic Belief and the Concept of Truth', in: G. Brüntrup/R. K. Tacelli (eds.), *The Rationality of Theism* (Dordrecht: Kluwer Academic Publishers, 1999), pp. 39-59 (p. 53), who speaks of a relative 'truth status': 'Only at the end of the day, that is, when *all* factors (data, aspects, alternatives, and the like) have been taken into account and examined, will it be possible to establish "the truth", that is, the fully determinate status of the sentences stated and the propositions articulated.'

III. Conclusion

With regard to the notion of inclusivity, the this model allows for the possibility that a particular religious truth claim as well as a religious belief can be considered as being 'approximately true'. By appealing to the three aspects – epistemic inclusivity, doctrinal contingency, and openness to learning – it is possible to philosophically construct and theologically defend an inclusivistic position while still upholding the ultimate truth of a certain *veritas capta*, yet without excluding the possibility that the *veritas ultima* might be more comprehensive and profound. Epistemic inclusivism composes the basis for that inclusivism found within the theology of religion and cannot be separated from it. Religious truth claims underlie every analysis of interreligious difference. Truth claims in all religious sectors, be they regarding transcendence, questions of salvation, or ethical precepts, imply that their presuppositions in this matter are true from the perspective of the respective religion.

In this respect, and contrary to John Hick's assessment quoted above, inclusivism is not a 'somewhat astonishing doctrine'. Hick maintains that essential attributes (like 'omnipotence' or 'being a person') cannot be ascribed to the divine reality and that religious truth claims are, at best, mythologically but not literally true.[36] We now see how it is that, for Hick's pluralism, religions are unable to refer *successfully* to the divine reality. Because of the transcategoriality of the divine reality, reference to what religions call 'God' or 'Allah' or whatever is unable, according to Hick's theory, to identify the divine reality in itself. So when Hick, for example, points out unequivocally that 'the ultimate reality, the Real, cannot be described as a personal God',[37] it follows that within Hick's pluralism the Christian attempt to refer to God as a person remains unsuccessful as it fails to identify God as he is in himself. As a result religions would only be capable of an unconsummated and unsuccessful reference to God. This claim would not only be conceptually unconvincing, it would also radically contradict the self-understanding of religious people. Against exclusivism, and without relinquishing the exclusivity that is logically inherent in her truth claims, the inclusivist can (i) accept a plurality of heterogeneous attitudes and thus co-exist at least with a minimal pluralism, (ii) on the basis of her own doctrinal contingency even learn from this other position and supplement or deepen her own teaching, and (iii) when faced with another *religious* belief or conviction, ascribe to that other position an inclusivity of truth claims of the home religion. That is, she can consistently

---

36 Cf. Hick, *Interpretation*, pp. xix-xxii, 348.
37 Ibid., p. xxii.

concede that members of other religions make successful although incomplete references to God.

Divergent truth claims of religions harbour a particular potential for both ethical and political conflict. They do so on the one hand when combined with a radically exclusivist attitude, and when they involve both strong and exemplary beliefs, thus creating a clash of world views upon which identities are constructed. They do so on the other hand when the members of the religious communities concerned lack sufficient intellectual and social competence to manage these conflicts both cognitively and politically, and to call into question an unjustified coherence of strong religious and political beliefs. The inclusivist model is empirically and epistemically the most viable position to adopt in response to the challenge of the plurality of religious truth claims. In my opinion, the challenge of the plurality of religious views consists first and foremost in the problem of whether the members of a religious community are willing to acknowledge their particularity *de facto*, without therefore having to relinquish the truth claim of their own religion. In this respect the concept of epistemic inclusivism offers major advantages.

Exclusive Inclusivism

Anita Renusch

Religious inclusivism is often presented by its advocates as if it were much more advantageous than religious exclusivism. Though its openness to other religions does not go as far as religious pluralism would require – the theory developed by Hick, Knitter and others – inclusivism is said to outstrip religious exclusivism to a considerable degree. Ever since inclusivism was vindicated for the first time, there have been doubts whether this characterization is right. My aim is to articulate these doubts more explicitly by clarifying the putative distinction between religious exclusivism and inclusivism. I argue that the claim that there are significant epistemic differences rests on an overly restrictive notion of exclusivism and a misleading use of metaphors like 'an element of truth'. I conclude that the similarities make it advisable for inclusivists to focus their attention on the problems shared with exclusivism instead of dissociating themselves from exclusivism.

I. Preliminaries

In the 1980s the two students of John Hick, Race and D'Costa,[1] introduced the nowadays widely used terminology of *exclusivism, inclusivism* and *pluralism* in the literature to differentiate attitudes towards problems of religious diversity that had been discussed for a long time before in philosophy and theology (and still are today). Historically and very roughly exclusivists can be described as those religious believers favouring their own religion, pluralists as claiming that all religions are in a sense equally valid, and inclusivists as taking a position in between. But this characterization is very rough and perhaps even false, as we will see later when looking at more detailed accounts. Since their introduction, these three concepts are often used to name three alternative responses to the same problem. In this paper I argue that this should be done more cautiously, particularly when it comes to an evaluation of inclusivism.

---

1   Gavin D'Costa, *Theology and Religious Pluralism: The Challenge of Other Religions,* Signposts in Theology (Oxford, New York: Blackwell, 1986) and Alan Race, *Christians and Religious Pluralism: Patterns in the Christian Theology of Religions* (London: SCM Press, 1983 & 1993).

In light of there being many different approaches towards the challenges arising from religious diversity it is not so clear whether exclusivists, pluralists and inclusivists are concerned with the same issue. There is a bunch of different questions all being somehow attached to the philosophical or theological problem of religious diversity: How can the diversity of religions be explained? How can religious beliefs be justified in the face of religious diversity? What do the facts of religious diversity imply for the question of who is going to be saved or liberated, the religious goal entailed by many religions? These are obviously not the only questions being discussed under the heading *religious diversity* in the above mentioned fields, nevertheless, they represent the most urgent and therefore the most prominent ones. Inclusivists do not only place their emphasis differently with respect to these questions than pluralists and exclusivists do, they also seem to presuppose answers to questions the other two argue for in much more detail. From pluralism inclusivists take their assumption that all people are going to be saved (although they differ in their belief whether this is done through some particularity of their religion, e.g. the works of Jesus Christ, or not). From exclusivism inclusivists borrow the claim that particular religious beliefs are justified in the face of religious diversity, while rival claims are not. Although a similar argument could be developed with respect to inclusivism and pluralism, in this paper I am going to concentrate my efforts on showing how inclusivism resembles exclusivism, regardless of the differing claims of some inclusivists.[2]

The taxonomy of exclusivism and inclusivism is muddied by the intermingling of three dimensions – the doctrinal, the soteriological and the experiential dimension. In the past, being an exclusivist often meant believing that one's own religion is true while others are false (doctrinal or alethic exclusivism) and asserting that only members of one's own religion could be saved (soteriological exclusivism or particularism) and taking one's own religious experiences to be authentic while the religious experiences of adherents of other religions are seen as illusions (experiential exclusivism). However, recently, and in some instances in the past as well, these three dimensions may break apart. People offered defences of doctrinal exclusivism without pledging allegiance to soteriological particularism.[3] So, there is certainly a tendency among current philosophers of religion to concentrate on what seems the epistemically most interesting

---

2   Cp. e.g. Reinhold Bernhardt, 'Jesus Christ as "vere Deus" as a Challenge for Interreligious Dialogue', *Approaching Religion*, 1 (2011), 41–49.

3   And, of course, on the other side there are defences of religious pluralism and inclusivism concentrating solely on soteriological issues, too. But those are not in the main focus of this text.

question, namely 'How can religious beliefs be justified in the face of religious diversity?', to the neglect of what seems to be a theological problem of the first order – the challenge to explain issues arising with regard to religious diversity and salvation.[4] I follow this trail to the extent that I assume it is possible to endorse doctrinal exclusivism without being a soteriological exclusivist. However, there is an important caveat to be considered. Although it is true that the concepts of salvation and liberation are central for many religions, more empirical research would have to be carried out to show whether they really have that prominent role in other religions as they have in Christianity. Pluralist John Hick claims this to be the case, yet it is not clear whether he is right. However, even if Hick was right in this regard, the connection between affirming certain doctrine and eternal bliss needs to be investigated. Do other religions relate doxastic commitment and salvation in the same way as Christianity does? And is there a similar sense of injustice many Christians feel considering the putative fact that non-Christians might not be saved? With respect to these questions surrounding issues of salvation incompatible truth-claims virtually appear as a smaller challenge, which will therefore be addressed first. However, it should be kept in mind that incompatibilities between religious beliefs obtain their importance at least partly for the connection between beliefs and salvation. At stake is not only whose beliefs are true but further who is going to be saved thanks to his or her right beliefs (provided that beliefs have any influence for the question of salvation at all).

The main challenge for defences of *doctrinal* religious exclusivism arises from the fact that there are sincere, virtuous, and intelligent people whose beliefs are incompatible with the exclusivist's religious beliefs and who, like the exclusivist herself, maintain a seemingly coherent and well-based religious belief-system. As there seems to exist no agreed method, no widely accepted evidence and no non-question-begging argument for deciding which of the contradictory claims are false and which are true, and respectively which of the belief-forming processes are reliable and which are not, the exclusivist seems to be guilty of arbitrarily favouring her own religious beliefs. On which epistemic basis is she holding her religious beliefs to be true while claiming that the beliefs of her religious opponents are false? While this important question needs to be answered in a more in-depth study than possible within the scope

---

4   Representatives of this approach are, for instance, Alvin Plantinga, 'Pluralism: A Defense of Religious Exclusivism', in *The Philosophical Challenge of Religious Diversity*, ed. by Philip L. Quinn and Kevin Meeker (Oxford, New York: Oxford University Press, 2000), pp. 172–92; and Jerome Gellman, 'In Defense of Contented Religious Exclusivism', *Religious Studies*, 36 (2000), 401–417.

of this paper, at least a first step is taken in the following, by investigating whether inclusivism and exclusivism present two different approaches to its answer. And my reply is that they do not. Defences of doctrinal inclusivism can be subsumed under defending exclusivism.

II. Doctrinal Exclusivism

What exactly does a doctrinal exclusivist maintain? Consider the following accounts of religious exclusivism:

I. The doctrines of one's own religion are true and any other religious doctrines are false.

II. An exclusivist holds 'that one religion has it mostly right and all other religions go seriously wrong'.[5]

III. '[T]he exclusivist holds that the tenets or some of the tenets of one religion – Christianity, let's say – are in fact true; he adds, naturally enough, that any propositions, including other religious beliefs, that are incompatible with those tenets are false.'[6]

IV. The exclusivist says: 'In either case, if I do adopt a certain set of beliefs, I have to believe that I and those who agree with me are right and that the rest of the world is wrong.'[7]

Though historically a) is the formulation most exclusivists would have used to describe their stance, in this restrictive form it is not very reasonable. If there are shared doctrines in the exclusivist's home religion and another religion the exclusivist would either have to admit that one of her convictions is wrong or that the other person entertains true beliefs too. As there are many shared beliefs amongst different religions the claim that all of the doctrines of other religions are not true is certainly false and therefore not worth pursuing. A form of inclusivism that is directed against this kind of exclusivism is certainly right albeit not being very interesting. Acknowledging the existence of over-lapping propositions strikes me as basic for any discussion concerning religious diversity and most educated exclusivists would have no problem in doing so. Although not very precise, b) entails a better formulation because it does not require

---

5   Philip L. Quinn and Kevin Meeker, 'Introduction', in *The Philosophical Challenge of Religious Diversity*, ed. by Philip L. Quinn and Kevin Meeker (Oxford, New York: Oxford University Press, 2000), pp. 1–28 (p. 3).

6   Alvin Plantinga, *Warranted Christian Belief* (New York: Oxford Univ. Press, 2000), p. 440.

7   Peter van Inwagen, 'A reply to Professor Hick', *Faith and Philosophy*, 14, no. 3 (1997): 299–302 (p. 299).

the exclusivist to exclude *any* true beliefs in other religions. What does 'mostly right' mean? Does this phrase accommodate the exclusivist's concession that some of her own beliefs could also be wrong? If yes, which ones? Besides, what does it mean in general that one 'religion has it right and that another one goes seriously wrong'? The best translation into epistemic terms might be something like 'one set of propositions entails largely true propositions whereas other sets entail almost solely false ones'. Any rational exclusivist would have to specify this very bold claim and c) seems to offer an elegant solution as to how this might be done. First, its expression 'tenets of a religion' narrows its scope. Second, it specifies the claims or propositions considered to be false by the exclusivist, namely those propositions incompatible with the tenets or core claims of her faith. There is no need to demote all other religious claims for the exclusivist. Asserting that the tenets of her religion are true merely requires her to think that all claims negating those tenets are false. Any just divergent or even compatible religious claims could be true nonetheless.

What about formulation d), which basically claims that one or more of one's beliefs are true and those incompatible with them are false? Although it expresses one of the fundamental conditions of assertions in general, it falls short to put into words what religious exclusivism amounts to. Religious beliefs do not appear in isolation, they are mostly connected to others. Thus, religious exclusivists affirm a set of beliefs as opposed to single beliefs. Religious exclusivists do not just want to assert that some of their beliefs are true and others are not, they also claim superiority for their religion or all the beliefs central to their religion in some sense and that clearly goes beyond just asserting that one or some propositions are true whereas incompatible ones are false. As Byrne points out, it is even more complicated, since 'conflict over the truth of religious propositions implies, although it does not entail, that there will be conflict about which religious believers have genuine religious experience and which believers are on a genuine path to salvation'.[8]

Something like c), which is put forward by Plantinga, thus on the one hand seems just broad enough to express religious exclusivism (against the too simple and narrow version in d)), and on the other hand it is not built too broad like b) and implausible like a). To summarize, the doctrinal exclusivist claims that the tenets or core beliefs of her religion are true and that incompatible propositions are false. This account still contains a good amount of vagueness as there is not only inter- but also intra-religious diversity. In most religions there is

---

8   Peter Byrne, 'A Philosophical Approach to Questions About Religious Diversity', in *The Oxford Handbook of Religious Diversity*, ed. by Chad Meister (New York, Oxford: Oxford University Press, 2011), pp. 29–41 (p. 30).

considerable debate among the adherents about the question of what the core claims of a particular religion are. However, the Roman Catholic Church's Magisterium, for instance, defines a set of dogmata specified as central and many other denominations have similar authoritative sources. Another interesting question is to what extent those pronouncements are mandatory for every single believer and thus shape her picture of what the core claims are. Since none of these issues can be addressed here the formulation c) has to be accepted as the best account, despite some remaining vagueness inherent to its 'tenets' and 'core claims'.

Inclusivists mostly see their view as an improvement to exclusivism. To find out whether they have a different position with respect to the doctrinal dimension of the problem of religious diversity and what their position is like, the main ideas of inclusivism are illustrated in what follows using the influential approach of Karl Rahner as representative. None of the other inclusivists like D'Costa, Dupuis and Bernhardt has received as much attention as Rahner, whose theory was adopted in core as the official position of the Roman-Catholic Church at the Second Vatican Council (1962-65).[9] All other inclusivist concepts were more or less influenced by Rahner's work and could be seen as developments of it. In any event, most of what I have to say about Rahner's inclusivism should apply to those other versions of inclusivism, too.

III. Rahner's Inclusivism

Karl Rahner was one of the (if not even *the*) greatest and most influential Catholic theologians of the 20th century. The German Jesuit courageously approached and wrote about new religious topics when others did not even recognize their importance. In some areas – including other religions – he went even further than many of his disciples did later. His thoughts about non-Christians, however, did not derive from extensive study of other religions or a huge number of encounters with their practitioners, but resulted from what he thought the Christian gospel says about the greatness and fullness of God's grace.

Rahner himself did not use the term 'inclusivism' in his writings, but he is certainly seen as the most powerful inclusivist in the 20th century. The catholic

---

9   The official catholic position as well as theological discussions received a variety of inputs since Vatican II, followed by developments which can be traced in several papal documents. Written in the sometimes hard to understand theological language, it is difficult to say whether the Catholic Church still formally endorses inclusivism based on these documents alone.

theologian attempted to promote a certain Christian stance towards the phenomenon of religious diversity and accomplished that task clearly in the spirit of a catholic-dogmatic interpretation.[10] Rahner did not try to occupy a neutral position as an exercise in religious studies, neither did he engage in empirical history. Instead, he views every bit of foreign religion through the spectacles of a Roman Catholic theologian. The Christian perspective is not up for discussion for Rahner. Christians, so the Jesuit assumes, cannot abandon their belief of the *presence of Jesus Christ in the history of God's grace and for all people*.[11] Rahner's explicit Christian viewpoint is something we should not forget in what follows and there is a good chance we will not, as Rahner's attitude towards other religious believers heavily depends on his treatments of *standard loci* in Christian theology – the concept and influence of God's grace.

Rahner's teaching of why God's grace embraces all people[12] is based on his conviction that a loving God wants salvation for all people including salvation for people having lived thousands of years ago as well as people living now everywhere in the world. As a consequence, Rahner says, this God exposes every single human to his grace despite any sinfulness or limitations. That is, everyone could feel graced – whether she accepts or rejects that offer – since God reveals himself to every person and offers inner community.[13] Rahner rejects any theological approaches depicting non-Christians as rejecting God's grace as cruel and implausible. Likewise he disapproves of theories claiming that God would not even offer his grace to many people outside the Christian Church because of their alleged wicked nature or because God foresees the rejection of his offer. Rahner also rejects assertions that the offer becomes ineffective in many cases because of personal guilt or that grace and human nature are not entangled and one comes after the other but seldom at the same time.

The gospel – Rahner lets us know – allows a far more optimistic view of God and salvation. As Knitter says, 'God really does want to save all people

---

10   Karl Rahner, 'Das Christentum und die nichtchristlichen Religionen', in *Schriften zur Theologie*, V, ed. by Karl Rahner, 2nd ed., (Einsiedeln: Benziger, 1964), pp. 136–58 (p. 138); and Karl Rahner, *Grundkurs des Glaubens: Einf. in d. Begriff d. Christentums*, 12. Aufl. (Freiburg im Breisgau: Herder, 1982), p. 304.

11   ibid.

12   In my following interpretation of the works of Rahner I benefit from Paul F. Knitter, *Introducing Theologies of Religions*, 9. print. (Maryknoll, N.Y: Orbis Books, 2009), pp. 68–75. Knitter was once a student of Rahner and later started to defend a pluralistic theory.

13   Karl Rahner, 'Das Christentum und die nichtchristlichen Religionen', p. 145.

[... I]f God really *wants* to save all people, God will *act*, will do whatever is necessary, to make this possible.'[14] Clearly, therefore, grace cannot be restricted to the boundaries of the Catholic Church. For Rahner, that means that grace is both offered and accepted by people outside the church and not restricted to Christians.

Postulating this was not a completely new theological move. What was new, however, was how Rahner saw the role of non-Christian religions in accepting grace. By contrast with previous Roman Catholic teaching, Rahner does not see non-Christian religions as irrelevant to or counter-productive for achieving salvation through Christ. Instead Rahner regards them as *ways of salvation* – a startling claim for most of his Roman Catholic comrades at his time. In his argument, he assumes that a proper relationship to God can only be cultivated historically and socially.[15] People attain salvation in community with others mediated through historical bodies like religions, he says. Even though salvation is through Jesus Christ – Rahner thought – there must have been bearers of the Christian revelation before Christ's coming, because God certainly wants to save all people regardless of when their life in history took place. To Rahner, this suggests that religions had this function before Christ, and there is no reason why they should not have it now. Non-Christian religions had their role in embodying grace before Christ was known and they still play this role today for people who have no acquaintance with the Christian gospel. They are no obstacles to achieving salvation as many theologians before Rahner had proclaimed (and even do so today). Instead they should be seen as proper ways to salvation. If every human being really is living in prospect of salvation in her earthly life, then many religions must be vehicles of conveying supernatural grace ('Momente übernatürlicher, gnadenhafter Art') – Rahner argues – and by practicing them their adherent can attain God's grace.[16] As Knitter points out, from Rahner's stance '[Buddhists] are saved not despite their Buddhism, as had previously been said, but because of their Buddhism'.[17]

Rahner thought it was in part an empirical question whether experiences of grace really can be found in religions and so he did not even attempt to investigate it. His part was to establish the claim that it was possible at all. He believed from a catholic dogmatic perspective non-Christian religions had to be considered as a place where people could experience divine presence.[18]

---

14   Paul F. Knitter, *Introducing Theologies of Religions*, p. 68.
15   Karl Rahner, *Grundkurs des Glaubens*, p. 306.
16   Karl Rahner, 'Das Christentum und die nichtchristlichen Religionen', p. 153.
17   Paul F. Knitter, *Introducing Theologies of Religions*, p. 71.
18   Karl Rahner, *Grundkurs des Glaubens*, p. 312.

Rahner mentions three constraints of other religions in this context. First, besides instances of grace and experiences of God's presence, religions contain or reveal elements of sin and human depravity. Error belongs to religion as much as truth does. Rahner does not want to give an overall positive evaluation of every single element in religions, not even in Christianity. However, acknowledging that religions produce negative effects too should by no means keep us from valuing their positive sides. Second, error, depravity and other negative elements are not equally distributed. Thus claims of religious legitimacy are justified to different degrees. Not all religions are equally valid truth-bearers, Rahner notices.[19] Third, he mentions as a turning point that moment when a person first encounters the Christian gospel. Rahner maintains that her religion may enable a non-Christian to cultivate proper relationship to God up to that moment when she encounters the Christian gospel for the first time.[20] Once the gospel has been heard, practicing another religion loses its previous legitimacy for that person – the other religion's purpose has been *fulfilled* as Knitter says.[21]

Remarkable or even brazen as this may seem, this conclusion follows from Rahner's view of how Christ works in other faiths, and his understanding of why becoming Christian might increase one's personal chances for salvation despite the fact that practicing another religion might also do so. To a consideration of these views we now turn.

There is one strong assumption Rahner defends at length in the first part of his *Foundations* of *Christian Faith*: viz., that Christianity is the only absolute religion, truly given by God and designed for all people. Any salvation whatsoever has its source in the God of Christendom mediated through Jesus Christ. This is how salvation through Christ works in other religions as well.[22]

---

19   It is an interesting but for our purpose less important question whether Rahner himself considered religions along some kind of scale as it was implied by the documents of Vatican II.

20   Karl Rahner, 'Das Christentum und die nichtchristlichen Religionen', p. 145.

21   According to Knitter, Rahner concedes that the gospel is often carried over in an European style so that it is hard to understand when coming from another cultural background. Paul F. Knitter, *Introducing Theologies of Religions*, p. 75.

22   Rahner tries to come by the problem of how Jesus as a historical figure can work in pre-Christian religions as well by pointing to the Aristotelian distinction between efficient and final cause. Karl Rahner, *Grundkurs des Glaubens*, pp. 309f. According to Paul F. Knitter (*Introducing Theologies of Religions*, p. 73), herein we find the key for a distinction between soteriological exclusivism and inclusivism. Whereas exclusivists require Christ functioning as an efficient cause and therefore excluding pre-Christians from receiving grace the inclusivist Rahner takes the causing relation in terms of final

Participation in God's grace or experiences of his presence are intimately connected to Christ the saviour according to Rahner, whether or not the graced person knows this in her lifetime. As grace is always mediated through Christ, people can be Christians without realizing it. They can be what Rahner calls *'anonymous Christians'*.[23]

Rahner's position questions missionary efforts as missionaries will not only meet non-Christians but also anonymous Christians, that is, people already graced who have some sense of God's presence. But if those people can attain salvation, and if they know at least in part (a fact Rahner urges missionaries to take into account), why should Christians continue to proselytise? Rahner, like many other Catholics, was convinced that humans are looking for truth. Because in Christianity we have the clearest and fullest expression of God's love, Rahner believes that missionaries are responsible to help non-Christians to achieve full awareness and commitment of their being Christians and so to grasp the Christian gospel in its whole meaning. Anonymous Christians should be led to a new phase in their development.[24] Proselytising thus is in no way redundant, says Rahner, not least because a clearer and more explicit recognition is pivotal in increasing a person's chances of getting saved.[25] In summary, Rahner thinks that other religions are legitimate in that they anticipate some elements of the Christian message even though they lose this legitimacy when adherents encounter Christianity.[26] They have provisional character according to Rahner. One of his followers, the Catholic priest Jacques Dupuis, went beyond Rahner's scheme exactly at this point by denying that the other religions' legitimacy is provisional, a move that attracted the attention of the Congregation for the Doctrine of the Faith in 2001.[27]

However, Rahner makes his assumptions so strong that there can be no doubt about his stance. Christianity for Rahner is the superior, or better the primary religion, implying our familiar formulation of exclusivism: The tenets of Christianity are true and adherence to it is more valuable than adherence to another religion. Though Rahner argues against many of his predecessors that

---

causation and thus has no problem to include people living previously to Christ's death and resurrection.

23   Karl Rahner, 'Das Christentum und die nichtchristlichen Religionen', p. 154.

24   ibid., p. 155.

25   ibid., p. 156.

26   Karl Rahner, 'Kirche, Kirchen und Religionen', in *Schriften zur Theologie*, VIII, ed. by Karl Rahner, 2nd ed., (Einsiedeln: Benziger, 1964), pp. 355–73.

27   Cp. 1. Appendix included in Jacques Dupuis, Ulrich Winkler and Sigrid Rettenbacher, *Unterwegs zu einer christlichen Theologie des religiösen Pluralismus*, Salzburger theologische Studien Interkulturell 38:5 (Innsbruck: Tyrolia-Verl., 2010).

it is not the church alone that possesses truth – a fact that moderate and recent exclusivists would not deny – he still holds that the church is 'the historically tangible *vanguard* and the historically and socially constituted explicit expression of what the Christian hopes is present as a hidden reality even outside the visible Church'.[28] In other words, Christians have the clearest and most true picture of God and his love for human people.

With respect to the question of conflicting truth-claims one might have expected a different stance given the inclusivists' claim to offer a model that is able to cope with the problems exclusivism has difficulties with. However, the most noted inclusivist of the 20th century, Karl Rahner, seems to be pretty much what we called earlier a doctrinal exclusivist. He sticks to his own religious beliefs in the face of religious diversity. When the question is whether we should do so or whether another response is rational he answers in the same way as exclusivists do pretty much to the pluralist's and agnostic's dismay. My point in this essay is not that one response is right rather than another. Rather, I am suggesting that so far as the doctrinal dimension is concerned, there is no difference between a somewhat moderate exclusivism and many versions of inclusivism. Inclusivism's wallflower existence in philosophy of religion thus is not just a result of the fact that 'no one has yet undertaken to provide the same *detailed* defense of inclusivism that is evident in Hick's defense of pluralism or Alston's defense of exclusivism'.[29] Instead, Basinger is right to assume that there are just 'two basic [religious] responses to the reality of religious diversity: religious exclusivism and religious pluralism'[30] – at least as far as the doctrinal dimension is concerned.[31]

Defenders of inclusivism might want to object that inclusivists concede that there are 'elements of truth' in other religions, a concession allegedly not made by exclusivists. Rahner himself called for forms of proselytising that give non-Christians credit for already knowing parts of the truth about God. This idea was accepted at Vatican II with the bishops proclaiming that 'elements of truth

---

28   Karl Rahner, 'Das Christentum und die nichtchristlichen Religionen', in *Schriften zur Theologie*, V, ed. by Karl Rahner, 2nd ed. (Einsiedeln: Benziger, 1964), pp. 136–58; translation taken from Paul F. Knitter, *Introducing Theologies of Religions*, p. 74.

29   Philip L. Quinn and Kevin Meeker, 'Introduction', in *The Philosophical Challenge of Religious Diversity*, ed. by Philip L. Quinn and Kevin Meeker (Oxford, New York: Oxford University Press, 2000), pp. 1–28 (p. 27), italics Quinn/Meeker.

30   David Basinger, *Religious Diversity: A Philosophical Assessment,* Ashgate Philosophy of Religion Series (Aldershot, Hants: Ashgate, 2002), p. 4.

31   Below I will consider the question of whether 'inclusivism' and 'exclusivism' are better used when naming a certain attitude or behaviour towards other religious believers, instead of something going beyond a purely epistemological distinction.

and grace' (Ad Gentes 9) can be found in other religions, that they contain 'seeds of the Word' (Ad Gentes 11) and that their teachings 'reflect a ray of the Truth that enlightens all people' (Nostra Aetate 2). Even though the Roman Catholic Church thereby turned down certain strong versions of exclusivism – ones that insist that no claims whatsoever could be true outside the Church – talk about 'elements of truth' was not completely new. In the early second century Justin coined the expression of a 'word in germ' (*logos spermatikos*), and other theologians embraced similar ideas since then.[32] However, what exactly is the idea behind such rather metaphorical talk? Irlenborn offers what he calls a philosophical defence of religious inclusivism in which he tries to specify this alleged distinctive feature between exclusivism and inclusivism.[33]

IV. 'An Element of Truth'

Irlenborn provides insights into our main question on how inclusivism is to be distinguished from exclusivism by claiming that 'they [inclusivism and exclusivism, A.R.] differ roughly in that the other religion is in its core tenets untrue for the exclusivist, but only partially untrue for the inclusivist', *core tenets* being specified as those 'doctrines and teachings to which assent is religiously required of all believers'.[34] So his definition of inclusivism reads as follows: 'I am going to call the position that holds that there is a compatibility among competing religious truth claims epistemic inclusivism' and a bit further on he says '[t]he inclusivist position opens up the only conceptual possibility for a believer upholding the exclusivity of her own truth claim (against pluralism), without declaring the divergent belief, or the central truth claims of that belief to be false (against exclusivism)'. Irlenborn summarizes the answer to our question by postulating that 'inclusivism differs from (at least a traditional and more restrictive) exclusivism on the question, "whether it is possible for an alien religion to include any true claim among its doctrines and teachings"'.[35]

While explicitly defending what he calls *epistemic inclusivism*, Irlenborn remains unspecific when it comes to exclusivism. It becomes clear in the last quoted sentence that he wants his distinction between epistemic inclusivism and exclusivism to apply to 'traditional and more restrictive' sorts of exclusivism.

---

32   Cp. Henri d. Lubac, *Geheimnis aus dem wir leben*, 2. Aufl., Kriterien 6 (Einsiedeln: Johannes-Verl., 1990) for a historical review.

33   Bernd Irlenborn, 'Religious Diversity: A Philosophical Defense of Religious Inclusivism', *European Journal for Philosophy of Religion*, Vol. 2, no. 2 (2010), 127-140.

34   ibid., p. 128.

35   ibid., pp. 130f.

Irlenborn specifies this in a footnote by saying 'A "traditional exclusivist" holds that only her own religion is true if there are no core claims of an alien religion which are compatible with the core claims of Christianity (for example, the claim that salvation is only available through faith in Christ)'.[36] However, Irlenborn nonetheless seems to presuppose a more restrictive version throughout his paper, treating the exclusivist as saying that any foreign religious doctrines are false. At the beginning of this text we distinguished four versions of exclusivism including the one Irlenborn seems to have in mind when proposing his distinctive feature. However we dismissed this version because shared beliefs would either have to be evicted by the exclusivist or she would have to admit that there were in fact true beliefs among the other people's beliefs although she claimed them to be false. So I agree with Irlenborn that his epistemic inclusivism outplays this kind of exclusivism. However, by referring to a non-serious version of exclusivism, Irlenborn circumvents the most demanding challenge of distinguishing inclusivism and something like the Plantingian account of exclusivism. According to the latter the core claims of one's religion are true while incompatible religious beliefs are false. Both Irlenborn's and Rahner's inclusivism presupposes this exclusivistic assumption although Irlenborn stresses that an important feature is added in inclusivism, namely that of divergent religious beliefs being partially true, or to put it differently that foreign religions contain 'elements of truth'. Consider as one of Irlenborn's example the claim:

'B) The one God is not triune.'[37]

According to Irlenborn only the (Christian) inclusivist is able to say that this claim must be false on the one hand – as it is at odds with classical Christian theology – while on the other hand acknowledging an 'element of truth' in it, namely the belief that there is only one God. The Christian Exclusivist on the contrary, says Irlenborn, can only deny that (B) is true and therefore defends a less viable position than inclusivism. But this view seems to rest on a misunderstanding. B) could be treated as a conjunction of

B_1) There is one God.

and

B_2) This one God is not triune.

The theistic exclusivist would deny the second conjunct but could perfectly agree with the first. So where is the problem? Why does Irlenborn claim that

---

only inclusivists can account for 'an element of truth' in B)? Following Searle's theory of reference in *Speech Acts*, Irlenborn puts the case of the inclusivist in terms of having fully consummated reference, which identifies the object unequivocally while others refer successfully without having complete reference.[38] For example, one can refer successfully to a tower looking rectangular and looking round depending on how far one stands in relation to that tower. However, even if we would adopt that analogy, all parties could agree on the existence of a tower, with one claiming it to be rectangular while the other party believes it to be round. If this is meant by inclusivism accommodating for an *element of truth* in other religions and other religious beliefs, however, why should only inclusivism be able to account for this? The exclusivist would just distinguish several parts of B) judging that some parts are true and others are not. What else is the inclusivist doing? Given the distinctions between several versions of exclusivism stated in the beginning, Irlenborn's claim that a view accepting 'that "false statements" about [an] object may be partially true [...] is available only to the inclusivist but not to the exclusivist'[39] is false. Though Irlenborn's assumption might be right regarding certain restrictive versions of exclusivism it certainly does not hold for many of the nowadays vindicated forms. The latter are not oblivious to there being shared beliefs among the members of different religions.

However, locating overlapping propositions (Irlenborn's approach) is only one of several attempts that have been made to translate metaphors like 'seeds of truth' into literal language. Another one regards the study and understanding of other religions as a possible way of supplementing one's own by means of discovering propositions that have been neglected by one's home religion so far. The claim is that dealing with foreign images and myths could lead to a better and more complete understanding of one's home religion.[40] A similar view is put forward by the catholic theologian Robert Schreiter as part of his contextual theology. In the course of investigating how Christianity is received and adapted by non-Christian cultures Schreiter takes a religious tradition as a kind of code system that offers a way to communicate for a community,

---

38   ibid., pp. 136f.

39   ibid., p. 138.

40   'Take a now out-dated example from science: is light a wave or particles? Looking at it through the lens of the wave theory, you get insight into one set of data; looking at it through the lens of the particle theory, you get another. So I was thinking that the Hindu myth of creation as Shiva's dance gives one insight into what God is doing in creation, an insight Christianity has missed. If one were to try [to turn] the metaphor into propositions, I suppose they would be compatible with [a] Christian belief set, but they have been missed, left out.' Marilyn McCord Adams, in correspondence.

similar to any language.[41] Using such a code does not only enable communication and mutual understanding, it also plays an important part in creating group identity. According to Schreiter, this explains why foreigners often fail to comprehend the mechanism keeping that group together. It is because the foreigners do not know the codes. With regard to the question of how to interpret the inclusivist's search for partial truth in other religions, Schreiter states something remarkable about the scope of religious code systems. Every code system, he says, can be supplemented further. Not a single one is complete.[42] Supplementation could come from other cultures, traditions and religions. This can be interpreted as meaning that what is said in other religious traditions could bring into light what is only implicitly comprised in the inclusivist's own religion.

Again, it can be questioned whether this strategy is available only to the inclusivist and not the exclusivist. Exclusivism necessarily neither opposes the existence of overlapping propositions nor that one's own religious beliefs can be made more complete by insights owed to the study of other religions. The exclusivist could certainly concede that some of her religious beliefs became more explicit while studying other religions, she could also expand her religious code system or even modify minor parts of it. Like dealing with the grammar of a foreign language generates greater sensitivity for the particulars of one's own language, religious people can become more familiar to her own religion by studying other religions. However, nothing in the very concept of exclusivism hinders the exclusivist from acknowledging there being partial truth in other religions as the inclusivist does. It is certainly one of the merits of inclusivist approaches to stress the question of how to regard other religions and their adherents. And since they gave a good deal of thought to this question their ideas are much more explicit at this point compared to the thoughts of many exclusivists. However, with regard to the epistemically most important question, namely, whether one's own religion could rationally be regarded as true in the face of religious diversity, a remarkable harmony exists between inclusivism and moderate versions of exclusivism. At any rate, metaphors like 'seeds of truth' are not distinctive features.

Someone might mention general difficulties regarding the translation of metaphors as a problem here, assuming that the meaning of a metaphor

---

41   Robert J. Schreiter and R. J. Schreiter, *Abschied vom Gott der Europäer: Zur Entwicklung regionaler Theorien*, 1. Aufl., Edition solidarisch leben (Salzburg: Pustet, 1992), pp. 84ff.

42   ibid., p. 184.

cannot be expressed in literal language. Attempts to translate them misconceive the nature of metaphors which often transport connotations that are difficult to put into words. Thus, the inclusivist might have thought of something other than the proposed translations – an idea perhaps which might have had nothing to do with the epistemological part of his position. However, what is that supposed to be? Metaphors, even though not always completely translatable, are comprehensible for their specific propositional content, which can be expressed in literal talk. And even if this translation does not capture all aspects of its meaning, the metaphor can only be successfully grasped when the person who endorses it and the recipient have similar ideas of its meaning and possible not fully translatable connotations. Besides, the borderline between metaphoric and non-metaphoric expressions is often not clear. 'Seeds of the truth' seems to be obviously metaphoric, but what about 'partial truth' – is it metaphoric or literal? Fortunately, for our purpose it is sufficient to know that metaphors do not generally escape translation, even if some aspects might. The fact the inclusivist's metaphors most often entail the concept of 'truth' seems to indicate that he wanted to make an epistemologically relevant claim. In that case, however, there seems to be no successful candidate for a proper translation except those discussed above. With respect to the epistemically most important question of whether they should claim their religious beliefs to be true in the face of religious diversity, inclusivists and liberal exclusivists are, thus, in remarkable agreement, since all possible interpretations of the inclusivist's metaphors are reconcilable with exclusivism. Therefore, the inclusivist's talk of 'seeds of truth' does not serve as the distinction to exclusivism.

In order to prevent any misunderstandings, I should say that I am not clinging to a certain term. Whether we call someone sticking to her own beliefs when confronted with religious diversity and thinking about her attitude towards other religious believers 'inclusivist' or 'exclusivist' does not matter much to me. Perhaps a totally different term would do best. My point is that both entail the same stance towards the problem of religious diversity. Holding the tenets of one's home religion to be true and thinking that incompatible beliefs are false – no matter how we call that attitude (most frequently it is called 'exclusivism'), the inclusivist as well as the exclusivist does nothing else. The attempt to outstrip exclusivism undertaken by inclusivists has failed from an epistemological point of view. No matter how the inclusivist's metaphors like 'seeds of truth' are to be interpreted, at best they express a certain curious and open-minded attitude towards other religious people, not a totally different epistemic strategy. Exclusivists and inclusivists have their main challenge in common; that is, justifying their preference for their own religious teachings and the superiority claim made with respect to their own religious beliefs. Put into Irlenborn's terminology: Why should inclusivists think that their perception of the tower (analogical: God or other transcendental entities) is the veridical one whereas divergent beliefs or perceptions are said not to capture the full truth? Or why should inclusivists think that their religious beliefs get supplements while thinking what is supplemented is basically right? No kind of metaphoric talk prevents the inclusivist being challenged by these questions. In order to prevent another misunderstanding I shall add that I do not want to claim that the problem of justifying superiority claims is restricted to inclusivism. However, if inclusivists believe it is less urgent for them than for exclusivists, they err.

V. Those who believe will be happy – or does it work without belief too? Universalism, Particularism and the role of belief

We have seen so far that doctrinal religious exclusivism and doctrinal religious inclusivism take the same stance with respect to the problem of conflicting truth claims despite the inclusivist's attempt to dissociate from the exclusivist's position. If they do not differ with respect to epistemological terms, what else marks the distinction? Two further possibilities are investigated here. The first one is based on differences with respect to soteriological questions. The second one questions whether it makes sense to look for a philosophical or theological criterion at all. Perhaps inclusivism is better understood when it is considered to be a certain psychosocial attitude in religious matters.

Reiterating the distinction between doctrinal religious issues and soteriological religious issues,[43] perhaps soteriological issues make the difference and the way in which they are connected to religious beliefs, even if harmony exists between religious inclusivism and religious exclusivism in the doctrinal realm. Contrary to the pluralist, the inclusivist as well as the exclusivist thinks that some kind of doxastic commitment is required to attain salvation. Neither holds religious beliefs to be irrelevant with respect to the question of whether salvation is possible. Being a Christian (or a Muslim or a Jew), whether anonymous or non-anonymous, might not be sufficient. In any case, according at least to Rahner, it will increase one's chances for attaining salvation. This being said, let us compare the relevant possibilities to combine soteriological and doctrinal considerations. Doctrinal exclusivists either adopt soteriological particularism or soteriological universalism (the view that all people can or will be saved).

---

43   Neglecting the experiential dimension of the problem of religious diversity happens
      for reasons of simplicity and does not change my results in any significant way.

Inclusivists will usually affirm universalism. Let us look at these three options in detail.

The first and most clear picture arises when we look at strong or extreme exclusivism understood as the combination of doctrinal and soteriological particularism.[44] Only those fulfilling the alleged doxastic requirements can attain salvation. Without commitment, no rescue – the soteriological exclusivist's message is as simple and its difference to inclusivism thereby obvious. Inclusivists believe that all people can be saved, soteriological exclusivists do not. This view had always been questioned by religious critics and even from the exclusivist companion's perspective itself. Among Christians, for instance, it is a most pressing and controversial question how soteriological exclusivism could be held given Christian teachings about God's goodness.[45] While Rahner – to name one Christian – thought that a very good and powerful God would save all people, including people living before Jesus Christ and people having no acquaintance with Christianity, the American philosopher William Lane Craig – to name another – defends God's being just and loving while salvation is said to be restricted to Christians.[46] It would be interesting to examine whether other religions struggle with similar problems. Buddhists believe, for example, in the seeking of enlightenment – *bodhicitta* – as a precondition to achieve emptiness or the nonexistence of the self – *śūyata*. "Both can only be attained in Buddhism", Buddhists say.[47] This clearly is an exclusive claim stating that

---

44 As it is expressed, for example, in the documents of the *Council of Florenz-Ferrara* in 1442 or in Luther's *Sermons for the Early Christmas Service*. In the philosophy of religion, William Lane Craig, *No Other Name: A Middle Knowledge Perspective on the Exclusivity of Salvation Through Christ* (Oxford: Oxford University Press, 1989 (2000)) is a defender of this form of exclusivism.

45 For a detailed articulation of this worry see Kenneth E. Himma, 'Finding a High Road: The Moral Case for Salvific Pluralism', *International Journal for Philosophy of Religion*, 52 (2002): 1–33.

46 William Lane Craig, *No Other Name: A Middle Knowledge Perspective on the Exclusivity of Salvation Through Christ* (Oxford: Oxford University Press, 1989 (2000)). For arguments against the view, that God's goodness and soteriological particularism can be combined I would recommend Paul K. Moser, 'Religious Exclusivism', in *The Oxford Handbook of Religious Diversity*, ed. by Chad Meister, (New York, Oxford: Oxford University Press, 2011), pp. 77–88 (pp. 81–4); and Gavin D'Costa, *Christianity and World Religions: Disputed Questions in the Theology of Religions* (Malden, MA: Wiley-Blackwell, 2009). On my view, Craig's defence fails for the reasons mentioned there and for his use of the doctrine of middle knowledge which is incompatible with libertarian free will.

47 Cp. Gavin D'Costa, *The Meeting of Religions and the Trinity* (Edinburgh: T&T Clark, 2000), p. 90.

only Buddhists can attain the religious goal of Buddhism. Are there, however, analogous thoughts in Buddhism to that of Rahner, whose denial of soteriological particularism is derived from theological and dogmatic arguments? Would Buddhists think of it as unjust if only Buddhists could attain enlightenment? For many Christians today Rahner's line of thought seems the most convincing one probably because of the changes the notion of God has undergone containing less terrifying elements now. God was often described as wrathful and punitive in the past, depicted as being capable of damning the heathens, supported by a somewhat crude sense of justice which is hardly comprehensible from the perspective of a Christian nowadays, whose notion of God almost completely lacks these elements.

Not surprisingly therefore many doctrinal exclusivists have their affirmation of universalism in common with inclusivists, in Christian terms, they believe that all human beings can be saved through the work of Christ. Following Moser, I will call that stance 'inclusive exclusivism'.[48] This account does not have trouble integrating God's goodness like staunch exclusivism does. However, inclusive exclusivism raises the question whether salvation presupposes knowledge of the Christian gospel or not. Inclusivism – the alleged third possibility to combine soteriological and doctrinal issues – also has to face this question; nevertheless the more satisfying answer is available to the inclusive exclusivist. Salvation, inclusivists say, is possible for people who know nothing about Christ. However, if one was going to be saved without any such knowledge, it is doubtful whether there is any connection between belief and salvation at all (and perhaps it can even be doubted whether salvation happens through Christ at all). The question therefore is how and to what degree religious commitment is soteriologically effective. Inclusivists would often say that foreign religious beliefs function as *preparatio evangelica*, a way of preparation for the Christian gospel.[49] The Christian beliefs do not necessarily need to be explicit on this account. Their importance rather derives from the fact that they favour religious forms of life and thereby stimulate soteriologically relevant practices. However, the epistemological link remains unclear in this model.

Another but similar way of describing the soteriological effectiveness of beliefs is chosen by D'Costa, who locates himself in the exclusivistic camp in his recent works. Contrary to inclusivists, D'Costa stresses the importance

---

48   Paul K. Moser, 'Religious Exclusivism', in *The Oxford Handbook of Religious Diversity*, ed. by Chad Meister, (New York, Oxford: Oxford University Press, 2011), pp. 77–88 (p. 85).

49   Cp. D'Costa, *Christianity and World Religions*, p. 22.

of explicit knowledge for salvation and he adds that a proper response to the gospel could also take place after death in a post-mortem state.[50] Furthermore, he argues that exclusivism can accommodate what was said by inclusivism:

> inclusivists want to affirm the possibility of salvation outside the visible church [...] The objection would be that certain exclusivists allow for this and better explain the epistemologically necessary relationship to Christ that is required as a final means to salvation. Further, positive preparatory status to other religions is entirely compatible with some forms of exclusivism. If both these are the case, the argument amounts to suggesting that the classification is problematic: ... inclusivists are better grouped as [...moderate] exclusivists, for their aims and goals are fully attained under that heading.[51]

D'Costa goes even further and argues that inclusivists 'fail to explain how non-explicit Christological means can bring about Christological knowledge that is requisite for salvation. Exclusivism is the only position that seems to hold together all that is required'.[52]

However, this shortfall does not imply that delivering such an explanation is impossible for the inclusivist, it might be possible that there is one. But D'Costa rightly observes that conceding preparatory status could be done by inclusivists and moderate exclusivists alike. It is right that some forms of exclusivism would not share this concession as they would not admit that people are getting saved if they do not belong to their home religion. However, the more liberal end of the exclusivist spectrum and the less pluralistic end of inclusivism are very close together – close enough to the degree that they are almost indistinguishable as it was argued here. D'Costa demonstrates how it is possible to combine doctrinal exclusivism and universalism.[53]

Should we call this meanwhile popular combination 'exclusivism' or 'inclusivism'? 'Exclusivism' might be more appropriate due to the following reasons: First, the inclusive exclusivist's insistence on explicit commitment (even if possibly post-mortem) combined with universalism certainly fits better with Christian tradition than the inclusivists mere affirmation of universalism.[54]

---

50   ibid., p. 29 + part IV. A similar though less detailed theory is advocated by Paul
       K. Moser, 'Religious Exclusivism', in *The Oxford Handbook of Religious Diversity*,
       ed. by Chad Meister, (New York, Oxford: Oxford University Press, 2011), pp. 77–88
       (pp. 85–7).
51   D'Costa, *Christianity and World Religions*, p. 24.
52   ibid., p. 25.
53   Or *universal-access exclusivism* as he calls it.
54   Cp. Paul K. Moser, 'Religious Exclusivism', in *The Oxford Handbook of Religious
       Diversity*, ed. by Chad Meister, (New York, Oxford: Oxford University Press, 2011),
       pp. 77–88 (pp. 85f.).

The second reason is more of a sociological kind. Inclusivism was developed and advanced to overcome some of exclusivism's difficulties, so one might have expected that inclusivism offers something new, not just a disguised exclusivism. But at least with respect to doctrinal issues this seems not to be the case. Inclusivism does not offer a new epistemic theory to deal with the problem of religious diversity. Introducing a new or different term – *inclusivism* – rather leads to confusion and perhaps was just done in order to euphemize the somewhat unpopular exclusivist position. Concerning soteriological issues, changes have occurred since Rahner first presented his inclusivistic approach, and the popular opinion among Western Christians changed. Today soteriological particularism is much less popular than it was decades or even centuries ago – which is not the case with doctrinal exclusivism, whose only alternative seems to be pluralism and not doctrinal inclusivism, as there is no position deserving that name, as we have seen. If 'inclusivism' referred to an attitude towards salvation only it would be right to say that many exclusivists became inclusivists. However, one could also interpret exclusivists as having adopted the right theological stance towards salvation encouraged by later named inclusivists like Rahner. D'Costa's account shows that it is possible to accept doctrinal exclusivism, thereby making one's epistemological stance distinctive and clear, while at the same time endorsing universalism.

VI. Just an attitude?

Is there another possibility to make sense of the distinction between inclusivism and exclusivism apart from those discussed in this paper so far? Do we have to march in a totally different direction? Two attempts should be mentioned here. With respect to the level of incompatible theologies, a considerable part of what is done under the name 'inclusivist approaches' are attempts to reinterpret theological dogmata so that logical contradictions between different theologies vanish.[55] It is hardly conceivable, however, that all incompatibilities can be brought to disappear in this way. Furthermore, one might question the acceptance of these revisionary theological accounts. Very few people hold a system of religious beliefs deprived of central elements or reinterpreted at many points. Most religious people want to know whether their actual beliefs allow religious diversity, and not whether a scaled down version or a different variant of their faith is justified.

---

55 Take as one example Bernhardt's *representation Christology* in Bernhardt, 'Jesus Christ as "vere Deus" as a Challenge for Interreligious Dialogue'.

Sometimes, finally, *inclusivism, exclusivism and pluralism* seem to name different psychosocial attitudes. The Basel theologian inclusivist Bernhardt, for instance, distinguishes between three different levels when using the typology:[56] Behaviour or attitude, validity (Geltung) and the level of theological judgement about relationships with other religions. Bernhardt classifies exclusivism as a dismissive and reserved attitude towards other religious believers, as it would claim exclusive validity and be backed by a theological framework saying that there is just one way to salvation and one possible set of true beliefs respectively. Bernhardt depicts inclusivism, traditionally understood, as an attitude of connection seeking superordination, claiming superiority of its own religious doctrines and regarding its own faith as fulfilment of any human-God relation.

Bernhard himself tries to offer what he describes as an *inclusivistic model combining a mindset that seeks connection with theological inclusivism without claiming superiority.*[57] However, it remains unclear how this inclusivism should work without claiming superiority. Bernhardt's attempts to establish this claim are far from being convincing. As we have previously shown, the inclusivist like the exclusivist believes that the tenets of his religion are true whereas he believes incompatible religious beliefs to be false. We called this 'doctrinal exclusivism'. Nothing commits the doctrinal exclusivist necessarily or in a unique way to a certain attitude concerning interreligious dialogue – an open-minded and curious as well as a dismissive attitude is possible. However, it commits the doctrinal exclusivist (and therefore also the inclusivist) to thinking that the person who does not believe as she does fails to believe something that is true and therefore that the person errs. Hence, the exclusivist will hold herself to be superior in a certain sense, as she thinks she has true beliefs the other person lacks. She need not exclude the possibility that she could err, but the doctrinal exclusivist claims per definition that her beliefs are true and those of her opponent are false. This does not automatically mean that she believes herself superior with respect to wisdom, morality or in general to being a better person. With respect to all these matters the exclusivist might consider herself to be on a par with her interlocutor or even below him. However, epistemically she takes herself as having the advantage of knowing the truth. Although this can be brought forward in a most humble way, without any claims of self-

---

56   Reinhold Bernhardt, *Ende des Dialogs? Die Begegnung der Religionen und ihre theologische Reflexion,* Beiträge zu einer Theologie der Religionen, 2 (Zürich: TVZ Theol. Verl., 2005), pp. 104ff.

57   'Es gibt eine religionspsychologische Inklusivhaltung und einen religionstheologischen Inklusivismus ohne Verbindung mit einer geltungstheoretischen Superioritätsbehauptung – etwa in Form des von mir favorisierten "mutualen Inklusivismus"' ibid., p. 114.

confidence, the kind of superiority-thinking involved cannot be put off without self-deception.

Nonetheless, the suggestion of drawing a distinction between inclusivism and exclusivism in terms of characterizing different psychological attitudes is an interesting one. Although there are many exclusivists who approach other religious believers eager for knowledge and ready to learn, it is certainly one of the merits of inclusivistic approaches to stress the question of how to regard other religions and their adherents. And since they gave a good deal of thought to this question their ideas are often much more explicit at this point compared to the thoughts of many people in the exclusivist camp. Some exclusivists could learn from so called *inclusivists* at this point, even though this does not hold for all.[58]

58   Many thanks to Marilyn McCord Adams, Thomas M. Schmidt, Heidi Stoeckl, the audience of a presentation given at Goethe University Frankfurt, and the members of a research group founded by the John Templeton Foundation who all read and discussed versions of this paper and thus prevented many embarrassing mistakes. The still remaining errors and inadequacies are due to my inability to embrace all their many precious insights in an appropriate way.

Methodological Pluralism
and the Subject Matter of Philosophy of Religion

Vladimir K. Shokhin

Anglo-American philosophy of religion, being one of the most advanced field of the today's contemporary philosophy and having great merits in rational apology of theism, does not differ substantially in its subject matters (arguments for the existence of God, Divine attributes, theodicy, faith and knowledge, etc.) from the traditional *theologia naturalis*[1] provided with elaborated contemporary epistemological (like internalism or externalism) or methodological (like 'evidentialism') foundations.[2] Meanwhile, beginning in the 1980s, more and more persons who call themselves Christian philosophers embark (not without encouragement from Alvin Plantinga[3]) on philosophical foundation and interpretation of those subjects which had always been the indubitable domain of *theologia revelata*, viz. the dogmas of Holy Trinity, Incarnation, Atonement,

---

1   One may refer here at least to *Disputationes metaphysicae* (chapter XXX) by Francisco Suarez (1597) as the most authoritative text in the field. The same was also true with his followers. So while disputatio LIX of *Disputationes in universam philosophiam* by Guiseppe Polizzi (1675-1676) dealt with the existence of God, the next one with the Divine attributes, and this curriculum was reproduced also in *Quaestionum philosophicarum* (Lib.V, quest. 2.39-44) by Silvestro Mauro (1670), not to mention others.

2   Authors convinced of the identity of philosophy of religion with the substantiation of philosophical theism are too numerous to be named separately. One can refer to comprehensive historiographical surveys of the subject, like: W.J. Wainwright, *Philosophy of Religion: An Annotated Bibliography of Twentieth-Century Writings in English* (New York-London: Garland Publishing, Inc., 1978), and their continuations: A.P.F. Sell, *The Philosophy of Religion 1875-1980* (London: Croom Helm, 1988), or E.T. Long, *Twentieth-Century Western Philosophy of Religion 1900-2000* (Dordrecht: Kluwer, 2000). It is very typical that some compilers of anthologies on rational theology are so persuaded that their topic is an integral part of subject matters of philosophy of religion that they, e.g., coordinate their presentation of the problems of evil and theodicy with handbooks on philosophy of religion. See: *The Oxford Handbook of Philosophical Theology*, ed. by Thomas P. Flint and Michael C. Rea (Oxford: Oxford University Press, 2009), p. 3 (cf. p. 4). It deserves mention in this regard that the five-volumed history of philosophy of religion edited by Oppi and Trakakis is also a history of philosophical theology from the ancient up to today's stages.

3   See: A. Plantinga, 'Advice to Christian Philosophers', *Faith and Philosophy*, Vol.1 (1984), 253-271.

Resurrection, the sacrament of Eucharist, prayers, etc. In classical theology such subject matters were strictly divided, but now they are included on the basis of equality into the same field of 'philosophy of religion', and this is testified by many anthologies under this title. Herewith there is a minority of Anglophone writers on philosophy of religion who consider it a suitable area of knowledge to discuss religious feelings, religious phenomena and compare different religious traditions.[4] A still more complicated diversity of approaches to the subject of philosophy of religion is being manifested in what is called the Continental tradition. Here we have some philosophers of authority who are still sure that philosophy of religion is nothing other than a field within the area of traditional theology; some others, with Ingolf Dalferth, prefer to see in it a philosophical investigation of 'speech about God'; some follow such eminent religious philosophers as Bernhard Welte, Rudolph Schaeffler, and Franz von Kutschera to regard it as a theological project in the context of religious studies; some, on the contrary, consider it a religious studies project in the context of theology; some regard it as an integral section of religious studies;[5] others prefer to consider it a philosophical investigation of the phenomenon of religion without theological commitments, or, with Wilhelm Dupré, a combination of metaphysical and 'culturometrical' studies of religion; some others regard it as hermeneutical investigation of symbolical language of religion,[6] a field of hermeneutical phenomenology,[7] while there are many authors who try to use philosophy of religion as a resource for the solution of general philosophical issues, to whom Arie Molendijk should be counterposed because of his insisting on such a mission of philosophy of religion as an investigation of religion in socio-public space, and in this regard it is not too separable from sociology of religion.

Elsewhere I endeavoured to reconstruct 13 views on the goals and assignments of philosophy of religion in Anglo-American and 16 in the Continental tradition,[8] but I'm sure I was very far from the completion of such a catalogue

---

4   Among older authors, F. Ferré may be referred to, then R. Blackstone, P. Burke, R. Sharlemann and R. Neville. It was Paul Griffiths who emphasized comparative study of religions as a special competence of philosophy of religions.

5   Here in the first place Wilhelm Trilhaas' fundamental *Religionsphilosophie* (1972) is to be singled out, then works by H. Schrödter and R. Pummer.

6   Paul Ricoeur is to be mentioned here in the first place and Christian Adriaanse among our contemporaries.

7   French authors from A. Duméry up to N. Depras are to be marked out in this group, as well as the German philosopher H. Waldenfels, to name only first-rate figures.

8   V. K. Shokhin, *Introduction to Philosophy of Religion* (Moscow: Alpha-M, 2010), pp. 50-119, 136-197 (in Russian).

then, because enormous writing on this field is being published, and no one, I believe, is currently able to make an account of it. So such pluralism of approaches is natural, and, to say more, in a sense desirable, inasmuch as it testifies to the scale of corresponding intellectual activity.

Nevertheless, some logical criteria could be taken into account in judging the validity of these avowed, and, what is taking place much more often, implicit approaches. It seems more or less clear that philosophical theory of religion should differ from religious studies because of its non-empirical methods. On the other hand, *philosophy-on-religion* is not the same as *philosophy-in-religion, and* if we say that philosophy of religion corresponds to the first kind of philosophizing while philosophical theology to the second one, we'll obtain not too bad a point of departure to solve the 'boundary dispute' between them, and avoid the confusion of ideas which is undesirable for anyone who wishes to embark on either of these different 'philosophical undertakings'. Given that such a simple distinction is acknowledged, one can realize that philosophy of religion in a proper sense should, by definition (and in accordance with the very combination of the corresponding words), in my opinion, deal with religion and not God or even 'discourse' or 'speech' of God, in the same way as phenomena of science, politics and education make subjects of such 'philosophies of the genitive case' (as I prefer to call 'philosophies of something') as philosophies of science, politics and education. It is true that the philosophical study of religion has been closely connected with the philosophical science of God during many centuries, but already Sextus Empiricus (from the second to third century A.D.) differentiated between two issues, i.e. whether gods exist and how people conceive their ideas of them,[9] in other words differentiated between *theology* and *religiology*.[10] That being said, this does not mean that a person A who is a philosopher of religion cannot in his (her) other commitments develop some empirical religious studies or investigate arguments for the existence of God, or classifications of Divine attributes, subjects of his (her) scrutiny. Nor does it mean that there are not some common soils which could be tilled by a philosopher, theologian and one embarking on religious studies, certainly, each using his (her) specific 'farm implements'. The fact of the matter is that in his (her) *competence of a* philosopher of religion he (she) works with a specific 'map of topics'.

---

9   Sextus Empiricus, Adv. math. IX, 48.
10   The term *Religiologie* was introduced in the 1920s-1930s by some German Catholic theologians and endorsed in the 1970s, by the French scholar P. Bourgault and Canadian German-speaking P. Pummer. In English it was transferred in the 1960s. See, e.g.: R.A. McDermott, *Religion as an Academic Discipline,* Cross Currents (1968), Vol. 18, 11-33.

One way to mark their scope in the 21st century could be to turn to the reality of *Religiőse* (the term was coined by Fichte during the famous Atheism Controversy (der Atheismusstreit) in Jena in 1798/9,[11] and having no good English equivalent) and try to differentiate between its ontological levels. On the surface we have numerous empirical traditions and movements which are considered *religions* (in plural). Their common features, which give us a reason to identify them as religions and not something else, constitute the genus of *religion* (in singular). But bearing in mind that religion is as old as mankind, and even consistently antireligious movements cannot but substitute a traditional religion by 'quasi-religious' dogmas and practices, we have good reasons to talk also about *religiosity* as a profound level of human existence. Let's look at some objectives of philosophy of religion in accordance with these dimensions of religion beginning with it as an essence, then turning to it as a genus and at last to a body of empirical traditions.[12]

1. In its investigation of *religiosity*, philosophy of religion might have much in common with phenomenology of religion, because its core, as has been convincingly demonstrated firstly by Friedrich Schleiermacher and then by Rudolf Otto, is constituted by some inner feelings (like cosmic or numinous ones) more than by reasonings or moral obligations, though *homo religiosus* is not to be reduced only to one dimension of human nature. But philosophy has some specific objectives herein which couldn't be accomplished by any kind of religious studies. Firstly, it could try to find out the place of religion on the map of the intentional structure of the human being, e.g. to fit it into the framework of universal human needs and particular personal values, then the hierarchy of goods and goals, etc. Secondly, it has to work on religious experience as such, to define how it differs from other types of human experiences and line borders between it and adjacent ones. E.g., it is more or less clear that not everyone who is religious is at once also a mystic, but is vice versa true? In other words, is it not true that one can write mystic treatises, poems or stories, or even feel some profound laws governing her (his) life, coming from outside of this world, and remain in spite of all not religious? Let's remember

---

11   For the first time, according to my knowledge, in the *Appeal to the Public*, where Fichte repudiates imputations of atheism, aroused by the publishing in his journal of Karl Forberg's essay where religion was defined only as belief in moral progress of mankind. See: J.G. Fichte *Werke. Auswahl in sechs Bänden. Mit mehreren Bildnissen Fichtes*, Hrsg. und eingel. von F. Medicus (Leipzig: Fritz Eckhardt, 1908-1912), Bd. III, S. 175-176.

12   More detailed versions of the following points are presented in my book: V.K. Shokhin, *Introduction to Philosophy of Religion* (Moscow: Alpha-M, 2010), pp. 231-251 (in Russian).

that the whole movement of Hindu bhakti proved to become so successful because subtle mystic implications of the powerful Advaita philosophy (manifested, e.g., in hymns ascribed to Śaṅkara) had not met the religious needs of people because it made genuine religious worship in some sense superfluous. But is mystic consciousness the only kind of consciousness whose correlation with religious mentality deserves amplification? It is sufficient only to remember the ancient Roman distinction between *religiosi* and *superstiosi* (i.e. religious and superstitious men), articulated by Cicero, to answer 'No'. Anyway, defining religiosity, however difficult it is, remains claimed for philosophy of religion. Thirdly, a perennial issue for philosophy of religion is whether religiosity is reducible to some so called 'more real' movers of a human being (such as economic, social, political, psychophysical, etc.) or not. In the first case we have one or other kind of naturalistic reductionism which is in contradiction to the law of sufficient reason, because the supposed 'genuine' causes of religious world-outlook and practices contain less explanation of their effects than 'philosophers of suspicion', beginning with Critius and Eugemerus[13] up to followers of Marx, Freud and Dennett, have hoped to have. The need in the philosophical struggle against religion being with some thinkers insurmountable, philosophical justification of its non-reducibility will also be on the agenda forever.[14]

2. Turning to the next level of Religiöse, i.e. to *religion* as a genus, philosophy is challenged now by a suggestion in vogue that it is a sheer abstraction because in reality we have only various religious traditions which differ so greatly from each other that the very attempt to subordinate them to a general notion should

---

13   According to the Sophist Prodicus from Keos (circa 470-after 399 B.C.), the origin of religion lay in human adoration of needful products and inventors of goods, like Prometheus. Another Sophist, Critius (circa 460-403 BC), insisted, in opposition to Prodicus, that religion was established by that wise one who guessed that human laws were insufficient for keeping a crowd in awe and suggested adoration of some celestial beings for that purpose. Euhemerus' (circa 340-260 B.C.) theory is well known; its thrust was that deities had been primarily rulers and other famous men later deified for their merits.

14   Sextus Empiricus, whom I have already referred to, was the first one to touch the philosophical matter of religiosity by his shrewd criticism of the naturalistic reduction of religion to social needs and the physiological peculiarities of man promoted by the older Sophists, like Critius and Prodicus, Democritus, Euhemerus from Messina, Epicurus and others (Adv. math. IX. 34-43), and his criticisms (e.g., that in order to deify a ruler you have to have the very idea of divinity beforehand, etc.), in my opinion, are encouraging even today, in the face of advancing naturalism.

be the same as to neglect their specifics.[15] Not seldom is such an attitude
supported by ideological presuppositions; for example, that the general notion
of religion is enrooted in the traditional conception of one veridical religion
which is regarded as an 'outdated', 'europocentric', 'imperialist', 'sexist', etc.,
conception contradicting today's challenges of the multicultural world, religious
pluralism, rights of minorities, etc. The consistent religious nominalism under
discussion (not, I believe, without influence from the postmodernist
'unmasking' of universal normative concepts as expressions of 'big narratives'
serving as it were for the empowerment of man) is, as any species of radical
nominalism, obviously problematic even from a logical point of view. It is
the same as the proposition that we can safely get rid of the general concept
of colour to be satisfied with such varieties of it as red, blue, white, yellow
and so on, without answering the question of why then we call all of them
colours and not, e.g., smells. But the philosopher can step further and investigate
deep connections of this rejection of religion (in singular) with blossoming
contemporary secularism. One thing to be kept in mind is, however, that
the secularism under discussion is of a specific kind, its target being not so much
religion in general as Christianity in particular, as for the time being it is still
the main religious tradition of the Western world.

3. It is not sufficient to defend the existence of *religion* in the mass of *religions*.
One has to make clear what it is. And here every philosopher of religion faces
the problem of whether a good definition of it is possible at all. But what does
'good' mean here? Is it one such that it could satisfy everyone dealing with
the subject, or one that could satisfy at least some of them? We have a great
number of such definitions (no one has counted them) beginning with the first
one in the history of the world thought, which belonged to the early Cicero (for
whom religion was 'what gives people the possibility to serve and adore
the superior order of nature, one that is called divine')[16], which has advantages
over many later ones. Many philosophers dealing with religion have complained
about the special difficulties with defining it. They have been right inasmuch as
religion is irreducible to other so called 'objective' factors of human existence,
in opposition to the 'philosophers of suspicion' I talked about earlier. But one
equipped with analytical methodology can try to classify existent definitions
and then discern which of them are more comprehensive and fit for generalizing
the whole set of empirical traditions which have come down to us. Such

---

15   See, e.g.: R.C. Neville, 'Religions, Philosophies, and Philosophy of Religion',
      International Journal for Philosophy of Religion, Vol. XXXVIII, N 1-3 (1983), 165-181.

16   *Religio est quae superioris cuiusdam naturae, quam divinam vocant, curam cerimonianque
      affert* (Rhet.=De inv. II.53).

an 'inventory work' seems not only useful, but, I believe, also entertaining and deserving special attention from philosophers, but one criterion of differing between good conceptions of religion and bad ones is anyway valid. Religion being a very complicated organic whole, those explicit and implicit patterns of its understanding which reduce this whole to one or another part of it prove to be misleading. For example, both reducing religion to morality, which was held in great esteem during the Enlightenment, and to salvation/deliverance technologies taking place with Hickeanism[17] (in both cases at the expense of the doctrinal identities of religious traditions), ignore this 'holistic texture' of religious ethos.

4. Now, a philosopher may (contrary to a scientist) study not only what exists but also what ought to be, religion not being an exclusion to the rule. One could refer to the authority of Plato, who looked at things from the point of how they correspond to their *eidoi*, or ontological archetypes and norms. Also in this regard, the ancient etymologizing of the word *religio*, which was the same as defining-cum-contemplating its essence, should not be thrown away even if its estimations may differ from a purely linguistic point of view. For example, the famous etymology of the word *religio* offered by Lactantius, i.e. its production from the union between God and man[18] (on which the whole medieval and still later reflexion on religion fed), could also be, in my opinion, developed into two further 'unions': those between men around the worship of God and between spiritual capacities inside man resulting from veritable worship. But such 'contemplation of essences' also gives criteria for the criticism of a factual religion. For example, if the twofold main commandment of love to God and one's neighbour (which is also the commandment of two "unions") is being shifted at the expense of permanent gratitude to God (which is to be laid into the foundation of the first commandment) or judicious charity for neighbours (which is the same for the second one), we have a sure deviation from the eidos of the authentic religion. Although the derivation of *religio* offered by Cicero is more quastionable from the linguistic point of view, his insistence on "deliberation" as the core of religious attitude of consciousness is not also misleading, and when religious persons confine themselves only with the "outward piet

---

17   In reality, Hick only voiced much louder and with more authority what was many times expressed by Helen Blavatsky, Annie Besant, Sarvepalli Radhakrishnan, Alan Watts, and some other religious authors and leaders before him (so in this regard we have nothing familiar with a pretended 'Copernican upheaval').

18   ... *hoc vinculo pietatis obstricti Deo et religati sumus; unde ipsa religio nomen accepit* (Inst. IV.28).

y" and fulfilment of traditional ceremonies without pondering on the truths of their faith they also deviate from the authentic religion.

5. The work on the universals of religion, among which 'God', 'creation', 'emanation', 'miracle', 'faith', 'revelation', 'tradition', 'cult', 'community', 'salvation' are to be selected, not to mention many others, also seems unavoidable for a philosopher of religion. The main methodological problem here is whether a philosopher of religion has to start with 'ruling' them in the three theistic (Abrahamic) religions and then 'go abroad' with available instruments for measuring aberrations of these notions in other traditions or, in contrast, to look at them as quite neutral concepts of contemporary language, and then apply their meanings to the fabric of both theistic and other religions as enjoying equal rights from the very beginning. Both approaches have their advantages – the second in fitting these 'categories of religion' into comparativistic context from the very beginning, and the first one in providing a student of the subject with a good point of departure – but their amplification makes a subject of a separate methodological project. The only point to be emphasized now is that the second approach provides us with a much shorter way to the uncritical obliteration of religious peculiarities and a simplistic approach to the crucial texts of the world religions, as exemplified by the main works of Annie Besant, and to the invention of imaginary Religion besides real religions which has been a dream of many applicants for 'Copernican upheavals' in religious studies.

6. One of the concluding subjects among those pertaining to religion (in singular) could be its denial, i.e. atheism. As it is an acknowledged fact that religion is as old as mankind, and purely irreligious epochs in its history are not testified by archaeologists and anthropologists, the question about the origin of atheism is of more interest, in my opinion, than that of religion. Of especial interest is the problem of the deep motives behind an atheistic attitude to the world, and what I would call the main paradox of atheism consisting in a dogmatic semi-religious faith (against rational reason) in the nonexistence of the Judicious Designer of the world and hope for this nonexistence, which is conditioned primarily not by ordinary or scientific scepticism, but by hatred of, or at least a grudge against, God, i.e. the supposedly nonexistent object. The latter paradoxical attitude, testified by the history of ideas beginning with the father of atheists, Diagorus from Melos (the fifth century B.C.), via Diderot or Golbach, up to today's English atheists with Richard Dawkins at their head, demonstrates the irrationalism of an atheistic world attitude, in contradiction to the hopes of atheists themselves who are quite sure that they are champions of a purely scientific world outlook par excellence. One issue is whether the so-called quasi-religious consciousness, exemplified with Paul Tillich by Communism and Nazism and discovered by Sergius Bulgakov and Nicolai Berdyaev before him while analyzing the profound motive forces of the Russian revolutions, are enrooted more in this 'hatred of a non-existent object', in the profound constitution of homo religiosus (see ebove) independent of an explicit ideology or in both. And another one is the matter of prediction; that is, in what degree the contemporary consumer society can be a provider of the post-postsecular era.

7. Now, turning to religions (in plural), one can start with an amplification of the main patterns of world-outlook on which different empirical traditions are founded. I mean that the existent conceptions of 'theism', 'pantheism', 'dualism', 'polytheism', etc., need much reconsideration. For example, what is usually designated as 'pantheism' should in many cases be identified as 'monism', or the conception of All-unity which is equal to the acknowledgement that in the final analysis the whole world is reduced to only one substance. Then 'pantheism' (the world is not different from Godhead) is to be considered only one very rare species of it, besides much more proliferating panentheism (Godhead is developing in the world which is a kind of its body), acosmism (Godhead is the only reality while the world is an illusion) and 'emanatism' (the world is a non-illusory projection of Godhead). Concerning 'dualism', one should differentiate between the models where two principles of the world are mutually complementary and competitive,[19] and so on. Though theism is more definite a conception, one has also here to differentiate between its classical pattern and theistic elements interwoven into the fabric of alien types of world outlook. Numerous examples are not lacking, beginning with the acknowledgement of typical theistic attributes of God and even theodicy in the acosmic context of Advaita-Vedānta, up to a mixture of theistic and panentheistic features in the philosophy or Fichte or Solovyev, not to mention many other religious thinkers. Differentiating between historical and cultural forms of the same pattern is also needed: Hegelian panentheism is not the same as that of Sufist mystics, while that of process-theology differs from Hegelian variety.

8. From the main world outlooks, the types of religious mentality (exclusivism, inclusivism, pluralism, relativism) are to be distinguished, which, according to John Hick, Paul Knitter, Harold Coward and their numerous followers, are

---

19   The pattern of the first type of dualism is that of Sāṃkhya-Yoga (influential also for the medieval Hindu schemes) where two principles of the world, i.e. Puruṣa and Prakṛti are likened to a lame and blind one, cooperating with each other for attaining the same goal, and that of the second one the dualism of Manichaeism where the good and evil principles of the world are both active and in perpetual struggle.

variable among empiric religions.[20] It is an affair of a historian of religions to prove, e.g., that inclusivism has not been, against all endeavours of the mentioned persons, proficient in 'double standards', an invention of the Second Vatican Council or John Paul the Second, but has much deeper roots in the missionary strategies of ancient Buddhism and Hinduism, which, again, in contradiction to the same authors, have nothing to do with 'pluralism'.[21] A philosopher of religion has other pursuits, that is, obligations

---

20 In Hick's view, though all the traditions are necessarily marching to 'the new brave world' of the religion of the future, their starting points differ. So Hinduism, Jainism, Sikhism and Buddhism 'are already considerably more advanced than the faiths of Semitic origin in the development of a pluralistic outlook, and may be expected to continue to contribute to its spread' – J. Hick, *An Interpretation of Religion* (London / New Haven: Macmillan / Yale University Press, 1989), p. 378. So it is possible, the reader is made to realize, that they might help their brothers-in-participation in the Real who are more 'lingering' (Christians insisting on Jesus' divinity being first among them) in their progress.

21 Paul Hacker (1913-1979), one of the greatest Indologists of the twentieth century, persuasively demonstrated this while referring to texts of both traditions. As the *locus classicus* in Hinduism two passages were cited by him, both from the Bhāgavadgītā, where Krishna says about himself that 'Whatever form (of Godhead) a devotee seeks to worship with faith, that faith of him (needed for that) I make steady. Endowed with such faith, he seeks to propitiate it and obtains from it his desires, distributed (in reality) by me alone', and 'Also devotees of other divinities who sacrifice (to them) endowed with faith, they sacrifice (in reality) to me, though not according to (the authentic) law' (VII.21-22, IX.23). The German Indologist also documented the inclusivistic trend in the early Purāṇas, late medieval (from the 15th century A.D.) Vishnuite poetry of Tulsidas (in his Avadhi epic *Ramcaritmanas*) and Neo-Hindu writings of which, according to him, those of Sarvepalli Radhakrishnan were classically inclusivistic. Among the Pali Buddhist texts, Hacker singled out the *Tevijja-sutta*, wherein the Buddha persuades young Brahmanas that his teaching contains everything valuable in their 'native' lore including the knowledge of the three Vedas, in its initial, veritable and pure essence while their Brahmanic teachers managed only to distort it. But along with the 'doctrinal inclusivism' of the Buddhists, emphasized by Hacker, one can refer to numerous passages of the Pali canon where we have a 'narrative inclusivism'; e.g., when the Brahmanic gods take every opportunity to recite their eulogies before the Buddha and his arahants ('perfected ones'), to appeal to them as their teachers and attend the Buddha's funeral grieving deeply. Vassalage is also the main relation between Brahmanic gods and the previous Buddhas. (*Dīgha-Nikaya* II, 276-289, 46, 208-222, etc.). As a skilful missionary strategy, inclusivism was actively implemented in the propagation of Buddhism not only in India, but also in China (where Lao-tsu, e.g., was declared to be one more incarnation of the Buddha), Tibet (where local Bon divinities where included into the Buddhist pantheon), as well as in the South-eastern Asia, and now it is implemented in the West. See: V. K. Shokhin, 'On Some Features

to answer such questions as: should an exclusivistic attitude be understood only in a narrow sense (i.e., that only one tradition is true while all others are simply false) and not also in a wider sense (i.e., while there is only one veridical and salvational tradition, there are some genuine elements also besides)? Whether any genuine religious consciousness can be anything, in the final analysis, but exclusivist at least in the second sense? Is there a difference between such an exclusivism and inclusivism in a weaker sense? Is there, again, a difference between inclusivism in a stronger sense (a view that other traditions can not only contain some elements of the truth, but be also salvational) and relativism? Do both pluralism and relativism[22] deserve, in the final analysis, to be considered religious attitudes at all, and not only an outward (philosophical, sociological, political, etc.) approach to religions? I'm sure that these questions will prove very focal in the 21st century for both theologians and those occupied with religious studies, so a philosopher of religion may be also expected to meet them.

9. A philosopher of religion has much work also in the area of the classification of religions. For example, some consider only Christianity, Islam and Buddhism to be the so-called world religions, others enrol Judaism and Hinduism in this list also, while attempts to include Confucianism and Taoism along with other species are also not lacking (while for some feminists, like Grace Janzen, the very differing between the ranks of religions is against democracy). But what is a criterion for such enrolment, and how are we to designate those religions which don't correspond to it? The same puzzle is also with new cults or non-traditional religions, the question being what age and characteristics a religious movement or cult should have to be enrolled into the lists of old and traditional ones? One of the popular answers is that to be 'new' a religious movement has to emerge not earlier than after 1945, but I have not met a justification of such a chronology. Here religious studies are doubtlessly involved, but the general framework of answering such questions, I mean that of interrelations between religions and cultures, or, more strictly, the participation of religions in the development of civilizations, as well as the very differentiating between a 'religion', 'religious movement' and 'cult', is an object of philosophical scrutiny.

---

of Buddhist Missionary Work and Double Standards in Religious Studies', *Studies in Interreligious Dialogue*, Vol. 15, n. 2 (2005), 148-151.

22   The last attitude has been substantiated in some details in a special manifesto: J. Runzo, 'God, Commitment, and Other Faiths: Pluralism Versus Relativism', in *Philosophy of Religion: An Anthology*, ed. by Louis P. Pojman and Michael Rea, Fifth Edition (Belmont, CA: Thompson, 2008), pp. 542-554.

10. While philosophy-*on*-religion is by no means the same as philosophy-*in*-religion, the latter may be an important topic of the former. Here a new typology of religions is near at hand. For Jainism and Buddhism are constituted in their core just by the respective philosophies. Hinduism admits that not everything claimed by man for realizing his highest goals is available from reason and Vedic revelation is therefore needed, though its world-outlook cornerstones, like the teaching of All-unity and those of *karma and saṅsāra*, are in reality products of natural and not revealed reason. All the three theistic traditions are sure, in contrary, that philosophy can at best be an instrument of interpretation of Revelation which, on the whole, supersedes reason. And Christianity among them is enrooted in supernaturalism in such a degree that it is the only tradition that established frontiers between natural (i.e. rational) and revealed theology.[23] But this is only a sketch, for a more detailed comparison of religions from this point of view is needed, to say nothing about some intermediary (like Gnosticism) and artificial (like the natural religion of the Enlightenment) species.

All this being said, this doesn't mean that philosophy of religion has no other objectives. It has among other things also metatheoretical tasks, firstly in classifying varieties of some adjacent disciplines, 'the sciences of religion and sciences of spirit', inasmuch as it can, e.g., differ between various kinds of rational theology (*theologia rationis*) in dividing them into those where philosophizing is the end in itself (speculative theology), only the means of defending Tradition (apologetic theology), and both (natural and philosophical theologies). It can also undertake the further differentiation between its varieties, taking into account that the first treatise under the title *Theologia naturalis* was written by the Scotist Nicolas Bonetus in 1330 and printed in 1505,[24] while the first book entitled *Philosophical Theology* was published by the English theologian Frederick Robert Tennant in only 1928-1930, and that such a chronological gap cannot be purely accidental and makes one suggest that the second discipline has been somehow stimulated to make up for something lacking in the first one.[25] Philosophy of religion has, further, as any field

---

23   See Tertullian (Adv.Marc.I.18), who stated that God is to be learned of in the beginning
      from his deeds in the world (ex operibus), and then by means of preaching
      (ex praedicationibus), the idea being that the natural God-knowledge may be regarded
      only as a preliminary stage for that cognition which is available only from the Scriptures.

24   See: W. Schröder, 'Religion bzw. Theologie, natürliche bzw. vernünftige', *Historisches
      Wörterbuch der Philosophie*, Bd. VIII., hrsg. J. Ritter und K. Gründer, (Basel: Schwabe
      Verlag, 1992), pp. 714-715.

25   E.g., it is true that natural theologians also criticized their predecessors from the point
      of persuasiveness, but if we would opine that among two kinds of rational theology,

of philosophy, need of self-reflexion and, correspondingly, of a perpetual revisiting of its own history. But given that it has to correspond to its vocation, working on the levels of Religiöse will remain its main destination, and several points highlighted above indicate only to a crude scheme of the curriculum of its commitments.

---

the one concentrated mostly on the elaboration of argumentation could be better designated as natural theology and the other, dealing more with its critical analysis, as philosophical theology, we could get not too bad a distinction. Further, while natural theology seems to be in the strict sense a Christian phenomenon (as a notion correlative to its antonym, i.e. revealed theology, the very strictness of this opposition dating from the very beginnings of the Christian writings and having nothing of the kind in non-Christian traditions), philosophical theology an intercultural one. In reality, it would be ridiculous to call Plato, Chrysippus or Epicurus, who worked out arguments for the existence of gods, natural theologians (because they didn't know Revelation), but nothing is in our way to rank them among philosophical theologians. The same is also true with such Indian philosophers as, e.g., Uddyotakara, Jayanta Bhaṭṭa or Vācaspati Miśra, who proved the existence of Īśvara in their controversy with antitheists (the Buddhists and others). Now, given that names which we give to things do mean something, and classical natural theology (as I mentioned above in connection with Francisco Suarez and his followers) worked on the general rational foundations of theism, the same should also be true with it today. So if we state that the rational theology attempting to elaborate the domain of *theologia revelata* may be better designated as a philosophical rather than natural one, we'll reach another important point of demarcation.